SCOTT, CHAUCER, AND MEDIEVAL ROMANCE

SCOTT, CHAUCER, AND MEDIEVAL ROMANCE

A Study in Sir Walter Scott's Indebtedness to the Literature of the Middle Ages

JEROME MITCHELL

THE UNIVERSITY PRESS OF KENTUCKY

Frontispiece: Sir Walter Scott, from a portrait by John Watson (later Sir John Watson Gordon). Courtesy of the Scottish National Portrait Gallery.

Copyright © 1987 by The University Press of Kentucky

Scholarly publisher for the Commonwealth serving Bellarmine College, Berea College, Centre College of Kentucky, Eastern Kentucky University, The Filson Club, Georgetown College, Kentucky Historical Society, Kentucky State University, Morehead State University, Murray State University, Northern Kentucky University, Transylvania University, University of Kentucky, University of Louisville, and Western Kentucky University.

Editorial and Sales Offices: Lexington, Kentucky 40506-0024

Library of Congress Cataloging-in-Publication Data
Mitchell, Jerome.
  Scott, Chaucer, and medieval romance.
  Bibliography: p.
  Includes index.
  1. Scott, Walter, Sir, 1771-1832—Knowledge—Literature. 2. Scott, Walter, Sir, 1771-1832—Sources.
  3. Chaucer, Geoffrey, d. 1400—Influence—Scott.
  4. Romances—History and criticism. 5. Middle Ages in literature. 6. Medievalism in literature.
  7. Literature, Medieval—History and critcism.
  I. Title.
  PR5343.L56M58 1987   828'.709   87-8294
  ISBN 0-8131-1609-0

For
my mother
MARIE DICK MITCHELL

and my brother
JOHN LEE MITCHELL

and in memory of my father
EMERSON LEE MITCHELL

CONTENTS

✻

Preface ix

1. Scott's Knowledge of Medieval Literature 1

2. The Narrative Poetry 40

3. The Early Novels, 1814-1816 86

4. Novels of the Broken Years, 1817-1819 108

5. Novels of the High-Noon Period, 1820-1825 138

6. Novels of the Dark Days and Servitude, 1826-1832 183

7. Style and Structure in the Waverley Novels 213

8. Conclusion 242

Notes 249

Index 262

PREFACE

THIS BOOK is a study of Sir Walter Scott's indebtedness to Chaucer and to medieval romance, especially the Middle English romances, for story-patterns, motifs, character types, style and structure, and detail of one sort or another. In the first of eight chapters I establish as best I can the extent of Scott's knowledge of medieval literature, showing which romances he knew (and in which editions), which romances he knew of and had read in, and which ones he did not know. In the second chapter I discuss his poetry, especially the long narrative poems, in relation to Chaucer and medieval romance. Chapters 3 through 6 deal mainly with the Waverley Novels: the early novels, 1814-16; novels of the broken years, 1817-19; novels of the high-noon period, 1820-25; and novels of the dark days and servitude, 1826-32—my phraseology coming from John Buchan's beautifully written biography, *Sir Walter Scott* (London: Cassell, 1932). In these chapters I go through the novels one by one, showing what specifically Scott has drawn from Chaucer and medieval romance and how he has used it. In some of the novels the borrowing is superficial; in others it runs deep and is essential to what Scott is doing. Matters of style and structure relevant to the poems are discussed in the second chapter; the seventh is devoted to style and structure in the novels. In the last chapter I try to explain how Scott's reliance on Chaucer and medieval romance enhances and deepens his poems and novels and why it works so effectively.

John Gibson Lockhart, his son-in-law and biographer, once said about Scott's *Minstrelsy of the Scottish Border*: "No person who has not gone through its volumes for the express purpose of comparing their contents with his great original works, can have formed a conception of the endless variety of incidents and images now expanded and emblazoned by his mature art, of which the first hints may be found either in the text of those primitive ballads, or in the notes, which the happy rambles of his youth had gathered together for their illustration." Much the same can be said about Scott and medieval literature. I believe that medieval romance is the single most important literary source for the Waverley Novels, even more pervasive than Shakespeare (whose influence on Scott was great and profound), and that an understanding of Scott's debt to it is the key to an understanding of his immense appeal. Let me say too that I fully realize the danger inherent in a study of this sort. When one source area is put under a magnifying glass, it inevitably gets blown up out of proportion. As great as the influence of medieval literature is, it does not overshadow all other influences, for Scott's reading was vast and omnivorous. Here and there I have cited other possible sources.

While it has long been known that Scott knew medieval romance, other studies have been concerned with his medievalism in general rather than with specific indebtedness to specific romances. The present study deals, as much as possible, in specifics within the boundaries I have set. Some limitations in scope have been necessary and inevitable. I have not said very much about Scott and Italian romance, and for this subject I refer the reader to R.D.S. Jack's chapter on "The Novel and Scott" in his pioneering book, *The Italian Influence on Scottish Literature* (Edinburgh: Edinburgh Univ. Press, 1972). I have also not said much about Scott's debt to Old Norse; for this material the reader may consult John M. Simpson's "Scott and Old Norse Literature," included in the *Scott Bicentenary Essays*, edited by Alan Bell (Edinburgh: Scottish Academic Press, 1973). I have given very short shrift to chronicles and to long works that hover between romance and chronicle, like Barbour's *Bruce*. As for ballads, I have tried to limit myself to those that share motifs with romances that Scott knew and to those that are later versions of romances. ("The farther our researches are extended," Scott once wrote, "the more we shall see ground to believe, that the romantic ballads of later times are, for the most part, abridgments of the ancient metrical romances, narrated in a smoother stanza and more modern language.") Despite these and other limitations, a wealth of material is here, and the scope of the present study is very large.

I would like to express special thanks to the helpful and friendly staff of the National Library of Scotland, in Edinburgh, where I did the major part of my research. Most of the material I needed was there—and the library is close to where the house once stood, at the top of Guthrie Street, in which Walter Scott was born; it is only a short distance from George Square and the house, still standing, in which he lived as a boy and young man; it is only a stone's throw from the site of the old Tolbooth, long since demolished and removed, where Effie Deans was imprisoned for having allegedly murdered her newborn child; it is at the top of a steep street (Victoria Street and West Bow) leading into the Grassmarket, where Captain John Porteous was lynched by determined avengers before a mob of onlookers; it is a twenty-five-minute walk from the Salisbury Crags, where one awesome night Jeanie Deans met with the seducer of her sister and where on pleasant days young Walter Scott and his friend John Irving used to go to read old romances together and to compose new ones for each other's amusement. I must also thank the library staff at the University of Bonn, where I read the German dissertations that I cite in this book; many of these had to be ordered on interlibrary loan, sometimes from East Germany. I am also indebted to many individuals for help, especially James C. Corson, Kurt Gamerschlag, George O. Marshall, Jr., Patricia and Jean Maxwell-Scott, Coleman O. Parsons, Charles I. Patterson, Jr., and Donald E. Sultana. Without their advice this book would have been the poorer, and without their encouragement it might never have been. I hasten to add that all faults and shortcomings are entirely my own.

1

SCOTT'S KNOWLEDGE OF MEDIEVAL LITERATURE

HOW MUCH medieval literature was Scott familiar with, specifically, and how do we know? These basic questions must be answered at the outset, and no study of which I am aware considers them with any degree of completeness.[1] Fortunately, Scott himself has a lot to tell us. Scattered throughout the four volumes of his *Minstrelsy of the Scottish Border,*[2] that is, in the introductions, essays, and explanatory notes, he has numerous allusions to Chaucer and to medieval romance. Much can be found too in the lengthy introduction and notes to his edition (the first ever) of the Middle English poem *Sir Tristrem* (1804). Further allusions and quotations can be found in the explanatory notes to the long narrative poems—especially *The Lay of the Last Minstrel, Marmion,* and *The Lady of the Lake*—and in the texts of the poems themselves.

If one searches for allusions in the introductions and notes to the Waverley Novels, the complete picture begins to come more clearly into focus, and in the texts of the novels there are numerous specific allusions to Chaucer, romance, and other medieval literature. Scott compares Quentin Durward explicitly to the Squire of Low Degree, to cite one good example. His essays on Chivalry (1818) and Romance (1824) also give clear indication of his vast knowledge of medieval literature; both are filled with numerous allusions to and quotations from Chaucer and medieval romance. Additional material can be culled from some of the reviews Scott wrote (now most conveniently found, like the essays, in the *Miscellaneous Prose Works*).[3] I am thinking in particular of his review (1803) of the translations of *Amadis de Gaul* by Robert Southey and William Stewart Rose, his review (1804) of William Godwin's *Life of Chaucer*, his review (1806) of George Ellis's *Specimens of Early English Metrical Romances* and Joseph Ritson's *Ancient Engleish Metrical Romanceës*, and his review (1810) of Thomas Evans's *Old Ballads*. Finally, in his letters—as edited by Sir

Herbert Grierson in the 1930s—there are numerous references to medieval romance (but not to Chaucer), especially in his correspondence with George Ellis but also in letters to Richard Heber (the bibliophile), Joseph Ritson, Robert Southey, and others. One can now, at long last, conveniently locate these references by using James C. Corson's *Notes and Index*. Further material can be found in some of the unpublished letters.[4]

Scott's interest in medieval literature can be traced in Lockhart's *Life of Scott*,[5] although much of the information comes in quoted letters, which are better read in Grierson. Nevertheless, there is material enough not in the letters to make a search through Lockhart worthwhile (and a search it must be, since the index is not adequate). Also extremely useful is J.G. Cochrane's *Catalogue of the Library at Abbotsford*.[6] Numerous "books of chivalry and romance in various languages" are to be found on the shelves of Press N; editions of Chaucer and other medieval works are located elsewhere in the library Scott accumulated in his Abbotsford home. The *Catalogue* does not say when he actually acquired any given book, but cross-references to Lockhart's *Life of Scott* and to Scott's works themselves often provide the information; otherwise one can likely assume that he acquired the book, if it was published in his active lifetime, very soon after the date of publication.

Also useful is Dr. Corson's article "Scott's Boyhood Collection of Chapbooks"—that is, chapbooks (just over a hundred) that Scott acquired before he was ten years old. Among the interesting titles with regard to the present study are *The History of Roswal & Lillian*, *The Famous History of the Seven Wise Masters of Rome*, *The Famous and Renowned History of Hector Prince of Troy*, *The Explication of Thomas Rymer's Prophecies*, and an episode from *Valentine and Orson*. Almost two thousand additional chapbooks that Scott collected later have also been catalogued by Dr. Corson, but that catalogue has not yet been published. Scott became familiar with a great many important literary and historical works, including medieval romances, by having read them as a boy in chapbook versions, later turning to the works themselves—just as thousands of people today (like me) first became acquainted with important works of literature by reading them in the 1940s and 1950s in *Classic Comics* (later *Classics Illustrated*). Sometimes the chapbook versions differ in certain respects from the original romance; in at least one case an important motif in a Waverley Novel derives from a chapbook version rather than from the romance itself.[7]

Before the publication of *Waverley*, Scott was acquainted with a number of the romances in manuscript. He knew the Auchinleck MS well—it was in the Advocates' Library, in Edinburgh—and he edited from it the metrical romance *Sir Tristrem*. The poem is important because it derives from the version by Thomas of Britain (in large part lost), as do the versions by Gottfried von Strassburg and Brother Robert. Scott, on the contrary, thought that the Auchinleck poem was the source of the more famous continental versions and that it was originally composed by Thomas of Erceldoune in about 1250. In the fourth appendix to his introduction, Scott gives a list and description of the contents of the Auchinleck MS. Besides *Sir Tristrem* it includes a number of other well-known romances, in this order: *The King of Tars; Amis and Amiloun; Sir Degare; Floris and Blancheflur;* three romances dealing with Guy of Warwick which Scott has entitled *Gy of Warwike* (Guy before marriage), *Continuation of Gy's History* (Guy after marriage), and *Rembrun's* [sic] *Gy's Sone of Warwike* (Guy's son Reinbrun); *Bevis of Hampton; Arthur and Merlin;* the *Lai le Freine; Roland and Ferragus* (i.e., *Roland and Vernagu); Otuel a Knight; King Orfeo* (i.e., *Sir Orfeo);* and *Horn Child.* There are also fragments of romances dealing with Alexander the Great and Richard the Lion-Hearted (see note 4); *Owain Miles,* which Scott describes as a "legend or romance"; and *The Seven Wise Masters,* a "celebrated romance, or rather tissue of stories."

The Auchinleck MS now has the number 19.2.1. Scott made arrangements through Robert Southey for the acquisition by the Advocates' Library, in February 1806, of MS. 19.3.1, which includes among many other items three romances in tail-rhyme stanzas—*Sir Gowther, Sir Isumbras,* and *Sir Amadace*—and the delightful comic romance *The Huntyng of the Hare.* There is a partial list of contents at the beginning of the manuscript in Scott's hand; the manuscript itself belongs to the second half of the fifteenth century. Scott also knew in manuscript the long metrical romance *Clariodus* (now MS. 19.2.5), which was not printed until 1830 (Maitland Club, No.9). I do not know to what extent he was familiar with Advocates MS. 19.1.11, which was acquired in 1808. He certainly would have known *of* it, since Weber edited the poem *Sir Cleges* from it (see below), but he knew *Mandeville's Travels* from printed versions rather than from MS. 19.1.11, and I have found no evidence anywhere that he knew the third major work included, Thomas Hoccleve's *Regement of Princes.* Surely Scott would have commented somewhere on Hoccleve's magnum opus if he had known it, for he could not but have found it interesting, especially its long, charmingly diffuse "autobiographical" prologue.

The attraction of medieval literature was not unique to Scott. During his lifetime there was in fact much interest and activity on the part of antiquarians, dilettantes, and a few genuine scholars in getting the old romances into print—sometimes in the original versions, sometimes in modernized versions or translations, and sometimes in summaries interspersed with excerpts from the original. In the last quarter of the eighteenth century much of this activity occurred in France. Abridged and modernized versions of many an old prose romance were to be found in the

Bibliothèque Universelle des Romans, which was published in numerous issues between 1775 and 1789. Scott could have acquired from this one source a large part of his knowledge of medieval romance, including the French Arthurian romances and those relating to Charlemagne and Roland. He was certainly familiar with this ambitious periodical; occasionally he quotes from it. All issues but those of the last two years were readily available to him in the Advocates' Library, in Edinburgh. Other old romances in the prose tradition were modernized by the Comte de Tressan in his four-volume *Corps d'Extraits de Romans de Chevalerie* (1782).[8] Scott later acquired a copy of this for his library at Abbotsford. The titles that would have particularly interested him include *Tristan de Leonis, fils de Méliadus; Artus de Bretagne; Flores et Blanch-Fleur* (all in Volume 1); *La Fleur des Batailles, Huon de Bordeaux, Guérin de Montglave* (in Volume 2); and *Le Petit Jehan de Saintré* (in Volume 3). There was also the *Bibliothèque Bleue*, which Scott knew in the three-volume edition published in Liège in 1787; some of the titles that stand out are the *Histoire de Robert le Diable, et celle de Richard sans Peur, son fils*, the *Histoire de Jean de Calais*, and *Les Quatre Fils d'Aymon*. Several old romances from the poetic tradition, albeit in modernized prose versions, are to be found in Le Grand d'Aussy's *Fabliaux ou Contes;* Scott had the revised and enlarged five-volume edition of 1781.[9] The romance *Parténopex, Comte de Blois* makes up the second half of Volume 5.

Not this piece but many others were selected from Le Grand and translated into English verse by G.L. Way in his two-volume *Fabliaux or Tales* (1796, 1800).[10] After Way's death on April 26, 1799, George Ellis saw the second volume through the press and provided a preface, notes, and an appendix. Romances in Volume 1 include *Aucassin and Nicolette;* two poems involving Sir Gawain: *The Mule without a Bridle* and *The Knight and the Sword* (both being analogues to *Sir Gawain and the Green Knight*); and two Breton lais: *The Lay of Sir Gruelan* and Marie de France's *Lay of Sir Lanval*. Among the selections in Volume 2 are Marie's *Lay of Sir Gugemar, The Countess of Vergy, Griselidis* (the same story as Chaucer's Clerk's Tale but translated here from Le Grand)—all the work of Way; and, at the very end, Thomas Chestre's *Launfal Miles* (i.e., *Sir Launfal*), edited from Cotton MS. Caligula A.ii by Ellis, who indicates that the poem had not hitherto appeared in print. Scott was sent a copy of Way's *Fabliaux* by Richard Heber, whom he heartily thanks in a letter of July 28, 1800. "On my part," he adds, "I can only say that with all my admiration for the original which is great & for Mr. Ways translation which in many parts might do honor to Dryden, still I hold the notes & illustrations of your friend Mr. Ellis as even the most valuable part of the Publication."[11] They are indeed fascinating. There are notes on tournaments, judicial combat, and armor; on the finding of King Arthur's coffin during the reign of Henry II; on Tristan's homeland Lyonnesse, now submerged; on castles and towers of castles; on medicine and physicians; on medieval dress; on the degrees of rank in the feudal system; on various aspects of knighthood; and on what we now call "courtly love." A curiosity of the appendix is a fragment entitled "The Crusaders" (translated by Way), which consists of a debate between a crusader and a noncrusader (see the discussion of *The Betrothed* in Chapter 5).

The interest in medieval romance might not have developed so rapidly in Britain had Bishop Percy not published his *Reliques of Ancient English Poetry*. This was in 1765.[12] Many years later, in the autobiographical fragment that Lockhart includes as the first chapter of the biography, Scott fondly recalled a significant day in his boyhood: "The first time . . . I could scrape a few shillings together, which were not common occurrences with me, I bought unto myself a copy of these beloved volumes, nor do I believe I ever read a book half so frequently, or with half the enthusiasm" (*Life of Scott*, 1:53-54). In the last decade of the century John Pinkerton published a curious three-volume set entitled *Scotish Poems, Reprinted from Scarce Editions*.[13] The third volume includes two important metrical romances: *Golagrus and Gawain*, or, as Pinkerton gives the title, *Gawan and Gologras* (from the edition printed in Edinburgh by Chepman and Myllar in 1508); and *The Awntyrs off Arthur*, or again, with Pinkerton's title, *Sir Gawan and Sir Galaron of Galloway* (printed for the first time ever). Scott refers to both romances in a letter to Ellis of March 27, 1801 (*Letters*, 12:176).

During the next ten years three very important collections of romances were published. The first was by the notorious scholar and antiquary Joseph Ritson, whom Scott greatly respected although he was not blind to Ritson's personal shortcomings and idiosyncrasies. The three-volume work is entitled *Ancient Engleish Metrical Romanceës*.[14] Volume 1 includes *Ywain and Gawain* (from Cotton Galba E.ix) and *Sir Launfal* (from Cotton Caligula A.ii); Volume 2, *Libeaus Desconus* (from Cotton Caligula A.ii), *King Horn* (from Harley 2253), *The King of Tars* (from Bodleian 3938 [the Vernon MS]), *Emare* (from Cotton Caligula A.ii), *Sir Orfeo* (from Harley 3810); and Volume 3, *Le Bone Florence of Rome* and *The Earl of Toulous* (from Cambridge Univ. MS. Ff. 2.38 [formerly More 690]), *The Squyr of Lowe Degre* (from the edition of William Copland, c. 1560), *The Knight of Curtesy and the Fair Lady of Faguell* (from the edition of William Copland, 1568), and *Horn Child* (from the Auchinleck MS). Lockhart had no use for Ritson, whom he refers to as "this narrow-minded, sour, and dogmatical little word-catcher . . . this half-crazy pedant" (*Life of Scott*, 2:62); but Scott, who felt honored by Ritson's visit in 1801 at Lasswade, was kinder and fairer in evaluating his older friend's accomplishments. To him Joseph Ritson was

> a man of acute observation, profound research, and great labour. These valuable attributes were unhappily combined with an eager irritability of temper, which induced him to treat antiquarian trifles with the same seriousness which men of the world reserve for matters of importance, and disposed him to drive controversies into personal quarrels, by neglecting, in literary debate, the courtesies of ordinary society. It ought to be said, however, by one who knew him well, that this irritability of disposition was a constitutional and physical infirmity; and that Ritson's extreme attachment to the severity of truth corresponded to the rigour of his criticisms upon the labours of others. [*Minstrelsy*, 1:28–29]

Ancient Engleish Metrical Romanceës was published about one year before Ritson went insane and died. The collection has proved to be one of his most significant scholarly achievements and belies the misgivings he expressed in the remarkable closing paragraph of the Advertisement: "Brought to an end with much industry and more attention, in a continue'd state of il-health, and low spirits, the editour abandons it to general censure, with cold indifference, expecting little favour, and less profit; but certain, at any rate, to be insulted by the malignant and calumnious personalitys of a base and prostitute gang of lurking assassins, who stab in the dark, and whose poison'd daggers he has allready experience'd" (1:iii–iv). Scott's own jucidious appraisal, in his review of 1806, is worth quoting: "Let it be remembered to his honour, that, without the encouragement of private patronage, or of public applause; without hopes of gain, and under the certainty of severe critical censure, he has brought forward such a work on national antiquities, as in other countries has been thought worthy of the labour of universities, and the countenance of princes."

George Ellis's *Specimens of Early English Metrical Romances* appeared in 1805.[15] The three octavo volumes did a lot to further the already established interest in the Middle English romances because Ellis happily adopted a method suited to a broad spectrum of readers: "The editor has followed, with little deviation, the plan adopted by M. Le Grand in his edition of the French Fabliaux; and has faithfully given, in plain prose, not only the general outline but even the smallest incidents of each story: but he has thought it necessary to intersperse, throughout the narrative, such passages of the originals as appeared to him worth preserving, either from their poetical merit,—from their representing correct pictures of ancient manners,—or from their being characteristic of the author's feelings, or of those of the nation" (Advertisement, 1:iii–iv). In his introduction Ellis has a lot to say about Geoffrey of Monmouth, and in the second appendix to the introduction he gives full descriptions of eight of Marie de France's lais: *Equitan, Bisclaveret, Les deux Amants, Ywonec, Laustic, Milun, Chaitivel,* and *Eliduc.* He refers the reader to Le Grand and Way for *Guigemar,* to his own version of the Middle English *Lai le Freine* for Marie's *Freisne,* to Le Grand and Way for *Lanval,* and to Scott's edition of *Sir Tristrem* for *Chevrefoil.* The early English metrical romances are divided into six groups. In "Romances Relating to Arthur," Ellis summarizes *Arthur and Merlin* (from Lincoln's Inn 150, with "some deficiencies" supplied through Scott "from the more antient and perfect copy in the Auchinleck MS") and the stanzaic *Morte Arthur* (from Harley 2252). Then come two "Saxon Romances": *Guy of Warwick* (from the two romances about Gy in the Auchinleck MS, Ellis having found in the account of Guy and Colbrand "a degree of spirit and animation which formed a striking contrast with the usual monotony of the minstrel compositions") and *Bevis of Hampton* (from Caius College Cambridge MS. 175, with omissions supplied from Richard Pynson's printed edition, c. 1503). *Richard Coer de Lyon* is the one "Anglo-Norman Romance" (Ellis knew it in Caius Cambridge MS. 175). This is followed by three "Romances Relating to Charlemagne": *Roland and Ferragus* (from the Auchinleck MS, a transcript having been supplied by Scott); *Sir Otuel* (i.e., *Otuel a Knight,* from the Auchinleck MS, with additional material from the Fillingham *Firumbras*); and *Sir Ferumbras* (i.e., *The Sowdon of Babylon,* from a transcript of the manuscript now called Garrett 140 [formerly Phillips 8357]). Ellis summarizes one "Romance of Oriental Origin," namely, *The Seven Wise Masters* (from the Auchinleck MS and from Cotton Galba E.ix). Finally, there are the "Miscellaneous Romances," which include *Floris and Blauncheflur* (from the Auchinleck MS, and with the help of Tressan's "elegant compendium"); *Roberd of Cisyle* (from Cambridge Univ. MS. Ff. 2.38 [formerly More 690]); *Sir Isumbras* (from Caius Cambridge MS. 175), collated with the early printed edition by William Copland in the Garrick Collection); *Sir Triamour* (from the early printed edition by William Copland, in the British Library); *The Lyfe of Ipomydon* (from Harley 2252); *Sir Eglamour of Artoys* (from the early printed edition by John Walley, in the Garrick Collection); the *Lai le Freine* (from the Auchinleck MS); *Sir Eger, Sir Grahame, and Sir Gray-Steel* (from the edition printed at Aberdeen in 1711); *Sir Degare* (from a transcript of an early black-letter edition by William Copland, in the Garrick Collection); *Roswall and Lillian* (from an early printed edition without place or date of publication, loaned to Ellis by Francis Douce [probably Bodley Douce PP 157]); and *Amis and Amiloun* (from Bodley 21900 [Douce 326]).

In his review of 1806, Scott interestingly compares Ellis's work with that of the Comte de Tressan:

In some respects, the works resemble each other considerably. They are both executed by men of rank and fashion, who formed their style not merely by perusing the best authors, but by frequenting the first company in their respective countries. . . . In other respects, Mr Ellis has a decided superiority over Mons. de Tressan. He is infinitely more faithful as an editor; and, as an author, exhibits much deeper research; which appears from his having chosen the metrical romances for his subject: whereas the count has confined his attention to those in prose, though far less ancient, and in every respect less interesting. [*Miscellaneous Prose Works*, 17:53–54]

Scott and Ellis met in 1801, following a correspondence of several months. Their friendship, which lasted until Ellis's death in 1815, was one of the most felicitous relationships ever between two distinguished men of letters. Their voluminous correspondence is a mine of antiquarian information about English and French romances, and it gives detailed indication of the state and progress of medieval studies in Britain in the early part of the nineteenth century. After Ellis's death a number of transcripts of romances made by himself and others—material he had used in preparing the *Specimens*—came into Scott's hands; they are listed in Cochrane's Abbotsford Library *Catalogue*.

On August 21, 1804, Scott wrote to Ellis, "I have lighted upon a very good amanuensis . . . he was sent down here by some of the London Booksellers in a half starved state but begins to pick up a little" (*Letters*, 12:263). "There was something very interesting," Lockhart wrote years later, "in his appearance and manners: he had a fair, open countenance, in which the honesty and the enthusiasm of his nation were alike visible; his demeanour was gentle and modest; and he had not only a stock of curious antiquarian knowledge, but the reminiscences, which he detailed with amusing simplicity, of an early life chequered with many strange-enough adventures" (*Life of Scott*, 4:147). This was Henry Weber, born in 1783 in St. Petersburg of a German father and an English mother; he was employed by Scott from 1804 until the end of 1813 (he became insane and eventually died in an asylum in York in 1818).

Weber's three-volume edition of *Metrical Romances* appeared in 1810.[16] Lockhart called it a "wild project" because it was not successful in financial terms, but it was a very respectable piece of scholarship for the times. The first volume contains *Kyng Alisaunder*, Parts I and II (from Lincoln's Inn MS. 150, with missing parts filled in from Bodley 1414 [Laud Misc. 622; formerly Laud I.74]), and in an appendix to his introduction, Weber includes a summary (by Scott?) of *The Scottish Alexander Buik*, printed by Alexander Arbuthnet c. 1580. Also in Volume 1 are *Sir Cleges*, which Weber calls a "fabliau" (from Advocates MS. 19.1.11) and the *Lai le Freine* (from the Auchinleck MS, with defects supplied by the editor from the French, "as nearly as possible in the style of the original"). The second volume contains *Richard Coer de Lyon*, Parts I and II (mainly from Caius Cambridge

MS. 175). Weber mentions the early printings by Wynkyn de Worde, the second of which (1528) describes "the savage meal which Richard made upon the heads of the Saracens, and the feast he prepared for the messengers of Soliman"—not included in Weber's edition. Also in Volume 2 are *The Lyfe of Ipomydon* (from Harley 2252) and *Amis and Amiloun* (mainly from the Auchinleck MS). Volume 3 contains *The Proces of the Seuyn Sages* (i.e., *The Seven Wise Masters*, from the Auchinleck MS, with help from Cotton Galba E.ix); *Octouian Imperator* (i.e., *Octavian*, from Cotton Caligula A.ii—the Southern version); *Sir Amadas* and *The Huntyng of the Hare* (both from Advocates MS. 19.3.1).

"Happy should the editor be," Weber writes in his introduction (1: lxvii), "if he were called upon, in consequence of the present collection, to proceed in rescuing these ancient records of language, manners, and tradition from oblivion." He then lists in a footnote several romances that he had already transcribed for the press: "Artour and Merlin; Sir Bevis of Hampton; Sir Ferumbras; Sir Eger, Sir Grahame and Sir Graysteel; Charlemagne, (called by Mr Ellis, Roland and Ferragus); Otuel, with the continuation of Charlemagne; Sir Triamoure; Sir Eglamour; Sir Owaine; Sir Tundale; Sir Degare; Sir Isumbras; Sir Gowther; Robert of Cisyle; Roswal and Lillian; Florice and Blancheflour, &c." Many of the transcripts Weber cites are to be found in two MS volumes that are shelved in Press N at Abbotsford (but not Artour and Merlin, Sir Ferumbras, Sir Eglamour, Sir Isumbras, Sir Gowther, and Florice and Blancheflour). Most of these romances had appeared in abstracted form in Ellis's *Specimens*, but not *Sir Gowther* (which I presume Weber transcribed from Advocates MS. 19.3.1) and not *Sir Owaine* (or *Owain Miles*, which was easily accessible to him in the Auchinleck MS) and not *Sir Tundale* (i.e., *The Visions of Tundale*, to be found in Advocates MS. 19.3.1 and in Cotton Caligula A.ii).

One more publication of "poor Weber" (as Scott often called him) deserves mention, although it falls a bit outside the boundaries I have set. Lockhart describes it thus:

The last of Weber's literary productions were the analyses of the Old German Poems of the *Helden Buch*, and the *Nibelungen Lied*, which appeared in a massive quarto, entitled Illustrations of Northern Antiquities, published in the summer of 1814, by his and Scott's friend, Mr Robert Jameson [i.e., Jamieson]. Scott avowedly contributed to this collection an account of the Eyrbiggia Saga, which has since been included in his Prose Miscellanies . . . but any one who examines the share of the work which goes under Weber's name, will see that Scott had a considerable hand in that also. The rhymed versions from the Nibelungen Lied came, I can have no doubt, from his pen; but he never reclaimed these, or any other similar benefactions, of which I have traced not a few; nor, highly curious and even beautiful as many of them are, could they be intelligible, if separated from the prose narrative on which Weber embroidered them, in imitation of the style of Ellis's Specimens of Metrical Romance. [*Life of Scott*, 4:153–54]

As fascinating as this book is, Weber is chiefly remembered for the *Metrical Romances*.[17]

E.V. Utterson's two-volume edition of *Select Pieces of Early Popular Poetry* (1817)[18] probably had little if any influence on Scott; he already knew the four romances included: *Sir Triamour, Sir Isumbras, Sir Degare,* and *Sir Gowther.* Of more importance to his development were some English versions of individual romances that had appeared earlier. The year 1803 saw the publication of William Stewart Rose's poem *Amadis de Gaul,* "freely translated from the first part of the French version of Nicolas de He[r]beray," and Robert Southey's complete translation in prose of the Spanish version by Garciordonez de Montvalo. Scott thought that Rose followed too closely the French prose of Herberay when as a poet he should have taken more liberties, but he was favorably impressed with Rose's notes. In part of his review of these two publications he contrasts verse romances with prose romances, which were composed later (after 1450) and which tended to be lengthier, more detailed, and sometimes more refined in moral tone, although not beyond reproach. But, Scott continued,

> the advantage, thus gained by the prose romances, was often lost, by carrying too far the principle on which it was grounded. Having once regularly completed a story, good taste and judgment required them to stop, and choose for their future labours some subject unconnected with what was already perfect. But this was not the genius of the age. When they had secured an interesting set of characters, the authors could not resist the temptation of bringing them again upon the stage; and hence, the endless continuations with which Amadis and the other romances of that class, were saddled, and of which Mr Southey complains with so much justice. Only four books of Amadis are genuine. The remaining twenty are an interpolation, containing the history of his descendants, in all respects greatly inferior to the original. [*Miscellaneous Prose Works*, 18:14–15]

Scott indeed admired the original: "The march of the story engages our attention; and the successive events are well managed to support each other and to bring on the final catastrophe" (18:30).

Scott eagerly awaited the publication in 1807 of Southey's version of *Palmerin of England,* but he was somewhat disappointed, finding it of less interest than *Amadis de Gaul.* Rose's version of *Partenopex de Blois* also appeared in 1807, freely translated from the version in French by Le Grand d'Aussy (not included in Way's *Fabliaux*). In 1814 Utterson's edition of Lord Berners's *Arthur of Little Britain* was published in the limited number of two hundred copies, and Scott acquired one for his library; he would also have known this work in the French version by Tressan. The year 1817 saw the publication of Southey's long-awaited edition of the *Morte Darthur*, which Scott had long known from William Stansby's edition of 1634 and which he himself had considered editing before he found out that Southey was already well under way with the project. Utterson's edition for the Roxburghe Club of the Middle English verse romance *Cheuelere Assigne* may have come too late (1820) to have had much influence on Scott.

It is clear that the period 1790 to 1820, to think in round numbers, was one of unprecedented activity on the part of enthusiasts for medieval romances. I must not forget the three-volume *History of Fiction* by Scott's countryman John Dunlop. Concerned exclusively with prose narratives from the Greek romances to the first novels of the eighteenth century, it appeared first in 1814 and again two years later in a revised and augmented edition.[19] Scott apparently had some misgivings about the first edition, but they did not prevent him from writing a letter of introduction on Dunlop's behalf in 1815 to Richard Heber: "Mr Dunlop the bearer, author of the History of Fiction is desirous of the advantage of being known to you. You will find him a very well informed & gentlemanlike young man" (*Letters*, 12:354; these are rather lukewarm words for Scott). The second edition is immensely useful because of its summaries of the Continental as well as the English prose romances. Most of what Scott knew about medieval romance he had learned earlier, but Dunlop's work is an admirable manifestation of the spirit of the age. Whatever else it may or may not have been, Romanticism indeed was, as Heinrich Heine said, a return to the Middle Ages.

To Scott (writing in his Essay on Romance), a romance was "a fictitious narrative in prose or verse; the interest of which turns upon marvellous and uncommon incidents." A novel, on the other hand, was "a fictitious narrative, differing from the Romance, because the events are accommodated to the ordinary train of human events, and the modern state of society." Scott thought of medieval romance, especially "the ancient *Romance of Chivalry*," as "the parent of those select and beautiful fictions which the genius of the Italian poets has enriched with such peculiar charms"; it was also the parent of the heroic romance of the seventeenth century, which "with few exceptions" he considered "the most dull and tedious species of composition that ever obtained temporary popularity."

In the annotated and alphabetized lists that follow, I have attempted to document in convenient fashion, and as precisely as I can, Scott's knowledge (or lack of it) of the medieval romances. In the first group are those that Scott certainly knew: he refers to them specifically, he quotes from them, and his discussions of them reveal a thorough knowledge. In the second group are romances that Scott must have known, for he had access to them in manuscript or owned them in editions published within his early or middle life, but these he does not discuss anywhere and indeed scarcely mentions. Next come those romances that Scott knew of and had read in, to a greater or lesser degree, but his references and discussions give no indication of thorough knowledge. There are still others that he knew of but had probably read little of, if any; either his brief allusions give no telling evidence that he was familiar with their contents, or they appeared in print too late in his life to have been of any influence on him. Finally, there is a group of romances that he apparently did not know at all. Some readers would perhaps classify certain romances differently, but it is my hope that what follows, with all its shortcomings, will prove useful; if it provokes controversy, even that should prove constructive in the long run.

Group 1: Romances Known Well and Cited Often

Amadis de Gaul. The versions by Rose and Southey are reviewed in detail by Scott for the *Edinburgh Review* (October 1803). There is reference to and quotation from "the famous romance of Amadis de Gaul" (the French version by Nicolas de Herberay) in a note to I.lxxxvii (Fytte First, stanza lxxxvii) of *Sir Tristrem;* Rose's version is alluded to in a note to II.lxv. Mentioned in the Essay on Chivalry (1818) and discussed in the Essay on Romance (1824). An abridged version by the Comte de Tressan is in the *Bibliothèque des Romans.* The versions by Herberay, Rose, and Southey are at Abbotsford; also at Abbotsford is Francis Kirkman's translation from the French of Part VI: that is, *The Famous and Renowned History of Amadis de Gaule, Conteining the Heroick Deeds of Arms and Strange Adventures, aswell of Amadis himself, as of Perion his Son, and Lisvart of Greece* (London: J. Bell, 1652). This relates the adventures of Perion (the Knight of the Sphere) and his nephew Lisvart (the Knight of the True Cross). It ends with the birth of Amadis of Greece (son of Lisvart and Onoloria, daughter of the Emperor of Trebisond) and his abduction by rovers, or blackamoors, at a fountain. See *Esplandian* below. (Esplandian was Amadis's first-born son, older brother to Perion, and the father of Lisvart.) See also *Dom Flores de Grece* below. (Flores, or the Knight of the Swans, was another son of Esplandian, and the younger brother of Lisvart.)

Amis and Amiloun. In the Auchinleck MS. Scott quotes it in his introduction to the ballad "Sir Hugh le Blond," cites it again in reference to "the institution of brotherhood in arms" in the introduction to "Græme and Bewick" (both in *Minstrelsy*, vol. 3), and discusses and quotes it in the notes to *Sir Tristrem*. It appears in both the Ellis and the Weber collections, is cited by Scott in reference to judicial combat in the notes to *Marmion*, and is referred to in the Essay on Chivalry: "The beautiful romance of *Amis and Amiloun*, in which a knight slays his own child to make a salve with its blood to cure the leprosy of his brother-in-arms, turns entirely on this extravagant pitch of sentiment."

Arthour and Merlin. In the Auchinleck MS. Scott alludes to it in a note to the essay "On the Fairies of Popular Superstition" (*Minstrelsy*, vol. 2); in a note to "Christie's Will" (*Minstrelsy*, vol. 4); in the introduction to *Sir Tristrem* (with reference to the English language gaining ground over French) and also in the notes to II.xxvii and III.lxxviii. It appears in Ellis and is singled out for special praise in Scott's review of Ritson and Ellis: "This is a romance in the very best style of minstrelsy, so far as language, and even incident, are concerned. The marvellous birth of Merlin, surreptitiously begotten by a fiend upon a maiden, under the most extraordinary circumstances, is one of those feats of witchery which arrest the imagination." Scott mentions it several times in his *Letters* (see *Bevis of Hampton* below). A transcript by Ellis is in the Abbotsford library. A transcript by Weber is cited by Weber, but its whereabouts are not known.

Aucassin and Nicolette. In Barbazan's *Fabliaux et Contes*[20] (Scott owned the four-volume edition published in Paris in 1808) as *Aucasin et Nicolete*, in verse (with music) and prose (1:380-418). Included in Le Grand in modern French prose and translated in Way, with an interesting note (by Ellis) on female and Jewish physicians. Also in the *Bibliothèque des Romans*.

Bevis of Hampton. In the Auchinleck MS. Scott alludes to it negatively in a letter to George Ellis of October 22, 1801: "I now send with two additional sheets of Arthour a packet of Sir Gy which is except perhaps Bevis of Hampton the dullest Romance of priis which I ever attempted to peruse"; refers to it in the introduction to "Kempion" (*Minstrelsy*, vol. 3); quotes from it in the notes to I.x and I.xxix of *Sir Tristrem;* alludes to it in the introduction to Canto I of *Marmion;* and mentions it in the Essay on Chivalry. It appears in Ellis; transcripts by both Weber and Ellis are at Abbotsford. Scott discovered it during the winter of 1831–32 at the Royal Library of Naples, in a fifteenth-century manuscript (XIII.B.29), which was copied for him by one Signor Sticchini "in a beautiful hand and very exactly, although Sticchini did not understand a word of the language";[21] this transcript is also at Abbotsford, as is a 24-page chapbook version printed at Newcastle (according to Corson's unpublished catalogue) entitled *The History of the Life and Death of that Noble Knight Sir Bevis of Southampton.*

The Bruce. By John Barbour. It is referred to in a letter to George Ellis, May 26, 1805. A letter to Jacob Grimm, April 29, 1814, in which Scott writes negatively of John Pinkerton's edition (1790), tells of his encouraging Dr. John Jamieson to do an edition, which did appear in 1820. Both are at Abbotsford, and also a black-letter quarto edition from 1758. *The Bruce* is a mixture of chronicle and romance; it is not included in the volume on romances in Severs's *Manual of the Writings in Middle English.*[22]

Clariodus. In Advocates MS. 19.2.5. Scott refers to it in the introduction to "Fause Foodrage" (*Minstrelsy*, vol. 3) as *Clariodus and Meliades;* he quotes it at length in the note to I.xiv of *Sir Tristrem*. He knew this poem from the manuscript and was interested in the "elaborate reference to the etiquette of chivalry and tournaments, of feasting and clothing" (Severs's *Manual*, p. 158). The first printed edition, done in 1830 for the Maitland Club, came too late for him to make use of.

La Fleur des Battailes. In the *Bibliothèque des Romans* and in Tressan. A note to "Sir Hugh le Blond" (*Minstrelsy*, vol. 3) comments: "In the romance of Doolin, called *La Fleur des Battailles*, a false accuser discovers a similar impatience to hurry over the execution, before the arrival of the lady's champion"; this is followed by a quotation in French prose. Scott quotes from it again in the notes to I.lxiii and III.xlii of *Sir Tristrem*. An old quarto edition published in Paris is at Abbotsford, as is the modernized version by the German poet Johann Baptist von Alxinger: *Doolin von Maynz,* 2d ed. (Leipzig, 1797). "Whatever may be the merit of [Alxinger's] poem," wrote Dunlop, "the Histoire de Doolin is not an interesting romance" (1:448). Scott apparently saw more in it to command attention than did Dunlop.

Floris and Blauncheflur. In the *Bibliothèque des Romans*, Tressan, and Barbazan. The Middle English version is in the Auchinleck MS. It is quoted briefly in the headnote to "Erlington" (*Minstrelsy*, vol. 2); referred to in connection with chess in the note to I.xxix of *Sir Tristrem*; and mentioned in the Essay on Romance. A transcript by Weber is cited by Weber. It is included in Ellis and in C.H. Hartshorne's *Ancient Metrical Tales* (1829).

Golagrus and Gawain. In Pinkerton, with the names reversed: *Gawan and Gologras*. This is also the title form that Scott used (though he calls attention to the sloppiness of Pinkerton's edition in a letter to George Ellis,

March 27, 1801). *Minstrelsy,* vol. 4, refers to it as a romance "rendered almost unintelligible by the extremity of affected alliteration." The Essay on Romance says of it, together with *Sir Gawain and Sir Galeron of Galloway:* "These Romances . . . have all the appearance of being original compositions, and display considerable poetic effort. But the uncouth use of words dragged in for the sake of alliteration, and used in secondary and oblique meanings, renders them extremely harsh in construction, as well as obscure in meaning."

Guerin de Montglave. In the *Bibliothèque des Romans* and Tressan. Scott alludes to "extracts" from this romance in his notebooks of 1792 (see *Life of Scott,* 1:274) and calls it "the fine old romance of *Guerin de Montglaive"* in a note to II.xii of *Sir Tristrem.* In 1812 Scott purchased through Richard Heber the Roxburghe copy of the old quarto edition published in Paris (see *Letters,* 12:336–37 n.4).

Guy of Warwick. Sampled in Warton's *History of English Poetry.*[23] In the Auchinleck MS as three separate romances. For references in letters to George Ellis, see *Bevis of Hampton* above and note 4. It is referred to *passim* in *Sir Tristrem,* and it appears in Ellis. Scott's review of Ritson and Ellis calls it "a very long romance, and in general as dull as may be, with even more than the usual huge proportion of battles and tournaments. Yet it may be read with pleasure in Mr Ellis's abridgement, though the original would have defied the patience of most antiquaries. The combat betwixt Guy and Colbrond the Danish champion, is told in a more animated strain, and in a different stanza." A stanza from this section, which Scott considered "the cream of the romance," is quoted in the Essay on Romance. A very worn prose version of some 150 pages, lacking the title page, is at Abbotsford; it was "printed for A. Bettesworth at the Red-Lyon in Pater-Noster-Row." The title page of a copy in perfect condition in the British Library reads *The Noble and Renowned History of Guy Earl of Warwick* (London, 1729). The story was also well known in chapbook form; two are listed in Corson's unpublished catalogue of Scott's chapbooks.

Horn Child (or *Horn Childe and Maiden Rimnild*). In the Auchinleck MS and in Ritson. (See also *King Horn* in Group 2 below.) The story of Horn is discussed by Scott in connection with the French version in a letter to Ellis, March 19, 1804; Scott does not seem to distinguish here between *Horn Child,* a tail-rhyme romance, and *King Horn,* which is in couplets.

The Hunting of the Felon Sow of Rokeby by the Friars of Richmond. In Thomas Evans's *Old Ballads,* revised and enlarged by his son R.H. Evans (London,

1810), 3:270–81. It is discussed by Scott as a "burlesque romance" in his review of Evans's *Old Ballads* (*Quarterly Review*, May 1810) and included in its entirety in a note to Canto V of *Rokeby*.

The Huntyng of the Hare. In Advocates MS. 19.3.1. Described by Scott in a letter to Ellis, October 17, 1805: "Moreover there is a merry tale of hunting a hare, as performed by a set of country clowns, with their mastiffs, and curs with 'short legs and never a tail.' The disgraces and blunders of these ignorant sportsmen must have afforded infinite mirth at the table of a feudal baron, prizing himself on his knowledge of the mysteries of the chase performed by these unauthorized intruders." It is included in Weber; discussed by Scott in his review of Evans's *Old Ballads;* mentioned in a note to Canto V of *Rokeby;* and cited in the Essay on Romance as an example of a comic romance.

Huon de Bordeaux. In the *Bibliothèque des Romans* and Tressan. Scott quotes it in notes to I.xxvii of *Sir Tristrem* and refers to it again in the note to I.xxix. It is referred to and quoted by Rose with regard to Huon's magic horn in the notes to Canto I of *Partenopex de Blois*. In 1812 Scott purchased through Heber the Roxburghe copy of the old quarto volume *Les Prouesses et Faictz du noble Huon de Bordeaulx, Per de France, Duc de Guyenne* (Paris, 1516). He wrote to Heber, July 1, 1812: "I will stand the Huon with delight for in my opinion it is the most beautiful of the old Romances & paying a round sum for it compared with what is given for similar works is like the difference between a Countess and your most estimable Fuzer." He mentions it in the Essay on Chivalry. Apparently he did not know Lord Berners's translation.

Lai le Freine. The Middle English poem is in the Auchinleck MS. It is referred to in the essay "On the Fairies of Popular Superstition" (*Minstrelsy*, vol. 2) and quoted in the introduction to "Lord Thomas and Fair Annie," (*Minstrelsy*, vol. 3). Scott arranged for a transcript (by Weber) from the Auchinleck MS to be sent to Ellis (see letters to Ellis of March 1804 and May 16, 1804); it appears in both Ellis and Weber.

Lais of Marie de France. *Guigemar* and *Lanval* are in Le Grand and in Way, *Chevrefoil* (in Ellis's translation) in *Sir Tristrem*, and the others in Ellis.

Libeaus Desconus. Summarized at length by Percy in his essay (in *Reliques*) "On the Ancient Metrical Romances" (he calls it an epic poem). In Ritson. Scott mentions it in a letter to Ellis, July 20, 1805, and in the Essay on Romance. It was discovered by Scott during the winter of 1831–32 at the Royal Library of Naples in another manuscript (XIII.B.29), which was copied for him by Sticchini (see *Bevis of Hampton* above); this transcript is at Abbotsford.

The Lyfe of Alisaunder (or *King Alexander*). A 200-line fragment is in the Auchinleck MS. "There is in our Ms one sheet of Alisaundre being the conclusion of the romance, if you think it of consequence I can have it transcribed & forwarded to you," Scott wrote to Ellis, August 21, 1801. Scott also knew *The Buik of Alexander* (or *The Scottish Alexander Buik*) in the printed version (c. 1580) by Alexander Arbuthnet; he discusses and briefly summarizes it in a letter to Ellis, May 26, 1805. The entire *King Alexander (Kyng Alisaunder)* is in Weber, who also knew *The Buik of Alexander,* which is summarized at some length in an appendix.

The Lyfe of Ipomydon. Quoted at length in Warton; quoted by Scott in a note to I.xlii of *Sir Tristrem*. It appears in both Ellis and Weber.

The Marriage of Sir Gawaine. In Percy's *Reliques*. It is mentioned by Scott in letters to Ellis of May 11, 1801, and May 27, 1804, and discussed in the "Introductory Remarks on Popular Poetry" (*Minstrelsy*, vol. 1): "It would be now, no doubt, desirable to have had some more distinct account of Dr. Percy's folio manuscript and its contents; and Mr. Thomas Percy, accordingly, gives the original of the 'Marriage of Sir Gawain,' and collates it with the copy published in a complete state by his uncle, who has on this occasion given entire rein to his own fancy, though the rude origin of most of his ideas is to be found in the old ballad." Other versions of the story known to Scott include the Wife of Bath's Tale (and Dryden's translation of it), Gower's Tale of Florent and the Loathly Hag, and the ballad "King Henrie" (*Minstrelsy*, vol. 3). He apparently did not know *The Weddynge of Sir Gawen and Dame Ragnell*, which was first published in 1839.

Malory's *Morte Darthur.* At the turn of the century Scott's opinion of Malory was negative; the *Morte Darthur,* he wrote on January 27, 1804, to the Rev. Richard Polwhele, is "a bundle of extracts made by Sir T. Mallory, from the French romances of the Table Round, as Sir Lancelot du Lac, and the other folios printed on that subject at Paris in the beginning of the 16th century. It is therefore of no authority *whatever*, being merely the shadow of a shade, an awkward abridgement of prose romances, themselves founded on the more ancient metrical *lais* and *gests*." He began to relent in his introduction to *Sir Tristrem:*

The *History of Tristrem* was not, so far as I know, translated into English as a separate work; but his adventures make part of the collection, called the *Morte Arthur,* containing great part of the history of the Round Table, extracted at hazard, and without much art or combination, from the various French prose folios on that favorite topic. The work was compiled by Sir Thomas Malory, or Maleore, in the ninth year of the reign of Edward IV., and printed by Caxton . . . Those unaccustomed to the study of romance, should beware of trusting to this work, which misrepresents the adventures, and traduces the character, of Sir Gawain, and other renowned Knights of the Round Table. It is, however, a work of great interest, and curiously written in excellent old English, and breathing a high tone of chivalry.[24]

The last sentence signals a change of attitude on Scott's part. Despite his mixed feelings about the *Morte Darthur* he quotes from it in several notes to *Sir Tristrem* and seems much impressed with Sir Ector's well-known and moving eulogy of Sir Lancelot (although following his Stansby edition he attributes it to Sir Bors). He also quotes two lengthy passages about Lancelot in the notes to Canto I of *Marmion*. On November 18, 1807, he wrote to Richard Heber: "Palmerin you have seen of course it is I think far inferior to Amadis & infinitely so to the Morte Arthur in which I take great pleasure." And by the time he wrote the Essay on Romance (1824) Scott was calling Malory's "celebrated" *Morte Darthur* "indisputably the best Prose Romance the language can boast."

The Stanzaic *Morte Arthur*. Quoted by Warton, included in Ellis, and mentioned by Scott in his review of Ellis. The first genuine edition was by G.A. Panton, in 1819, for the Roxburghe Club. Scott also knew the ballad "King Arthur's Death" in Percy's *Reliques*, and he quotes two lines from it in a letter to Southey, April 10, 1811.

Otuel a Knight. In the Auchinleck MS. Scott cites it in letters to Ellis, March 27 and April 20, 1801, as having a "highly spirited" beginning, and quotes it in a note to III.xlii of *Sir Tristrem*. It appears in Ellis as *Sir Otuel*, with additional material from the Fillingham *Firumbras;* it was copied for Ellis from the Auchinleck MS by Robert Leyden (younger brother of the famous John Leyden); that copy, together with a copy of the continuation from the Fillingham MS, is at Abbotsford, as well as a transcript by Weber.

Palmerin of England. Scott knew this in Southey's four-volume version (1807), which was essentially the old version from Shakespeare's times by the indefatigable Anthony Munday, which Southey "corrected" from the original Portuguese of Francisco de Moraes. Scott wrote to Southey in November 1807: "I have to thank you for Palmerin, which has been my afternoon reading for some days. I like it very much, although it is, I think, considerably inferior to the Amadis. But I wait with double anxiety for the Cid, in which I expect to find very much information as well as amusement. One discovery I have made is, that we understand little or nothing of

Don Quixote except by the Spanish romances. The English and French romances throw very little light on the subject of the doughty cavalier of La Mancha." (See also Scott's letter to Heber, quoted above under Malory's *Morte Darthur*.)

Partenopex de Blois. In Le Grand, vol. 5. It was freely translated from Le Grand by William Stewart Rose in 1807. Scott alludes to Rose's version in the introduction to Canto I of *Marmion* and quotes it in the Essay on Chivalry. I find no indication that Scott knew the Middle English version.

Le Petit Jehan de Saintré. Scott owned the three-volume Paris edition of 1724. It is also in Tressan, and his version is in the *Bibliothèque des Romans*. Scott refers to it in a note to "Auld Maitland" (*Minstrelsy*, vol. 1): "Until [he performed] some distinguishing exploit . . . a young knight was not said to have *won his spurs;* and, upon some occasions, he was obliged to bear, as a mark of thraldom, a chain upon his arm, which was removed, with great ceremony, when his merit became conspicuous. These chains are noticed in the romance of *Jehan de Saintré*." It is cited by Rose in his notes to *Amadis of Gaul* and discussed and quoted by Scott in connection with the etiquette of "courtly love" in the Essay on Chivalry. Scott seems not to have been interested in the second half of the work, which deals with the lady's love affair with the young bourgeois abbot (the only really memorable character) and with Jehan's eventual revenge (which is toned down in Tressan's version).

Rauf Coilyear (or *The Taill of Rauf Coilyear*). Reprinted by David Laing in 1822 from a recently discovered early edition. It is referred to by Scott in a letter to John Richardson of February 27, 1823, and mentioned in his 1830 introduction to *Ivanhoe*.

Reinbrun. This is the third part of *Guy of Warwick* (see above).

Richard Coer de Lyon (or *Richard the Lion-Hearted*). Fragment in the Auchinleck MS. Discussed by Scott in letters to Ellis, October 17, 1802 (in which he is especially intrigued with Richard's use of beehives as artillery: "certainly the strangest bombs that ever were invented") and November 29, 1802: "Your deduction[s] from the variations in the Cuer [Coeur] de Lion Romances are very ingenious and interesting and I certainly cannot gainsay your conclusions especially as I never saw the full Romance of King Richard. I have sometimes thought that the original of the Knight who married the Devil may perhaps be traced to a distorted account of the marriage of Guy de Lusignan with the fairy Melusina which undoubtedly is a tale of great antiquity." It appears in Ellis and is discussed at length by Scott in his review of Ritson and Ellis, with emphasis on "the bloody cruelties practiced by the champions of Palestine upon an enemy." It is also in Weber, who omits "the savage meal which Richard made upon the heads of the Saracens, and the feast [of boiled Saracen heads] he prepared for the messengers of Soliman [i.e. Saladin]." Ellis's transcript of the MS at Caius College, Cambridge, is at Abbotsford.

Robert of Cysille (or *Roberd of Cisyle*). Quoted at some length by Warton. It appears in Ellis and is cited by Scott in connection with Sir Gowther's penance in a letter to Ellis, October 17, 1805. Transcripts by both Weber and Ellis are at Abbotsford. The first printing of the whole poem did not occur until 1839.

Roland and Ferragus (or *Roland and Vernagu*). In the Auchinleck MS. Scott described it in a letter to Ellis, October 22, 1801: "The Romance of Feragus in our Ms is I find a versified edition of a chapter of Turpins Chronicle entitled de bello Ferracuti Gigantis et de optima disputatione Rolandi. The Latin version & the poem resemble each other even in the minute particulars. It commences with a detail of Charlemagnes conquests in Spain not forgetting the circumstance of his efficacious prayers converting the obstinate city of Lucerne into a lake of fire and brimstone." It appears in Ellis (to whom Scott wrote, May 25, 1803: "Young Leyden is at work upon Ferragus & this transcript shall be speedily sent to you"). A transcript by Weber is at Abbotsford.

Roswall and Lillian. In Scott's boyhood collection of chapbooks; Scott also owned a chapbook version printed at Newcastle and entitled *The Pleasant History of Roswal and Lillian*, according to Corson's unpublished catalogue. Discussed in a letter to Ellis of August 25–September 8, 1801: "I am anxious you should include among your Romances, one called Roswal & Lilian: my reason is that it is the last metrical Romance of Chivalry which retaind popularity in Scotland & indeed was sung in Edinr. within these 20 years by a sort of reciter in the streets. I can send you a modern copy—the Duke of Roxburgh has a black letter Copy of some antiquity" (Edinburgh, 1663, according to Corson; later acquired by the Advocates' Library). Referred to in a note to II.xiii of *Sir Tristrem*. It appears in Ellis, and transcripts by both Ellis and Weber are at Abbotsford. It was printed by David Laing from the Duke of Roxburgh's copy in 1822.

The Seven Wise Masters. In Scott's boyhood collection of chapbooks. In the Auchinleck MS. Scott arranged to have the Auchinleck version copied for

Ellis (see letters of May 27 and June 18, 1804), who included it in his *Specimens*. It is cited by Scott in his review of Ritson and Ellis as a romance "long known among the school-boys of this country." It also appears in Weber.

Sir Amadace. In Advocates MS. 19.3.1. Described by Scott in a letter to Ellis of October 17, 1805, as "a poem called Sir Amadis—not Amadis of Gaul, but a courteous knight, who, being reduced to poverty, travels to conceal his distress, and gives the wreck of his fortune to purchase the rites of burial for a deceased knight, who had been refused them by the obduracy of his creditors." Printed for the first time in Weber.

Sir Eger, Sir Grahame, and Sir Gray-Steel (or *Eger and Grime*). As early as 1800 Scott had correspondence about this romance with Bishop Percy, who sent him an account of the version in the Folio MS. Scott refers to "the tune of old Graysteil" in a letter to Ellis, August 25–September 8, 1801; he discusses the romance in a letter to Ellis, November 29, 1802: "I have studied the Romance with great pleasure & I am by no means surprised at the high interest which it seems to have excited in Scotland for the situations are sometimes good and drawn with great force. The dying picture of Graysteel tearing up the grass in his agonies is horribly fine. I wish the conclusion had been less obscure. I think it probable that in the great tournament which Sir Graham had proclaimd in the land of Bealme he fell by the lance of his friend Sir Eger without their knowing each other. As for Graysteel his name seems to have past into a proverb for gallantry & courage." Mentioned also in the introduction to *Sir Tristrem*. Mrs. Ellis wrote out a transcript for Scott of the edition of 1711. Transcripts by Ellis and Weber are also at Abbotsford.

Sir Eglamour of Artoys. Scott wrote to Ellis in December 1802: "Did I ever mention that the oldest Book known to have been printed in Scotland (about 1511 I think) contains the Romance of Sir Eglamore & would you wish to have a copy of it" (he means the Chepman and Myllar print of 1508). He quotes it in a note to III.xli of *Sir Tristrem*. It is sampled in Ellis, and the whole romance was copied by Weber, who considered it "wretched." Scott refers to it in the Essay on Romance, with the observation that no French original had ever been discovered.

Sir Ferumbras (or *The Sowdon of Babylon*). Mentioned in letters to Ellis of April 20 and July 13, 1801. It is referred to as "the famous romance of Fierabras" in a note to II.xiii of *Sir Tristrem* and quoted briefly in the Essay on Romance. A transcript by Ellis is at Abbotsford; a transcript by Weber is cited by Weber.

Sir Gawain and Sir Galeron of Galloway (or *The Awntyrs off Arthure at the Terne Wathelyne*). In Pinkerton's *Scotish Poems*. The opening lines are quoted by Scott in a letter to Ellis, May 27, 1804, in connection with Tarn Wadling, but mistakenly attributed to *Golagrus and Gawain*. For references to it in *Minstrelsy*, vol. 4, and the Essay on Romance, see *Golagrus and Gawain* above. Printed by Laing in 1822 as *The Awntyrs of Arthur.*

Sir Gowther. In Advocates MS. 19.3.1. Scott wrote to Ellis, October 17, 1805: "There is a tale of Sir Gowther, said to be a Breton Lay, which partly resembles the history of Robert the Devil, the hero being begot in the same way; and partly that of Robert of Sicily, the penance imposed on Sir Gowther being the same, as he kept table with the hounds, and was discovered by a dumb lady to be the stranger knight who had assisted her father the emperor in his wars." A transcript by Weber is cited by Weber. In Utterson's *Select Pieces*. A copy of *Roberte the Deuyll: A Metrical Romance*, edited by J. Herbert (London, 1798), is at Abbotsford.

Sir Isumbras. In Advocates MS. 19.3.1. Mentioned by Scott in a letter to Ellis, October 17, 1805. It appears in Ellis and in Utterson. A transcript by Ellis is at Abbotsford. A transcript by Weber is cited by Weber.

Sir Launfal. In Le Grand and Way, from Marie de France, in modernized versions. Thomas Chestre's poem was edited by Ellis and printed in an appendix to Way; it is also in Ritson. In the essay "On the Fairies of Popular Superstition" (*Minstrelsy*, vol. 2), Scott says: "In the tale of *Sir Launfal*, in Way's *Fabliaux*, as well as in that of *Sir Gruelan*, in the same interesting collection, the reader will find the fairy of Normandy, or Bretagne, adorned with all the splendour of Eastern description." He quotes Chestre's version in a note to II.ix of *Sir Tristrem*.

Sir Orfeo. In Auchinleck MS (as *King Orfeo*). In a letter to Ellis, March 27, 1801, Scott cites it as "Orfeo & Herodeis (a Gothicised edition of Orpheus & Euridice) where Herodeis is carried off by the fairies." It appears in Ritson and is discussed and quoted by Scott in "On the Fairies of Popular Superstition" (*Minstrelsy*, vol. 2).

Sir Otuel. See *Otuel a Knight*.

Sir Tristrem. In the Auchinleck MS. Summarized by Scott in a letter to the Rev. Richard Polwhele, January 27, 1804. His first edition was published in Edinburgh by Archibald Constable in 1804; only 150 copies were printed. Subsequent editions appeared in 1806, 1811, 1819, and later in the century. Contains a long introduction, several appendices, a detailed summary, and elaborate notes. Scott attributed this important Middle English poem to Thomas of Erceldoune and argued (erroneously) that it was the source for the better-known French and German versions. Scott also knew the Oxford *Folie Tristan* and the long fragment from Thomas of Britain that begins with a quarrel between Brengwain and Ysolt; he includes Ellis's abstracts of both in *Sir Tristrem*. Also included are a Welsh triad involving Tristan, Gawain, and Arthur—the Welsh together with a parallel English translation; Ellis's translation of Marie de France's *Lai de Chevrefeuille*; and, beginning with the edition of 1811, Weber's essay on the German versions. For whatever Scott knew about Gottfried von Strassburg's *Tristan* and Heinrich von Freiberg's continuation, I suspect he was indebted to Weber; he probably did not read this material in the original, even though he acquired editions of Gottfried in the 1820s. I have found no evidence that he knew Eilhart von Oberge's *Tristrant*, or Brother Robert's Old Norse version, or the Icelandic rendering of it, although he would have seen these versions mentioned in the essay by Weber, who knew very little about them himself. I have found no certain evidence that he knew Béroul's version. He of course knew the prose Tristan, as it appears in Malory, and he was more or less familiar with some of the medieval French prose versions as well as the modernization by Tressan. He apparently read in *Meliadus de Leonnoys* and *Ysaie le Triste*. He knew of a Spanish Tristan of 1528 and an Italian version of 1552 and 1555, but he did not read them or even see them, so far as I can determine; they are listed in his introduction with little or no comment.

The Squyr of Lowe Degre. Quoted at some length by Warton and included in Ritson. Scott quotes from it in *Quentin Durward* and refers to it in the Essay on Romance, with the observation that no French original has ever been discovered.

The Tournament of Tottenham. In Percy's *Reliques*. Scott discusses it as a "burlesque romance" in his review of Evans's *Old Ballads*. He refers to it in a note to Canto V of *Rokeby* and in the Essay on Romance.

Valentine and Orson. In Scott's boyhood collection of chapbooks. In the *Bibliothèque des Romans*. A ballad version is in Percy's *Reliques*. "Valentine & Orson is the last prose Romance which kept its ground with the common people," Scott wrote to Ellis, August 25–September 8, 1801. He quotes from a French edition of 1631 in a note to "Christie's Will" (*Minstrelsy*, vol. 4). An English edition "printed by A.M. for E. Tracy, at the Three Bibles, on London-bridge" (1700?) is at Abbotsford, and at least three chapbooks are listed in Corson's unpublished catalogue.

Ywain and Gawain. In Ritson. Mentioned by Scott in a letter to Ellis, July 20, 1805, and praised highly in his review of Ritson and Ellis: "The first romance in the collection is Ywain and Gawain, a most beautiful tale of chivalry, from which Warton has given copious extracts in his History of English Poetry. It is certainly the finest romance in the work, perhaps the most interesting which now exists." He goes on to summarize the work in some detail. He mentions it in the Essay on Romance.

Group 2: Romances Known but Seldom Cited

Arthur of Little Britain. In the *Bibliothèque des Romans* and in Tressan (much condensed). Lord Berners's translation of the original French, edited by E.V. Utterson (1814), is at Abbotsford. Scott mentions it in the Essay on Romance.

Le Bone Florence of Rome. In Ritson.

Chevalere Assigne. Edited by Utterson for the Roxburghe Club in 1820. See Scott's letter of September 19, 1831, to David Laing: "Happening to have two reprints of Mr Utterson of the Chevelere assigne (du Cygne) I send you one as a duplicate [is] of no use to me which you may consider as valuable."

The Earl of Toulous. Summarized in Warton; included in Ritson. It is *not* mentioned or quoted by Scott in connection with the ballad "Sir Hugh le Blond" (*Minstrelsy*, vol. 3), which has a similar story. ("Sir Aldingar," in Percy's *Reliques*, also involves a lady who is accused falsely and is about to be put to death.)

Emare. In Ritson; quoted by Rose in the notes to Canto I of *Partenopex de Blois*.

The Foure Sonnes of Aymon. Scott owned the French edition published at Lyon in 1581. Another version is included in the *Bibliothèque Bleue*. I have found no indication that he knew William Caxton's translation.

Gamelyn. Included in *The Works of Geoffrey Chaucer*, edited by John Urry (London, 1721), a copy of which is at Abbotsford. Also in Alexander Chalmers's *English Poets* (1810), vol. 1; this too is at Abbotsford. Scott refers to "the Cokes Tale of Gamelyn" in a note to Canto V of *The Lady of the Lake*.

Graelent. In Barbazan. A modernized prose version is in Le Grand (with the name Gruélan), and it is translated in Way. (See *Sir Launfal* in Group 1 above.)

King Horn. In Ritson. (See *Horn Child* in Group 1 above.)

The King of Tars. Quoted at length in Warton. In the Auchinleck MS. In Ritson.

The Knight of Curtesy and the Fair Lady of Faguell. In Ritson.

*Octavian (*or *Octouian Imperator).* In Weber (the Southern version). Scott also knew and owned the modern English prose version by the Rev. J.J. Conybeare (the Anglo-Saxon scholar), abridged from a French manuscript in the Bodleian Library (Oxford: Collingwood, 1809). It is bound together with vol. 3 of Weber's *Metrical Romances* at Abbotsford.

Sir Cleges. In Advocates MS. 19.1.11. In Weber.

Sir Degare. Summarized by Warton. In the Auchinleck MS. It appears in Ellis and in Utterson. Transcripts by Ellis and by Weber are at Abbotsford.

Sir Triamour. In Ellis and in Utterson. A transcript by Weber is at Abbotsford.

Group 3: Romances Known to Some Extent

Chrétien de Troyes. Discussed briefly by Scott in the introduction to *Sir Tristrem*, where he mistakenly ascribes to Chrétien *Le Chevalier à l'Epée*. He refers hesitatingly (but correctly) to *Erec et Enide* in a note to "Auld Maitland" (*Minstrelsy*, vol. 1), in connection with the concept of "jeopardy": "The romantic custom of achieving, or attempting, some desperate and perilous adventure, without either necessity or cause, was a peculiar, and perhaps the most prominent, feature of chivalry. It was not merely the duty, but the pride and delight, of a true knight, to perform such exploits, as no one but a madman would have undertaken. I think it is in the old French romance of *Erec and Eneide*, that an adventure, the access to which lay through an avenue of stakes, garnished with the bloody heads of the knights who had attempted and failed to achieve it, is called by the inviting title of *La joie de la Cour.*" Scott mentions Chrétien in connection with the Tristan-story in letters to Ellis, July 1803, and to the Rev. Richard Polwhele, January 27, 1804. Prose versions of *Erec et Enide*, *Le Chevalier de la Charrette* (or *Lancelot*), and *Le Chevalier au Lion* (or *Yvain*, on which the

Middle English poem *Ywain and Gawain* is based) were in the *Bibliothèque des Romans*, but not *Cligés*, which Scott never mentions.

Dom Flores de Grece, surnommé le Chevalier des Cignes. Scott owned a copy of this book, which was apparently *written* (not translated) by Nicolas de Herberay and published in Paris in 1552. I do not know whether he was familiar with the English edition of 1664. (This was the third English edition; I have found no references to the first and second editions.)

Esplandian. Mentioned by Scott in a letter to Ellis, August 27, 1803— "Where I have been, the people talked more of the praises of Ryno and Fillan (not Ossian's heroes, but two Forest greyhounds which I got in a present) than, I verily believe, they would have done of the prowesses of Sir Tristrem, or of Esplandian, had either of them appeared to lead on the levy *en masse*"—and again in the Essay on Romance. Scott must have known the French version that constitutes Part V of the multivolume edition of Herberay's *Amadis de Gaule* and its many sequels (Lyon, 1577-81; Paris, 1615); this edition takes up a whole shelf of Press N at Abbotsford. I do not know whether he knew *Esplandian* in the English versions of 1598 and 1664; neither is listed in the Abbotsford Library *Catalogue*.

Les Faits et Prouesses de Jourdain de Blaves. In the *Bibliothèque des Romans*. In a note to III.x of *Sir Tristrem* Scott gives the title, indicating that the work was published in Paris in 1520—his information apparently coming from the headnote in the *Bibliothèque des Romans*. Not listed in the Abbotsford Library *Catalogue*. (A beautifully bound copy of the Paris volume in mint condition is in the British Library.)

Gyron le Courtois. In the *Bibliothèque des Romans*. In the introduction to "Græme and Bewick" (*Minstrelsy*, vol. 3), Scott notes: "The romance of *Gyron le Courtois* has a similar subject. I think the hero, like Græme in the ballad, kills himself, out of some high point of honour towards his friend." (Actually he only wounds himself, and recovers to undertake new adventures, according to Dunlop.) Mentioned in the Essay on Romance. Not listed in the Abbotsford Library *Catalogue*. (A copy of the version published in Paris, 1519, is in the Newbattle Collection, currently in the possession of the Marquis of Lothian. I have not seen it; Scott may have.)

Helyas, The Knight of the Swan. Freely translated by Robert Copland from the French, and printed by William Copland c. 1550; reprinted in 1827 in an edition by W.J. Thoms. This is an expanded version of the *Chevalere Assigne*, the verse romance listed in Group 2 above, with much additional material. In the Essay on Romance Scott refers to it (erroneously) as having been compiled by Lord Berners. It is not listed in the Abbotsford Library *Catalogue*. The story is similar to that of the German poem *Lohengrin*, a copy of which Scott did have (the edition by Görres, published in Heidelberg in 1813) but which he probably did not read much of, if any, since the medieval German would have been very difficult for him.

Lancelot du Lac. In the *Bibliothèque des Romans*. Scott mentions it in a note to II.xcviii of *Sir Tristrem* and in a letter to Southey, December 15, 1807: "Do you follow the metrical or the printed books in your account of the Round Table? and would your task be at all facilitated by the use of a copy of Sir Lancelot, from the press of Jehan Dennis, which I have by me?" The three-volume Abbotsford copy was published in Paris in 1533. (See also *Perceforest* below.)

The Mabinogion. This was to have been translated and published by William Owen, the Welsh scholar, but he never completed the project. Scott knew of it and, according to a letter to Jacob Grimm, April 29, 1814, had "seen some curious specimens in [Ellis's] possession." He alludes specifically to *iron horses, magic cauldrons*, and *Bran the Blessed* in a letter to Ellis, September 14, 1803. The first translation (Lady Charlotte Guest's) was not published until 1839.

Meliadus de Leonnoys. In the *Bibliothèque des Romans*. Referred to (perhaps) in a letter to Heber, January 7, 1805: "I have still some books of yours Sir Tristrem & his father King Meliadus also Richard sans peur, will you let me know how they will reach you safely" (*Letters*, 12:269-70; not listed in Corson's *Notes and Index*). Scott cites the edition published by Denis Janot in Paris, 1532, in the introduction to *Sir Tristrem* (copies are in the Newbattle Collection and the British Library but not at Abbotsford).

Melusine. Summarized in part in the essay "On the Fairies of Popular Superstition" (*Minstrelsy*, vol. 2), which cites the *Bibliothèque des Romans*. Referred to, quoted, and summarized by Rose in notes to *Partenopex de Blois* and alluded to by Scott in a letter to Ellis, November 29, 1802 (see *Richard Coer de Lyon* in Group 1 above). I do not know whether Scott knew other French versions; he seems not to have known either the Middle English translation of the prose version of Jean d'Arras or the Middle English stanzaic *Romans of Partenay, or of Lusignan* (based on the French of La Coudrette, which itself is based on Jean d'Arras).

Ogier le Danois. In the *Bibliothèque des Romans*. Scott briefly refers to it in connection with chess in a note to I.xxix of *Sir Tristrem*. "The infamous and traitorous character assigned in the prose romance to the knights templar, make it probable that it was written in the time of Philip the Fair, in whose reign that order was suppressed, on account of real or alleged enormities" (Dunlop, 1:450). Not listed in the Abbotsford Library *Catalogue*. (The edition published in Troyes, 1626, is in the National Library of Scotland. Scott may have known it, but probably not, for it is not listed in the 1807 or earlier catalogues of the Advocates' Library, and the librarians at the National Library do not know how or exactly when this particular copy, which once belonged to Louis-César de la Baume-le-Blanc, Duc de Voujours and afterwards Duc de la Vallière (1708–80), came into Scotland; it *is* listed in the Advocates' Library catalogue of accessions to 1871.)

Perceforest. Quoted at some length (on raw venison) in a note to Canto IV, of *The Lady of the Lake.* It is discussed also in the Essay on Romance, where Scott is intrigued with the way in which the work was introduced to its readers, namely, "as the contents [in translation] of a newly-discovered manuscript." Further, "it is in the prose folios of *Lancelot du Lac, Perceforest*, and others, that antiquaries find recorded the most exact accounts of fights, tournaments, feasts, and other magnificent displays of chivalric splendour; and as they descend into more minute description than the historians of the time thought worthy of their pains, they are a mine from which the painful student may extract much valuable information. This, however, is not the full extent of their merit. These ancient books, amid many pages of dull repetition and uninteresting dialect, and notwithstanding the languor of an inartificial, protracted, and confused story, exhibit from time to time passages of deep interest, and situations of much novelty, as well as specimens of spirited and masculine writing." Scott cites here the Paris edition of 1528; he owned the edition published in Paris in 1531–32, which he quotes in *The Lady of the Lake.* Both are in six volumes. An abridged version is in the *Bibliothèque des Romans*.

Richard sans Peur. Included in the *Bibliothèque Bleue* (1787). Scott refers to it in connection with military traits of fairies in "On the Fairies of Popular Superstition" (*Minstrelsy*, vol. 2), and in a letter to Heber, January 7, 1805, he mentions "Richard sans peur," presumably a separately printed book; both T.F. Henderson (the later editor of the *Minstrelsy)* and Grierson suggest the *Histoire du redouté Prince Richard sans Peur, Duc de Normandie*, published in Paris by Nicolas and Pierre Bonfons (1590?), but there were other editions as well. Richard was the son of Robert le Diable.

Sir Gaheret. Referred to by Scott in the note to I.xxix of *Sir Tristrem:* "But the most splendid game of chess, and which puts to shame even that which the late King of Prussia and Marshal Keith were wont to play, with real soldiers, occurs in the romance of Sir Gaheret. That champion was entertained in the enchanted castle of a beautiful fairy, who engaged him in a party at chess in a large hall, where flags of black and white marble formed the chequer, and the pieces, consisting of massive statues of gold and silver, moved at the touch of the magic rod held by the player. Sir Gaheret, being defeated, was obliged to remain the fairy's prisoner, but was afterwards liberated by his cousin Gawin, who checkmated the mistress of the enchanted chess-board." I do not know what romance Scott had in mind. Gaheret is Gawain's youngest *brother* in the French prose *Lancelot*; he also figures prominently in the *Histoire des Quatre Frères* (Gauvain, Agravain, Gueret, and Galheret) in the *Bibliothèque des Romans*, and Malory's Gareth owes much to him.[25]

Sir Pleindamour. Referred to by Scott in the Essay on Romance, with the observation that no French original has ever been discovered. I do not know what romance he had in mind. There is a Sir Pleyndamour mentioned at the end of Chaucer's *Sir Thopas*, and there is a Sir Plaine d'Amour in Malory's story of La Cote Mal Tayle; but I know of no separate romance dealing with a Sir Pleindamour. (Maybe Scott meant to say *Sir Eglamour.*)

Tirant lo Blanch. Mentioned in the introduction to Canto IV of *Marmion*: "I spelling o'er, with much delight, / The legend of that antique knight, / Tirante by name, yclep'd the White" (lines 170–72). The Essay on Chivalry calls it a romance much praised by Cervantes. The work was originally written in Catalan (not in English, not in Portuguese), according to Joseph A. Vaeth.[26] Scott knew and owned the 1737 French translation by the Count de Caylus; an abridged version is in the *Bibliothèque des Romans*. Much of the story is quite similar to *Guy of Warwick* (see Group 1 above).

Troy-Book. Among Scott's boyhood collection of chapbooks was *The Famous and Renowned History of Hector, Prince of Troy; or, The Three Destructions of Troy*. Scott quotes about a dozen lines from the opening of the Laud *Troy-Book* in the note to I.iv of *Sir Tristrem*. I doubt that he knew the whole poem—it is 18,664 lines long—and I do not know whether he knew the two Scottish Troy fragments. Additional chapbooks are listed in Corson's unpublished catalogue.

William of Palerne. Mentioned by Weber in the introduction to his *Metrical Romances*. In 1817 Scott wrote two letters to James Bailey of Trinity College, Cambridge, to arrange to have a copy made of "William and the

Wer-wolf"—apparently without success, for on April 25, 1822, he wrote to David Laing: "At Cambridge I would have you by no means fail to get a Transcript of the old poem calld William and the Werwolf. I am extremely curious to see it and would long since have had it transcribed if I could have found an amanuensis in whose fidelity I could have placed confidence but such men as Leyden, Weber or David Laing are not of every days occurrence: the labour of the antiquarian transcriber must be a labour both of learning & of love both of head and affections as well as of the fingers." He mentioned the romance in another letter to Laing, September 19, 1831, shortly before he went abroad. The first edition was done by Frederic Madden for the Roxburghe Club in 1832. Selections had appeared in C.H. Hartshorne's *Ancient Metrical Tales* in 1829.

Ysaie le Triste. Discussed by Scott in the introduction to *Sir Tristrem:* "This is a romance of faërie. Ysaie is under the protection of certain powerful fays, who have assigned him, for his attendant, Tronc le Nain, a dwarf, whose deformity is only equalled by his wit and fidelity. This page of Ysaie le Triste is subjected to a law of extreme, and, it would appear, very unjust severity. Whenever his master was fickle in his amours, and he by no means copied the fidelity of his father Tristrem, the dwarf was unmercifully beaten by the fairies, his sovereigns. Upon the whole, the romance is very inferior to that of *Sir Tristrem.*" Ysaie's promiscuity is referred to again in the note to I.x. The Abbotsford copy, entitled *L'Histoire de Isaie le Triste, Filz de Tristan de Leonnoys,* was published in Paris by Jehan Bonfons (1550?); the edition that Scott cites in *Sir Tristrem* was published in Paris by Galliot du Pré, 1522. An abridged version is in the *Bibliothèque des Romans.*

Group 4: Romances Known Only Slightly

Athelston. I have found no reference by Scott to this romance. It was included by C.H. Hartshorne in his *Ancient Metrical Romances,* published in 1829. Scott would therefore have known of it but too late for it to have influenced his work.

Havelok. Referred to briefly by Scott in a letter to Sir Francis Freeling, February 27, 1828: "I have the note about the Saxon poem and will with pleasure take my copy at £6.6." This was the edition (the first ever) by Frederic Madden for the Roxburghe Club, in 1828; Scott was sent a copy on December 12 (see *Letters,* 12:69 n.1), too late to have had any influence on his work. He knew the short poem about Argentile and Curan, included in Percy's *Reliques* and taken from William Warner's *Albion's Eng-*

land. "Warner's poem is . . . the story of Havelok and Goldeburgh, told with the names used in Gaimar's version—Aldebrict, Edel, Argentille and Curan" (Johnston, *Enchanted Ground*, p. 88); actually, Warner's account is a *much diluted* version of the Havelok story. *Albion's England* is included in the fourth volume of Chalmers's *English Poets*, which is at Abbotsford. I do not know whether Scott was familiar with Gaimar's *Estorie des Engles*; probably not.

Sir Gawain and the Green Knight. Scott first became aware of this finest of all the Middle English verse romances in 1831. Grierson cites a letter from Madden which "informs us that shortly after Madden's discovery of Sir Gawaine [at the British Museum] he wrote to Sir Walter and offered to edit it for the Bannatyne Club. The proposal was declined as the Club had not sufficient funds" (*Letters*, 11:494 n.1). During the negotiations, Scott wrote to Lockhart on March 25: "I took the liberty to suggest as a most valuable & important contribution an old Scottish romance extant in the Museum named Sir Gawaine & the Green Knight. It was in part copied by Dr Maddocks [i.e. Madden] of the Musæum who I mak[e] no doubt would be glad to part with what he has copied for a small sum. . . . I would account this to be a great curiosity and if the Marquis of Stafford undertook [it] I should be happy to give any assistance in my power. . . . I think it one of the most legitimate contributions which the Club could secur[e] or the munificent Marquis bestow." On April 5 he wrote to Charles Kirkpatrick Sharpe: "I have been laying anchors to leeward to persuade Lord Stafford to print Sir Gawain and the Green Knight supposed to [be] written by Clerk of Tranent lamented in the poem of the Makers by Dunbar"; but these plans fell through, according to a letter to David Laing, September 19: "I wrote you some time since that Lord Stafford had given up thoughts of the Green Knight." In October Scott was in London before going abroad; on the 17th he went to the British Museum, where Madden was struck by "the uncouthness of his appearance and figure" and by his "slow and thick manner of speaking—and broad Scotch accent."[27] I do not know whether they discussed *Sir Gawain* or whether Madden showed him Cotton Nero MS. A.x; apparently not. The Bannatyne Club did eventually issue the poem, edited by Madden, in 1839—seven years after Scott's death.

In the above entry on *Sir Tristrem* I have called attention to Spanish and Italian versions of the Tristan-story that Scott knew of but had probably not read, or even seen. I wonder too about some of the titles he cites in the Essay on Romance. Did he know well Heliodorus's *Theagenes and Chariclea*, or the romances of Antonius Diogenes, or the three Oriental romances:

Antar, Sha-Nameh, and *Méjnoun and Leilah?* If he had read *Antar, A Bedoueen Romance* (which is in his library at Abbotsford), one might expect him to have said something about it; he certainly would have been interested in it. This romance was translated from Arabic by Terrick Hamilton, Oriental Secretary to the British Embassy at Constantinople, and published by John Murray in four volumes (1819–20). Since the original work is very long, this translation covers only the early life of Antar, from his birth to his marriage to Ibla. Antar flourished around 600 A.D., that is, before Islam had become established. The description in the editor's introduction (p. iv) of the early inhabitants of the Arabian peninsula would certainly have been noticed by a writer who understood so well the Scottish people of earlier times: "The characteristics of the real Arabs or Bedowins are here presented in their native simplicity. An eager desire for the property of their neighbour; an unconquerable fondness for strife and battle; a singular combination of profuse hospitality, with narrow economy—quick perception—deep cunning—great personal courage, a keen sense of honour, respect for their women, and a warm admiration and ready use of the poetical beauties of their unrivalled language." The narrative is interspersed, in Scott's own manner, with lyrical poems composed by Antar (translated by Hamilton into very poetic prose). "It is certain," wrote W.A. Clouston in 1887, "that European chivalry owed much to the Arabs; and that many scenes and incidents from 'Antar' and other Arabian romances were appropriated by the early Spanish authors of similar works, which they had derived from their Moorish conquerors; and we may fairly consider 'Antar' as the prototype of European romances of chivalry."[28]

Group 5: Romances Apparently Not Known

The Grene Knight. This condensed version of the famous romance has been preserved in Bishop Percy's Folio MS, but Percy did not include it in the *Reliques.* The first edition was by Madden, in 1839.

Lancelot of the Laik. This Scottish verse romance has come down to us in a single manuscript (Cambridge Univ. Kk.1.5.vii). The first edition was by J. Stevenson, for the Maitland Club, in 1839.

The Alliterative *Morte Arthure.* This excellent romance has survived in a single manuscript (Lincoln Cathedral 91). The first edition, by J.O. Halliwell, did not appear until 1847.

Sir Degrevant. This romance has some typical motifs and characters that can be found in Scott—the secret love of an enemy's daughter, the three-day tournament, the faithful squire, the faithful waiting-maid—but the first edition was by J.O. Halliwell, in 1844, for the Camden Society.

Sir Torrent of Portyngale. This romance also has motifs that can be found in Scott—a father's unwillingness to permit his daughter to marry her true-love, a loss of children, a combat between father and son, a recognition scene, the reunion of a family—but the first edition was by J.O. Halliwell in 1842. The same motifs can be found in *Sir Eglamour,* which Scott did know and from which *Sir Torrent* probably derives.

The Weddynge of Sir Gawen and Dame Ragnell. See *The Marriage of Sir Gawaine* in Group 1 above.

So much for Scott's knowledge of the romances. And what about Chaucer? The earliest edition in Scott's library at Abbotsford is by John Stow (1561), which was printed by John Kyngston for John Wight. Next is Thomas Speght's edition of 1602 (his second). Both of these black-letter volumes go back to the 1532 edition by William Thynne for the *Canterbury Tales, Troilus and Criseyde,* and other basic works by Chaucer (and other writers), but each contains additional material as well. John Lydgate's *Siege of Thebes,* for example, appears for the first time with Chaucer in Stow's volume, while Chaucer's "A.B.C." appears for the first time ever in Speght. Also included in the latter is the *Flour and the Leafe,* first published in Speght's edition of 1598. Scott also had the edition of 1721 by John Urry, which was the first in roman letter and the first to include the *Tale of Gamelyn;* he had Thomas Tyrwhitt's second edition of the *Canterbury Tales* (1798) and George Ogle's modernizations of them (1741). A later edition at Abbotsford is Alexander Chalmers's, the first volume of his mammoth *Works of the English Poets from Chaucer to Cowper* (1810). In addition, there are the *Illustrations of the Lives and Writings of Gower and Chaucer* by the Rev. Henry J. Todd (1810) and William Godwin's four-volume *Life of Chaucer* (1803), which Scott reviewed in 1804 for the *Edinburgh Review.* Prominently displayed in Scott's study was a print of Thomas Stothard's *Canterbury Pilgrims.* "It is much to the credit of British painting," he wrote in a note to Dryden's Preface to the *Fables,* "that Mr. Stothard, of London, has been able to execute a picture representing this celebrated group on their journey to Canterbury with the genius and spirit of a master, and all the rigid attention to costume that could be expected by the most severe antiquary."[29]

The works of Scott both creative and critical are full of allusions to "Father Chaucer," as he fondly called him. In the essay "On the Fairies of Popular Superstition" (*Minstrelsy,* vol. 2), he cites, not surprisingly, the Merchant's Tale and *Sir Thopas.* In the introductory note to "King Henrie"

(*Minstrelsy,* vol. 3) he remarks that "the legend will remind the reader" of the Wife of Bath's Tale, and in a note to "The Flowers of the Forest" (*ibid.*) he quotes from the Wife of Bath's Prologue to explain the word *preaching*. In an appendix to "Christie's Will" (*Minstrelsy,* vol. 4) he quotes from the Franklin's Tale to help illustrate his point about the power of some skilled individuals in olden times to cause people "to see the thing that is not." He mentions the Knight's Tale in the note to I.xiv of *Sir Tristrem,* and he refers to and quotes from it at some length in the Essay on Chivalry:

> Where the honour or love of a lady was at stake, the fairest prize was held out to the victorious knight, and champions from every quarter were sure to hasten to combat in a cause so popular. Chaucer, when he describes the assembly of the knights who came with Arcite and Palemon to fight for the love of the fair Emilie, describes the manners of his age in the following lines:
>
> "For every knight that loved chivalry,
> And would his thankes have a passant name,
> Hath pray'd that he might ben of that game,
> And well was him that thereto chusen was.
> For if there fell to-morrow such a case,
> Ye knowen well that every lusty knight
> That loveth par amour, and hath his might,
> Were it in Engellonde, or elleswhere,
> They wold hir thankes willen to be there.
> To fight for a lady! Ah! Benedicite,
> It were a lusty sight for to see."

Interestingly, Scott does not consider the possibility of irony here. I wonder what he would have thought of Terry Jones's interpretation of this passage,[30] or of the tale as a whole—or of the Knight himself, in view of his having referred to his son Walter (in a letter to Heber, October 29, 1823) as "a fine person and just the stuff out of which would have been made in former days 'a verie parfite gentil knight.' " Later in the essay he invokes the Knight's Tale in discussions of armor and of proper procedure in tournaments. All in all, this tale—this romance—was Scott's favorite of the Canterbury tales. He alludes to it and quotes from it frequently in the Waverley Novels, either in the original Middle English or in Dryden's modernization, and he shows a predilection for the story-pattern of two young men vying for the hand in marriage of the same girl. The reasons for his attraction to this particular tale lie deep (see Chapter 3).

The *Canterbury Tales* captured Scott's imagination more than did *Troilus and Criseyde* or the dream poems or anything else by Father Chaucer. In his spirited review of Godwin's *Life of Chaucer,* Scott censures Godwin for having taken so little notice of the Canterbury pilgrims:

The characters . . . of the several pilgrims, so exquisitely described, that each individual passes before the eyes of the reader, and so admirably contrasted with each other; their conversation and manners, the gallantry of the Knight and Squire, the affected *sentimentality* of the Abbess, the humour of mine Host and the Wife of Bath; the pride of the Monk, the humility of the Parson, the learning and poverty of the Scholar, with the rude but comic portraits of the inferior characters, are, in the history of the life and age of Chaucer, of which they form a living picture, passed over in profound silence, or with very slight notice. [*Miscellaneous Prose Works*, 17:70]

Scott's view of Chaucer's pilgrims is the same as Dryden's:

I see . . . all the Pilgrims in the "Canterbury Tales," their humours, their features, and the very dress, as distinctly as if I had supped with them at the Tabard in Southwark. . . . Some of his persons are vicious, and some virtuous; some are unlearned, or (as Chaucer calls them) lewd, and some are learned. Even the ribaldry of the low characters is different: the Reeve, the Miller, and the Cook, are several men, and distinguished from each other as much as the mincing Lady-Prioress and the broad-speaking, gap-toothed Wife of Bath. But enough of this; there is such a variety of game springing up before me, that I am distracted in my choice, and know not which to follow. It is sufficient to say, according to the proverb, that here is God's plenty.

This comes from Dryden's Preface to the *Fables* (in Scott's edition), and it is still one of the best critical appreciations of Chaucer that we have.

As editor of Dryden's *Works*, Scott knew well his worthy predecessor's translations from Chaucer: *Palamon and Arcite* (the Knight's Tale), *The Cock and the Fox* (the Nun's Priest's Tale), *The Wife of Bath's Tale*, and *The Character of A Good Parson* (this translation and elaboration of Chaucer's portrait of the Parson in the General Prologue more readily brings forth Scott's phrase "the humility of the Parson" than does the original Middle English). Another poem included in the *Fables—The Flower and the Leaf*—was thought of by both Dryden and Scott as the work of Chaucer, but we know now that it is not. Scott's footnotes to Dryden's preface and the headnotes and footnotes to the Chaucerian pieces are worth reading for the insight they give us into his critical opinion of Chaucer. He considered the Knight's Tale, whether in the original or in Dryden's modernization, "one of the finest pieces of composition in our language." He considered the Nun's Priest's Tale "a poem, which, in grave, ironical narrative, liveliness of illustration, and happiness of humorous description, yields to none that ever was written." In the headnote to Dryden's *Wife of Bath's Tale* he politely mentions *The Marriage of Sir Gawaine* and Gower's Tale of Florent and the Loathly Hag, but he reserves his highest praise for Chaucer's version: "What was a mere legendary tale of wonder in the rhyme of the minstrel, and a vehicle for trite morality in that of Gower, in the verse of Chaucer reminds us of the resurrection of a skeleton, reinvested by miracle with flesh, complexion, and powers of life and motion." The next sentence is especially perceptive in contrasting the works of Chaucer with those of his contemporaries: "Of all Chaucer's multifarious powers, none is more wonderful than the humour with which he touched upon natural frailty, and the truth with which he describes the inward feelings of the human heart; at a time when all around were employed in composing romantic legends, in which the real character of their heroes was as effectually disguised by the stiffness of their manners, as their shapes by the sharp angles and unnatural projections of their plate armour."

When Scott thought of Chaucer, he thought primarily of the *Canterbury Tales*. His allusions to *Troilus and Criseyde* and the other poems are fewer and sometimes rather curious: "The Creside of Chaucer, a long performance, is written expressly to be read, or else sung" (from the note to II.xiii of *Sir Tristrem*). In his introduction to Dryden's reworking of Shakespeare's *Troilus and Cressida* he labels Chaucer's *Troilus* "a long and somewhat dull poem." Although some passages from the poems and novels do recall *Troilus*, it is Geoffrey Chaucer the author of the *Canterbury Tales*, despite his "fault" of "coarseness,"[31] who plays such an important role in shaping Scott's own creative works.

Scott's knowledge of medieval literature does not stop with Chaucer and the romances already cited. One favorite writer was Lady Juliana Berners, whose important *Book of St. Albans* he quotes at length in the notes to *Sir Tristrem* in connection with the art of hunting. He borrowed a copy of her book from Ellis in 1801; he bought Haslewood's reprint in 1815; and he admired her work so much that he named one of his many dogs after her. He also knew well the *Chronicle of England;* it is in the Auchinleck MS and in Ritson. He refers to the *Cursor Mundi* in his review of Rose's and Southey's versions of *Amadis* and quotes a passage as it appears in Warton. He was more or less familiar with Dante but not fond of him. Lockhart cites a letter from Miss Anna Seward to Henry Francis Cary, the translator of Dante, in which she writes about a visit from Scott in 1807. "Miss Seward adds, that she showed him the passage in Cary's Dante where Michael Scott occurs, and that though he admired the spirit and skill of the version, he confessed his inability to find pleasure in the Divina Comedia. 'The plan,' he said, 'appeared to him unhappy; the personal malignity and strange mode of revenge presumptuous and uninteresting'" (*Life of Scott*, 3:14–15). Near the end of his life, while he was in Italy, he admitted to Captain Edward Cheney that "of Dante he knew little, confessing he found him too obscure and difficult" (Cheney's notes, quoted in Lockhart, 10:187).

Only infrequently does Scott allude to the "sententious" Gower's *Confession Amantis*. He read in it, certainly, but except for the Tale of Florent and some lines from Book VI referring to the Tristan-story (which he quotes in the note to II.1 of *Sir Tristrem)*, it made little impression on him; on the whole he found it "dull." Of Robert Henryson he had a much higher opinion. In the note to III.lxxx of *Sir Tristrem*, in connection with Tristrem's disguising himself as a leper, he calls attention to the memorable moment in Henryson's *Testament of Cresseid* when Troilus, after a successful skirmish with the Greeks, rides up to a group of lepers begging for alms. Among them is Cresseid; she "looked on Troilus. He met her glance," Scott continues, "and could not recognise the beauty he had adored, in the leprous wretch before him; but her look instinctively revived in his bosom 'the spark of love,' which had long lain dormant. His arm grew weary of bearing his shield, his heart glowed, and his colour changed; he knew not himself the cause of his disorder; but throwing his purse into the skirt of Creseide, rode heavily onwards to the city. She recognised her lover, and died in despair." Actually she did not recognize Troilus at once, because her illness had apparently damaged her eyesight, and she had to be told who the generous man was after he had departed. The text of the *Testament* was available to Scott in all his editions of Chaucer's works. He also knew of Henryson's *Fables*; ten are in the Bannatyne MS, and there was an edition by Andrew Hart in 1621.

He was quite familiar with William Dunbar, as a number of references in the *Letters* clearly indicate, but he has very little to say about Hoccleve and Lydgate, "who, with equal popularity, but with merit incalculably inferior, supported the renown of English poetry after the death of Chaucer."[32] He could have read Hoccleve's *Regement of Princes* in Advocates MS. 19.1.11, but I find no evidence that he did. The *Letter of Cupid* was readily at hand in his editions of Chaucer, but he never mentions the poem. In a note to II.1 of *Sir Tristrem* he points out a brief allusion to the Tristan-story in Lydgate's *Temple of Glas*, but he found Sir John Mandeville's *Travels* of much more interest than either Hoccleve or Lydgate. He refers to Mandeville in his introduction to the ballad "Kempion" (*Minstrelsy*, vol. 3), and he quotes a passage from the prose *Travels* in a note to "Christie's Will" (*Minstrelsy*, vol. 4), describing the ability of *jogulours* and *enchantours* of the "Grete Chan" to cause people "to see the thing that is not." In a letter to John Richardson of December 23, 1814, he remarks that "there is something hard & meagre & cold & affected in the French diction that might remind one of the polar climate of Mandeville where the very words were frozen & required to be thawed before they could be understood," but here Dr. Corson (*Notes and Index*, p. 108) is quick to point out that the frozen words are not in Mandeville but rather in "a fiction of Addison and Steele, based on an imaginary manuscript of Mandeville."

Scott knew of *Piers Plowman* and no doubt read some of it. Percy discusses it in his essay (included in the *Reliques*) "On the Alliterative Metre, without Rhyme, in Pierce Plowman's Visions"; Scott refers briefly to the work and its author ("Robert" Langland) in a footnote to Dryden's Preface to the *Fables* and even more briefly in the introduction to the second part of "Thomas the Rhymer" (*Minstrelsy*, vol. 4). Scott owned the 1550 edition by Robert Crowlye; the ornate edition by Thomas Dunham Whitaker of the C-text was published in London by John Murray in 1813. I think it is safe to say, though, that *Piers Plowman* did not interest Scott very much. David Laing included *The Pistill of Susan* in his *Select Remains of the Ancient Popular Poetry of Scotland*, which was published in Edinburgh in 1822, but Scott knew of the poem earlier: Ballantyne had once printed it for Ritson, but "[having groaned] in spirit over the peculiarities of his type & orthography," he discontinued work on Ritson's larger project, *Select Scotish Poems*, in which *Susan* was to have appeared.[33] As I have noted earlier, Scott knew the poem *Sir Owain*, or *Owain Miles*, which is a mixture of romance and legend; it is in the Auchinleck MS, and there is a transcript by Weber at Abbotsford. Scott quotes the poem at length in the introduction to "A Lyke-Wake Dirge" (*Minstrelsy*, vol. 3) to illustrate the concept of the Bridge of Dread; in a note to "Clerk Saunders" (in the same volume) he quotes its description of terrestrial paradise. Scott no doubt knew *Sir Tundale*, a similar type of poem, which is in Advocates MS. 19.3.1; Weber transcribed it also. First editions of both poems appeared not long after Scott's death. In the essay "On the Fairies of Popular Superstition," Scott refers to Gervaise of Tilbury, and he quotes John Trevisa briefly in a footnote to his introduction to *Sir Tristrem*.

The list of Scott's reading in medieval literature continues, but I shall stop, since I intend for my emphasis to be on Chaucer and especially the romances, and even here I have set up limitations: I have said nothing or next to nothing about his knowledge of the German and Old Norse romances, the Italian romances, or *The Cid* and his beloved *Don Quixote*. Scott's traveling in the golden realm of medieval romance was long and extensive. "All that was adventurous and romantic," he recalls, "I devoured without much discrimination, and I really believe I have read as much nonsense of this class as any man now living" (*Life of Scott*, 1:62).

We shall see that Scott was immensely indebted to Chaucer and the romances in his narrative poems and in the Waverley Novels. Sometimes he mentions the particular romance he has in mind; when he does not, it is not always easy to catch him in the act of borrowing. I say *borrowing*, not blatant stealing, of which some of his contemporaries (he avers) were guilty. "When I *convey* an incident or so I am [at] as much pains to avoid detection as if the offence could be indicted in literal fact at the Old

Bailey" (*Journal*, p. 215). I am of course aware that there were other influences on Scott besides medieval literature and that sometimes there are alternative sources for a particular motif or detail or point of style. I cannot always pin Scott down to a medieval source to the exclusion of other possible sources. In such cases it is altogether conceivable that three or four or more literary works from different periods of literary history were on his mind at the same time. If so, I am inclined to believe that medieval romance weighed most heavily because of his utter fascination with literature of this sort during his formative years. Although he also read widely in other literature at an early age, ballads and old romances were his passion.

In the following chapters I point out what Scott has borrowed and show how he has used the borrowing. When he has covered his tracks, I cannot always say for certain which particular romance is involved—I cannot indict him at the Old Bailey—but the accumulation of interesting parallels provides good circumstantial evidence in support of my belief that medieval romance is the most important literary source for the Waverly Novels.

2
THE NARRATIVE POETRY

SCOTT's indebtedness to Chaucer and medieval romance in his poetry is greatest in the long narrative poems, although some influence is apparent as well in other poems and the verse dramas.[1] Since Scott's poems are not so well known in the late twentieth century as they once were—they have not withstood the test of time as successfully as have the novels—a canto-by-canto summary precedes each major discussion as a convenience for readers and a means of highlighting the material to be discussed.

The Lay of the Last Minstrel (1805)

The aged Minstrel is described in the *Introduction*. *Canto First:* He begins his story by recalling the situation at Branksome Hall in the mid-sixteenth century. The Ladye's husband, Lord Walter Scott of Buccleuch, is dead, and her daughter Margaret is in love with Lord Cranstoun, whose family has been unfriendly to the Scotts of Buccleuch. The Ladye, who is opposed to a match between Margaret and Cranstoun, possesses magical powers, which she learned from her father. She sends one of her knights, William of Deloraine, to Melrose Abbey on a secret mission: namely, to get an important book from the tomb of the renowned wizard Michael Scott. She warns him not to look into it. *Canto Second* opens with the famous verse-paragraph describing Melrose Abbey. An aged Father, known as the Monk of St. Mary's aisle, leads Deloraine to the tomb of Michael Scott, which they open. Deloraine takes the Mighty Book from the "cold hand" of the dead man, who seems to frown, and the Father dies very shortly thereafter. Meanwhile Margaret has a secret rendezvous with Cranstoun. His mischievous Dwarf, or Goblin-Page, is introduced. *Canto Third:* Cranstoun fells Deloraine as he is returning to Branksome Hall and leaves his Dwarf to look after him. The Dwarf steals the Mighty Book, looks into it, and finds a spell which can make things appear otherwise than they really are. He takes the wounded Deloraine back to Branksome Hall stealthily. Then he pretends to be a playmate of the young heir and leads him away.

The boy is soon apprehended by the English, who are in the vicinity. The Dwarf then returns to the castle and impersonates the young heir, acting so wildly that many think the boy is possessed. Meanwhile the Ladye draws a splinter of Cranstoun's lance from Deloraine's bosom; he will be cured. The Seneschal of Branksome Hall announces that the English are nearby, and preparations are made to fight against them. *Canto Fourth:* Cohorts and friends come to the aid of the Ladye. When the Seneschal goes out to face the English, he learns that the young heir is in their hands. It is decided that things will be settled by a solemn combat between Deloraine and Richard Musgrave, an Englishman who claims that Deloraine has done him wrong. If Musgrave wins, the boy will remain a hostage; if Deloraine wins, the English will give him back and leave the vicinity. *Canto Fifth:* Cranstoun gets into Branksome Hall through the magic of his Dwarf, who makes him appear like a knight friendly to Margaret's family. A solemn combat then takes place between Musgrave and Cranstoun, who has disguised himself as Deloraine. Musgrave is killed. In this way Cranstoun patches up the feud between his family and the Scotts of Buccleuch. He and Margaret will marry. *Canto Sixth:* During the ensuing festivities we are entertained with melancholy songs. Suddenly it becomes dark, and the Dwarf is mysteriously whisked away, presumably by the vengeful ghost of Michael Scott. The mood changes to one of solemnity, as the various people present vow to go on a pilgrimage to Melrose Abbey to pray for Michael's soul. The Minstrel's lay closes with a "Hymn for the Dead" sung by the holy fathers of Melrose Abbey.

A few sentences from Scott's preface to the first edition of the poem serve admirably as a point of departure, not only for the present discussion but for those that follow:

As the description of scenery and manners was more the object of the author than a combined and regular narrative, the plan of the Ancient Metrical Romance was adopted, which allows greater latitude in this respect than would be consistent with the dignity of a regular Poem. The same model offered other facilities, as it permits an occasional alteration of measure, which, in some degree, authorises the change of rhythm in the text. The machinery, also, adopted from popular belief, would have seemed puerile in a poem which did not partake of the rudeness of the old Ballad, or Metrical Romance.

For these reasons the poem was put into the mouth of an ancient Minstrel, the last of the race, who, as he is supposed to have survived the Revolution, might have caught somewhat of the refinement of modern poetry, without losing the simplicity of his original model. [As quoted in Robertson's edition of Scott's poetry]

In content *The Lay of the Last Minstrel* does resemble a medieval romance. The underlying story-pattern of a young man and a young lady falling in love but being hindered by parents opposed to their relationship can be found in many a ballad and metrical romance. Closely connected with this is the story-pattern of enmity and reconciliation, which underlies many medieval romances. There has been long-standing enmity between the Cranstoun and Scott families, and there must be a reconciliation if Lord Cranstoun is to win his truelove's hand in marriage. Margaret, moreover, is typical of the heroines of romance, with her "golden hair," "fair cheek," and "blue eyes." Still another story-pattern prevalent in medieval romance, especially some of those based on Breton lais, involves the imposition of a taboo, the breaking of it, and a resulting catastrophe. The Ladye warns William of Deloraine not to look at the book from the tomb of Michael Scott:

> What he gives thee, see thou keep;
> Stay not thou for food or sleep:
> Be it scroll, or be it book,
> Into it, Knight, thou must not look;
> If thou readest, thou art lorn!
> Better had'st thou ne'er been born. [I.xxiii]

But Cranstoun's Goblin-Page, not knowing about the taboo, does look into the Mighty Book, and at the end of the poem he is "lorn." Although Scott makes no mention of the fight between Tristan and Morold, I suspect it was in his mind when he had a "splinter" of Cranstoun's lance get lodged in Deloraine's *bosom*; if it had been his *brain*, there would be no doubt whatever. The Ladye of Branksome Hall, like Iseult and Iseult's mother and many another lady of medieval romance, cures him: "She drew the splinter from the wound, / And with a charm she stanch'd the blood" (III.xxiii). She cures the trusted knight who has been wounded by a man who is a member of an unfriendly family but who, ironically, is soon to wed her daughter—again the Tristan-story, I would contend, but with much distortion and variation.

For the basic conception of Cranstoun's mischievous Goblin-Page, Scott was indebted, as he tells us in a note to Canto II, to local tradition, namely, the "universally credited" legend of Gilpin Horner; but medieval romance is full of mischievous dwarfs as well. Also the Goblin-Page makes himself appear like the Young Baron, and he causes his master Cranstoun to appear like a knight friendly to the Scotts of Buccleuch, so that he will have no difficulty entering Branksome Hall. The motif of a person through magic being able to make himself or another person look like someone else is in medieval romance. In Malory's *Morte Darthur* the renowned wizard Merlin is very adept at shape-changing; everyone will recall how he helps Uther Pendragon get into Igrayne's presence: "This nyght ye shalle lye with Igrayne in the castel of Tyntigayll. And ye shalle be lyke the duke her husband, Ulfyus shal be lyke syre Brastias, a knyghte of the dukes, and I will be lyke a knyghte that hyghte syr Jordanus, a knyghte of the dukes."[2] That Merlin was on Scott's mind is clear from a note to Canto II: "Notwithstanding his victory over the witch of Falsehope, Michael Scott, like his predecessor, Merlin, fell at last a victim to female art."

As the story evolves, the dispute between the English and the Scots is settled by a solemn combat between two men, one from each side. Scott could have drawn this motif from romance (for example, the combat between Earl William of Warwick and the Moorish King of Canary in *Tirant lo Blanch*), or from real life itself in the Middle Ages, or from I Samuel 17 (the fight between David and Goliath). In the account of the combat between Musgrave and Cranstoun and in his depiction of the festivities thereafter, the Minstrel slows down the flow of action with passages of description. This is in the general manner of some medieval romances, such as Chaucer's Knight's Tale.

But Scott's indebtedness to Chaucer in *The Lay of the Last Minstrel* goes further. The third verse-paragraph of Canto I begins:

> Nine-and-twenty knights of fame
>   Hung their shields in Branksome hall;
> Nine-and-twenty squires of name
>   Brought them their steeds to bower from stall;
>   Nine-and-twenty yeomen tall
>   Waited, duteous, on them all.

Why *nine-and-twenty*, one might ask, instead of four-and-forty, or two-and-thirty, or one-and-fifty? I think that Scott was recalling the General Prologue to the *Canterbury Tales:*

> At nyght was come into that hostelrye
> Wel nyne and twenty in a compaignye,
> Of sondry folk, by aventure yfalle
> In felaweshipe, and pilgrimes were they alle,
> That toward Caunterbury wolden ryde. [I, 23-27]

A few lines later Chaucer begins his character portraits, with the Knight, the Squire, and the Yeoman coming first—Scott's order exactly. Moreover, the *Lay* ends with an account of a pilgrimage, not to Canterbury, but to Melrose Abbey, the "ruin'd pile" which Scott describes most memorably in the first verse-paragraph of Canto II:

> If thou would'st view fair Melrose aright,
> Go visit it by the pale moonlight;

> For the gay beams of lightsome day
> Gild, but to flout, the ruins grey.
> When the broken arches are black in night,
> And each shafted oriel glimmers white;
> When the cold light's uncertain shower
> Streams on the ruin'd central tower;
> When buttress and buttress, alternately,
> Seem fram'd of ebon and ivory;
> When silver edges the imagery,
> And the scrolls that teach thee to live and die;
> When distant Tweed is heard to rave,
> And the owlet to hoot o'er the dead man's grave,
> Then go—but go alone the while—
> Then view St. David's ruin'd pile;
> And, home returning, soothly swear,
> Was never scene so sad and fair!

Very noticeable here, and rhetorically effective, is the series of *when* clauses beginning at the fifth line; we read on for ten lines before we come to the main clause: "Then go . . ." I would contend again that Scott was recalling (perhaps subconsciously) the famous opening lines of the General Prologue, in which Chaucer uses the same suspended sentence structure:

> Whan that Aprill with his shoures soote
> The droghte of March hath perced to the roote,
> And bathed every veyne in swich licour
> Of which vertu engendred is the flour;
> Whan Zephirus eek with his sweete breeth
> Inspired hath in every holt and heeth
> The tendre croppes, and the yonge sonne
> Hath in the Ram his halve cours yronne,
> And smale foweles maken melodye,
> That slepen al the nyght with open ye
> (So priketh hem nature in hir corages);
> Thanne longen folk to goon on pilgrimages,
> And palmeres for to seken straunge strondes,
> To ferne halwes, kowthe in sondry londes.

There are some minor parallels as well. In the middle of Canto III the young heir, at this point a captive, speaks arrogantly to an English archer: "And, if thou dost not let me go, / Despite thy arrows and thy bow, / I'll have thee hang'd to feed the crow!" (III.xix). The archer replies, "Gramercy for thy good-will, fair boy!" (III.xx). This sarcasm seems to echo Chauntecleer's reply to Pertelote's advice, well-meaning but unpleasant, that he take a strong laxative: " 'Madame,' quod he, 'graunt mercy of youre loore' " (VII, 2970). And in Canto V, after Cranstoun has felled Musgrave in mortal combat, a holy Friar rushes to the dying man to shrive him and thereby "smooth his path from earth to heaven": "In haste the holy Friar sped; / His naked foot was dyed with red" (V.xxiii). Scott's image here is reminiscent of Chaucer's hyperbole in his account of the duel, soon to be stopped by Theseus, between Palamon and Arcite: "Up to the ancle foghte they in hir blood" (I, 1660). But I cannot say categorically that Scott is indebted here to Chaucer, because the image is standard in popular tales and poetry. We do know that Scott was familiar with both the Knight's Tale and the Nun's Priest's Tale, especially in the "translations" by Dryden, whose works he was engaged in editing near the time of publication of the *Lay*.

Moving from imagery to structure, one finds Scott's verse is a mixed bag of familiar forms. The verse-paragraphs of each canto vary in length, often combining four-stress couplets, balladlike quatrains, and tail-rhyme patterns. The four-stress couplet was used by Gower in the *Confessio Amantis*, and it was a staple of medieval romances; a multitude of them are written in it. The quatrain that alternates four-stress lines with rhyming three-stress lines ($a^4b^3c^4b^3$) was the staple of ballads. The tail-rhyme stanza was common in a number of romances that have come down to us, most of which Scott knew, and is the most intriguing of the three.[3]

The medieval tail-rhyme stanza is difficult to define to everyone's satisfaction because there are many variations, but the form most generally known, as found in a group of twenty-three Middle English romances,[4] consists of twelve lines divided into four groups of three. Each group is composed of a couplet, four feet to a line, followed by a shorter line of three feet, the so-called tail-line (or *b*-line). The four couplets usually have different rhymes, while the four tail-lines always have the same rhyme. Here is a typical stanza:

> For goddes loue in trinyte,
> Al þat ben hend, herkeniþ to me,
> I pray ʒow par amoure:
> What whilom fel beʒond þe see
> Of two barons of grete bounte
> And men of grete honoure.
> Her faders were barons hende,
> Lordinges com of grete kende
> And pris in toun and toure.
> To here of þe children two,
> How þey were in wele and woo,
> Ywys, it is grete doloure.[5]

The twelve-line tail-rhyme stanza is characterized by conventional expressions, special narrative devices, syntactical peculiarities, definite structural patterns, and a stereotyped vocabulary.[6] To begin with, there are frequent summonses to attention, often found in the tail-lines: "Now herkeneþ how hyt was" (*Launfal*, line 6); "Y pray yow take hede" (*Erl of Tolous*, 12). Assertions of the truth, sometimes in the tail-lines, are also common: "Launfal, forsoþ, he hyȝt" (*Launfal*, 27); "as y you say" (*ibid.*, 49); "wythoute fable" (*ibid.*, 85); "Forsoþe, wythoute lye" (*ibid.*, 1038). Comments on the nature of an action are frequent: "Wyth joye & greet solas" (*ibid.*, 9); "Wyth chere boþe glad & blyþe" (*ibid.*, 66); "Wyth solas & wyth pryde" (*ibid.*, 1020). These tail-lines also illustrate the minstrel's fondness for pairs. General emotional comments in the tail-lines are not unusual: "Woo worth wederes yll" (*Emare*, 336); "þat was a fowll lesynge" (*Launfal*, 765). Oaths and curses are very frequent: "Os y am trewe knyght" (*Erl of Tolous*, 54); "Be God, thus thynketh me" (*ibid.*, 144); "Telle me, syr, for Goddys grace" (*ibid.*, 185). References to the time of an action are frequent: "Wythoute more soiour" (*Launfal*, 258); "Hyt was ydo wythout lette" (*ibid.*, 340); "He nolde no lengere abyde" (*ibid.*, 459). Reference occurs occasionally in a tail-line to the poem's source: "As telleth þys storye" (*Emare*, 162); "In romans as we rede" (*ibid.*, 216); "þus seyd þe Frenssch tale" (*Launfal*, 474). A typical way of introducing a character was to begin the introduction in the couplet and then give the name in the tail line: "Wyth Artour þer was a bacheler, / And hadde ybe well many a ȝer: / Launfal, forsoþ, he hyȝt" (*Launfal*, 25-27). Hyperbole is a frequent device: "So gret a lord was nane" (*Emare*, 30); "So fre lady was nane" (*ibid.*, 36); "Men sawe þo nowher her make" (*Launfal*, 21). Other characteristics are the frequent use of direct discourse, inverted word order, and verse repetition. Direct discourse helped the minstrel make his poem lively enough to hold the attention of an unlettered (and perhaps unruly) audience. The meter and rhyme often demanded inverted word order: "Of hur to haue a syght" (*Erl of Tolous*, 213); "In schryfte thus tolde sche me" (*ibid.*, 1032); "Hys enemyes to assayle" (*ibid.*, 1113). Repetition of verses is especially noticeable in *Emare:* "That semely were to se" occurs four times (93, 135, 141, 471).

The tail-line makes the tail-rhyme stanza what it is; any study of this stanza is largely a study of the tail-lines. The minstrel tried to put important parts of a unit of thought in this position of emphasis; if the tail-line is not climactic, it is usually ornamental, descriptive, or parenthetical. "The stanza," Trounce remarks, "is often a picture of four small panels framed and unified by the tail-lines" (p. 176). Enjambment is not only rare between stanzas but also exceptional between the three-line units of the same stanza.

This is the stanza Chaucer so humorously parodied in *Sir Thopas*. The conventional elements are of course ludicrous when overworked, but they did enable the minstrel to compose and recite his work with a minimum of effort. As Bliss points out in the introduction to his edition of *Sir Launfal*:

> Many of the peculiarities of style and convention to be found in these romances are to be explained by the circumstances for which they were composed, and the modern reader must learn to adapt himself before he can expect to appreciate them to the full. In particular a general slowness, repetitiveness, and discursiveness must be accepted and even relished. These romances were not composed for quiet reading in a study, but for recitation, often in the disturbed atmosphere of, perhaps, a village inn, to a mixed audience of no more than average intelligence; the minstrel was therefore bound to hold up the progress of his story with what seems to be mere padding, so as to give the important events time to sink in; he was well advised to repeat the most vital points two or three times. [pp. 31-32]

Some of the characteristics and conventions of tail-rhyme romances can be found in the *Lay*, though not to the blatant extent that is typical of its Middle English forerunners. Like his medieval counterpart, Scott's ancient Minstrel has a fondness for alliteration. He uses internal rhyme occasionally ("And hark! and hark! the deep-mouth'd bark"; III.xv), and his occasional inverted word order, with the preposition following its object, is reminiscent of tail-rhyme patterns ("Five hundred feet him fro"; III.xvi). Sometimes he summons his audience to attention in the manner of a medieval minstrel ("Hearken, Ladye, to the tale"; IV.x), and he has a predilection for rhetorical questions, which help to hold an audience's attention. His transitions from scene to scene are often typical of tail-rhyme romances ("Now leave we Margaret and her Knight, / To tell you of the approaching fight"; V.xiii). Once in a while he describes a character for several lines before telling who he is (as in IV.ix). He also uses a certain amount of conventional diction ("the gentle ladye bright"; V.xiii) and the near-verbatim repetition that is typical of epic poetry, medieval romance, and especially ballads. When the Ladye of Branksome Hall sends William of Deloraine on the mission to Melrose Abbey, she says:

> "Greet the Father well from me;
>   Say that the fated hour is come,
> And to-night he shall watch with thee,
>   To win the treasure of the tomb." [I.xxii]

And when Deloraine finds the holy Father, he addresses him thus:

> "The Ladye of Branksome greets thee by me;
>   Says, that the fated hour is come,
> And that to-night I shall watch with thee,
>   To win the treasure of the tomb." [II.iv]

Repetition of this sort is both pleasing and effective, as well as an aid to memorizing.

The Minstrel uses a number of rhetorical devices that are to be found in Middle English poetry—such as anaphora, onomatopoeia, and *effictio* (the description of a person's outward appearance); in at least two places he employs *occupatio*, a standard method of condensing in medieval poetry that is especially noticeable in the Knight's Tale. For example, the Minstrel declines to describe the combat between Musgrave and Cranstoun in all its gory detail, yet in the process of declining, he does in fact tell something about it:

> Ill would it suit your gentle ear,
> Ye lovely listeners, to hear
> How to the axe the helms did sound,
> And blood pour'd down from many a wound;
> For desperate was the strife and long,
> And either warrior fierce and strong. [V.xxi]

And of the festivities following Cranstoun's victory over Musgrave, he maintains:

> Me lists not at this tide declare
>   The splendour of the spousal rite,
> How muster'd in the chapel fair
>   Both maid and matron, squire and knight;
> Me lists not tell of owches rare,
> Of mantles green, and braided hair,
> And kirtles furr'd with miniver;
> What plumage wav'd the altar round,
> How spurs and ringing chainlets sound;
> And hard it were for bard to speak
> The changeful hue of Margaret's cheek—
> That lovely hue which comes and flies
> As awe and shame alternate rise! [VI.iv]

These lines are especially reminiscent of the famous passage in which the Knight describes Arcite's funeral in detail while pretending all along to pass over it (I, 2919-64).

The Lay of the Last Minstrel, then, is an intriguing imitation of a medieval metrical romance. While it draws somewhat on local tradition, it owes much of its content to medieval romance, as well as its leisurely pace, its passages of description, and the verse forms copied freely from balladry and romance. Scott could have written the whole poem in imitation Middle English, as his own conclusion to *Sir Tristrem* (which lacks the final

The Narrative Poetry 49

stanzas in the Auchinleck MS) clearly shows—it is a remarkable tour de force—but he chose to tell the story through a minstrel who flourished more than two hundred years after 1485 and thus would have known no Middle English. If the time-worn conventions of medieval romance are not superabundant in the *Lay*, it is because Scott's ancient Minstrel (as he says in his introduction) "might have caught somewhat of the refinement of modern poetry." So forcefully and so convincingly did Scott establish a new brand of romance in *The Lay of the Last Minstrel* that in those to follow he could himself assume the role of minstrel. The ancient narrator was no longer needed.

Marmion (1808)

Canto First ("The Castle"): Lord Marmion arrives at Norham Castle, where he is well received by Sir Hugh the Heron, who is lord of the castle. The year is 1513. Marmion has been sent by King Henry VIII on a mission to the Scottish king, James IV. A Palmer will be his guide into Scotland. (We learn later that the Palmer is none other than De Wilton, his rival for the hand of Clara de Clare.) *Canto Second ("The Convent"):* The Abbess of Saint Hilda and a group of nuns, including Clare, are on their way by sea to Lindisfarne, Saint Cuthbert's Holy Isle. The Abbess and two other officials pass solemn judgment there on Constance de Beverley and a male accomplice. She had been in orders but had left the convent because of her love for Marmion, whom she followed around for a while disguised (rather inadequately) as a young page. He soon tired of her, though, and began to woo Clare for her land, but Clare was already in love with De Wilton. Marmion then defeated De Wilton in a judicial combat, documents having been forged that made De Wilton seem a traitor. (We learn later that Constance herself had produced the false documents and had them given to Marmion, so that she would have a hold over him.) To avoid marrying Marmion, Clare then fled to Whitby's convent, where she narrowly escaped being murdered by Constance's accomplice. Constance and her accomplice are sentenced to be walled up alive in the depths of Lindisfarne. The sentence is carried out. *Canto Third ("The Hostel, or Inn"):* Marmion and his party stop at an inn, Marmion feeling remorse for what he has done to Constance (although he does not yet know that she has been buried alive). The Host tells a supernatural tale, which unnerves Marmion, about an Elfin Knight. Later that evening, when Marmion goes out to try to find the Elfin Knight, he has a strange encounter and is overcome. (We learn later that his antagonist was no Elfin Knight but rather De Wilton alias the Palmer, who hates Marmion enough to kill him but has solemnly promised a dying benefactor never to kill his deadliest enemy.)

Canto Fourth ("The Camp"): Marmion and his party leave the inn to stay at Crichtoun Castle until King James finds time to see Marmion. Their host is Sir David Lindesay. *Canto Fifth ("The Court"):* King James is celebrating in Edinburgh, at Holy-Rood. His mistress, Lady Heron, sings the famous poem "Lochinvar." Marmion gives him the message from King Henry. Marmion is to stay at Tantallon, along with the nuns from Canto II (who have been captured), under the protection of old Douglas, who is opposed to his king's war against the English. So fate has brought Clare into Marmion's power. The Abbess tells the Palmer about the forged documents relating to De Wilton that came into her hands after the execution of Constance. She hands them over to the Palmer, not realizing that he is De Wilton. Clare is separated from the other nuns, despite much protest from the Abbess. She will remain in the company of Marmion during the forthcoming battle. *Canto Sixth ("The Battle"):* Marmion is mortally wounded at Flodden Field. The Scottish forces are defeated, and their king is killed. Although she detests Marmion, Clare administers to him as he is dying. In his last moments he learns of Constance's fate. At the very end Clare and De Wilton are married.

All six cantos are preceded by introductions, in four-stress couplets, addressed successively to William Stewart Rose, the Rev. John Marriot, William Erskine, James Skene, George Ellis, and Richard Heber. Rose, Ellis, and Heber shared Scott's interest in medieval literature (see Chapter 1), so it is no surprise that these introductions should contain references to the romances. The one addressed to Rose (Canto I) is especially rich in this regard:

> But thou, my friend, can'st fitly tell,
> (For few have read romance so well,) . . .
> How on the ancient minstrel strain
> Time lays his palsied hand in vain;
> And how our hearts at doughty deeds,
> By warriors wrought in steely weeds,
> Still throb for fear and pity's sake;
> As when the Champion of the Lake
> Enters Morgana's fated house,
> Or, in the Chapel Perilous
> Despising spells and demons' force,
> Holds converse with the unburied corse;
> Or when, Dame Ganore's grace to move,
> (Alas, that lawless was their love!)
> He sought proud Tarquin in his den,
> And freed full sixty knights; or when,

The Narrative Poetry

> A sinful man, and unconfess'd,
> He took the Sangreal's holy quest,
> And, slumbering, saw the vision high,
> He might not view with waking eye.

Keyed to these lines are two notes in which Scott prints lengthy, and widely separated, extracts from the *Morte Darthur:* Malory's account of Lancelot's adventure at the Chapel Perilous, and Lancelot's unsuccessful attempt to achieve the Holy Grail. Scott's genuine enthusiasm for Malory by this time is obvious: "The romance of the Morte Arthur contains a sort of abridgement of the most celebrated adventures of the Round Table; and, being written in comparatively modern language, gives the general reader an excellent idea of what romances of chivalry actually were. It has also the merit of being written in pure old English; and many of the wild adventures which it contains are told with a simplicity bordering upon the sublime" (Note I). In the closing lines of his introduction to Canto I Scott alludes to the giant Ascapart, to Bevis of Hampton, and to Rose's own renditions of *Amadis of Gaul* and *Partenopex de Blois*. In the story itself the horse that Marmion rides in his nocturnal encounter with the supposed Elfin Knight is named Bevis. The introduction to Canto IV indicates that Scott has been reading *Tirant lo Blanch*, and he mentions Marie de France and Blondel in the introduction to Canto V. Using a bit of conventional self-deprecation, Scott called his poem an "Essay to break a feeble lance / In the fair fields of old romance" (introduction to Canto I).

Like Scott himself, Marmion's young squire Fitz-Eustace is a lover of medieval romance. The beautiful natural setting at the beginning of Canto IV brings to his mind his recent reading in "a huge romantic tome" printed by either Caxton or Wynkyn de Worde:

> "A pleasant path," Fitz-Eustace said;
> "Such as where errant-knights might see
> Adventures of high chivalry;
> Might meet some damsel flying fast,
> With hair unbound, and looks aghast;
> And smooth and level course were here,
> In her defence to break a spear.
> Here, too, are twilight nooks and dells;
> And oft, in such, the story tells,
> The damsel kind, from danger freed,
> Did grateful pay her champion's meed." [IV.iv]

Later, when contemplating the melancholy Clara de Clare, he swears by the Virgin Mary that "Some love-lorn Fay she might have been, / Or, in

Romance, some spell-bound Queen" (VI.iii). And Scott's initial description of Clare during her voyage to Lindisfarne draws on standard medieval lore about the lion:

> Harpers have sung, and poets told,
> That he, in fury uncontroll'd,
> The shaggy monarch of the wood,
> Before a virgin, fair and good,
> Hath pacified his savage mood. [II.vii]

The judicial combat, prior to the main story, in which Marmion fought against De Wilton and overcame him even though De Wilton was innocent, held a particular fascination for Scott—and for Constance de Beverley:

> Say ye, who preach Heaven shall decide
> When in the lists two champions ride,
>   Say, was Heaven's justice here?
> When, loyal in his love and faith,
> Wilton found overthrow or death
>   Beneath a traitor's spear? [II.xxviii]

Scott makes no specific reference anywhere in *Marmion* to the evasive shifts that Tristan and Iseult use to get out of difficult situations, but in a note to Canto V he does observe that "various curious evasive shifts, used by those who took up an unrighteous quarrel, were supposed sufficient to convert it to a just one. Thus, in the romance of 'Amys and Amelion,' the one brother-in-arms, fighting for the other, disguised in his armour, swears that *he* did not commit the crime of which the Steward, his antagonist, truly, though maliciously, accused him whom he represented." Scott had discussed this passage in more detail in his edition of *Sir Tristrem*, in a note commenting on the "equivocal oath" that Ysonde swears at Westminster:

> Swete Ysonde sware,
>   Sche was giltles woman;
> —"Bot on to schip me bare,
>   The knightes seighe wele than;
> What so his wille ware,
>   Ferli neighe he wan,
>   Sothe thing:
>   So neighe com neuer man,
> Bot mi lord the King."[7]

The one who bore her to the ship was of course Tristrem in disguise, who dropped her, fell on her, and exposed her *queynt* to all the knights present

(II.ciii). (Scott has made superb use of equivocal ruses of this sort in two of the Waverley Novels.)

There is a poignant reference to the story of Roland near the end of the poem:

> O, for a blast of that dread horn,
> On Fontarabian echoes borne,
>   That to King Charles did come,
> When Rowland brave, and Olivier,
> And every paladin and peer,
>   On Roncesvalles died!
> Such blast might warn them, not in vain,
> To quit the plunder of the slain,
> And turn the doubtful day again,
>   While yet on Flodden side,
> Afar, the Royal Standard flies,
> And round it toils, and bleeds, and dies,
>   Our Caledonian pride! [VI.xxxiii]

Despite Scott's sympathy for his countrymen, he recognizes their faults: their king is in need of help, but they are too busy "plundering the slain" to come to his rescue.

Scott's debt to Chaucer in this poem has already been discussed by Georg Martin Hofmann.[8] He points out parallels between Chaucer's Squire and Marmion's two squires, Fitz-Eustace and Blount:

> Wel koude he sitte on hors and faire ryde.
> He koude songes make and wel endite,
> Juste and eek daunce, and weel purtreye and write. . . .
> Curteis he was, lowely, and servysable,
> And carf biforn his fader at the table.
> [General Prologue to the *Canterbury Tales*, I, 94-96, 99-100]

> For well could each a war-horse tame . . .
> Nor less with courteous precepts stor'd,
> Could dance in hall, and carve at board,
> And frame love-ditties passing rare,
> And sing them to a lady fair. [*Marmion*, I.vii]

He is also quite right in seeing parallels between Chaucer's Friar, who "knew the tavernes wel in every toun / And everich hostiler and tappestere" (I, 240-41), and Scott's Friar John of Tillmouth: "He knows each castle, town, and tower, / In which the wine and ale is good" (I.xxi). Both love to talk and sing and play:

> Chaucer: In alle the ordres foure is noon that kan
>   So muchel of daliaunce and fair langage. [I, 210-211]

> Scott: He is a man of mirthful speech,
>   Can many a game and gambol teach. [I.xxii]
> Chaucer: Wel koude he synge and pleyen on a rote. [I, 236]
> Scott: None can a lustier carol bawl. [I.xxii]

Moreover, as Hofmann shows, Friar John owes something to the Friar John of *The Friars of Berwick*, an amusing poem sometimes attributed to Dunbar. The earlier ecclesiastic was also a connoisseur of food and drink and adventure; and one evening while innkeeper Simon Lawder (or Lawrell or Lawrear) was away, he was amusing himself with Alison, Simon's pretty wife, only to be frustrated by Simon's sudden and unexpected return and by other complications that cause him to flee for his life. Scott's Friar John, prior to the time of the story,

> In evil hour . . . cross'd the Tweed,
> To teach Dame Alison her creed.
> Old Bughtrig found him with his wife;
> And John, an enemy to strife,
> Sans frock and hood, fled for his life. [I.xxi]

That Scott knew *The Friars of Berwick* is certain, for he cites it in a note to Canto III to illustrate "the accommodations of a Scottish hostelrie, or inn, in the sixteenth century."[9]

Hofmann is less convincing when he compares Chaucer's Knight and Marmion, and Harry Bailey and Scott's Host of Canto III; the parallels simply aren't there. Also unconvincing is his suggestion that Scott's Abbess of St. Hilda owes something to Chaucer's Prioress, though I do think Scott had the Prioress in mind, early in Canto II, in his description of the nuns, "these holy maids":

> And one would still adjust her veil,
> Disorder'd by the summer gale,
> Perchance lest some more worldly eye
> Her dedicated charms might spy;
> Perchance, because such action grac'd
> Her fair-turn'd arm and slender waist. [II.ii]

Also very likely inspired by Chaucer, but not noticed by Hofmann, is a detail in the chain of events that occurred prior to the time of the main story. Accused of a treacherous conspiracy, De Wilton sent a messenger (presumably, his squire) to his castle for letters that would prove his innocence. To his consternation, the squire returned bearing—unwittingly—false documents that made De Wilton seem guilty. As the Abbess tells the supposed Palmer (in tail-rhyme verse):

> His squire, who now De Wilton saw
> As recreant doom'd to suffer law,
>   Repentant, own'd in vain,
> That, while he had the scrolls in care,
> A stranger maiden, passing fair,
> Had drench'd him with a beverage rare;
>   His words no faith could gain. [V.xxii]

The "stranger maiden" was Constance de Beverley, and all this is very reminiscent of a famous episode in the Man of Law's Tale. Constance, the heroine, gives birth to a son while her husband Aella is away. She sends a messenger to tell him the good news, but on the way the messenger stops at the castle of Constance's wicked mother-in-law, who gets him drunk and replaces the message with one saying that Constance has given birth to a monstrous child. Aella sends word back that mother and child should nevertheless be well looked after. Again the messenger stops at the mother-in-law's castle, and she exchanges this message with one stipulating that mother and child should be set adrift on a raft. Scott might have borrowed the exchange-of-messages motif from Gower's version of the story or from the tail-rhyme romance *Emare*, but I think it more likely that he was indebted to Chaucer. Surely it is no coincidence that the heroine of the Man of Law's Tale and Marmion's former mistress are both named Constance. Moreover, Scott's interruption of his narrative in VI.xxx, beginning "O Woman! in our hours of ease, / Uncertain, coy, and hard to please," recalls the Man of Law's frequent interruptions, especially his apostrophes to the two wicked mothers-in-law; nothing of the sort occurs in Gower or *Emare*.

    A few other stylistic touches are perhaps owing to Chaucer. Early in the story Sir Hugh the Heron uses a proverbial expression in connection with his wayward wife (his "lady bright," as he facetiously calls her): "No bird, whose feathers gaily flaunt, / Delights in cage to bide" (I.xvii). These lines recall similar but lengthier passages in the Squire's Tale (V, 611ff) and the Manciple's Tale (IX, 163-74). Scott's reference to Saint Thomas of Canterbury (I.xxiv) and the oath "By Becket's bones" (IV.i) also remind us of Chaucer's world. And the conventional expression used by the King—"Soothly I swear, that, tide what tide, / The demon shall a buffet bide" (III.xxii)—occurs in *Sir Thopas*: "And there he swoor on ale and breed / How that the geaunt shal be deed, / Bityde what bityde!" (VII, 872-74). It can also be found in some of the romances, especially tail-rhyme romances, which Chaucer was parodying.

    The verse form of *Marmion* is mainly a mixture of four-stress couplets and tail-rhyme verse. Sometimes Scott uses a conventional six-line stanza:

> Not so the Borderer: bred to war,
> He knew the battle's din afar,
>   And joy'd to hear it swell.
> His peaceful day was slothful ease;
> Nor harp, nor pipe, his ear could please
>   Like the loud slogan yell. [V.iv]

And sometimes he varies the pattern by adding an extra *c*-line, as in the passage about the "stranger maiden," quoted above. Other conventions reminiscent of tail-rhyme romance are similar to those in *The Lay of the Last Minstrel*, such as the obvious transitions between parts of his story:

> Leave we these revels now, to tell
> What to Saint Hilda's maids befell. [V.xviii]

> Shift we the scene. The camp doth move. [V.xxvii]

Sometimes, in a manner like that of the medieval minstrel, Scott writes about a new character at some length but withholds the name until the end. Marmion himself, approaching Norham Castle, is described from the viewpoint of the Warder in I.iii, but we are not given his name until the middle of I.iv, in a tail-line, when the Warder joyfully tells the others at the castle that "Lord MARMION waits below!" Then Scott goes on to describe at some length his main character's outward appearance—a type of description that Geoffrey of Vinsauf, the thirteenth-century rhetorician, called *effictio*, as opposed to the description of inner qualities, or *notatio*. Scott tells us that Marmion "was a stalworth knight, and keen" (I.v). This word order is very much in the manner of Middle English romances (see Chapter 7).

Occasionally, Scott links his verse-paragraphs by repeating a key word or phrase from the last line of one in the first line of the next: "At night they might in secret come" (V.xix, last line); "At night, in secret, there they came" (V.xx, first line). This device is used throughout *Pearl*, which Scott did not know, but is also frequent in *Sir Tristrem*, which he knew best of all the Middle English verse romances. Not long before the battle of Canto VI there is a passage describing the "Scottish host" in which the *-ing* verb form is conspicuous: "Their front now deepening, now extending; / Their flank inclining, wheeling, bending, / Now drawing back, and now descending" (VI.xviii). Scott sometimes uses this stylistic device in depicting vigorous action—as does Malory (again, see Chapter 7). One should also take note of Scott's very effective use of the so-called "inexpressibility topos," at the moment when Clare and De Wilton see each other again after long separation:

> Expect not, noble dames and lords,
> That I can tell such scene in words:
> What skilful limner e'er would choose
> To paint the rainbow's varying hues,
> Unless to mortal it were given
> To dip his brush in dyes of heaven? [VI.v]

Self-deprecation is involved here also. Passages of this sort are frequent in Middle English literature, the most forceful one I know of occurring in Malory's version of the Tristan-story: "And to telle the joyes that were betwyxte La Beall Isode and sir Trystramys, there ys no maker can make hit, nothir no harte can thynke hit, nother no penne can wryte hit, nother no mowth can speke hit" (*Works*, p. 302).

Marmion, then, like *The Lay of the Last Minstrel*, is a successful modern imitation of a medieval romance. The motifs, the detail, the stylistic devices that Scott has judiciously drawn from medieval romance and from Chaucer make the imitation effective. One further important motif underlies almost the entire story: that of the undesired marriage, which occurs in a host of medieval romances. Marmion is hell-bent on marrying Clare, but she is in love with De Wilton. She goes into a convent to escape the unwanted suitor, but to little avail, for he has the support of the king. When she falls into his hands near the end, things look bad indeed. This same motif is of course central to "Lochinvar" (V.xii): fair Ellen is about to be married, against her will, to "a laggard in love and a dastard in war," but young Lochinvar rescues her in the nick of time and with heart-warming aplomb. The happy ending of this famous poem within a poem foreshadows the happy ending of the larger poem. The unwanted suitor is dead, and Clara de Clare and Ralph de Wilton are finally united in marriage.

The Lady of the Lake (1810)

Canto First ("The Chase"): Just when it seems that a stag will be forced to turn at bay it escapes a hunter and his dogs. The hunter's exhausted horse expires. On foot then, the hunter (who is actually King James V in disguise) comes to Loch Katrine and sees beautiful young Ellen in a skiff. She is uneasy when she discovers that the stranger is neither her father (Lord James of Douglas) nor her friend Malcolm Græme. She tells him, though, that he was expected, since the old minstrel Allan-Bane had foreseen his plight. The stranger is graciously received at Ellen's island home by Lady Margaret, "mistress of the mansion" and mother of Ellen's other suitor, Roderick Dhu. The stranger then announces that he is James Fitz-James, the Knight of Snowdoun. When he retires to bed he dreams of Ellen being transformed into a warrior "with darken'd cheek and threatening eyes," but after praying he falls asleep, no longer troubled by dreams. *Canto Second ("The Island")* opens with Allan-Bane's song to the departing Fitz-James. Ellen expresses embarrassment that she had been somewhat moved by him, while Allan-Bane bemoans the fallen fortune of the Douglas family. They then talk about the brave chieftain, Roderick Dhu, who wants to marry her but who has little hope because she does not love him, although the Douglas clan is indebted to him. Roderick then approaches the island by boat together with his followers. Douglas (Ellen's father) and Malcolm also arrive. Roderick wants Douglas to join him in a bold enterprise against the king, but Douglas refuses; he also tells Roderick that Ellen cannot be his bride. Roderick and Malcolm then get into a violent altercation, which Douglas stops. Malcolm swims away. *Canto Third ("The Gathering")*: Roderick seeks aid in his enterprise from Brian the Hermit, who deals in religious practices bordering on witchcraft. Brian pronounces an anathema on all who will not heed Roderick's call. Malise, Roderick's henchman, then goes forth to rouse people to Roderick's cause. Later Roderick overhears Ellen singing an "Ave Maria" and has a foreboding that this is the last time he will hear her voice. *Canto Fourth ("The Prophecy")*: Brian's prophecy is: "Which spills the foremost foeman's life, / That party conquers in the strife." Douglas leaves the wooded retreat, and Ellen fears he has gone to the king to give himself up for the cause of peace. Allan then sings to her the faerie ballad of Alice Brand, after which Fitz-James returns. He woos Ellen, but she tells him that there is another. As he departs, he gives her a ring that will give her access to the king. Fitz-James suspects his guide Murdoch of treachery when Murdoch cries out suddenly near the site of Fitz-James's dead horse. The half-crazed Blanche of Devan warns Fitz-James of coming dangers. When Murdoch tries to shoot him, the arrow just grazes him and kills Blanche instead. Fitz-James then kills Murdoch (see the prophecy). Later he is given hospitality by one of the enemy, who turns out in *Canto Fifth ("The Combat")* to be Roderick Dhu. The two end up fighting man to man, despite Fitz-James's attempt to find another way of settling their differences, and Fitz-James wins. The mortally wounded Roderick is carried away by some of Fitz-James's men who appear at the call of his bugle. The scene then shifts to the popular games, at which Douglas excels even in old age. He becomes angry when his dog Lufra is mishandled, and a melee threatens, since many people present are sympathetic with Douglas. The king muses on the fickleness of the mob. *Canto Sixth ("The Guard-Room")*: The king's soldiers at Stirling are introduced. Ellen shows her ring to their captain, Young Lewis, and demands an audience with the king. Allan-Bane is ushered to the apartment of Roderick Dhu, who expires during the course of Allan's battle-song. Fitz-James leads Ellen into the presence of the king, revealing that he himself is the king. He tells Ellen that he and Douglas have become reconciled, and at the end we learn that Ellen and Malcolm will marry with the king's approval.

The story opens with a hunt, during which an important character gets separated from the rest of his party and enters into a strange adventure. The motif is frequent in medieval romance; it can be found in the *Morte Darthur*, which Scott had been reading not long before. The strange adventure sometimes begins with the hero coming to a body of water where a strange ship awaits him, sometimes with someone aboard and sometimes not, and the ship usually takes him to a place (a castle, a city) where more adventure is in store for him. The motif of the magic ship and the motif of the hunt need not be connected, but in *Partenopex de Blois*, which Scott had been reading in Rose's version, they are. Partenopex, nephew to the King of France, is separated from a hunting party while he is chasing after a boar. He gets lost and must spend the night in the forest of Ardennes. The next day, still lost, he comes to the sea and beholds a wondrous ship. He boards it, and it takes him to a castle where he sees beautiful mosaics depicting scenes from romances and where later he meets Melior, his faerie mistress.

To return to Scott: Ellen adds to the illusion of romance when she says to the stranger knight, "On heaven and on thy lady call, / And enter the enchanted hall!" (I.xxvi). A few lines later she compares her absent father with the giants Ferragus and Ascabart, and in an accompanying note Scott quotes from the Auchinleck *Romance of Charlemagne* (i.e., *Roland and Vernagu*) and *Bevis of Hampton*. After the knight has been introduced to Dame Margaret and has introduced himself as James Fitz-James and begins to show interest in Ellen, she "[turns] all inquiry light away" with words that add also to the illusion of romance:

> Weird women we! by dale and down
> We dwell, afar from tower and town.
> We stem the flood, we ride the blast,
> On wandering knights our spells we cast;
> While viewless minstrels touch the string,
> 'Tis thus our charmed rhymes we sing. [I.xxx]

In her song that follows ("Soldier, rest! thy warfare o'er"), she refers again to the rustic dwelling as an "enchanted hall." There is something of the mock heroic here as well, which might have been inspired by Chaucer's Nun's Priest's description of the lowly widow's cottage as a hall and bower.

Another motif is that of the undesired marriage, but unlike its use in *Marmion*, it does not loom large throughout the entire poem. We know already by the end of Canto II that Douglas will not force Ellen to marry Roderick Dhu if she does not love him. Related to this motif, however, is a story-pattern quite frequent in Scott: two young men—equally or nearly equally accomplished, attractive, and worthy—in love with the same girl. The reader naturally wonders which one of them will eventually marry her. This is the story-pattern that underlies Chaucer's Knight's Tale and holds the reader's attention until the very end (see Chapter 3). Roderick's chances for Ellen seem slight when Douglas declines to support him, but a lot happens after Canto II that might have changed things, and Roderick is not safely out of the way until his death in Canto VI.

The ring that Fitz-James gives Ellen has a close family resemblance to rings in medieval romance. Sometimes a lady is made aware that her lover is nearby or that there is a message from him when she sees a familiar ring worn either by himself in disguise or by someone he has sent to her. She may then grant that person a private interview in order to find out more about what is going on. Disguised as a beggar, Horn reveals himself to Rymenild (Rimnild) by means of a ring that she had given him. In *Sir Tristrem*, Ganhardin easily wins the attention of Ysonde when he appears in her presence with the ring that Tristrem has entrusted to him to give to her, and a meeting of the lovers is soon arranged (see Scott's edition of the poem, III.lxxii-lxxvii). There is also the motif of enmity and reconciliation. Owing to slander and to rebel kinsmen, a feeling of ill-will toward James of Douglas has been nurtured in the king's heart. The enmity gives way to a happy reconciliation between the two at the end. Finally, there is the important motif of the king in disguise, which in this case pervades the entire poem. In a long note Scott gives a barrage of historical information about the real James V, but he refers also to "the beautiful Arabian tale of *Il Bondocani*," and he knew well that the motif is widespread in folklore. Indeed, it is essential to the Scottish metrical romance *Rauf Coilyear*, rediscovered in 1821, in which Charlemagne, having become separated from his party, is given simple lodging for a night by the saucy hero, who does not realize who his guest is and who later, at court, is much surprised to find out.

Foreboding dreams, such as the nightmare in which James sees Ellen as a warrior, are frequent in medieval literature. Ellen does not turn into a warrior later in the story, but the dream has some basis in that she is the daughter of old Douglas, whose fierce kinsmen have been inveterately unfriendly to James, and she is loved by Roderick Dhu, a brave but ruthless chieftain. Later we are told that Allan-Bane has had an "idle dream / Of Malcolm Græme in fetters bound" (IV.x). This dream does foreshadow an event that comes to pass—but the fetters are not of the prison but of marriage:

> His chain of gold the King unstrung,
> The links o'er Malcolm's neck he flung,
> Then gently drew the glittering band,
> And laid the clasp on Ellen's hand. [VI.xxix]

The circumstances surrounding the conception of the savage monk Brian the Hermit, whose mother was believed to have met his Phantom Sire at night in a "dreary glen" where the bones of dead men lay scattered about, are based on local legend, as Scott tells us in a note; but one cannot help recalling also the romances *Sir Gowther* and *Robert the Devil*, in which the very strange hero is conceived when the mother is approached by a devil. There is a lot of Celtic faerie lore in Allan-Bane's ballad about Alice Brand. In one note Scott refers to *Sir Orfeo* and quotes a striking passage from the Auchinleck version that is lacking in the manuscript used by Ritson in his edition of the poem. King James's observations on the fickle crowd at the games recall vaguely the similar observations of Chaucer's Clerk with regard to patient Griselde and the support she receives and then does not receive from her monomaniac husband's fickle subjects.

Yes, medieval literature lurks in the background nearly everywhere in *The Lady of the Lake*, but sometimes the references are clearly articulated, as in Ellen's comparison between her father and the formidable giants Ferragus and Ascabart. Sometimes, too, Scott portrays a character by having him talk medieval romance, as does Marmion's youthful squire Fitz-Eustace. In the *Lady*, Young Lewis, the captain of the soldiers at Stirling, addresses Ellen with mildly satirical allusions to romance:

> Welcome to Stirling towers, fair maid!
> Come ye to seek a champion's aid,
> On palfrey white, with harper hoar,
> Like errant damosel of yore?
> Does thy high quest a knight require,
> Or may the venture suit a squire? [VI.ix]

But his attempt to ingratiate himself in this way falls flat, because it comes at a time when other matters weigh very heavily on her mind.

Near the beginning of Canto IV one character likens Brian the Hermit to a "raven on the blasted oak, / That, watching while the deer is broke, / His morsel claims with sullen croak." This comparison of the fanatical, awe-inspiring Hermit Monk to a raven, with all its dark associations, is fitting in every way; it owes much to *Sir Tristrem*, as a note tells us—specifically, to the lines about the raven's bone at the end of the famous passage describing the breaking of the stag. Later in the same canto Scott glosses his allusion to "the harden'd flesh of mountain deer" with a lengthy quotation from the lengthy French prose romance *Perceforest*. In Canto V, Douglas wins at wrestling and receives from the king as prize "a golden ring"—a detail that Scott backs up with a note that quotes briefly from the *Tale of Gamelyn*. Elsewhere in the notes he refers to "the huge metrical record of German Chivalry, entitled the Helden-Buch." The allusions to old ballads, medieval history, and medieval lore go on and on. Even the poem's title, *The Lady of the Lake*, comes almost certainly from the *Morte Darthur*, as readers of Malory might suspect, but there is a lady of the lake briefly mentioned in *Palmerin of England* as well.[10]

Again, the main verse form Scott uses is the four-stress couplet, the staple of the Middle English verse romances; some tail-rhyme verse is intermixed but not so much as in *The Lay of the Last Minstrel* and *Marmion*. Other verse forms are occasionally introduced for variety's sake, including Spenserian stanzas at the beginning of each canto. Infrequently, two verse paragraphs are linked by the repetition of a key word in the last line of one in the first line of the next (e.g., "alone" in I.vi and vii). Scott continues to use anaphora and rhetorical questions effectively, and his transitions from one part of the story to another are clear, as in the tail-rhyme romances. Alliteration is plentiful, with Scott showing a predilection for words beginning with *f*.

In style, then, *The Lady of the Lake* is basically similar to the *Lay* and *Marmion*—but Scott adds a few other tricks. Upon the death of his horse Fitz-James exclaims, "Woe worth the chase, woe worth the day, / That costs thy life, my gallant grey!" (I.ix). The phrasing seems unusual today, but it was by no means unheard of in Middle English, as the following admonishment of Pandarus to his niece Criseyde clearly shows:

> Wo worth the faire gemme vertulees!
> Wo worth that herbe also that dooth no boote!
> Wo worth that beaute that is routhelees!
> Wo worth that wight that tret ech undir foote!
> [*Troilus and Criseyde*, II.344-47]

Another apparent echo of Chaucerian diction occurs in Roderick's "short" speech to Douglas, Ellen, Malcolm, and others in II.xxviii: "The dales, where martial clans did ride, / Are now one sheep-walk, waste and wide." The last phrase is reminiscent of the Knight's description of Thebes, "with his waste walles wyde" (I, 1331). At the end of the canto, when Malcolm abruptly leaves the island, he "[strips] his limbs to such array / As best might suit the watery way." Scott may have borrowed the phrase "watery way" from Dryden's "translation" of the Nun's Priest's Tale: Chanticleer tells Dame Partlet of a man who has a dream in which a strange figure appears to him and says: "I come, thy Genius, to command thy stay; /

Trust not the Winds, for fatal is the Day, / And Death unhop'd attends the watry way."[11] Scott used the same flowery phrase a few years later in *The Field of Waterloo*, near the end of the poem. I hasten to add that it is not to be found in Chaucer, whose apparition says simply, "If thou tomorwe wende, / Thow shalt be dreynt; my tale is at an ende" (VII, 3081-82).

Finally, there is Ellen's "Ave Maria" (III.xxix)—perhaps the most widely known and loved of all hymns to the Virgin, medieval and otherwise, because of Schubert's musical setting. The genre was well established in the Middle English period. Hundreds have come down to us; most are anonymous, but famous poets—Chaucer, Hoccleve, and Lydgate—wrote them. Chaucer has one in the prologue to the Prioress's Tale, another in the prologue to the Second Nun's Tale. In the Man of Law's Tale, just before Constance is set adrift on her boat for the second time, she utters a prayer to the Virgin—something not to be found in Chaucer's source, Nicolas Trivet's Anglo-Norman *Chronicle*, or in Gower's version of it. Chaucer's addition is worthy in itself, and it heightens the emotional intensity of the story. Scott's "Hymn to the Virgin" incorporates some of the conventional diction associated with the genre—"maiden mild," "undefiled," "stainless," the alternation between "Maiden" and "Mother"—but the poem is not cloyed with it. And like the hymn of Constance, Ellen's "Ave Maria," overheard by Roderick, contributes to the drama and atmosphere of the story at the particular point where it occurs. The "Ave Maria" is probably the most typically medieval of all the lyrics and set pieces that Scott inserted into his narrative.

In sum, we find in *The Lady of the Lake* basically the same imitations of medieval romance as in *The Lay of the Last Minstrel* and *Marmion*, with some variation and with some branching out into new ways.

The Vision of Don Roderick (1811)

Scott drew the first part of *The Vision of Don Roderick* from legendary history, as he explains in an introductory note, specifically the purported vision of Don Roderick, the sinful last of the "Gothic" kings of Spain, shortly before his defeat in 714 by the Moors. But he has expanded the original vision, adding two parts: one, a vision of the heyday of Spain and Portugal during the early modern period, with conquests in the New World (marred, however, by cruelty); the other, a vision of the conquest of the Iberian peninsula by Napoleon, together with the brave resistance of the Spanish and the Portuguese, and with the bravery of the English and especially the Scots who came to their aid.

Although Scott is indebted mainly to history and legend, he may have been influenced to some extent by the prophetic visions of an ominous sort that can be found quite often in medieval romance. These, however, are usually in the form of dreams, whereas Don Roderick's vision is not a dream vision. The fact that Don Roderick "had the temerity to descend into an ancient vault," where he has the vision, recalls the Middle English poem *Owain Miles*, in which the hero descends into the "fearful hole" that is St. Patrick's purgatory. He goes alone, however, whereas Don Roderick is accompanied by a prelate—like Tundale in *The Visions of Tundale*, who is accompanied by a guardian angel. The Spanish legend may have caught Scott's attention because of his knowledge of the two Middle English poems, but there is no reference to either of them in the text of *Don Roderick* or in the notes. Nor does Scott's poem owe anything, so far as I can see, to Chaucer's dream visions. Interestingly, though, Scott was planning toward the end of his life a poem about Rhodes, which *was* to have been a dream vision.

From the standpoint of style *The Vision of Don Roderick* is quite different from *The Lay of the Last Minstrel*, *Marmion*, and *The Lady of the Lake*. Scott uses the Spenserian stanza throughout, and his many personified abstractions—Fear, Remorse, Shame, Guilt, Conscience, and Despair in stanza v of the long second section; Conscience, Fear, Remorse (stanza vi); Ambition (stanza vii), Conscience (stanza viii), Valor and Bigotry (stanza xxvii); Ambition (stanza xl), Slaughter and Ruin (stanza l), and Destruction (stanza liv)—were probably inspired by Spenser; they look forward to *Rokeby*.

Rokeby (1813)

"The Scene of this Poem is laid at Rokeby, near Greta Bridge, in Yorkshire, and shifts to the adjacent fortress of Barnard Castle, and to other places in that vicinity. . . . The date of the supposed events is immediately subsequent to the great Battle of Marston Moor, July 3, 1644" (from the Advertisement). *Canto First:* Bertram Risingham tells Oswald Wycliffe that he has murdered Philip of Mortham during the course of the battle against King Charles's forces. The wily Oswald is scheming to get Mortham's land; Bertram, the wealth that Mortham has won in the New World. Oswald's dreamy son, Wilfrid, is in love with Matilda, daughter of the Knight of Rokeby, but his affections are unrequited. We learn that Mortham's late sister had been Rokeby's wife and mother of Matilda. *Canto Second:* Wilfrid accompanies Bertram on the way to Rokeby's castle. Bertram, normally a bold man, is shaken when he thinks he sees Mortham, and in an unguarded moment he tells Wilfrid that he has slain Mortham. In the ensuing encounter between Wilfrid and Bertram, Mortham (who has survived the assassination attempt) saves Wilfrid from certain death and then disappears. Bertram runs off into the woods.

Oswald then appears with an entourage including Rokeby's page, Redmond O'Neale, who insists on pursuing Bertram but does so in vain. We learn that Rokeby, who fought on the (losing) side of the king, is to be entrusted to Oswald. Thus Oswald can more easily force Matilda into marrying Wilfrid and thereby aggrandize his own family's position and power. *Canto Third:* Having eluded young Redmond, Bertram falls in with one Guy Denzil, who invites him to join a group of malcontents and outlaws from both sides and to be their leader. Denzil tells Bertram that Mortham's hard-won treasure is at Rokeby's castle; that Mortham entrusted it to Matilda, whom he has designated his heiress. Young Edmund of Winston is introduced; he lives with the outlaws in the forest and entertains them with his singing. *Canto Fourth:* We learn how Redmond, as a young child, was entrusted for his upbringing to Rokeby (who was repaying a favor owed to Redmond's Irish family). Matilda and Redmond have grown up together, and she obviously favors him over Wilfrid. We learn also of Mortham's history. Having been misled by a treacherous friend (who is later revealed as Oswald), he became convinced of his wife's faithlessness and impetuously killed both her and her brother, whom he mistook for her lover. His son was abducted and apparently lost forever. (It turns out that the son is Redmond, whose mother was an Irish woman with whom Mortham had eloped, much against her father's wishes; later the father had relented and sent his son to England to see his sister in private.) *Canto Fifth:* The wealth at Rokeby is to be moved to Barnard Castle. The canto opens with Matilda, Redmond, and Wilfrid at Rokeby's castle for a last evening. A minstrel appears, seeking hospitality; it is Edmund. The head servant, Harpool, is reluctant to admit him but finally does so. Edmund has second thoughts about the deceitful role he is playing, but he ultimately betrays the castle to his outlaw friends. Help arrives, but the castle burns to the ground. The outlaws are killed by their opponents—all save Edmund and Guy Denzil, who are taken captive, and Bertram, who escapes. *Canto Sixth:* Oswald threatens to put Redmond and Rokeby to death if Matilda refuses to marry Wilfrid, but during the ensuing confrontation scene (in a dilapidated abbey church) Wilfrid dies of wounds received at Rokeby and of inner emotional conflict. Oswald is determined to go ahead with the executions. (He has already executed Guy Denzil, and he has learned that Redmond is Mortham's son and heir.) Bertram, however, having been told about Oswald's machinations by Edmund, arrives suddenly and shoots Oswald dead; he himself is killed by Oswald's retainers when his horse stumbles. Mortham arrives and is reunited at long last with Redmond; Redmond and Matilda are married.

The summary shows that Scott has used a number of motifs typical of medieval romance. Mortham's son Redmond is abducted when he is a small boy, and he grows up not knowing who he is. Much later he finds out, and he is finally reunited with his father. Since this motif underlies the entire story, it might better be called a story-pattern, and of course this story-pattern, with multitudinous variations, is a staple of medieval romance. Both Valentine and Orson are separated from their parents at a very early age; they grow up not knowing who they are but are eventually reunited with both mother and father. I mention this particular romance because I think it lurks elsewhere too in the background of Scott's poem. Redmond and Matilda are childhood friends; they grow up together and become attached to one another forever. Their long-standing relationship recalls such pairs of lovers as Floris and Blancheflur, Aucassin and Nicolette, Amadis and Oriana—and Valentine and Eglantine. Moreover, the events of Mortham's tragic history—his having been convinced by a supposed friend (Oswald Wycliffe) of his wife's supposed infidelity, his failure to look into things properly, his lamentably rash and brutal action in the wake of the false information, and his subsequent remorse for what he has done—recall the opening pages of *Valentine and Orson*, in which an evil archbishop convinces Emperor Alexander of Constantinople that his wife Bellyssant is an adulteress. Without any attempt to verify the wily archbishop's fabrication, Alexander pitilessly expels Bellyssant from his court and realm, even though she is in an advanced stage of pregnancy. In the unhappiest of circumstances she gives birth to twin sons, who are soon lost to her and grow up elsewhere, not knowing their parentage. When the emperor finds out that his wife was *not* unfaithful to him, he expresses great remorse for his rash and brutal action. Needless to say, one is reminded also of *Othello*. My hunch is that Scott had both Shakespeare's play and the medieval romance in mind.

There is also the motif of the unwanted marriage, with Oswald Wycliffe trying to coerce Matilda into marrying Wilfrid, who, although of "soft mould," is a rather decent young man. Again, as in the Knight's Tale, we have two eligible, attractive young men in love with the same girl. Redmond has won Matilda's heart, but Wilfrid has the support of his powerful father. The reader hopes (and suspects) that Redmond will triumph, for it is only poetic justice that an affair of the heart should win out over the political stratagems of a wicked parent. But how will Scott dispose of Wilfrid? Unlike Arcite, the sensitive would-be lover in *Rokeby* dies of injuries received in a skirmish and of emotional agony, not of injuries received in a fall from a horse; Arcite's fate, with modifications, is transferred to Bertram Risingham, who must also be disposed of. Before Bertram is killed he himself kills Oswald Wycliffe, and thus helps save Redmond and Rokeby from certain execution. The motif of a sympathetic character being saved from death at the last moment can be found in, for example, *The Tale of Gamelyn:* Gamelyn's brother Ote is about to be hanged but is rescued by Gamelyn himself, who takes over the proceedings and orders all the jurors to be hanged, including the wicked oldest brother. As in *Rokeby* the tables are turned, and the wicked characters meet with death, fittingly, at the very spot where they would have executed a sympathetic character. *Rokeby* ends in typical medieval fashion—with the marriage at long last of Redmond and Matilda.

Sometimes Scott defines a character by showing how he or she relates, or not, to medieval romance. When the Knight of Rokeby turns against Wilfrid as a candidate for his daughter's hand because Wilfrid's father has joined the side opposed to the king, Redmond begins to hope and dream:

> And Redmond, nurtured while a child
> In many a bard's traditions wild,
> Now sought the lonely wood or stream,
> To cherish there a happier dream,
> Of maiden won by sword or lance,
> As in the regions of romance. [IV.xiv]

When Edmund seeks hospitality at Rokeby's castle with the deceitful intention of paving the way for his outlaw friends, old Harpool is very reluctant to admit someone who does not know the comic romance *The Felon Sow of Rokeby and the Friars of Richmond.*

> "For all thy brag and boast, I trow,
> Nought know'st thou of the Felon Sow. . . .
> If thou canst tell it, in yon shed
> Thou'st won thy supper and thy bed." [V.ix]

In a note Scott discusses this mock romance and then prints a version of it in its entirety. The time of the story is about 1500, the setting is Rokeby forest and the banks of the Greta, and a major character is one Ralph Rokeby, an ancestor of Scott's Knight of Rokeby. Harpool's reference to the old tail-rhyme romance helps flesh out his character, it provides a desirable comic touch in an otherwise very serious story, and along with Edmund's songs it contributes to the uneasy calm before the storm. (Even Bertram Risingham, a fierce and ruthless man, is partially but significantly defined by Scott as he relates to stories he heard during his voyages to the Spanish Main. The superstitious side of his personality has in fact been nurtured by many an old tale "of portent, prodigy, and spell," especially that of the Phantom Ship, or Flying Dutchman; but these are Gothic legends rather than medieval romances.)

A few minor points deserve mention. The surname Wycliffe is interesting, and one thinks immediately of John Wycliffe. How ironic that Scott should assign the name of the famous fourteenth-century religious reformer to the archvillain of this poem! In Canto V, when Edmund is at Rokeby's castle and knows that Bertram and the outlaws are about to enter and take it over, he expresses remorse for his deceitful role in the affair, especially because he has betrayed the "angel" Matilda: "And now—O! would that earth would rive, / And close upon me while alive!" (V.xxvi). The striking image recalls what actually did happen to the old prophet Amphiorax in the story of the siege of Thebes. There are brief accounts of this in "Jankyn's Book" (in the Wife of Bath's Prologue) and in *Troilus and Criseyde*, and Scott would also have known the longer account of Amphiorax's fate in Lydgate's fine narrative poem *The Siege of Thebes*. Aside from the *Felon Sow* and a quotation from Froissart, there are few allusions to medieval literature in the voluminous notes; in this respect the underpinning of *Rokeby* differs markedly from that of the major poems we have already examined.

Let us return now to the Knight's Tale, which, I have contended, lurks in the background. That it was on Scott's mind is clear from his specific reference in the verse-paragraph that introduces the big confrontation scene of Canto VI:

> Oh for the pencil, erst profuse
> Of chivalry's emblazon'd hues . . .
> [That] bodied forth the tourney high
> Held for the hand of Emily!
> Then might I paint the tumult broad
> That to the crowded abbey flow'd. [VI.xxvi]

Emily of course is the heroine of the Knight's Tale, one of the dullest characters ever conceived by a major author and matched, or in fact topped, only by Scott's Knight of Rokeby, Matilda's father, who has even less personality. Scott's expressed wish that he had Chaucer's powers of description recalls the Nun's Priest's wish that he could be gifted with Geoffrey of Vinsauf's colors of rhetoric in order to describe adequately the horrible mishap that befalls Chauntecleer. Scott goes on to tell a good bit about the people who come to the abbey to witness the executions, just as that master of *occupatio*, Chaucer's Knight, depicts Arcite's funeral in detail while protesting that he will not.

These comments bring us to the question of style. *Rokeby* uses the four-stress couplet primarily, but Scott breaks the pattern occasionally with Wilfrid's and especially Edmund's lyrics, some of which are quite attractive. Tail-rhyme verse is passé (we find it only in *The Felon Sow of*

Rokeby, relegated to a note), but alliteration, as in the earlier major poems, is conspicuous and sometimes a bit overdone, as when Wilfrid's "feeble frame was worn so low / With wounds, with watching, and with woe" (VI.xxx). Scott continues to use anaphora; he occasionally uses inverted word order typical of medieval romances: " 'Twas then that fate my footsteps led / Among a daring crew and dread" (IV.xxiii); and, though infrequently, he binds two verse-paragraphs by repeating a key word from the end of one in the first line of the next. He uses near-verbatim line repetition effectively during the course of a speech of Bertram to Oswald: "I trust not an associate's truth," and later, "I trust to no associate's truth" (I.xx). Also effective is his description in IV.viii of the old, wounded Irishman ("His plaited hair in elf-locks spread / Around his bare and matted head," etc.) who brings Redmond, still a boy, to Rokeby's castle. I will not quote it in full, but it is a good example of what Geoffrey of Vinsauf means by *effictio*. Conspicuous too is the appearance of numerous personified abstractions: Conscience and Fancy (I.i); Superstition, Curiosity, Fear, Pleasure, and Pain (II.x); Guilt, Excess, Regret, Sorrow, Fear (again), and Blasphemy (III.xiv); Vice (III.xv); Philosophy, Grecian Beauty, and Childhood (IV.iii); Memory (V.i); Indifference and Sympathy (VI.xxvi); and Sedition (VI.xxviii). In this respect *Rokeby* resembles *The Vision of Don Roderick* but differs from the first three major poems. Scott no doubt copied the technique from Spenser, whom he refers to in II.vi and in some of the notes, and from Milton, whose Satan is a prototype for Bertram Risingham: "While Bertram show'd amid the crew, / The Master-Fiend that Milton drew" (III.xiv). An interesting structural feature is Scott's bringing together for the first time, for the climactic scene in the abbey church, virtually all the important characters of the poem. Rokeby and Redmond are there, about to be executed; Oswald Wycliffe is presiding at the occasion; Wilfrid and Matilda are also present; Bertram arrives a bit later; and finally Mortham appears. Three of the characters are soon disposed of—Wilfrid conveniently drops dead, and Oswald and Bertram are killed—permitting a happy ending as Mortham is reunited with Redmond, his long-lost son, and Redmond and Matilda are free to marry. This bringing together of the various characters and strands of a complicated story for a final resolution is a technique common in medieval romance that Scott often uses (see Chapter 7).

With *Rokeby* there was a slight but noticeable falling-off of interest on the part of Scott's readers. He himself analyzed the causes in his introduction of 1830. He surmised that the English subject matter was intrinsically less interesting to his readers than the somewhat exotic manners and customs of the "primitive" Scots, and that the public had grown weary of the genre after his three major efforts and a number of imitations (by less gifted writers). Moreover, Lord Byron had arrived on the literary scene. I wonder too whether simply the time of the story, the mid-seventeenth century rather than the late Middle Ages, might have had significant bearing on the poem's reception—not to belabor the noteworthy fact that *Rokeby* owes somewhat less than *The Lay of the Last Minstrel*, *Marmion*, and *The Lady of the Lake* to Chaucer and medieval romance.

The Bridal of Triermain (1813)

Introduction: Arthur, the narrator of the poem, addresses his highborn ladylove, whose name is Lucy. Although Arthur is not of noble birth, Lucy favors him over her highborn friends. He will tell her a story "Of errant knight, and damozelle; / Of the dread knot a Wizard tied, / In punishment of maiden's pride." *Canto First:* Sir Roland de Vaux, Baron of Triermain, has a dream about a strange and incredibly beautiful lady. The old minstrel Lyulph enlightens him as to its meaning with a tale of five hundred years earlier about King Arthur's relationship with a strange lady named Guendolen. This story begins in Canto First and concludes in *Canto Second:* Arthur is received in a mysterious castle and is entertained there by Guendolen, whose father, "a Genie of the earth," trained her to ensnare "in slothful sin and shame / The champions of the Christian name" (II.iii). Arthur stays a long time and gets Guendolen pregnant; as he is leaving to resume his duties as king, she offers him a drink. When a drop accidentally falls on his horse, the horse "[bolts] twenty feet upright!" Arthur drops the goblet, the contents of which burn and blight the earth, and Guendolen and the mysterious castle disappear. Fifteen years pass. A beautiful girl named Gyneth arrives at Arthur's court; she is his daughter by Guendolen. Since Arthur had promised Guendolen that, if their child should be a daughter, he would give her hand in marriage to the best of his warrior knights, a tournament is held. Arthur asks Gyneth to order the fighting to cease before there is any killing; she haughtily refuses, and there is much bloodshed until Merlin appears, stops the tournament, and punishes Gyneth by putting her in a deep sleep from which only a brave man will be able to awaken her. She is confined in a mysterious castle in the Valley of St. John. Canto Second ends with the narrator asking Lucy to marry him. *Introduction to Canto Third:* It seems that the narrator and Lucy are now married. He will resume his tale about Roland de Vaux. *Canto Third:* Roland has a hard time finding the castle. He sees it in the glow of a meteor, but then it disappears. He sees it in a morning mist, but it disappears. In anger he strikes a rock, which breaks, and he discovers a staircase—which leads him to the castle. He is warned by an inscription on the gate not to enter, but he does so anyway and encounters four dark-skinned maidens, with ferocious tigers, who warn him not to proceed further. He defeats the tigers, and the maidens seem pleased. Next he encounters four maidens with riches who urge him to go no further, but he does not succumb to their temptation. Then he encounters fair damsels who tempt him to dally with them for a while in sensual pleasure, but he leaves them and enters a dark passage where the going is hard and rough. Finally, he encounters another four maidens, three of whom offer him kingdoms and power—which he refuses. The fourth maiden then announces that Gyneth's waking hour has come. Roland sees Gyneth; she awakens; the mysterious castle vanishes. *Conclusion:* The narrator tells Lucy that Roland weds Gyneth.

The Bridal of Triermain is heavily indebted to Arthurian romance, but I doubt that the poem has a single specific source any more than does Malory's *Tale of Sir Gareth*. If there was any single romance foremost in Scott's mind, it was probably the *Morte Darthur*. In one of his few notes he quotes at some length Roger Ascham's acid censure of the delight Malory took in "open manslaughter and bold bawdrye." Arthur's strange experience in departing from Guendolen recalls Sir Percivale's adventure with a supposed gentlewoman in *The Tale of the Sankgreal*. When he made the sign of the cross, "the pavylon turned up-so-downe and than hit chonged unto a smooke and a blak clowde" (Vinaver's edition, p. 550). This passage can be compared with Sir Bors's adventure, a few pages later, with a lovely lady who wanted to go to bed with him. When he blessed himself, "anone he harde a grete noyse and a grete cry as all the fyndys of helle had bene aboute hym. And therewith he sawe nother towre, lady, ne jantillwomen, nother no chapell where he brought hys brothir to" (p. 571). Both these "ladies" tried their utmost to ensnare a good Christian knight, and their attempts ended unsuccessfully with strange supernatural happenings. Perhaps they are prototypes for Scott's Guendolen, who probably owes her name to the Guendolen of Richard Hole's "poetical romance" entitled *Arthur; or, The Northern Enchantment* (London, 1789). Sir Roland's trials and temptations before winning the fair lady remind one in a very general way of *The Tale of Gareth*, and his adventures at the Castle of St. John recall vaguely the strange adventures of Gareth's prototype, Libeaus Desconus, in the magic hall where he eventually frees the Lady of Sinadoune from enchantment.[12]

The idea is brought out more than once, and voiced by his lovely temptresses themselves, that things would have gone awry for Roland if he had followed their advice and discontinued his quest. Scott was probably inspired here by a passage from Lancelot's adventure at the Chapel Perilous:

Beyond the chappell-yerd, there met him a faire damosell, and said, "Sir Launcelot, leave that sword behind thee, or thou wilt die for it."—"I will not leave it," said Sir Launcelot, "for no threats."—"No?" said she; "and ye did leave that sword, Queen Guenever should ye never see."—"Then were I a fool and I would leave this sword," said Sir Launcelot. "Now, gentle knight," said the damosell, "I require thee to kiss me once."—"Nay," said Sir Launcelot, "that God forbid!"—"Well, sir," said she, "and thou haddest kissed me thy life dayes had been done."

(This is the passage as quoted by Scott himself, apparently from the 1634 Stansby edition of Malory, in the first note to *Marmion*.) After overcoming all difficulties successfully in the manner of an exemplary knight of the Round Table, Sir Roland finally wins his Gyneth. Neither she nor any other daughter of Arthur can be found in Malory, but Scott's idea of having Arthur beget a child out of wedlock, in this case a daughter who would cause him much trouble and heartache later, may well have been inspired by Malory's account of Arthur and Mordred.

Like Theseus in the Knight's Tale, Arthur wants the tournament for the hand of Gyneth to be conducted without loss of life, but Gyneth finds that sort of tournament too tame. Arthur must acquiesce, since he had made a solemn promise to Guendolen that he would arrange the tournament, and he had not stipulated that it take place without loss of life. Thus his promise was a rash one—and the motif of the rash promise is very frequent in medieval literature, not only in Malory and other Arthurian stories such as the Wife of Bath's Tale and *The Marriage of Sir Gawaine* but in such well-known non-Arthurian stories as the Franklin's Tale and *Sir Orfeo*. Gyneth's deep enchanted sleep brings to mind the story of Brünhilde, in Wagner's version. Both heroines are put to sleep as a punishment for wrongdoing, but the punishment is tempered by mercy, for they can be awakened by a champion who has the strength and courage necessary to overcome formidable dangers. The well-known fairytale about the Sleeping Beauty is an obvious analogue.[13] Scott's story ends when Roland frees Gyneth from the enchantment and wins her hand in marriage—such an ending being altogether appropriate, as our narrator explains in the Conclusion:

> My Lucy, when the maid is won,
> The minstrel's task, thou know'st, is done;
> And to require of bard
> That to his dregs the tale should run,
> Were ordinance too hard.

The Bridal of Triermain, then, like many medieval romances, ends with a marriage. Moreover, there has been a marriage in the poem's framework—

the narrator has married his Lucy between Cantos II and III—providing a variation upon the double marriage that so often concludes a medieval romance.

In addition to the sort of tail-rhyme verse quoted above ($a^4a^4b^3a^4b^3$), Scott makes much use of the six-line tail-rhyme stanza and also of an eight-line stanza ($a^4a^4a^4b^3c^4c^4c^4b^3$), usually in conjunction with four-stress couplets. The six-line stanza is the stanza of Chaucer's *Sir Thopas*, and that *Sir Thopas* was on Scott's mind is clear from the motto that appears on the title page to the first edition of his poem:

> An elf-quene wol I love ywis,
> For in this world no woman is
>   Worthy to be my make in toun:
> All other women I forsake,
> And to an elf-quene I me take
>   By dale and eke by doun.[14]

While tail-rhyme stanzas are certainly conspicuous in the *Bridal*, its resemblance in content to Chaucer's parody is really too vague to have warranted the motto; no wonder it was later dropped. *The Bridal of Triermain* differs from the other major poems so far discussed in that there is a lot of anapestic and dactylic movement, as in the opening lines of Canto I: "Where is the maiden of mortal strain / That may match with the Baron of Triermain?" Alliteration and anaphora are conspicuous, and occasionally one finds rhymes reminiscent of Chaucer, such as "story" and "before ye," then "before ye" and "glory" (III.xxxiv). In at least one place there seems to be an echo of Chaucer's diction. Although Roland is at first unsuccessful in seeing the enchanted castle,

> Yet still his watch the warrior keeps,
> Feeds hard and spare, and seldom sleeps,
>   And drinks but of the well. [III.iv]

One is reminded of Chaucer's patient Griselde, who drank "wel ofter of the welle than of the tonne" (IV, 215).

Especially effective is Scott's use of repetition, of the sort familiar in romance and even more so in ballads, in connection with Arthur's oath to Guendolen:

> I swear by sceptre and by sword,
> As belted knight and Britain's lord,
> That if a boy shall claim my care,
> That boy is born a kingdom's heir;

> But if a maiden Fate allows,
> To choose that maid a fitting spouse,
> A summer-day in lists shall strive
> My knights, the bravest knights alive,
> And he, the best and bravest tried,
> Shall Arthur's daughter claim for bride. [II.vii]

Fifteen years later Gyneth has occasion to remind him of the oath he swore to her mother:

> King Arthur swore, *By crown and sword,*
> *As belted knight and Britain's lord,*
> *That a whole summer's day should strive*
> *His knights, the bravest knights alive!* [II.xxi]

Although *The Bridal of Triermain* is heavily indebted to Arthurian material, the Tristan-story is given rather short shrift. Nevertheless the "love-lorn Tristrem," "Morolt of the iron mace," and "Dinadam with lively glance" are at least mentioned in II.xiii as attending Arthur's court at Whitsuntide, just before the arrival of Gyneth on her white palfrey. Also mentioned are Galaad, Lanval, Mordred, Brunor, Bevidere, Cay, Banier, Bore, Carodac, Gawain, Hector de Mares, Pellinore, and Lancelot. The section indeed is what we would now call an epic catalogue. "The characters named in the stanza," says Scott in a note, "are all of them more or less distinguished in the romances which treat of King Arthur and his Round Table, and their names are strung together according to the established custom of minstrels upon such occasions." As an example he quotes two stanzas from *The Marriage of Sir Gawaine,* but there are fuller and better examples in Malory, and Scott himself provides another in II.xxv, when he lists the knights who are felled in the tournament before Merlin rises from the "quaking earth" and puts an end to the slaughter.

If *Rokeby* is less dependent on Chaucer and medieval romance than are the major poems discussed earlier, the present poem goes to the opposite extreme. I have called *The Lay of the Last Minstrel, Marmion,* and *The Lady of the Lake* "imitations" of medieval romances, but *The Bridal of Triermain* is more than an imitation; it is a new Arthurian romance by a gifted poet who, like Sir Thomas Malory, had immersed himself in older Arthurian romances and then, like Malory in *The Tale of Gareth,* decided to write one on his own.

The Lord of the Isles (1815)

"The story opens in the spring of the year 1307, when Bruce, who had been driven out of Scotland . . . returned from the Island of Rachrin on the coast of Ireland, again to assert his claims to the Scottish crown" (from the headnote). *Canto First:* A wedding is about to take place at Artornish Castle. Edith, sister of the Lord of Lorn, is to marry Ronald, Lord of the Isles, but she is unhappy because she is convinced that Ronald does not love her. Two strange men and a young woman sail up to the castle and seek hospitality. They are admitted by the Warder, who is certain by their appearance that they are of noble birth and worthy of the high company in the castle. *Canto Second:* The strangers are Robert and Edward Bruce and their sister Isabel. A melee almost ensues when their identities become known. An elderly Abbot, who arrives later on the scene, openly recognizes Robert Bruce as Scotland's rightful king. The Lord of Lorn is angered, because he and his family are allied with England. The marriage is disrupted. *Canto Third:* Edith disappears from the castle; Ronald offers aid to Robert Bruce; and Edward takes Isabel to the safety of a convent. We learn that Ronald has a romantic interest in Isabel. Ronald, his young page Allan, and Robert Bruce then go to Skye, where they have an encounter with five evil men who are allied to the Lord of Lorn. Allan is murdered. Ronald and Bruce avenge his death by killing the five men. As they leave the scene, they take with them a young mute lad who had been held captive by the evil men. (The young man is actually Edith in disguise; she pretends that she cannot speak.) *Canto Fourth:* Robert Bruce is rejoined by his brother Edward. Numerous warriors from the various isles congregate to aid their rightful ruler. Robert talks privately with Isabel at the convent and sounds her out about Ronald. She is willing to consider his suit only if he can gracefully get out of his prior arrangements with Edith and if Edith releases him of her own free will. *Canto Fifth:* Isabel recognizes the timorous young lad as Edith. Meanwhile Robert Bruce and his followers are preparing to set forth to the mainland. They take a strange light to be their signal, but it turns out that the light was not the signal, and no one ever finds out what caused it. The young page (Edith) falls into the hands of the English leader Clifford. Still refusing to reveal her identity, she is about to be executed, but she is rescued just in time by Bruce and his men. Clifford and his followers are defeated and slain. *Canto Sixth* tells of events leading to the Battle of Bannockburn and then of the battle itself. When Edith exhorts Scottish bystanders and onlookers to help out, they believe that a miracle has occurred, for it seems as if the "mute" page has spoken. The English forces under King Edward II are defeated. Ronald and Edith will marry after all, and Isabel steps conveniently into the background by taking holy vows.

Scott's primary source for *The Lord of the Isles* was Barbour's *Bruce*, which he knew in Pinkerton's three-volume edition of 1790 and which he quotes at length in the notes. Since that famous fourteenth-century poem is usually considered more a chronicle than a romance, it lies rather outside the limits of the present study; I have made no detailed comparison. In addition to borrowings from Barbour, however, Scott's poem contains a number of motifs associated with genuine medieval romance, most of which we have observed in his earlier poems; they appear here with interesting twists. To begin with there is again the impending undesired marriage. Ronald is not enthusiastic about the marriage because (we learn later) he is in love with Isabel, and Edith is not enthusiastic because she is convinced that Ronald does not love her. As the story unfolds, however, he has a change of heart, and we have a much desired marriage of the same two at the end. Underlying everything is the story-pattern not of two eligible young men in love with the same girl but the opposite—two attractive young ladies and one man—and we naturally wonder which of them he will eventually marry. (Scott used this modified Knight's Tale story-pattern again in *The Pirate*; see Chapter 5.) Near the end of Canto V, Edith, disguised as a young man and pretending that she cannot speak, is about to be put to death; she is saved at the last moment. On the surface this appears to be a situation typical of medieval romance, but in fact it is different in that Edith could probably save herself if she would only speak and reveal her true identity to her captors, who at the time are allied with her brother and his followers. The motif of a person who pretends for one reason or another to be mute may have been inspired by the Middle English Breton lai *Sir Gowther* (and the related story of *Roberte the Deuyll*), although the situations are quite different. The emperor's daughter in fact *is* mute when we are first introduced to her. When she finally does speak, after a bad fall and a period of unconsciousness, her newfound ability seems to be a miracle. Sir Gowther is also mute throughout much of the story, but his silence is a penance imposed upon him by the Pope. (Another possible influence here is Ben Jonson's *Epicœne, or The Silent Woman*, although again the situations are very different, and the character (Epicœne) who pretends for a while to be almost mute is a boy disguised as a young lady.)

Some sense of the medieval background comes out occasionally in the dialogue. In discussing intimate matters with Ronald, Robert Bruce alludes to Ronald's having endeared himself to Isabel, before the time of the story, as an unknown champion:

> I guess the Champion of the Rock
> Victorious in the tourney shock,
> That knight unknown, to whom the prize
> She dealt,—had favour in her eyes. [IV.xv]

Later, when Bruce talks with Isabel at the convent, he alludes again to the unknown knight, whom Isabel now knows to have been Ronald. That the three unknown strangers who arrive at Artornish Castle in Canto I are of noble birth is immediately perceived by the Warder:

> Worship and birth to me are known
> By look, by bearing, and by tone,
> Not by furr'd robe or broider'd zone;
>   And 'gainst an oaken bough
> I'll gage my silver wand of state,
> That these three strangers oft have sate
>   In higher place than now. [II.vii]

The executioner in *Anne of Geierstein* makes a similar observation (see Chapter 6), and the sentiment in both instances is one with which Malory would agree.

The Warder's comment is in tail-rhyme verse, as is much of the rest of the poem. Following his earlier practice Scott regularly combines the four-stress couplet with varieties of tail-rhyme verse, and as in *The Lady of the Lake* he uses Spenserian stanzas in the brief introductions to each canto. (I find the introduction to Canto IV especially attractive, in particular the Alexandrine "Or Children whooping wild beneath the willows green.") Alliteration is conspicuous, with Scott showing again a predilection for the letter *f*: "How fierce its flashes fell" (II.viii); "The affrighted females shriek and fly" (II.xvi). Anaphora works well at the climactic moment in the story when Bruce and his men find out that the strange light was *not* a signal for them to come to the mainland—but they vow to continue their enterprise:

> "Prove we our fate—the brunt we'll bide!"
> So Boyd and Haye and Lennox cried;
> So said, so vow'd, the leaders all;
> So Bruce resolved . . . [V.xvi]

This is followed in the next verse-paragraph by effective repetition of the clause "It ne'er was known" with regard to the strange light that no one can explain.

Like Geoffrey of Vinsauf and another Geoffrey after him, Scott's Abbot, proclaiming Robert Bruce Scotland's rightful ruler, is a master of rhetoric; contributing especially to his passionate intensity is the frequent repetition of the word "bless'd" in the invocation that begins, "I bless thee, and thou shalt be bless'd," and ends, "The Power, whose dictates swell my breast, / Hath bless'd thee, and thou shalt be bless'd!" (II.xxxii).

Scott again shows a fondness for rhetorical questions, sometimes answering them himself with a resounding "No," as in the following rather silly passage, which is sandwiched between four-stress couplets and a passage of tail-rhyme verse:

> Is it the lark that carols shrill,
>   Is it the bittern's early hum?
> No!—distant, but increasing still,
> The trumpet's sound swells up the hill,
>   With the deep murmer of the drum. [VI.xx]

Catalogues of names appear occasionally (somewhat in the manner of Malory and as in Scott's own *Bridal of Triermain*), the most engaging of which—because of its concise, well-chosen descriptive details—is the short list of the Scots who support Robert Bruce to the hilt in his dangerous game:

> The might of Douglas there was seen,
> There Lennox with his graceful mien;
> Kirkpatrick, Closeburn's dreaded Knight;
> The Lindsay, fiery, fierce, and light;
> The Heir of murder'd De la Haye,
> And Boyd the grave, and Seton gay. [IV.xix]

One does not have to look hard to find Miltonic echoes in *The Lord of the Isles*. Compare these lines:

> Scott: Black waves, bare crags, and banks of stone. [III.xiv]
> Milton: Rocks, caves, lakes, fens, bogs, dens, and shades of death.
>   [*Paradise Lost*, II, 621]
> Scott: Hurl'd headlong in some night of fear. [III.xv]
> Milton: Hurled headlong flaming from the ethereal sky.
>   [*Paradise Lost*, I, 45]

Not so arresting, perhaps, are the Chaucerian echoes, but they are also to be found. Robert Bruce tells the leader of the murderous band on the Isle of Skye "that on a pilgrimage / Wend I, my comrade, and this page" (III.xxiv), recalling Chaucer's narrator who was "Redy to wenden on my pilgrymage / To Caunterbury with ful devout corage." Scott concludes the present poem with two Spenserian stanzas in which he laments the death of the Duchess of Buccleuch (whom he does not name). The opening lines—

> Go forth, my Song, upon thy venturous way;
> Go boldly forth; nor yet thy master blame,

> Who chose no patron for his humble lay,
> And graced thy numbers with no friendly name—

recall a famous passage at the end of *Troilus and Criseyde:*

> Go, litel bok, go, litel myn tragedye,
> Ther God thi makere yet, er that he dye,
> So sende myght to make in som comedye!
> But litel book, no makyng thow n'envie,
> But subgit be to alle poesye.

Robinson's notes point out that Chaucer was by no means the only medieval writer to have used this formula, but I think that *Troilus and Criseyde* is the most likely place for Scott to have found it. If so, I wonder about the beautiful ending of Canto IV. Before the fighting begins, Robert Bruce visits his sister at the convent; after leaving her, he gives voice to his thoughts in an impressive, heartfelt soliloquy, and

> Then down the hill he slowly went,
> Oft pausing on the deep descent,
> And reach'd the spot where his bold train
> Held rustic camp upon the plain.

These are the last four lines of the canto, and in the context of the story they convey powerful feeling. The diction is simple; so is the sentence structure. I know of nothing quite like it except the ending of Book IV of *Troilus and Criseyde*. Criseyde must leave Troy for the Greek camp, and Troilus has spent his last night with her:

> For whan he saugh that she ne myghte dwelle,
> Which that his soule out of his herte rente,
> Withouten more, out of the chaumbre he wente.

To me this is the saddest, most beautiful passage in all of Chaucer. Perhaps Scott thought so too.

In sum, *The Lord of the Isles* owes a lot to medieval literature, not only to Barbour's *Bruce* for its historical content but to Chaucer and medieval romance for other content, general atmosphere, and matters of style and structure. "Although the poem cannot be said to have made a favourable impression on the public," Scott wrote in 1830 for a new edition, "the sale of fifteen thousand copies enabled the author to retreat from the field with the honours of war." One more poem was to come before the final retreat.

Harold the Dauntless (1817)

The *Introduction* consists of seven Spenserian stanzas on the subject of "Ennui." The narrator's own way of combatting Ennui is interesting in the context of the present study:

> Each hath his refuge whom thy cares assail.
> For me, I love my study-fire to trim
> And con right vacantly some idle tale,
> Displaying on the couch each listless limb,
> Till on the drowsy page the lights grow dim,
> And doubtful slumber half supplies the theme,
> While antique shapes of knight and giant grim,
> Damsel and dwarf, in long procession gleam,
> And the romancer's tale becomes the reader's dream.

Canto First: Harold's father, Count Witikind, is a Norseman who has established himself in northern England by fire and sword. Late in life he decides to become a Christian if the Church will grant him "broad lands on the Wear and the Tyne." Harold rudely confronts his father in the presence of the Bishop of Durham, but Witikind answers him in kind and casts him off. Harold departs, angry that his father has renounced the Norse gods. Young Gunnar, son of Harold's former nurse Ermengarde, decides to join Harold in the wilds. At first Harold is reluctant to receive him, but he is impressed with the younger man's fidelity. Years pass. When the old Prelate dies, Aldingar becomes Bishop of Durham. After the death of Witikind the churchmen scheme to disinherit Harold. Canon Eustace warns that Harold will cause trouble, but it is decided that the Church should take back the broad lands. *Canto Second:* The damsel Metelill is introduced. Wulfstane, her father, hunts illegally; her mother, Jutta of Rookhope, is a sorceress. One day, by a fountain deep in the woods, Metelill sings about Lord William, her suitor. Harold appears suddenly and declares that he wants her for his bride. She goes home to discuss the matter with her parents. When Harold arrives and demands her hand in marriage, her parents plead for time. Jutta goes out and calls on a heathen god, the mighty Zernebock, who answers that he has little power in Harold's case. Jutta is disgusted with the god. *Canto Third* opens with an apostrophe to the "grey towers of Durham." Harold and Gunnar are in a natural setting. Gunnar sings a song, after which he comments on Harold's wild mood, and Harold replies that "bold Berserkar's rage divine" sometimes inspires him. Gunnar then sings another song, in which he suggests that a Danish maid would be preferable to Metelill. Harold is displeased. *Canto Fourth:* A fearless Harold arrives at the conclave in Durham. He shows the churchmen the head of Anthony Conyers and a hand of Sir Alberic Vere, to whom the Church had newly granted Witikind's lands. Harold threatens the churchmen, but then leaves them to deliberate. Cellarer Vinsauf advises drugging Harold and putting him in chains. Walwayn the Leech advises poisoning him. Prior Anselm has the idea of imposing a task on Harold which he, as a knight, can hardly refuse. When Harold returns, a minstrel sings a ballad entitled "The Castle of the Seven Shields." Harold determines to find the castle and its wealth. *Canto Fifth:* While Harold is in search of the castle, "a Palmer form" (not seen by Gunnar) warns him to change his ways. The Palmer reminds Harold that although his father had been evil, he finally repented. The apparition disappears, leaving Harold unnerved. Next he happens upon the wedding festivities of Metelill and William. He slays Metelill's father, then fights with William until Gunnar intervenes. By mistake Jutta drinks Walwayn's poison and dies with a horrible shriek. *Canto Sixth:* Harold finds the castle and its "fiend-built towers." Upon entering, he and Gunnar see the corpses of kings and witches. Harold speaks of women's faithlessness, which caused the trouble; Gunnar in response relates the faith of a Danish maid named Eivir. The next morning Harold tells Gunnar that they must leave the castle. He has had nightmares: his soul was about to be taken to hell, but then the Palmer appeared and was revealed to be Witikind, who is doomed to wander the earth until Harold changes his ways. Also in the vision Witikind hinted at something strange about Gunnar. Suddenly Odin appears, seizes Gunnar, and warns Harold not to abandon his ancient gods. Harold overcomes Odin. It turns out that Gunnar is the Danish girl Eivir. For the first time, Harold experiences fear and love. He determines to be christened and wed the next day. In the brief *Conclusion* the narrator addresses Ennui again. There are no notes.

The medieval Germanic background to the poem is evident in the references to Valhalla (III.v) and to various gods and goddesses: Freya (I.ix), Lok (I.xv), Odin (I.ix) and Thor (I.ix); Odin actually appears near the end. During the conclave at Durham, Prior Anselm compares Harold indirectly to two famous heroes of medieval romance:

> He may not, he will not, impugn our decree,
> That calls but for proof of his chivalry;
> And were Guy to return, or Sir Bevis the Strong,
> Our wilds have adventure might cumber them long. [IV.xi]

But Harold more nearly resembles Sir Gowther and Robert the Devil, both of whom were sired by a devil.

> Men swore his eye, that flash'd so red
> When each other glance was quench'd with dread,
> Bore oft a light of deadly flame,
> That ne'er from mortal courage came. . . .
> And they whisper'd, the great Master Fiend was at one
> With Harold the Dauntless, Count Witikind's son. [I.xix]
>
> And "Oh! forgive," she faintly said,
> "The terrors of a simple maid,
>   If thou art mortal wight!" [Metelill to Harold, II.viii]
>
> Not to mere mortal wight belong
> Yon gloomy brow and frame so strong. [Wulfstane to Jutta, II.xiv]
>
> Oft seems as of my master's breast
> Some demon were the sudden guest. [Gunnar to Harold, III.vii]
>
> Were the arch-fiend incarnate in flesh and in bone,
> The language, the look, and the laugh were his own.
>   [Aldingar to the conclave at Durham, IV.vii]

Clearly, Harold is perceived as a demon. Like Sir Gowther and Robert the Devil he has brute strength, and he slaughters people without mercy. Later, after a supernatural warning, he decides to give up his evil ways and become a Christian and marry the girl he loves. This sudden about-face in his career also recalls *Sir Gowther* and *Roberte the Deuyll*.

Harold's parents are both mortal, but his initial meeting with Metelill by the fountain and her uncertainty as to whether he is mortal bring to mind those Breton lais that begin with a liaison between a mortal and a fairylike creature, although the other elements of the story-pattern—the imposition of a taboo, the thoughtless breaking of the taboo, and the resulting crisis—are not to be found. The deceased Witikind as the Palmer, Harold explains to Gunnar, is

> Doom'd for his sins, and doom'd for mine,
> A wanderer upon earth to pine
> Until his son shall turn to grace,
> And smooth for him a resting-place. [VI.xi]

The idea of a ghostlike figure who wanders the earth and wants to die, but cannot, recalls the old man in Chaucer's Pardoner's Tale. Other analogues include the story of the Flying Dutchman, which was well known to Bertram Risingham from his travels across the ocean prior to the events at Rokeby. At the end of the story, when Harold realizes that the faithful Gunnar is actually Eivir, a beautiful young woman, he brings to mind

Wagner's Siegfried in that "he fears who never fear'd, / And loves who never loved" (VI.xviii). The medieval background of Scott's poem is further enhanced by the idea, strongly suggested by the grim fate of the kings at the Castle of the Seven Shields, that "human bliss and woe" are "closely twined" (in Scott's words) or that "evere the latter ende of joye is wo" (in the Nun's Priest's words). Harold's ensuing harangue on the perfidy of women is typically medieval antifeminism. The entire poem is a heterogeneous mixture of motifs from medieval literature—something which Scott did a better job of in *Ivanhoe*, which he was soon to write.

In style, *Harold the Dauntless* reveals little that is essentially different from Scott's other long poems. The meter is a mixture of iambic and anapestic tetrameter couplets, tail-rhyme verse, and Spenserian stanzas; as always, alliteration is conspicuous. During the conclave at Durham, however, the narrator breaks in with first-person comments after the proposals for getting rid of Harold; this procedure is unusual in Scott's long poems, though it does occur in his novels—and it occurs occasionally in the *Morte Darthur*.

Scott considered *Harold the Dauntless* and *The Bridal of Triermain* less important than his other long poems; they were "trifles, which, like schoolboys' kites, served to show how the wind of popular taste was setting."[15] In *Harold* "the manner was supposed to be that of a rude minstrel or scald" (but it is hardly that), as opposed to the *Bridal*, "which was designed to belong rather to the Italian school" (and yet it owes most to the *Morte Darthur*). Whatever their ultimate merit, neither of the two poems could have been written had Scott not been so deeply and passionately immersed in medieval romance.

The Plays

Scott's plays, although not without interest, are less important than the rest of his creative output. Nevertheless, like the rest of his verse, they are indebted to medieval literature and history to some degree. *Halidon Hill: A Metrical Drama in Two Acts* "is designed," Scott tells us in the note, "to illustrate military antiquities, and the manners of chivalry." The time is the fourteenth century, and Scott's principal sources are Froissart, Fordun, and Pinkerton's *History of Scotland*. Edward III appears as a character, and there is a Knight Templar, Symon de Vipont, whom the reader silently contrasts with Scott's famous Templar, Brian de Bois-Guilbert. One might look on the play's emotional content as a sensitive blending of the *topos* of youth and age with the motif of enmity and reconciliation. By far the most engaging characters are two Scottish chieftains, Young Gordon and the older Alan Swinton, whose families have been involved in a deadly feud.

For a long time Gordon has nourished hatred in his heart for Swinton for having slain his father, but when he actually meets the older man, he cannot help respecting him—indeed, he becomes fond of him. The gradual reconciliation the two men achieve before facing the English forces in a hopeless conflict is a beautiful achievement on Scott's part. The element of what we now call courtly love appears when Gordon, shortly before the battle, reminisces about his sweetheart Elizabeth:

> To listen to her, is to seem to wander
> In some enchanted labyrinth of romance,
> Whence nothing but the lovely fairy's will,
> Who wove the spell, can extricate the wanderer.
> Methinks I hear her now!

Swinton's reply well illustrates the difference in age between the two:

> Bless'd privilege
> Of youth! There's scarce three minutes to decide
> 'Twixt death and life, 'twixt triumph and defeat,
> Yet all his thoughts are in his lady's bower,
> List'ning her harping!

The bravery of Gordon and Swinton in the face of certain defeat and death is chivalry in the finest sense. It anticipates the bravery of Raymond Berenger, in *The Betrothed* (see Chapter 5), when he keeps his rash promise to fight in chivalric fashion even though he knows that his opponent will have the decided advantage. It also anticipates the bravery of the Knights of St. John in their inspired but utterly hopeless defense of their fortress, St. Elmo, in Scott's last (unpublished) novel, *The Siege of Malta* (see Chapter 6).

MacDuff's Cross, which Scott calls "a dramatic sketch," was first published in 1823. The setting again is medieval Scotland, and like *Halidon Hill* this play hinges on the motif of enmity and reconciliation. Richard Lindesay and Maurice Berkeley are mortal foes because Berkeley has supposedly slain Lindesay's brother; but it turns out that the monk Waldhave, who is on stage from the very outset, *is* the Lindesay presumed to have been slain. He finally reveals who he is, and the play ends in a grand spirit of reconciliation. About *Auchindrane, or The Ayrshire Tragedy* I have indeed very little to say. Auchindrane refers to his fearless son Philip as "a second Bevis" and later speaks of Scottish nobles "stout as old Graysteel" in what is probably a reference, though indirect, to the romance *Eger and Grime*; but I can find no further allusions or indebtedness to medieval literature in this most ambitious of all Scott's plays.

In *The Doom of Devorgoil*, on the other hand, Scott uses a number of motifs typical of medieval romance—with a light touch: the play is his only comedy. Eleanor, wife of Oswald of Devorgoil, whose family has fallen on hard times, is trying to marry their daughter off to the foolish up-and-coming preacher Gullcrammer, but Flora is in love with Leonard, a ranger; so we have the motif of the undesired marriage. Gullcrammer and then Leonard are solemnly warned by the old palmer Durward of dangers awaiting them at the Castle of Devorgoil: the analogues of such warnings are numerous in medieval romance. There is also the missing-heir motif: Leonard turns out to be the heir of the Aglionby family, most of whom lost their lives through the cruelty of Oswald's grandsire. Old Durward, who was formerly the Prior of Lanercost and who saved Leonard from disaster, holds the key to Leonard's identity. The enmity between the families of Aglionby and Devorgoil ends in reconciliation: Leonard, heir of Aglionby, will marry Flora, only child of Oswald of Devorgoil. Moreover, Lancelot Blackthorn, Leonard's best friend, will marry Kathleen, who is Eleanor's niece and Flora's best friend. So there will be a double wedding, again in the tradition of medieval romance.[16]

This study of Scott's poetry does not pretend to have tracked down every borrowing from Chaucer and medieval romance, for Scott's reading was vast and his memory prodigious. Nevertheless, I hope I have shown convincingly that the influence of medieval romance on Scott the Poet is overwhelming—that it is the source without which Scott would have written poetry (if any) of a different sort altogether. In the next chapters the case for bringing Scott to the Old Bailey escalates. What has proved true for the poems is also true of the novels.

3

THE EARLY NOVELS
1814-1816

SCOTT'S interest in medieval literature is manifest even in his earliest serious attempts at prose fiction: namely, the chapters he composed to complete Joseph Strutt's unfinished "romance" *Queenhoo-Hall* (which is set in fifteenth-century England), and the "fragments" of his own unfinished "romance," which he had planned to entitle *Thomas the Rhymer.* But this and the next three chapters are concerned with his truly important works of prose fiction, the Waverley Novels. My approach differs from that of Alice Chandler, whose fine book *A Dream of Order* deals more with Scott's medievalism in general than his specific indebtedness to specific romances.[1] I have unabashedly indulged in source-hunting wherever possible, but I am interested too in the *use* that Scott made of the medieval material; often I point out or suggest intriguing parallels between Scott and medieval romance without trying to pin him down to a specific source.

Waverley (1814)

From the very outset of his first novel Scott's mind clearly is on medieval romance: "I have, therefore, like a maiden knight with his white shield, assumed for my hero, WAVERLEY, an uncontaminated name" (chap. 1). During the course of an episode in the Highlands, he likens his hero again to a medieval knight: "It was up the course of this last stream that Waverley, like a knight of romance, was conducted by the fair Highland damsel, his silent guide" (chap. 22). In earlier years the hero's reading had included "Spenser, Drayton, and other poets who have exercised themselves on romantic fiction" and especially Froissart, "with his heart-stirring and eye-dazzling descriptions of war and of tournaments" (chap. 3), and these readings had somewhat distorted his perception of reality. "My intention," Scott tells us, "is not to follow the steps of that inimitable author [Cervantes] in describing such total perversion of intellect as misconstrues the objects actually presented to the senses, but that more common aberration from sound judgment which apprehends occurrences indeed in their reality, but communicates to them a tincture of its own romantic tone and colouring" (chap. 5). Thus Waverley, rather superficially, looks on his ill-considered journey into the Highlands as a romantic quest, while in reality it is a journey fraught with immense peril, and in a deeper sense it indeed *is* a quest like those in medieval romance—one in which our hero will move from youthful innocence to experience and from ignorance to self-knowledge.

Where he arrives at the end, however, is really not owing to any latent qualities of greatness. Shortly before he is introduced to Prince Charles Edward at Holyrood Palace, he contemplates "the strangeness of his fortune, which seemed to delight in placing him at the disposal of others, without the power of directing his own motions" (chap. 39). And later he witnesses the agonizing death of Sergeant Houghton, one of his followers from home before he himself changed sides and joined the forces of the Pretender—this being "an incident," Scott tells us, that "gives rise to unavailing reflections." "Oh, indolence and indecision of mind," laments Waverley, "if not in yourselves vices, to how much exquisite misery and mischief do you frequently prepare the way!" (chap. 45). In his realization of the power of fortune in shaping his life and in his admitted inability to make up his own mind, he is not unlike Chaucer's Troilus, who is completely incapable of formulating or carrying through any sort of plan that would keep Criseyde from having to go to the Greek camp and who is ultimately convinced that he is fated to lose her. Waverley and Troilus are hardly stereotypical heroes (and their weaknesses make them all the more fascinating), but they do attain self-knowledge at the end—Troilus after death, looking down on earth from the eighth sphere, and Waverley after a period of gradual disillusionment followed by the overwhelming defeat of the Pretender's forces. In view of Scott's imperfect knowledge of *Troilus and Criseyde*, however, I would hesitate to state emphatically that there was any connection in his mind between Waverley and Troilus. The resemblance is limited, and perhaps coincidental.

During the course of his conversation with the dying Houghton, Waverley learns that his seal, which he had lost earlier in the cave of the robber Donald Bean Lean, had been misused by the Jacobites, so that he appeared a traitor to king and country. The misuse of a seal is a motif that Scott would have known from *Valentine and Orson*, in which the evil King Hugon of Hungary gets hold of Orson's seal and forges a letter from him that makes Clerimonde believe that her fiancé Valentine is dead. And making a worthy man appear a traitor is a motif that Scott would have known from *Huon of Bordeaux*, in which Huon himself is discredited on the basis of trumped-up charges; and from *Melusine*, in which Raymond's father, Henry of Leon, is framed and ruined by the evil Josselin Dupont—a wrong that remains unavenged until Raymond, with supernatural help from his newly wedded wife Melusine, gains back what is rightfully his by defeating Josselin's son and nephew in judicial combat.

If Waverley is likened by Scott to a knight of romance, it is Charles Edward who embodies Waverley's own "ideas of a hero of romance" (chap. 40). "The ladies, also, of Scotland very generally espoused the cause of the gallant and handsome young prince, who threw himself upon the mercy of his countrymen rather like a hero of romance than a calculating politician" (chap. 43). Earlier in the novel Waverley's uncle, Sir Everard, is also compared to a hero of romance, especially as regards the "grace and delicacy" with which he "withdrew his claim to the hand" of a young lady when it was clear that she preferred another suitor, a young soldier of fortune whom we see much later as Colonel Talbot. The motif of two worthy men vying for the hand of a lady is of course central to the Knight's Tale, and I think it no coincidence that Scott's young lady's name is Emily and that she is as dull as her counterpart in Chaucer.

For a while Waverley and Fergus MacIvor vie for the hand of Rose Bradwardine, so we have the Knight's Tale in duplicate; but there is a more profound way in which Chaucer's story of Palamon and Arcite, his "poetic pageant demonstrating the pursuit of the noble life,"[2] can be viewed in connection with *Waverley*. Chaucer clearly has set up an interesting series of opposites. We have youth represented by Palamon and Arcite versus age as represented by Theseus. We have folly versus wisdom, innocence versus experience, impetuousness and restraint, passion and reason, the romantic and the realistic, courtly love and marriage. The teller of the story, the Pilgrim Knight, must be a man in his sixties to have fought in all the battles that Chaucer cites in his portrait of him. Like Theseus he has become wise through age and experience. And behind the Knight is Chaucer himself—a man in, say, his late forties who has also become wise through experience, who has outgrown youthful passion and impetuousness. I once heard a learned professor argue that everything in the tale points to a rejection of courtly love and an approval of marriage—and by implication, then, a rejection of everything represented by Palamon and Arcite and an approval of the virtues represented by Theseus. But this is too simplistic a view of the story. The most deeply moving, the most memorable lines in the Knight's Tale are the speeches and complaints of the two young lovers, Palamon and Arcite. Chaucer has given us some of his very finest lyric poetry in these passages. There is a real attractiveness—something genuinely beautiful—in the youthful, unrestrained outpourings of feeling which we hear from Palamon and Arcite. If there is anything to be rejected in what they represent, is it not rather the danger and the chaos to which folly and innocence and impetuousness and passion can lead?

Sometimes a deeply moving passage is followed by flippant remarks that deliberately destroy the high seriousness, as if the Knight were saying to himself, "What a sentimental old fool I am for allowing myself to get carried away in my characterization of young Arcite. I had better change the tone immediately, before my audience notices that tears have come to my eyes. I am older now and wiser and more experienced, and I see the shortcomings and potential dangers in the code of Palamon and Arcite, but damn it! I can't help being attracted to them. I used to be this way myself. Now I know, or *should* know, better." We must not forget that even Theseus shows impetuousness at one point in the story. When he happens upon the two young knights fighting a duel—one having escaped from prison and the other having been freed but with the stipulation that he never return to Athens—his first reaction is to have them put to death immediately; but on second thought the voice of reason and wisdom tells him to handle the situation differently. When he finds out that the duel is over a girl, he admits that he too was once a lover; but he has long since outgrown such foolishness—he knows better now—and he enjoys poking fun at the excesses of romantic courtly love. I think, then, that Chaucer does *not* reject the code of Palamon and Arcite, because it too is an important part of the total experience of life, but he points out the dangers to which it can lead. It is a phase of life that one must experience, but ultimately outgrow, if one is to have a really worthwhile life. And yet maturity and responsibility and wisdom are arrived at not without a certain lingering nostalgia for what was beautiful in the earlier phase of life—in the wilderness, to introduce another often-used metaphor. Whatever else it may be, the Knight's Tale is certainly about the growing up of two impetuous young men. One of them dies along the way, and his death seems undeserved and unfair, but that's how life is. At the end of the tale a number of years have elapsed, and Palamon, finally married to Emily, has gradually moved toward the code of Theseus and of the Knight and, presumably, of Chaucer himself.

Readers of Scott criticism, especially of *Waverley*, probably see my drift already. In *Waverley* Scott has presented a conflict between two cultures, two life-styles, two nations. Although there is much to be commended in the romantic, heroic code of the Scottish Highlands with its emphasis on bravery and loyalty, it is nevertheless fraught with inherent perils, and it must ultimately give way to progress, to the Hanoverian solution, to the less heroic English code. It is often said that Scott's attitude toward his subject matter is ambivalent. As a mature, intelligent man he realizes that the old order must give way to the new, but his heart is still with the old order, or at least with what was beautiful in it. In the words of Robin Mayhead, "*Waverley* is the work of a writer deeply attracted by the wild, the picturesque, the stirring, yet who is at the same time acutely suspicious of their charms; a man who believes that the individual unduly swayed by them will at best be incomplete and at worst court sheer disaster. Scott is both Romantic *and* anti-Romantic. He is at once a Romantic at heart, and a vigilant critic of his own Romanticism." Such, I think, or something very like it, is Chaucer's stance in the Knight's Tale. If the mature Waverley, Mayhead tells us, "has stopped 'Castle-Building,' there is nothing . . . to make us suppose him to have become emotionally dried up. Rather the reverse, in fact. Growing away from the sillier side of personal romanticism does not have to mean emotional atrophy."[3] In the context of the present discussion, these remarks just as readily fit Theseus and the Knight and Geoffrey Chaucer. I am not saying that Scott derived the theme, the intellectual content, of his first novel from Chaucer's Knight's Tale, but I think there is an analogy here: something that could not but have struck a deep, if subconscious, responsive chord in Scott; something in the final analysis more elemental than the motif of two attractive young men vying for the hand of the same girl.

It is something more elemental too than the other miscellaneous allusions and parallels to medieval romance. Doughty old Baron Bradwardine is explicitly compared to Hardyknute, and his reading embraces Barbour's *Bruce* and Blind Harry's *Wallace* rather than the romances of courtly love. And there is the Bodach Glas—the spirit, Fergus MacIvor explains to Waverley, of a slain Lowland chief which "has crossed the Vich Ian Vohr of the day when any great disaster was impending, but especially before approaching death" (chap. 59). The Bodach Glas is reminiscent of the legend that grew up about Melusine. One authority quoted by Walter W. Skeat (in his edition of *The Romans of Partenay, or of Lusignan*) observed that "whenever one of her descendants, or a king of France, was about to die, she appeared on the great tower in a widow's habit, and uttered long and terrible cries; that she was thus seen before the siege of Lusignan; and that, when her castle was about to be demolished, she was seen longer than ever before, shrieking aloud in so lamentable a voice that she cleft all hearts with pity." Another writer quoted by Skeat describes the White Lady of German tradition, "who appears in many houses when a member of the family is about to die, and . . . is thought to be the ancestress of the race."[4] The obvious difference here is that the Bodach Glas is not an ancestor of Fergus but rather the ghost of a man who had been slain by one of his ancestors.[5] The brief, humorous comparison of Miss Cecilia Stubbs, Waverley's first flame, with St. Cecilia (chap. 5) and the assertion that in his whistling "our hero's minstrelsy no more equalled that of Blondel, than poor Davie [Gellatley] resembled Coeur de Lion" (chap. 63) are not important, perhaps, but they are further indications of Scott's immersion in medieval lore, and they do provide a mock-heroic touch. It's hard to conceive of a more effective juxtaposition of romance and reality than the name Cecilia Stubbs (unless it would be Williamina Belsches, Scott's one great affair of the heart, from which he never fully recovered).

Although Scott says in his general preface that he "cannot boast of having sketched any distinct plan of the work," he does conclude the novel with the marriage of his hero, in the manner of medieval romance and much other literature, and most of the novel's characters are on hand at the end. Besides Waverley and Rose Bradwardine, we see her father the Baron, the Reverend Mr. Rubrick, the Reverend Mr. Morton, Frank Stanley, Lady Emily and Colonel Talbot, Bailie Macwheeble, Davie Gellatley, Major Melville, Saunders Saunderson—indeed, most of the people who have had connection with Waverley's life from the time he first set foot in Scotland; even Fergus MacIvor, now dead, is present in the form of an impressive full-length painting. This bringing together of characters at the conclusion of a story has an obvious parallel in Malory's *Tale of Sir Gareth*, in which virtually all the people whom Gareth has encountered from the time he arrived unknown at Arthur's court (and they are legion) are on hand for his marriage to the Lady Lyonesse. Scott's remark in the general preface should not be taken very seriously; it is the old *topos* of self-deprecation, found in Chaucer and in other fine writers of the Middle Ages.

Guy Mannering (1815)

This wonderful tale of love and hate, of prejudice and loyalty, of greed and revenge and cruelty and murder, follows the familiar story-pattern of exile and return. A boy is abducted at age five by smugglers; he is taken from Scotland to Holland, where he grows up not knowing who he is; as a young man he serves in the British army in India; he returns to Scotland in his early twenties still not knowing who he is, but he finds out and gains back what is rightfully his, not without difficulty, and marries the girl he loves.

There are parallels in a number of medieval romances (although often the hero does know his identity, as in *King Horn* and *Bevis of Hampton*). In the third part of *Guy of Warwick*, Guy's son Reinbrun is kidnapped at the age of seven by merchants. He is found years later in Africa by his father's faithful steward Heraud. After many adventures along the way he and

Heraud and Heraud's son Haslak manage to get back safely to England. Scott's choice of the name *Guy* may be owing to this romance, although I would not want to insist on the point. Nevertheless, Guy of Warwick is a missing heir's father; and Guy Mannering becomes father-in-law to the young man who has been a missing heir. In both romance (part 3) and novel, the missing heir looms much larger than the father figure—although, strange to say, it is the father figure's name that appears in both titles. Another romance involving expulsion and return is *Amadis of Gaul*, in which the infant Amadis is put into a cradle that floats into the sea, whence he is rescued by the Scottish knight Gandales; he is educated at the Scottish court, not knowing until much later in the story who he is. Of course, the missing heir is also a common motif in folk narrative. There are aspects of it in the biblical story of Joseph; it appears in ballads such as "Fause Foodrage," which Scott included in *Minstrelsy of the Scottish Border;* it is central to such pieces of "sophisticated" literature as *The Winter's Tale* and *The Gentle Shepherd*. It is entirely possible that the Bible, old romances, ballads, Shakespeare, and Allan Ramsay all had a part in shaping Scott's creative imagination; but, as I have argued earlier, ballads and old romances must have loomed large, in view of Scott's absolute passion for this sort of literature in his formative years. The same can be said for other motifs that are conspicuous in medieval romance and in Scott, although they can be found elsewhere as well.

Instead of the motif of the undesired marriage, which figures prominently in *Horn* and in *Bevis*, we have in *Guy Mannering* what might be looked on as an intriguing substitution: the undesired sale of an estate, Ellangowan, which falls into the hands of the evil upstart lawyer Glossin but finally reverts to its rightful owner when Vanbeest Brown is recognized as Harry Bertram, the long-lost heir, and after Glossin has been discredited and murdered. The story of Harry Bertram also exemplifies the male Cinderella motif, which Donald Sands has aptly described as "the eventual rise of an ill-starred youth [like Horn or Havelok] to power and stature."[6] The story also belongs in the tradition of the "fair-unknown" stories. Malory's Sir Gareth knows all along who he is, but his prototype Gyngelayne, the bastard son of Sir Gawain, does not and is thus knighted as Libeaus Desconus. This romance, so much admired by Percy, is the story of a young man's "search for his own identity, a quest to discover his name and his parentage" (to quote Larry Benson)[7]—as is the story of Harry Bertram.

In *Sir Eglamour of Artois* the story of Degrebelle, Eglamour's son by the long-suffering Christabelle, becomes more interesting than that of his father. When just a baby he is whisked away by a griffin and carried to Israel, where the king finds him and brings him up as his heir. At age fifteen Degrebelle still does not know who he is. Later he marries his own mother, who fortunately recognizes his coat of arms (which depicts a griffin holding a child in its claws) before the marriage has been consummated. Moreover, Degrebelle has an armed conflict with his father, neither one knowing who the other is, until Christabelle recognizes Eglamour too (they had not seen each other in fifteen years) by the device on his shield (which depicts a mother and child adrift in a boat). In *Guy Mannering*, as I have said, young Harry Bertram grows up not knowing who he is. While in India, moreover, he has a duel with the man who will become his father-in-law; and Guy has been led to believe that there had been some serious flirtation between the young officer and Mrs. Mannering, who, if she had lived, would have become his mother-in-law. In fair-unknown stories the mother often reveals who the hero is. Gareth's mother comes to her half-brother Arthur's court in high dudgeon when she hears of her son's having been confined to the kitchen before he set out on his adventures; it is she who reveals to an astonished court the identity of the brave young knight who is still away. In *Amadis of Gaul* it is not the mother but rather the old sorceress, Urganda, who knows who the hero is. And in *Guy Mannering*, of course, it is Meg Merrilies who holds the key to young Brown's real identity (his mother having died long since in giving birth to his younger sister Lucy): "I shall be the instrument," she tells Brown mysteriously (chap. 28), "to set you in your father's seat again."

This beloved old gypsy, Meg Merrilies, is one of Scott's truly marvelous characters, and her stature is enhanced by her kinship with figures from medieval romance. Although her appearances are not frequent, she dominates the story, as does Urganda in *Amadis of Gaul*. In chapter 53 she is explicitly compared with the loathly lady of Percy's ballad *The Marriage of Sir Gawaine* (from which eight lines are quoted), but unlike the hag of the famous story she does not finally turn into a beautiful lady—not physically, at least. But Meg has a genuine beauty of character—of soul, if you will—which Harry Bertram and his friends fully appreciate at the end, and his good fortune is in large part owing to the fact that like the knight of the old story he keeps a solemn promise made to her earlier, at her request, to leave whatever he was doing and follow her whenever she should next call for him. Near the end of the novel she appears suddenly and demands that he honor his promise: "And immediately Meg Merrilies, as if emerging out of the earth, ascended from the hollow way and stood before them" (chap. 52)—the *them* being Harry and Lucy Bertram, Julia Mannering, and Dandie Dinmont. Her various appearances are indeed notable for their mysteriousness and suddenness. She appeared "unexpectedly" to Bertram's father in chapter 8, at that very place where she now encounters young Bertram. In chapter 47 she appeared to Charles Hazlewood, having first "suddenly" roused him by her voice. And just prior to that encounter she had appeared in typical fashion to Dominie Sampson: "The door [to the Kairn of Derncleugh] . . . opened *suddenly,* and the figure of Meg Merrilies, well known, though not seen for many a revolving year, was placed *at once* before the eyes of the startled Dominie!" (chap. 46; emphasis added). This mysteriousness and this suddenness are reminiscent again of Urganda the Unknown, and also of Malory's Merlin, although unlike Merlin, Meg never appears in other than her own proper person. In chapter 54 she appears before Dirk Hatteraick in the cave, and during the course of the ensuing tense conversation she asks, "Did I not tell ye, when ye wad take away the boy Harry Bertram, in spite of my prayers—did I not say he would come back when he had dree'd his weird in foreign land till his twenty-first year? Did I not say the auld fire would burn down to a spark, but wad kindle again?" Scott has very probably borrowed this last image from the Knight's Tale. When Emily prays at the temple of Diana, two fires indicate the future course of events: "For right anon oon of the fyres queynte, / And quyked agayn, and after that anon / That oother fyr was queynt and al agon" (I, 2334-36). The second fire prefigures Arcite, who wins the tournament for the hand of Emily but then dies; the first fire, which concerns us here, refers to Palamon, who loses the tournament but finally wins Emily. In at least this one instance, then, Scott has enhanced Meg's dialogue with an echo from medieval literature.[8]

The novel contains a number of other motifs that are frequent in the old romances. We have a father (Guy Mannering) who tries to thwart the amatory inclination of a daughter (Julia). We have a hero (Harry Bertram) rescued just in time to prevent his death, when the smugglers set fire to the prison at Portanferry, where he is being detained. During this exciting scene (chap. 48) little Wasp, Dinmont's dog, who has "acted gloriously" earlier in the story (chap. 23), is mentioned several times—the lovable dog reminding the reader of such friendly animals in medieval romance as Ywain's inseparable lion-companion in *Ywain and Gawain* and the faithful lioness of *Octavian*. We also have something approximating the resuscitation of a dead person—a motif found in folklore and occasionally in romance.[9] When our hero accidentally encounters Glossin at Ellangowan, Glossin, "seeing such a sudden apparition in the shape of his patron, and on nearly the very spot where he had expired, almost thought the grave had given up its dead!" (chap. 41). When Jock Jabos sees Bertram at the Kairn of Derncleugh, where Meg is dying, "he [starts] back in amazement, with a solemn exclamation: 'As sure as there's breath in man, it's auld Ellangowan arisen from the dead!' " (chap. 55).

Larry Benson has called attention to the story-pattern of enmity and reconciliation that pervades Malory's *Book of Sir Tristram*.[10] In killing Sir

Marhalt, a worthy knight of the Round Table, Tristram has incurred the enmity of King Arthur, Sir Lancelot, and the other knights of Arthur's court, and he must be reconciled with them. There is also enmity between Tristram and Lamorak to be resolved, and between Tristram and Isode. Whether or not Scott had Malory's *Tristram* in mind, he certainly did use the pattern of enmity and reconciliation both in his poems, as we have already seen, and in his novels. Near the beginning of *Guy Mannering* the old laird of Ellangowan incurs the enmity of Meg Merrilies and the gypsies, and there must be a reconciliation. Vanbeest Brown incurs the enmity of Guy Mannering, even fighting a duel with him. Their reconciliation comes in the same chapter in which Brown is recognized as Harry Bertram, the long-lost laird of Ellangowan, and is reunited with family and friends (chap. 50). "Do you remember nothing of your early life before you left Scotland?" lawyer Pleydell asks our hero. He replies:

"Very imperfectly; yet I have a strong idea, perhaps more deeply impressed upon me by subsequent hard usage, that I was during my childhood the object of much solicitude and affection. I have an indistinct remembrance of a good-looking man whom I used to call papa, and of a lady who was infirm in health, and who, I think, must have been my mother; but it is an imperfect and confused recollection. I remember, too, a tall, thin, kind-tempered man in black, who used to teach me my letters and walk out with me; and I think the very last time—"

Here the Dominie could contain no longer. While every succeeding word served to prove that the child of his benefactor stood before him, he had struggled with the utmost difficulty to suppress his emotions; but when the juvenile recollections of Bertram turned towards his tutor and his precepts, he was compelled to give way to his feelings. He rose hastily from his chair, and with clasped hands, trembling limbs, and streaming eyes, called out aloud, "Harry Bertram, look at me! Was I not the man?"

"Yes!" said Bertram, starting from his seat as if a sudden light had burst in upon his mind,—"Yes, that was my name! And that is the voice and the figure of my kind old master!"

The Dominie threw himself into his arms, pressed him a thousand times to his bosom in convulsions of transport which shook his whole frame, sobbed hysterically, and at length, in the emphatic language of Scripture, lifted up his voice and wept aloud. Colonel Mannering had recourse to his handkerchief; Pleydell made wry faces, and wiped the glasses of his spectacles; and honest Dinmont, after two loud blubbering explosions, exclaimed, "Deil's in the man! he's garr'd me do that I haena done since my auld mither died."

This wonderful scene has analogues in the recognition of Tristrem at the court of King Mark (in the Middle English poem), owing to the loyalty of Sir Rohand, and in numerous other recognition and reunion scenes from medieval romance, including Christabelle's recognition of her son Degrebelle and then of Eglamour, and the subsequent family reunion. Still more memorable are Valentine's first realization that Orson is his brother, and their heart-warming reunion with their mother Bellyssant, and then Valentine's reunion with his father the emperor and his uncle Pepyn in Constantinople, and then Orson's reunion with father and uncle, and finally the emperor's reunion with Bellyssant, whom he had so wrongfully abused. The last is an especially moving recognition scene, with much weeping and swooning:

Than whan the Emperour apperceiued his wyfe Bellyssant he lepte of his hors in wepynge and syghinge tenderly And wythout that he might speke ony worde he enbraced the lady the whyche set her vpon both her knees. In that place assembled the Emperoure and the good lady that by the space of twenty yere and more hadde ben separate in sondre. Now it is not to be demaunded yf for to fynd the one the other they were Ioyous, and if that by profounde pyte they had theyr heartes touched & oppressed so that by naturall loue they fell vnto the earth in arme togyther in a swowne. And whan valentyne and Orson sawe the greate pyte of thir father and mother, moche tenderly and pyteyusly they beganne for to wepe, and harde besyde them they fel bothe in a swowne. The kinge Pepyn and dyuers other barons & knyghtes that behelde that thynge beganne moche tenderly for to wepe.[11]

In emotional intensity the scene in Scott also brings to mind the recognition and reunion near the end of Malory's *Tale of Sir Gareth:*

"What ar ye," seyde sir Gareth, "that ryght now were so stronge and so myghty, and now so sodeynly is yelde to me?"
"A, sir Gareth, I am your brother, sir Gawayne, that for youre sake have had grete laboure and travayle."
Than sir Gareth unlaced hys helme, and kneled downe to hym and asked hym mercy. Than they arose bothe, and braced eythir othir in there armys, and wepte a grete whyle or they myght speke; and eythir of them gaff other the pryse of the batayle, and there were many kynde wordys betwene them. . . .
So whan the kynge cam there, he saw sir Gawayne and sir Gareth sitt uppon a lytyll hyllys syde. Than the kynge avoyded his horse, and whan he cam nye to sir Gareth he wolde a spokyn and myght nat, and therewyth he sanke downe in a sowghe for gladnesse.
And so they sterte unto theire uncle and requyred hym of his good grace to be of good comforte. Wete you well the kynge made grete joy! And many a peteuous complaynte he made to sir Gareth, and ever he wepte as he had bene a chylde.
So with this com his modir, the quene of Orkeney, dame Morgawse, and whan she saw sir Gareth redyly in the vysage she myght nat wepe, but sodeynly felle downe in a sowne and lay there a grete whyle lyke as she had bene dede. And than sir Gareth recomforted hir in suche wyse that she recovirde and made good chere. [*Works,*, p. 222]

Unlike Harry Bertram, Gareth has known all along who he is, but most of the other characters have just found out. This is one of the finest scenes in all of Malory.

The last pages of *Guy Mannering* reveal the forthcoming marriages of Harry Bertram and Julia Mannering and of Charles Hazlewood and Lucy Bertram, so once again a Scott novel concludes in the manner of medieval romance. *Sir Eglamour of Artois* also ends in a double marriage, with Degrebelle marrying the princess Organata and Eglamour (legally) marrying Christabelle.

The Antiquary (1816)

Scott's third novel is full of references and allusions to romance and chivalry, as the title might lead one to suspect. In the apartment at Monkbarns of the antiquary Jonathan Oldbuck, there is a "grim old tapestry representing the memorable story of Sir Gawaine's wedding, in which full justice was done to the ugliness of the Lothely Lady; although, to judge from his own looks, the gentle knight had less reason to be disgusted with the match on account of disparity of outward favour, than the romancer has given us to understand" (chap. 3). Oldbuck's tapestry portrays the version of the story in Percy's ballad *The Marriage of Sir Gawaine* (to which Scott refers in *Guy Mannering*). His selection of a loathly lady to decorate his sanctuary's walls perhaps reflects his own misogyny, but the lady's transformation and the happy marriage at the end of the story might also reflect a subconscious wish on Oldbuck's part that his own affair of the heart had turned out better.

His antifeminism, which is so typical of medieval literature (as Francis E. Utley has shown us in his monumental study),[12] is in full sway when he introduces Mr. Lovel, the hero, to Miss Oldbuck—"I present to you . . . my most discreet sister Griselda—who disdains the simplicity as well as patience annexed to the poor old name of Grizel" (chap. 6)—but it is not to be taken very seriously. Part of the high humor comes from the ludicrous contrast between Miss Griselda Oldbuck, who well knows how to put her brother in his place, and the patient, submissive Griselda of Chaucer's Clerk's Tale. Oldbuck's attitude toward women emerges again, in the same scene at Monkbarns, when he tells his friend Sir Arthur Wardour, "Let them minister to us, Sir Arthur,—let them minister, I say; it's the only thing they are fit for. All ancient legislators, from Lycurgus to Mahommed (corruptly called Mahomet), agree in putting them in their proper and subordinate rank; and it is only the crazy heads of our old chivalrous ancestors that erected their Dulcineas into despotic princesses." Later, when Oldbuck and Sir Arthur argue over the meaning of the Pictish word *benval,* Lovel says, "Methinks, gentlemen, with submission, the controversy is not unlike that which the two knights fought, concerning the shield that had one side white and the other black. Each of you claim one half of the word, and seem to resign the other." We are reminded further of the world of romance when we learn the name of Sir Arthur's ancestor, Gamelyn de Guardover, and again when Oldbuck says something disparaging about Sir Gamelyn: "Out of the parlour-door flounced the incensed Sir Arthur, as if the spirit of the whole Round Table inflamed his single bosom."

Oldbuck's account (chap. 11) of his own ancestor Aldobrand Oldbuck, who won his bride Bertha through his skill as a printer, recalls vaguely those medieval stories in which a knight wins his ladylove by performing some sort of feat (or feats) better than do his competitors. And in the next chapter, when Scott describes the private conversation between Isabella Wardour and the old beggar Edie Ochiltree at the window of Sir Arthur's castle, Knockwinnock, he uses a striking comparison: "The young lady, as she presented her tall and elegant figure at the open window, but divided from the court-yard by a grating with which, according to the fashion of ancient times, the lower windows were secured . . . might be supposed, by a romantic imagination, an imprisoned damsel communicating a tale of her durance to a palmer, in order that he might call upon the gallantry of every knight whom he should meet in his wanderings, to rescue her from her oppressive thraldom." Scott refers elsewhere as well to Edie as a pilgrim or "grey palmer" (chap. 20), and there are still more references to pilgrims and pilgrimages—all reminding us of the frequent image in medieval literature of life itself as a pilgrimage. Sometimes the allusions take on an altogether different tone, as when Capt. Hector M'Intyre exclaims to his sister, who has just mentioned Lovel's saving of Isabella from drowning, "What! that romantic story is true then? And pray, does the valorous knight aspire, as is befitting on such occasion, to the hand of the young lady whom he redeemed from peril? It is quite in the rule of romance, I am aware" (chap. 19). Also there is the old prophecy—"If Malcolm the Misticot's grave were fun', / The lands of Knockwinnock are lost and won"—quoted (chap. 23) and referred to (chaps. 42, 52) by Edie, which is in the manner of the prophecies of Thomas of Erceldoune. These, then, are some of the allusions to romance and chivalry in *The Antiquary.* They are external and decorative, but they do tend to have a cumulative effect. And there are some other matters that lie deeper.

Underlying the entire story is the expulsion-and-return motif as it relates to young Lovel, who was born under strange circumstances, secretly abducted by a Spanish woman (Teresa D'Acunha), servant to his evil grandmother (the Countess of Glenallan), and who was led to believe that he was the son of his uncle (Geraldin Neville). It turns out that Lovel is actually the legitimate son of William Lord Geraldin and Eveline Neville. Shortly after their secret marriage a rumor was circulated by the old countess—aided by a faithful but misguided servant, Elspeth Cheyne (later Mucklebackit)—that Eveline was the natural daughter of Lord Geraldin's father; thus Lord Geraldin thought that he had married his own sister and was about to have a child by her. Eveline then tried to commit suicide but was saved by Elspeth; a son was born, the mother died, and the child disappeared. At the end of the novel Lovel finds out who he really is and can assume his rightful inheritance and position in society. The old Countess did not know about the secret marriage when she let out the false rumor, but she hated Eveline Neville so much that at one point she even suggested that Elspeth kill her, and when she heard of the birth of the child, she wanted Elspeth to do away with it—but Elspeth would not go so far as murder. This aspect of the plot has parallels in medieval romance. Bevis of Hampton's wicked mother wants her steward Saber to do away with her seven-year-old child, but Saber does not obey her command; when the child falls into the hands of pirates, we have the beginning of the expulsion-and-return motif. On his deathbed the King of Denmark entrusts his son Havelok to the care of Earl Godard, but the evil Godard, wishing to obtain the Danish throne for himself, "gives Havelok over to a fisherman named Grim to be killed. When Grim sees a miraculous light issuing from Havelok's mouth and a royal mark on his shoulder, he realizes that the child is destined to become king and therefore flees with him to England"[13]—again the beginning of the expulsion-and-return motif. In addition to these motifs, there is for a while the familiar story-pattern of Chaucer's Knight's Tale, in which two eligible young men compete for the favorable attention of the same young lady—in the novel, our hero Lovel and hot-tempered but likable Captain M'Intyre vying for the attention of Isabella Wardour. But Hector M'Intyre never has much of a chance, inasmuch as Isabella, unlike Chaucer's Emily (who does not care about either Palamon *or* Arcite), has clearly placed her affections with Lovel and wisely so, since he turns out to be much more eligible than Hector.

If Lovel is the romantic hero, Jonathan Oldbuck is the novel's real hero; and if medieval romance lurks in the background, Chaucer is in the forefront. Early in the story Oldbuck shows Lovel his library, comparing himself with Chaucer's Clerk:

It was chiefly upon his books that he prided himself, repeating, with a complacent air, as he led the way to the crowded and dusty shelves, the verses of old Chaucer,—

> For he would rather have, at his bed-head
> A twenty books, clothed in black or red,
> Of Aristotle or his philosophy,
> Than robes rich, rebeck, or saltery.

This pithy motto he delivered shaking his head, and giving each guttural the true Anglo-Saxon enunciation, which is now forgotten in the southern parts of this realm. [Chap. 3]

(The term "Middle English" was not used by Scott.) As we have already seen, Oldbuck contrasts his spinster sister with patient Griselda of the Clerk's Tale. In chapter 10 he takes Lovel to the Green Room, where Lovel will spend the night after having played such an important part in saving Sir Arthur and Isabella just in time (another motif from medieval romance). The room is decorated with a large and ornate Flemish tapestry of the sixteenth century—a hunting scene: "It seemed as if the prolific and rich invention of old Chaucer had animated the Flemish artist with its profusion; and Oldbuck had accordingly caused the following verses, from that ancient and excellent poet, to be embroidered, in Gothic letters, on a sort of border which he had added to the tapestry." There follow short quotations from *The Flower and the Leaf,* then thought to be by Chaucer, and from the dream sequence in *The Book of the Duchess:*

> And many an hart, and many an hind,
> Was both before me and behind.
> Of fawns, sownders, bucks, and does
> Was full the wood, and many roes,
> And many squirrells that ysate
> High on the trees and nuts ate.
>   [Lines 427-32, as quoted by Scott]

Perhaps Scott meant this excerpt to help foreshadow Lovel's strange dream, which Oldbuck interprets (chap. 14) with a perception worthy of Chaucer's Pertelote.

Scott imparts a tremendous amount of antiquarian knowledge to the reader in this novel, and most of it comes from the mouth of Jonathan Oldbuck. As Harry Ahlers observed some sixty-five years ago, "Da wir von ihm von vornherein als Antiquar und Gelehrten ein reiches Mass von Kentnissen erwarten, so erscheinen sie uns trotz ihrer grossen Zahl kaum aufdringlich."[14] Oldbuck, moreover, is a very convincing character. Scott did his job here as well as did Chaucer in his portrait of the Wife of Bath, in a somewhat different and more difficult situation. Despite the erudition of the long prologue to her tale—and she is not a book-learned person— everything seems natural and lifelike. The scriptural authorities who stand behind nearly every line she speaks do not encumber her harangue. The erudition that Chaucer works into her prologue is not *aufdringlich.*

The trickery which the scoundrelly Dousterswivel uses to convince Sir Arthur that there is treasure buried at the ruins of St. Ruth's priory brings to mind the Canon's Yeoman's Tale. Even though Oldbuck quotes *The Alchemist* at the end of chapter 33 and refers to Ben Jonson by name, and not to Chaucer, I think it not unlikely that Scott had Chaucer's tale in mind as well. The lack of specific reference may mean that he took pains to cover his tracks. One can indeed argue feelingly, without specific documentation, that the entire novel is Chaucerian—Chaucerian in the sense of Scott's deep and compassionate understanding of the ironies, paradoxes, sorrows, and foibles of the human condition.

The Black Dwarf (1816)

Near the end of chapter 5, Lucy Ilderton says to Isabella Vere, the novel's heroine: "In former times, in case of mutual slaughter between clans, subsequent alliances were so far from being excluded, that the hand of a daughter or a sister was the most frequent gage of reconciliation. You laugh at my skill in romance; but, I assure you, should your history be written, like that of many a less distressed and less deserving heroine, the well-judging reader would set you down for the lady and the love of Earnscliff, from the very obstacle which you suppose so insurmountable." The obstacle to which Lucy refers is the enmity between Isabella's father, the Laird of Ellieslaw, and the family of young Earnscliff. Isabella (who thinks that Lucy's reading of plays and romances has turned her brain) replies, "But these are not the days of romance, but of sad reality." Later, in a different context, Mr. Ratcliffe echoes Isabella's words: "These are not the days of romance."

And yet the underlying story-pattern of this short novel is that of the undesired marriage, a veritable staple of medieval romance. Isabella is being pressured by her father to marry his fellow Jacobite conspirator Sir Frederick Langley, whom she detests. At the climax of the story she agrees to the marriage in order (she thinks) to save her father's life. The Dwarf appears at the hastily arranged wedding and stops the misalliance from taking place, and the story ends with Isabella marrying Earnscliff—the enmity between his family and the Veres ending, as not-so-silly Lucy had averred, with a daughter as the "gage of reconciliation," and in this case a very willing gage. So the days of romance are not gone after all, although we are told otherwise and although on first glance the novel seems mainly indebted to Shakespeare, the misanthropic Black Dwarf obviously owing much to Timon of Athens.

There are some other echoes of medieval literature as well. In chapter 7 the Dwarf commands the unscrupulous Westburnflat to return Grace Armstrong (whom he has abducted) to her friends and her fiancé Hobbie Elliott—"and let her swear not to discover thy villainy." Westburnflat replies with a typically medieval antifeminist sentiment: "Swear? . . . but what if she break her faith? Women are not famous for keeping their plight." Earlier in the novel, in explaining how the stones of Mucklestane-Moor came to be, Scott tells a curious story about an old hag and her wayward geese:

> Incensed at the obstinacy with which they defied all her efforts to collect them, and not remembering the precise terms of the contract by which the fiend was bound to obey her commands for a certain space, the sorceress exclaimed, "Deevil, that neither I nor they ever stir from this spot more!" The words were hardly uttered, when, by a metamorphosis as sudden as any in Ovid, the hag and her refractory flock were converted into stone, the angel whom she served, being a strict formalist, grasping eagerly at an opportunity of completing the ruin of her body and soul by a literal obedience to her orders. [Chap. 2]

The passage brings vaguely to mind a curious episode at the end of the "Arthur and Accolon" section of Malory's *Tale of King Arthur* in which Morgan le Fay, being hotly pursued by Arthur for having done something especially nasty to him, changes herself and her followers to stone (temporarily) to elude capture. It also recalls the "old rebekke's" expressed *and heartfelt* wish, in the Friar's Tale, that the devil take the summoner of the tale to hell—the devil then following her instructions precisely, to the great consternation of the summoner. Scott's account (in the 1829 introduction) of David Ritchie, the original for the Black Dwarf, parallels Chaucer's description of the Miller in the General Prologue. Quoting Robert Chambers of Edinburgh, Scott relates that Ritchie's skull "was said to be of such strength, that he could strike it with ease through a panel of a door, or the end of a barrel"; Chaucer's Miller, we are told, can bash a door down "at a rennyng with his heed" (I, 551). Another allusion to the Miller can be seen in the Laird of Ellieslaw's remark about Westburnflat's doings: "He had other tow on his distaff last night" (chap. 12). This old proverbial expression occurs near the end of the Miller's Tale, with reference to Absolon: "He hadde moore tow on his distaf / Than Gerveys knew" (I, 3774-75). It appears elsewhere too in Middle English literature (e.g., in Hoccleve's *Regement of Princes*), but the Miller's Tale is the most likely place where Scott could have found it.

Old Mortality (1816)

In this, one of Scott's finest achievements, we have perhaps our best example of the Knight's Tale story-pattern of two sympathetic and eligible young men vying for the hand of one girl; but as usual Scott varies the pattern. Although Edith Bellenden esteems and respects Lord Evandale, her heart is always with Henry Morton. Moreover, Evandale and Morton are considerate of each other's feelings toward Edith, unlike Palamon and Arcite, whose real chivalry begins at Arcite's deathbed. As the story evolves, each owes his life to the other: Evandale saves Morton from being executed at the command of Colonel Grahame Claverhouse, and Morton saves Evandale from being hanged by the fanatical John Balfour of Burley. Throughout the story each tries to outdo the other in courteous, gentlemanly behavior, because each knows that the other's affection for Edith is genuine and honorable beyond question.

When Morton is brought as a prisoner to Tillietudlem (chap. 10), perhaps to undergo a death penalty, Jenny Dennison contrives a way for her mistress, Edith Bellenden, to see him. During the course of their conversation Morton tells her, "My guards spoke of a possibility of exchanging the penalty for entry into foreign service. I thought I could have embraced the alternative; and yet, Miss Bellenden, since I have seen you once more, I feel that exile would be more galling than death." Arcite's release from prison early in the Knight's Tale and his exile from Athens are probably more galling to him than continued imprisonment is to Palamon, for Palamon can look out from the tower every day and behold Emily. This would be my answer to the question which the Knight poses at the end of Part I:

> Yow loveres axe I now this questioun:
> Who hath the worse, Arcite or Palamoun?
> That oon may seen his lady day by day,
> But in prison he moot dwelle alway;
> That oother wher hym list may ride or go,
> But seen his lady shal he nevere mo. [I, 1347-52]

For a novel that owes so much to the Knight's Tale story-pattern, it is only fitting that the final chapter should have as its motto a quotation from Dryden's *Palamon and Arcite* (the "he" is Arcite):

> Yet cou'd he not his closing Eyes withdraw,
> Though less and less of *Emily* he saw:
> So, speechless, for a little space he lay;
> Then grasp'd the Hand he held, and sigh'd his Soul away.[15]

We know from the outset, then, that Lord Evandale will die in this chapter, and his death is somewhat reminiscent of Arcite's. Fate enters the lists and prevents him from receiving Morton's warning that his life is in great danger. He is shot by four adversaries at once and "[falls] from his horse mortally wounded." He has no dying speech, but in his final action he entrusts Edith to Morton: "Lord Evandale, taking their hands in his, pressed them both affectionately, united them together, raised his face as if to pray for a blessing on them, and sunk back and expired in the next moment." Interestingly, his sister, also present at his deathbed, is named Emily. Her grief is "clamorous," like that of Chaucer's Emily ("Shrighte Emelye, and howleth Palamon"), but it is "far exceeded in intensity by the silent agony of Edith" (and also, we can assume, of Morton).

The story contains much in the way of what we would now call courtly love. Edith, with her fair hair and blue eyes and "soft and feminine" features, resembles a typical heroine of courtly romance, although Scott is quick to point out that these beautiful features are "not without a certain expression of playful archness, which redeemed their sweetness from the charge of insipidity, sometimes brought against *blondes* and blue-eyed beauties" (chap. 2). Like many ladies in tales of courtly love, she is above Morton in the social order; he looks up to her and is ennobled by the relationship. Winning her is no easy task or quick matter, and circumstances necessitate periods of separation—reminding us of Andreas Capellanus's dictum that courtly lovers should see each other seldom. Also there is a necessity for secrecy, not because of a jealous husband or even a rival lover but owing rather to the unfortunate political situation and troubled times. Both lovers are aided by trusted friends in lower spheres of life: Edith by Jenny Dennison, her coquettish servant, who is like the lady-in-waiting of courtly love stories; and Morton by Cuddie Headrigg, his own servant, who is as faithful to him as ever was Gorvenal to Tristan. "I'll never desert a true-love cause," Jenny tells Edith when she helps arrange the secret meeting between her mistress and Henry Morton, then a prisoner (chap. 10). "Ye see I wad get my mither bestowed," Cuddie tells Morton when both of them are in captivity, "and then you and me wad gang and pouss our fortunes, like the folk i' the daft auld tales about Jock the Giant-Killer and Valentine and Orson" (chap. 14).

Besides referring directly to a famous medieval romance, Scott has utilized several romance motifs. Near the end of the novel Henry Morton returns to Scotland after several years of exile. His physical appearance having changed markedly, he does not think that anyone will recognize him. At Milnwood, however, he *is* recognized by the old housekeeper, Mrs. Alison Wilson, but not by the "small cocking spaniel, once his own property, but which, unlike to the faithful Argus, saw his master return from his wanderings without any symptom of recognition" (chap. 39). The allusion to Homer's *Odyssey* is clear,[16] but the story-pattern of a man returning to his native land after long absence and in disguise also reflects the Middle English *Sir Orfeo*, which Scott knew well. It may be that the Tristan-story, too, was in the back of his mind, specifically Tristan's return, late in the story, to Cornwall and his assumption of the guise of a beggar, or madman (depending on which version you are reading). The phrase "unlike the faithful Argus" could just as well have been "unlike the faithful Hodain." The whole last part of the novel, chapters 37 through 54, can be looked on as a variation on the exile-and-return story-pattern which, as we have seen, underlies all of *Guy Mannering* and *The Antiquary*. Moreover, Henry Morton returns "as if from the grave"; indeed, he had been assumed dead in a shipwreck. Another instance of the resuscitation-from-the-dead motif can be seen in the religious maniac Habbakuk Mucklewrath, who has been assumed dead but who revives and prophesies doom for Claverhouse before dying for keeps (see chap. 34). We also have the motif of the undesired marriage—Edith really does not want to marry Lord Evandale—although it is different from the stock situation in the romances inasmuch as Evandale is a completely worthy suitor. Morton saves him from death once, but his final attempt to do so is unsuccessful. Another good example of escape from imminent death is Morton's own rescue by Claverhouse from the fanatical Covenanters who are about to execute him (chap. 33).

A number of miscellaneous details hark back to earlier times and to medieval literature. References to pilgrims and pilgrimages are frequent, especially in the introductory material and most especially with regard to Robert Paterson, alias Old Mortality, the restorer of Cameronian monuments. Like many a lady of medieval romance Lady Margaret Bellenden, Edith's grandmother, is noted for her knowledge and practice of medicine. In chapter 35 Claverhouse recommends Froissart to Morton, who is again a prisoner:

> His chapters inspire me with more enthusiasm than even poetry itself. And the noble canon, with what true chivalrous feeling he confines his beautiful expressions of sorrow to the death of the gallant and high-bred knight, of whom it was a pity to see the fall, such was his loyalty to his king, pure faith to his religion, hardihood towards his enemy, and fidelity to his lady-love! Ah, *benedicite!* how he will mourn over the fall of such a pearl of knighthood, be it on the side he happens to favour, or on the other. But, truly, for sweeping from the face of the earth some few hundreds of villain churls, who are born but to plough it, the high-born and inquisitive historian has marvellous little sympathy,—as little, or less, perhaps, than John Grahame of Claverhouse.

Claverhouse's whole character, then, is defined with regard to his conception of Froissart. How different his reading is from the long-winded seventeenth-century romances that are the favorite pastime of Edith Bellenden—"nonsensical romances," according to her crusty old great-uncle, Major Bellenden; "ponderous folios," Scott tells us in a note, which "combine the dulness of the metaphysical courtship with all the improbabilities of the ancient Romance of Chivalry." During the course of the story Edith has to deal with real life, but ironically it too has more than a passing resemblance to romance, that is, to the earlier *medieval* romances. As in *The Antiquary* there is an interest in dreams, especially the dreams of Morton and Balfour during the momentous night when Morton secretly harbors the wanted man in the hayloft at Milnwood, unaware that Balfour is wanted for the murder of Archbishop Sharpe.

Earlier in the story, in Niel Blane's pub, Balfour is forced by Captain Bothwell to make a toast to the archbishop, whose murder has already taken place but is not yet known. Balfour carefully formulates his toast in language that recalls the evasive shifts of the Tristan-story: "The Archbishop of St. Andrews, and the place he now worthily holds: may each prelate in Scotland soon be as the Right Reverend James Sharpe!" (chap. 4). Near the end of the story, when Morton encounters Balfour in his mountain hideout, Balfour points to three notches on his sword and tells Morton proudly, "The fragment of steel that parted from this first gap rested on the skull of the perjured traitor who first introduced Episcopacy into Scotland" (chap. 43). Again we are reminded of the Tristan-story—specifically, the piece of Tristan's sword that lodges in the skull of Morold and causes his death. In the awesome fight between Balfour and Bothwell in chapter 16, "each of the combatants was considered as the champion of his respective party, and a result ensued more usual in romance than in real story. Their followers, on either side, instantly paused, and looked on as if the fate of the day were to be decided by the event of the combat between these two redoubted swordsmen. The combatants themselves seemed of the same opinion." The very language that Scott uses recalls Malory, as the combatants "rolled together on the ground, tearing, struggling, and foaming, with the inveteracy of thorough-bred bull-dogs."

In the opening pages we are told in the words of one Jedediah Cleishbotham that the story was written by a young teacher named Peter Pattieson, who based his work on anecdotes told by Robert Paterson, or Old Mortality; after Pattieson's untimely death, his unpublished manuscript passed into the hands of Cleishbotham, who saw it through the press in order "to answer funeral and death-bed expenses." Scott observes in the Essay on Romance that "modern authors were not the first who invented the popular mode of introducing their works to the world as the contents of a newly-discovered manuscript." He goes on to give an account of the supposed discovery of the long French prose romance *Perceforest*, which is a "fabulous history" of Britain prior to the time of King Arthur:

In the year 1286, Count William of Hainault had, it is averred, crossed the seas in order to be present at the nuptials of Edward, and in the course of a tour through

Britain, was hospitably entertained at an abbey situated on the banks of the Humber, and termed, it seems, Burtimer, because founded by a certain Burtimericus, a monarch of whom our annals are silent, but who had gained in that place, a victory over the heathens of Germany. Here a cabinet, which was enclosed in a private recess, had been lately discovered within the massive walls of an ancient tower, and was found to contain a Grecian manuscript, along with a royal crown. The abbot had sent the latter to King Edward, and the Count of Hainault with difficulty obtained possession of the manuscript. He had it rendered from Greek into Latin by a monk of the abbey of Saint Landelain, and from that language it is said to have been translated into French by the author, who gives it to the world in honour of the Blessed Virgin and for the edification of nobleness and chivalry.

Although the circumstances are obviously different, a fabrication of this sort is precisely what Scott has used in *Old Mortality*. But we have moved now to matters of style and structure, which I want to reserve for the next chapter.

4

NOVELS OF THE BROKEN YEARS
1817-1819

THE BROKEN YEARS are the three years during which Scott was seriously ill with gallstones, sometimes suffering excruciating pain that demanded heavy sedation. Upon seeing for the first time *The Bride of Lammermoor* printed and in finished form, Scott told James Ballantyne that "he did not recollect one single incident, character, or conversation it contained."[1] When he recovered from his ordeal he was a noticeably older man. Sickness notwithstanding, some of his finest work belongs to this unhappy period. I would rate *The Bride of Lammermoor* and *The Heart of Mid-Lothian* as his two finest achievements. *Ivanhoe* is easily his best known and most popular work. *Rob Roy* rates high on anyone's list, with its intrigue and adventure, its boldly hewn characters, and its interesting experiment with sustained first-person point of view. *A Legend of Montrose* is unforgettable because of one character, Captain Dugald Dalgetty; if it falls short of the others, it obviously was not intended to be so ambitious an undertaking. So important are these five novels that Scott would hold today a secure and honorable place in literary history on their strength alone.

Rob Roy (1817)

The story of Frank Osbaldistone, told by himself, begins and ends with a motif from medieval romance. There is enmity between Frank and his father, owing first to Frank's lack of interest in assuming a responsible role in his father's London business firm and later to the machinations of Rashleigh Osbaldistone, Frank's evil cousin. The enmity gives way to reconciliation between father and son near the end of the novel, after

Rashleigh's plot to ruin Frank's father has been discovered and thwarted. In chapter 7, shortly after Frank has arrived from London at Osbaldistone Hall, the home of his Jacobite uncle Sir Hildebrand Osbaldistone and his six cousins, he finds himself accused of having robbed a fellow traveler, the jittery man with the portmanteau whose name he later learns is Morris. In discussing Waverley's misfortunes I called attention to analogous episodes in medieval romance that involve a hero's being falsely accused or maliciously framed by misinformation; I cited specifically *Melusine* and *Huon of Bordeaux*. In *Rob Roy* I suspect that *Huon of Bordeaux* was on Scott's mind, inasmuch as Frank has been recalled by his father to London *from Bordeaux*. Moreover, in Frank's silly poem about the Black Prince, who "in Bourdeaux dying lay" (more of this anon), he alludes to Charlemagne, and in the romance it is Charlemagne to whom Huon has been made to appear a traitor. In chapter 18 that servant of servants Andrew Fairservice leads Frank by night through the Middle Marches on their way to Glasgow, and "at a much brisker pace" than Frank "would have recommended." The terrain is treacherous: "We made abrupt ascents and descents over ground of a very break-neck character, and traversed the edge of precipices where a slip of the horse's feet would have consigned the rider to certain death." We have here the perilous journey of medieval romance but with a humorous touch: Frank becomes increasingly frustrated and angry with Andrew for paying no attention to his commands to slow down. In chapter 27 a perilous journey begins in earnest when Frank, Andrew, and Bailie Nicol Jarvie ride northeastward from Glasgow through a "waste and wild" landscape into the Highlands, where real danger is in store for them.

There is an array of allusions to medieval literature—sometimes vague, but more often than not specific; sometimes straightforward, but often with humorous overtones. In chapter 16 Diana Vernon urges Frank to go back to London to prevent Rashleigh from ruining his father: " 'Everything is possible for him who possesses courage and activity,' she said, with a look resembling one of those heroines of the age of chivalry whose encouragement was wont to give champions double valour at the hour of need." Scott may have remembered the story of Gareth, who fights all the more valiantly against the Red Knight of the Red Launds when his ladylove, Dame Lyonesse, looks on (and double valor is indeed desirable against an adversary who has the strength of seven men), but analogues are numerous. Miss Vernon shows on more than one occasion her familiarity with *Valentine and Orson*. When she first meets Frank (in chap. 5) she forewarns him of "the Orsons you are to live amongst"—that is, his uncouth, boorish cousins at Osbaldistone Hall. And later (chap. 17), when giving him an important letter from Mr. Tresham, his father's business partner, she again alludes to the famous romance: "Here is a letter . . .

directed for you, Mr. Osbaldistone, very duly and distinctly, but which, notwithstanding the caution of the person who wrote and addressed it, might perhaps never have reached your hands, had it not fallen into the possession of a certain Pacolet, or enchanted dwarf of mine, whom, like all distressed damsels of romance, I retain in my secret service."

This conversation takes place in the library, the scene of much mystery and intrigue. On one occasion Miss Vernon uses "a difficult passage in the Divina Commedia" as a pretext for drawing Frank into the library so that she can talk with him in private. Both her conception of "the obscure Florentine" and that of Rashleigh, who claims to be skilled "at tracking the sense of Dante through the metaphors and elisions of his wild and gloomy poem," are exactly Scott's own conception of the great poet whom he found "too obscure and difficult"[2] and infinitely less inspiring than Ariosto, whose *Orlando Furioso* Frank is in the process of translating (probably not very well). The names *Hildebrand* and *Perceval* are worthy of comment and not without a touch of humor. Frank's doughty but not deeply intelligent uncle is named after the hero of the medieval German poem, "The Song of Old Hildebrand" in Weber's translation,[3] and his son Perceval, who dies from overindulging in brandy, hardly practices the virtue of temperance associated with the Perceval of romance. Andrew Fairservice alludes to Sir David Lindsay in evaluating Frank's versifying— "Gude help him! twa lines o'Davie Lindsay wad ding a' he ever clerkit" (chap. 21)—and Rob Roy quotes loosely from Villon in answering the Bailie's question as to when he will receive from Rob the thousand pounds he lent him: "Where it is . . . I cannot justly tell,—probably where last year's snaw is" (chap. 23). Frank applies Spenser to the Bailie's horsemanship: "Ere he 'clombe to the saddle,'—an expression more descriptive of the Bailie's mode of mounting than that of the knights-errant to whom Spenser applies it,—he inquired the cause of the dispute betwixt my servant and me" (chap. 27). Throughout Frank's narrative the reader cannot avoid comparing Rob Roy with the Robin Hood of balladry, who also was noted for helping people in distress, often helping the poor at the expense of the rich.

What about Chaucer? Frank's poem about the Black Prince (chap. 2) is in tail-rhyme stanzas, the first of which echoes lines that Scott had previously written in *Marmion* (in VI.xxxiii):

> Oh for the voice of that wild horn,
> On Fontarabian echoes borne,
>   The dying hero's call,
> That told imperial Charlemagne
> How Paynim sons of swarthy Spain
>   Had wrought his champion's fall.

The poem brings to mind *Sir Thopas,* and indeed the whole dramatic situation seems inspired by Harry Bailey's reaction to Chaucer the Pilgrim's attempt at tale-telling. Frank's father reads the poem aloud in his presence, stopping at every stanza to make sarcastic comments about the phraseology, and although unlike Harry Bailey he does not go so far as to say that his son's "drasty rymyng is nat worth a toord," he is singularly unimpressed. Further, Frank's description of an English inn on a Sunday (chap. 4) recalls vaguely Chaucer's General Prologue: "The guests, assembled from different quarters, and following different professions, formed, in language, manners, and sentiments, a curious contrast to each other, not indifferent to those who desired to possess a knowledge of mankind in its varieties." Much later in the story Frank knocks at the gate of a hostel in Glasgow late on a Sunday night. Dogs start barking furiously, and when the neighbors show they are disturbed, Frank trembles "lest the thunders of their wrath might dissolve in showers like that of Xantippe" (chap. 24). The hostess awakens and scolds "loiterers in her kitchen" for not going immediately to the gate, using "a tone of objurgation not unbecoming the philosophical spouse of Socrates." This little vignette seems indebted to a story in the book about bad women that was the favorite reading of Jankyn, the Wife of Bath's fifth husband:

> No thyng forgat he the care and the wo
> That Socrates hadde with his wyves two;
> How Xantippa caste pisse upon his heed.
> This sely man sat stille as he were deed;
> He wiped his heed, namoore dorste he seyn,
> But "Er that thonder stynte, comth a reyn!" [III,727-32]

Scott would have found this anecdote about Socrates more appealing than the dialogues. The next chapter (25) has a short quotation from *Palamon and Arcite* as its motto:

> So stands the *Thracian* Heardsman with his Spear,
> Full in the Gap, and hopes the hunted Bear,
> And hears him rustling in the Wood, and sees
> His Course at Distance by the bending Trees;
> And thinks, Here comes my mortal Enemy,
> And either he must fall in Fight, or I.[4]

These lines prepare us for the fight between Frank and Rashleigh over Diana Vernon, which might have resulted in the death of one of them had not Rob Roy (like Theseus) intervened. So again we have the Knight's Tale but with variation: Frank and Rashleigh, although equally capable, are by no means equally worthy in character. The use of *occupatio* at the beginning of chapter 36 also recalls the Knight's Tale: Frank says he "will not attempt to describe" the "romantic country" around Loch Lomond, but then proceeds at some length to do so.

In chapter 20 Frank and Andrew are at church in Glasgow. Frank wants to leave, but Andrew informs him that the doors are locked. "While I endeavoured," Frank writes, "to make a virtue of necessity, and recall my attention to the sermon, I was again disturbed by a singular interruption." "To make a virtue of necessity" is a proverbial expression at least as old as Chaucer; it occurs, in fact, in the Knight's Tale (I, 3042). In chapter 23 we have another proverbial expression: " 'Ye're mad, Rob,' said the Bailie, 'mad as a March hare,—though wherefore a hare suld be mad at March mair than at Martinmas, is mair than I can weel say' "; a variation occurs near the beginning of the Friar's Tale: "For thogh this Somonour wood were as an hare" (III, 1327). In chapter 26 the Bailie remarks that "it's an ill bird that files its ain nest," and his fellow Scot Andrew Fairservice uses an equally old expression in chapter 39: "I judged they had other tow on their rock"—a variation of the phrase "to have other tow on one's distaff" (already mentioned in the discussion of *The Black Dwarf*). Sometimes Scott's imagery is reminiscent of Chaucer: for example, the following conversation (chap. 7) between Miss Vernon and Frank:

"Do you know one Moray, or Morris, or some such name?"
"Not that I can at present recollect."
"Think a moment. Did you not lately travel with somebody of such a name?"
"The only man with whom I travelled for any length of time was a fellow whose soul seemed to lie in his portmanteau."

Recalling the preface to *Gil Blas*, Miss Vernon goes on to speak of "the soul of the licentiate Pedro Garcias, which lay among the ducats in his leathern purse"; but the reader is reminded also of Chaucer's Summoner:

> And if he foond owher a good felawe,
> He wolde techen him to have noon awe
> In swich caas of the ercedekenes curs,
> But if a mannes soule were in his purs;
> For in his purs he sholde ypunysshed be.
> [I, 653-57]

During the course of an impassioned conversation with the Bailie (chap. 31), Helen MacGregor (Rob's wife) exclaims, "But now we are free,—free by the very act which left us neither house nor hearth, food nor covering, which bereaved me of all,—of all,—and makes me groan when I think I must still cumber the earth for other purposes than those of vengeance."

The curious expression "to cumber the earth" brings to mind some words of Troilus when he learns that Criseyde must go to the Greek camp:

> Allas, Fortune! if that my lif in joie
> Displesed hadde unto thi foule envye,
> Why ne haddestow my fader, kyng of Troye,
> Byraft the lif, or don my bretheren dye,
> Or slayn myself, that thus compleyne and crye,
> I, combre-world, that may of nothyng serve,
> But evere dye and nevere fulli sterve? [IV, 274-80][5]

On a lighter note, Frank once refers to Andrew's lowly cottage as a *mansion* (chap. 18), indulging in a mock-heroic game worthy of Chaucer's Nun's Priest, whose "povre wydwe's narwe cotage" contains a "bour" and "halle."

In sum, *Rob Roy* is full of allusions to Chaucer and medieval romance, often in a humorous or witty context. Clearly, though, the medieval influence is not as deep-seated as in some of the other novels. It is not burningly essential, it does not belong to the novel's emotional core. It appeals more to the intellect and sense of humor than to the heart. Without it Frank's story would not be as much fun to read.

The Heart of Mid-Lothian (1818)

The medieval influence in this novel, Scott's masterwork, *is* deep-seated, but it is vaguer than in *Rob Roy*, and thus I shall be dealing, even more so than hitherto, with interesting parallels rather than specific sources. Studies of this sort can go too far, of course; apparent parallels may be fortuitous. In the third chapter of *Mid-Lothian*, for example, Captain Porteous forces small handcuffs onto the wrists of the contraband dealer Andrew Wilson just before he is led to his execution; the unhappy man suffers terribly. The incident, which in this case is historical, brings to mind the episode in Béroul's *Tristan* when Yseut, her wrists bound together so tightly "that blood was being squeezed from all her fingers,"[6] is led to her doom. So far as I can determine, Scott was not familiar with Béroul's version of the Tristan-story. The seeming parallel suggests that he was so deeply immersed in medieval romance that he sometimes instinctively and unwittingly used detail not only fitting but clearly in the manner of medieval romance, while indeed a romance that contains the particular detail can be shown to be one which he probably did not know.

If Béroul was unknown to him, it is virtually certain that he had another version of the Tristan-story in mind in chapter 20, when Jeanie Deans visits Effie in her cell in the Tolbooth shortly before the trial. A more intensely emotional meeting between two sisters under more trying circumstances cannot be imagined:

> Even the hard-hearted turnkey [James Ratcliffe], who had spent his life in scenes calculated to stifle both conscience and feeling, could not witness this scene without a touch of human sympathy. It was shown in a trifling action, but which had more delicacy in it than seemed to belong to Ratcliffe's character and station. The unglazed window of the miserable chamber was open, and the beams of a bright sun fell right upon the bed where the sufferers were seated. With a gentleness that had something of reverence in it, Ratcliffe partly closed the shutter, and seemed thus to throw a veil over a scene so sorrowful.

This "trifling action" recalls an episode in the Middle English poem *Sir Tristrem*. Hunters have discovered where Tristrem and Ysonde are hiding in the forest, and King Mark goes stealthily to see for himself. He finds them asleep in their "earthen house" but with a naked sword between them. A ray of sun shines through an opening and falls onto the lovely face of the queen; touched, Mark puts his glove into the opening to screen out the sun and departs silently. Only after they awaken and discover the glove do Tristrem and Ysonde realize that the King has been there.[7] Almost all attendant circumstances are different, but the trifling action itself, with its "gentleness that had something of reverence in it," is the same in both romance and novel.

After the momentous trial in which her sister is pronounced guilty and sentenced to be hanged, Jeanie determines to go to London "and beg her pardon from the king and queen" (chap. 25). In several places Scott refers to Jeanie's journey as a *pilgrimage;* Jeanie herself once uses the word in a letter to her father. We are told in chapter 26 that "she was no heroine of romance," but in the very next chapter we read that "there was something of romance in Jeanie's venturous resolution." Indeed, her heroic journey, with its besetting dangers and nightmarish atmosphere, does resemble the perilous journey of many a knight. Also, as in romance, there are some narrow escapes: the daring escape of George Robertson (Staunton) from execution with the help of his comrade Wilson, who sacrifices himself to save the younger man; Jeanie's escape from Mrs. Murdockson and Madge Wildfire on the way to London; Effie's reprieve, which commutes a death sentence to fourteen years' banishment; and much later the narrow escape of Effie (now Lady Staunton) from accidental death in the mountainous terrain near her sister's home.

Another motif that has parallels in medieval romance is the disguise of a leading young man as a woman. During the storming of the Tolbooth and the subsequent lynching of Porteous, George Robertson is dressed as a woman, in clothes borrowed from Madge Wildfire. When the rioters finally succeed in breaking into the prison, he finds his truelove Effie, who has already been apprehended for alleged child murder, and he excitedly urges her to flee. Although there is no time for conversation, Effie presumably realizes who he is; nevertheless she is determined to remain in prison. In *Agesilan of Colchos*, a romance belonging to the Amadis cycle, Agesilan, according to Dunlop, "was inspired with such an irresistible passion, that he repaired, in the disguise of a female minstrel, to the court of Queen Sidonia, the mother of his mistress [Diana], and was presented to her daughter as an amusing companion. Here he occasionally entertained the court ladies by the exercise of his musical and poetic talents, but at other times distinguished himself as an amazon, in combating the knights, who on various pretexts came to molest Sidonia." Dunlop goes on to say that "the circumstances of a lover residing with his mistress, and unknown to her, in disguise of a female, is frequent in subsequent romances . . . and its origin must be looked for in the story of the concealment of Achilles" (*History of Fiction*, 2:39). The circumstances are obviously different from those in Scott's novel, but it is interesting that Agesilan is said to distinguish himself "as an amazon"—interesting because Scott more than once refers to the disguised George Robertson as an amazon (see chap. 6). In *Amadis of Greece* the hero falls in love with a closely mewed-up Moslem girl named Niquea. He gains admittance to her in the disguise of a female slave—and gets her pregnant. "The situation of Niquea now requiring retirement from a father's observation," Dunlop observes, "she eloped with Amadis, and soon after arrived with him at Trebizond, where she was solemnly espoused, and gave birth to a son, named Florisel de Niquea" (2:33). More of Amadis of Greece later. In the second book of the *Heldenbuch*, Hughdietrich also disguises himself as a female in order to see his truelove, who is carefully kept in an almost impregnable fortress. The trick works, the girl gets pregnant, her pregnancy must be concealed, a baby (Wolfdietrich) is born in secret, and shortly after birth the baby is borne away by a wolf (he will be recognized later by a small cross on his body). My examples from *Amadis of Greece* and the *Heldenbuch* involve not only a hero disguised as a woman but also his gaining admittance to his truelove, who is in a hard-to-get-at place, his getting her pregnant, and the necessity for secrecy because of the girl's condition. The *Heldenbuch* example involves also the loss of the child shortly after birth. In *The Heart of Mid-Lothian* Scott has altered what appears to be the typical order of the events in romance in that his Byronic lover disguised as a female gains difficult access to his mistress *after* his sexual affair with her, after the period of concealed pregnancy, and after the birth of the child.

The difficult circumstances accompanying the birth of Effie's child have still more parallels in medieval romance. In *The Knight of the Swan* a queen (Beatrice) gives birth to seven children while her husband the king (Oriant) is away. During her unusually painful labor and childbirth, Beatrice never actually sees the babies; her evil mother-in-law (Matabrune), who has always been opposed to the marriage of Oriant and Beatrice, tells Beatrice that she has given birth to dogs and accuses her of having copulated with a dog. The children are carried out into the forest by one Markes, who has been given orders by Matabrune to kill them, but taking pity on them he does not do so. When Oriant returns, he puts his wife into perpetual imprisonment. In the meantime Matabrune, having learned that the children live, sends a group of men led by one Savary into the forest to kill them. Along the way the men see an incident that gives them second thoughts about carrying out Matabrune's orders: "They sawe muche people assembled . . . for to see a woman executed and brent by Justice. And wherfore sayd Savary, what harme hath she doone. And they sayd for that she hath murdred and slaine the childe that she bare in her own bely."[8] Sixteen years later Beatrice is formally accused by a knight named Makayre, who is in the service of Matabrune, of having copulated with a dog. She maintains her innocence, and in the ensuing trial by combat she is saved from death by one of her own sons, Helyas. The defeated Makayre is hanged, and Matabrune is burned alive in her castle. Although much of this story is obviously quite different from *The Heart of Mid-Lothian*, there are these similarities: (1) a woman goes into childbirth when the father is away; (2) she is assisted in difficult labor by an older woman (cf. Mrs. Murdockson) who is malevolent toward her; (3) the issue from her womb is taken away from her at once, and she does not know what has become of it; (4) she is accused falsely; (5) she is saved at the last moment from execution; (6) a long-lost son appears when he is in his teens; (7) the evil woman is put to death. (I find intriguing the scene in which the young mother is executed for having done away with her child; such might have happened to Effie Deans, who is presumed to have murdered her child.) In *The Heart of Mid-Lothian* the order of events is somewhat different in that Effie is saved from execution and Mrs. Murdockson is hanged long before the appearance of the long-lost son. Accompanying circumstances are of course quite different in the romance, and one motif important in Scott is absent: the necessity for secrecy during the heroine's pregnancy. We must look in other romances for that, and, as my previous discussion has already intimated, it is not difficult to find.

In *Amadis of Gaul*, the first romance in the Amadis cycle, the original hero himself is born under difficult circumstances. His mother Elisena, younger daughter of the King of Brittany, falls in love with Perion, King of Gaul, when he is visiting at the Breton court; they sleep together on the sly, and she becomes pregnant. Since "the laws of Brittany punish a violation of chastity with death" (as William Stewart Rose puts it), Elisena retires from her father's court to a "sequestered spot," where in time she gives birth to a male child. She is convinced by Dariolette, her trusted lady-in-waiting, that she must part with him immediately to avoid the rigor of the law, so the baby is put into a seaworthy cradle and set adrift, later to be rescued by a vassal of the King of Scotland, who is the husband of Elisena's older sister. Perion and Elisena later marry not knowing the whereabouts of their child.

Scott has given us tantalizingly similar material in *The Heart of Mid-Lothian*. Effie is the younger daughter of Davie Deans, a strict moralist. She falls in love with a man from a neighboring country (England) and becomes pregnant by him. She must conceal her pregnancy to avoid shame and the wrath of her father; she manages to do so at her place of employment in the city. When her time comes, she gives birth to a child in secret and is immediately forced by circumstances to part with it. She does not know what becomes of it. After various ensuing complications have been straightened out, she finally is able to marry the boy's father. Her son later turns up in Scotland, near the home of her older sister and brother-in-law. Elisena does have one confidante, Dariolette, who knows all her problems—unlike Effie, who tells no one, not even Jeanie. Thus, when Effie admits having given birth to a child, which has disappeared, she runs into grave danger because the law then assumes that she has done away with it; like Elisena, Effie faces a death penalty, but for a different reason.

Trouble accompanying the birth of a child seems to run in Amadis's family. His first son, Esplandian, is born in secret. In Dunlop's words, "Oriana having given birth to a son, the fruit of her stolen interviews with Amadis, delivered the child to her confidants, that he might be conveyed to a remote part of the country for the sake of concealment" (*History of Fiction*, 2:19). Unfortunately, the infant is snatched away by a lioness, but Esplandian overcomes this and many other problems, and life goes on. His own first-born son, Lisuarte, has to leave his ladylove Onoloria, daughter of the Emperor of Trebizond, after having gotten her pregnant. "The imprudent anticipation of Onoloria rendered concealment necessary," Dunlop tells us, "and, during the baptism of her infant, which was performed at a retired fountain, he was carried off by corsairs, and sold by them to the Moorish king of Saba" (2:28). The infant is Amadis of Greece, who, as we have already seen, lives to see better days and to get a girl in a bad situation like his father before him. Prior to his affair with Niquea he has a fight with his father, neither one knowing who the other is. Urganda the Unknown intercedes before one of them is killed, so the encounter ends in recognition and joy, as do similar encounters in "The Song of Old Hildebrand" and in *Sir Eglamour of Artois*, *Sir Torrent of Portyngale*, and *Sir Triamour*.

In *Valentine and Orson* the Empress Bellyssant gives birth in very trying circumstances to twin sons who almost immediately are lost to her. She does not know what becomes of them. Orson grows up like a wild man before he is recognized, fifteen years later. The long-lost son of Effie and George may well owe something to Orson so far as upbringing is concerned. But it is the other son, Valentine, who is destined to have an armed conflict with his own father, neither one knowing who the other is—and he kills his father. In a sense both George Staunton and the Emperor of Greece get what they deserve: George finally pays for his misspent youth, and the emperor for the unnecessary anguish and grief he caused his wife. In romance an armed conflict between father and son usually occurs during the course of the son's search for his father; in Scott just the opposite, during a father's search for his son. Whatever the variation, the motif of a fight between a father and son who do not know each other, is a staple of medieval romance, and Scott seized on it as a canny way of concluding a novel—a superb novel—but one that he himself must have realized had grown tedious in the last chapters.

The Bride of Lammermoor (1819)

Very early in this most beautiful and most melancholy story, which runs the gamut of human emotions, we learn that the favorite reading of the heroine, Lucy Ashton, is "of a romantic cast": "Her secret delight was in the old legendary tales of ardent devotion and unalterable affection, chequered as they so often are with strange adventures and supernatural horrors. . . . In her retired chamber, or in the woodland bower which she had chosen for her own . . . she was in fancy distributing the prizes at the tournament, or raining down influence from her eyes on the valiant combatants" (chap. 3). Ironically, the world around her becomes more and more like the world of romance, but she is destined to experience its darker side—"the fairy wand, with which in her solitude she had delighted to raise visions of enchantment" becoming finally "the rod of a magician, the bond slave of evil genii, serving only to invoke spectres at which the exorcist trembled" (chap. 30).

Although the time of the story is the late seventeenth century, Scott is indebted everywhere to medieval romance, which can hardly be said to lurk in the background. Much of the stuff that romance is made of is very apparent at or near the "plentiful and pellucid fountain," its Gothic housing long in ruins but the place itself still thought to be one of misfortune for the Ravenswood family. The trouble began early in the sixteenth century when a former Lord of Ravenswood had a liaison with a mysterious lady who appeared to him each Friday near the fountain. She told him that their relationship could continue indefinitely as long as she departed before the ringing of the vespers' bell from a nearby chapel. Having been warned by a holy father that the lady might be a fiend from hell, the Lord of Ravenswood arranges for the bells to be rung later; presumably, should the lady indeed be a fiend, she would assume her true shape after the usual time for vespers. But when the trap is set,

no change took place upon the nymph's outward form; but as soon as the lengthening shadows made her aware that the usual hour of the vespers chime was passed, she tore herself from her lover's arms with a shriek of despair, bid him adieu for ever, and, plunging into the fountain, disappeared from his eyes. The bubbles occasioned by her descent were crimsoned with blood as they arose, leading the distracted Baron to infer, that his ill-judged curiosity had occasioned the death of this interesting and mysterious being. The remorse which he felt, as well as the recollection of her charms, proved the penance of his future life, which he lost in the battle of Flodden not many months after. [Chap. 5]

The story-pattern is the familiar one, to be found in some Breton lais (and other romances), in which a mortal has an amorous liaison with a fairylike creature whose presence depends on the keeping of a taboo; it is later broken, with sorrow resulting for the mortal.[9] The fairylike creature can be masculine, as in the stories of Lohengrin and the Knight of the Swan, but is more often than not a mysterious lady, as in the well-known lais of Lanval and Graelent. I suspect here that Scott had the romance about Melusine in mind, since the Christian name of the Lord of Ravenswood, Raymond, is the same as that of Melusine's lover and husband; moreover, the romance ends on a sad note, as does Scott's story, unlike what we find in the story of Lanval, who is reunited with his fairy mistress at the end.

It is near this fountain that Edgar of Ravenswood saves Lucy and her father the Lord Keeper from being gored to death by a wild bull—an incident that elicits a sarcastic comment from Lady Ashton, much later, in conversation with her husband: "Saved your life! I have heard of that story . . . the Lord Keeper was scared by a dun cow, and he takes the young fellow who killed her for Guy of Warwick—any butcher from Haddington may soon have an equal claim on your hospitality" (chap. 22). Lady Ashton might also have compared Edgar to Bevis of Hampton, who slew a vicious wild boar early in his career, but Scott has silently used the romance of *Bevis* in other connections and does not want to alert the reader as to what he is doing. Interestingly her words reveal that Lady Ashton knows about Guy of Warwick from chapbooks or from some other later account (such as Samuel Rowlands's) rather than from the original medieval story, in which the hero kills a dragon and two giants but no dun cow. In chapter 20 Edgar and Lucy plight their troth at the "fatal" fountain. They break and divide between them a gold coin:

"And never shall this leave my bosom," said Lucy, as she hung the piece of gold around her neck, and concealed it with her handkerchief, "until you, Edgar Ravenswood, ask me to resign it to you—and, while I wear it, never shall that heart acknowledge another love than yours."

With like protestations, Ravenswood placed his portion of the coin opposite to his heart.

This incident recalls the passage in *Valentine and Orson* (chap. 91) in which Valentine askes Clerimonde to give him the ring with which he wed her. When she does so, he breaks it in two, keeping one half for himself and giving the other half to her. He tells her not to believe anything she should hear about him unless she sees his half of the ring. In a later romance, Richard Johnson's *Renowned History of the Seven Champions of Christendom* (chap. 3), St. George of England and the Mohammedan princess Sabra plight their troth with a broken ring: "And thereupon she broke a ring, and gave him one half as a pledge of her love, and kept the other half herself."[10] Just after Edgar has been expelled from Ravenswood Castle by an enraged Lady Ashton, he sees by the fountain an apparition which he takes to be Lucy but which turns out to be Blind Alice, ancient servant to the Ravenswood family, who unbeknown to Edgar has just died. In a later chapter Lucy is told the story of the fountain "at full length, and with formidable additions," by the old hag Ailsie Gourley. (I will have more to say about the use of a place as a unifying device in Chapter 7.)

The Bride of Lammermoor has probably the most heartrending example in all of Scott of the undesired marriage motif so common in medieval romance. In *King Horn*, Rymenild is twice about to be forced into marriage with undesirable husbands, both of whom (King Mody of Reynis and the treacherous Fikenild) are eventually killed by Horn. In *Florisel de Niquea*, according to Dunlop, "Florisel, on his arrival in Apolonia, found his mistress, Helena, on the eve of a marriage with the prince of Gaul, an infidelity to which she had been constrained by her father; but Florisel interrupted the marriage ceremony by carrying off the bride" (*History of Fiction*, 2:36-37). A marriage stopped in this way, with a young man carrying off his truelove from the scene of the ceremony itself, was an appealing topic for Scott, as in "Lochinvar" (see Chapter 2). The interruption of a marriage, but with different accompanying circumstances, is prominent in *The Black Dwarf* (chap. 17), in "The Noble Moringer," and in the story of Wilibert of Waverley, which so much captured the fancy of young Edward Waverley. At one point in *Valentine and Orson* (chap. 56) Clarimonde fains madness, so that she will not have to marry the King of Inde. In *Bevis of Hampton*, Josian actually has to go through with two unwanted marriages. With her first husband, King Yvor of Mombrant, she has no sexual relations, managing to preserve her virginity by means of a magic charm. Her second husband, the unfortunate Erle Myle, she strangles in bed on the night of their marriage. In *The Seven Champions*, Sabra is forced into an unwanted marriage with the black King of Morocco, but she manages to preserve her virginity and is eventually rescued by St. George. At one point during her lover's absence she was told that he had married someone else.

The unwanted marriages in the three last-named romances contain accompanying motifs—madness, murder, and false report—which Scott has used with variation in *The Bride of Lammermoor.* Lucy Ashton does go mad after having attempted to kill her newly wedded husband, Hayston of Bucklaw, and she dies shortly thereafter. During Edgar's absence, while she was a virtual prisoner at Ravenswood, she was told that Edgar had become engaged to a foreign lady. Besides the analogue in *The Seven Champions* there are similar false reports in older romances. During the long period of Bevis's imprisonment Josian is saddened when her father tells her that Bevis has returned to England and married the king's daughter. During Sir Tristrem's absence from Cornwall, in the Middle English poem, Ysonde is disconsolate when she hears from Sir Canados that Tristrem has taken a wife in Brittany. Lucy also becomes discouraged because she does not know what is going on. All letters to her from Edgar have been intercepted by Lady Ashton, as have the letters she has tried to send to him. Scott may have gotten the idea for the interception of messages from the Constance-story (see *Marmion* in Chapter 2), but if so he has altered the motif in that no messages are put in place of those intercepted. When Lucy becomes suspicious, she sends Edgar a duplicate of a former letter through the Reverend Bide-the-Bent, whom she completely trusts, but six weeks pass without a reply. Lady Ashton taunts her with a reference to *Valentine and Orson:* " 'And pray how long, Miss Ashton,' said her mother, ironically, 'are we to wait the return of your Pacolet—your fairy messenger—since our humble couriers of flesh and blood could not be trusted in this matter?' " (chap. 29). The shabby treatment that Lucy receives from Lady Ashton brings to mind the famous Paston Letters of the fifteenth century, especially the plights of Elizabeth Paston, whose formidable mother, Agnes Paston, did almost everything short of murder to force her to marry "a battered old widower"; and of Margery Paston, whose mother (Margaret Paston) tried desperately, but in vain, to have her private betrothal to Richard Calle annulled.[11]

Let us return now to the Tristan-story. The forester Norman, talking with Lucy's father, the Lord Keeper, deplores the lack of interest that the present proprietors of Ravenswood Castle show in hunting, and then he explicitly compares Edgar of Ravenswood with Tristan:

It was a disheartening thing... when none of the gentles came down to see the sport. He hoped Captain Sholto [Sholto Ashton, Lucy's older brother] would be soon hame, or he might shut up his shop entirely; for Mr. Harry [Henry Ashton, Lucy's younger brother] was kept sae close wi' his Latin nonsense, that, though his will was very gude to be in the wood from morning till night, there would be a hopeful lad lost, and no making a man of him. It was not so, he had heard, in Lord Ravenswood's time—when a buck was to be killed, man and mother's son ran to see; and when the deer fell, the knife was always presented to the knight, and he never gave less than a dollar for the compliment. And there was Edgar Ravenswood—Master of Ravenswood that is now—when he goes up to the wood—there hasna been a better hunter since Tristrem's time—when Sir Edgar hauds out [presents his piece; takes aim], down goes the deer, faith. But we hae lost a' sense of wood-craft on this side of the hill. [Chap. 3]

Scott goes on to tell us that Sir William "could not help observing that his menial despised him almost avowedly for not possessing that taste for sport, which in those times was deemed the natural and indispensable attribute of a real gentleman." Much is said here about Edgar of Ravenswood—and much is implied, because the very mentioning of Tristrem invokes memories in the reader of a sorrowful, tragic love story, and this is what *The Bride of Lammermoor* is.

In the hunting scene of chapter 9, after the stag has been felled, Bucklaw is given the honor of "breaking" it: "[He] was soon stript to his doublet, with tucked-up sleeves, and naked arms up to the elbows in blood and grease, slashing, cutting, hacking, and hewing, with the precision of Sir Tristrem himself, and wrangling and disputing with all around him concerning nombles, briskets, flankards, and raven-bones." The term *breaking* (that is, dissecting) is used in *Sir Tristrem* ("Bestes thai brac and bare"; I.xlii, line 1), and there is specific reference to *nombles* ("noubles"; I.xlv, line 7) and to the leavings for ravens (I.xlvi, lines 7-9). How this passage should be taken in the larger context of the novel is something of a problem. Is Scott, in comparing Bucklaw with Sir Tristrem, telling us, in an indirect way, that he is really not such a bad young man? Perhaps so; but the tone of the quoted passage does not lead one to feel that Bucklaw performs his task with the dignity of Sir Tristrem. Like Malory, Scott often used the *-ing* form of the verb in passages describing vigorous action; here the effect is mock-heroic. Moreover, just before launching into his task, Bucklaw speaks twice of *breaking up* the stag, when the correct expression, as Scott well knew, is simply *breaking* the stag. Perhaps Scott is telling us, rather, that Bucklaw has some of the trappings of gentlemanly decorum, but that he in fact is not a real gentleman. I leave the question open.

Surprisingly, perhaps, there is a humorous side to this melancholy story, and medieval romance is not far in the background. In chapter 7 Edgar and Bucklaw get into a sword-fight during which Bucklaw slips and falls and is in effect defeated. Edgar does not exploit his advantage, and Bucklaw is grateful for his life. Edgar then apologizes to Bucklaw for having used language that offended him, and the two end up on friendly terms, Edgar even inviting Bucklaw to Wolf's Crag. Such quick reconciliation after an armed confrontation that might easily have led to one party's death seems ludicrous to modern readers, but the *Morte Darthur* contains not a few such incidents. Malory's knights will sometimes spend the better part of a day slashing, tracing, traversing, foining, and hurling like two boars, yet all at once they stop—having suddenly decided that their differences were not so great after all—and kiss and make up. We read at the end of the chapter that Bucklaw is to be housed in the secret chamber at Wolf's Crag. Its discomforts and deficiencies, owing actually to Edgar's poverty, are plausibly apologized for by Caleb Balderston with a humorous antifeminist remark worthy of a medieval monk: "For wha . . . would have thought of the secret chaumer being needed? it has not been used since the time of the Gowrie Conspiracy, and I durst never let a woman ken of the entrance to it, or your honour will allow that it wad not hae been a secret chaumer lang." In chapter 9, when Edgar offers Sir William and Lucy shelter from the storm but warns them that refreshment at Wolf's Crag will be scanty, Caleb is really beside himself. Edgar has openly acknowledged his poverty, and there is in fact no adequate provision. " 'He's daft—clean daft—red wud, and awa wi't! But deil hae Caleb Balderston,' said he, collecting his powers of invention and resource, 'if the family shall lose credit, if he were as mad *as the seven wise masters!*'" (emphasis added). This is Caleb's only specific allusion to medieval romance, but his plight leads him to act in chapter 12 like a latter-day Sir Kay.

The motto to this unforgettable chapter is a quotation from Chaucer's Summoner's Tale:

> "Now, dame," quod he, "now *je vous dy sanz doute,*
> Have I nat of a capon but the lyvere,
> And of youre softe breed nat but a shyvere,
> And after that a rosted pigges heed—
> But that I nolde no beest for me were deed—
> Thanne hadde I with yow hoomly suffisaunce." [III, 1838-43]

The parasitic friar of the tale is telling the lady of the house what he would like for dinner. Scott could hardly have found a more apt motto for the delightful comedy that develops when Caleb in desperation enters the village of Wolf's-hope to try to procure much-needed provisions for Wolf's

Crag. "It was a dreadful degradation," Scott writes, "but necessity was equally imperious and lawless." The last clause echoes the old proverb "Necessity has no law"—or "Nede has na peer," as articulated by the young student John, from the north country, in the Reeve's Tale (a tale, incidentally, in which dialect is used for the first time in English literature for the purpose of characterization). Caleb visits at the house of Gilbert Girder, the cooper, and, taking advantage of the absence for a few moments of Mrs. Girder and her mother, he steals a spit bearing succulent roasted wildfowl as the young boy attending to it at the chimney looks on, too surprised and stupefied to prevent the robbery. When Mr. Girder comes home and finds out what has happened, he is terribly angry and is just barely deterred from beating his wife.

Scott borrowed this celebrated incident from the opening pages of *Golagrus and Gawain*. While on a knightly excursion, King Arthur and his entourage run out of food. They chance upon a stately city defended by a castle, and Sir Kay is sent ahead to negotiate for the provisions they need so desperately. Upon entering the castle Kay at first sees no one, but action starts when he enters a room with a fire burning in the chimney:

> Ane duergh braydit about, besily and bane,
> Small birdis on broche be ane bright fyre.
> Schir Kay ruschit to the roist, and reft fra the swane,
> Lightly claught, throu lust, the lym fra the lyre;
> To feid hym of that fyne fude the freik wes full fane.
> (A dwarf was scampering about and small birds were roasting on a spit. Sir Kay rushed up to the fire and grabbed one of the birds from the boy, who was holding it lightly in his hand. Kay tore the wing off and was glad to eat the tasty flesh.)[12]

The dwarf yells out, and the master of the castle arrives on the scene, terribly angry with Sir Kay for his presumption. Heated words pass, and the knight deals Kay a blow that lays him out on the floor. Scott adapted the episode to suit his purposes, but enough remains in the account of Caleb and the wildfowl to prove beyond any reasonable doubt that the Middle Scots verse romance was the source for chapter 12's main event—an event which, in a later edition of the novel, Scott felt it necessary to defend because of the adverse criticism the passage had received. His long footnote relates what he claims to be a "similar anecdote," but so far as I know he never divulged his true source.

A Legend of Montrose (1819)

Captain Dugald Dalgetty, Scott's loquacious soldier of fortune who steals every scene in which he appears, fits in some ways Terry Jones's conception of Chaucer's "medieval mercenary,"[13] but to Scott, the "verray parfit gentil knyght" of the Canterbury pilgrimage and Captain Dalgetty were two different personages. It would not have occurred to him that the caustic remarks made by the Earl of Menteith about the mercenary knight of the novel might conceivably fit Chaucer's Knight as well. Jones's book would have shocked (and interested) Scott just as it has its readers of our own time. I do not mean to imply that Scott is contrasting his mercenary knight with the perfect knight, for Dalgetty is not as bad as Menteith's remarks alone would lead us to believe. There is another side to Dalgetty as well, and this ambiguity makes him one of the most intriguing of all Scott's characters.

Medieval analogues to the story material are not hard to find. Angus M'Aulay's foolish boast to his English friends (as related by the old Highland servant Donald in chapter 4) "that he had mair candlesticks, and better candlesticks, in his ain castle at hame than were ever lighted in a hall in Cumberland" and his accompanying wager of two hundred marks bring to mind the motif of the rash promise, which can be found in so many medieval stories, especially those that have their roots in Celtic material. The circumstances preceding the birth of Angus's younger brother Allan are also noteworthy. The mother is six months pregnant when she is shocked by the sudden sight of her brother's severed head, with "a piece of bread between the lifeless jaws," on the dinner table before her. (He has been murdered by the so-called Children of the Mist, a wild and homeless clan.) Her horrifying experience brings on a period of insanity from which she has not fully recovered at the time of Allan's birth, and these events together with her stories about them have a direct bearing on Allan's later mental health. Similar brutality can be found in romance. The Fair Lady of Faguell is served and eats something which her vengeful husband later tells her was the heart of her platonic lover, the Knight of Curtesy. And in *Richard Coer de Lyon* Saladin's ambassadors, on a visit to Richard's camp, are served in all pomp and ceremony the boiled heads of captured Saracen princes. They are as shocked as Allan's mother, and even more so by the action of Richard, who eats a piping-hot head with gusto as they look on, frightened and speechless.

Again we have the familiar Knight's Tale story-pattern of two young men, in this case Lord Menteith and Allan M'Aulay, in love with the same girl, Annot Lyle; but the pattern is varied this time in that neither lover is beyond reproach. Allan is hard to put up with when "his hour is on him" or "his hour of darkness approaches" or when "the shadow falls upon him" or "the cloud is upon his mind"—different ways of saying the same thing. And Menteith is not much more sympathetic. He says a bit too often that he cannot consider marrying Annot Lyle because of the obscureness of her birth. Although she is as dull as Chaucer's Emily, it turns out that she is the long-lost daughter of Sir Duncan Campbell, and is thus like a missing heiress of romance. The key to her identity is held, as in romance, by an older person—in this case Ranald M'Eagh, one of the Children of the Mist. Moreover, she has a birthmark on her left shoulder—making her real identity indisputable—and the analogues in medieval romance are many. Wolfdietrich of the *Heldenbuch*, having been borne away when a baby by a wolf, has a small cross on his body by which he is later recognized. The renowned Esplandian, son of Oriana and Amadis of Gaul, is abducted when only a small child by a lioness, but later he is recognized by his mother "by means of certain characters on his breast" (Dunlop, 2:20). Esplandian's illustrious grandson, Amadis of Greece, has "the representation of a sword on his breast" (Dunlop, 2:28). Young Valentine of *Valentine and Orson* confides to Eglantyne, "I bere a crosse vpon my shoulder, the whiche is also yelowe as the fyne golde" (chap. 17). (Another famous shoulder birthmark is Havelok's, but Scott did not know this romance.) Annot Lyle and Lord Menteith have their wedding at the end, although not without trouble from Allan, who is not the best of losers.

We hear faint echoes of the Tristan-story (for example, Annot plays the harp and sings, thereby soothing Allan in his hour of darkness, just as Tristan's music soothes King Mark), and there are a few general references in chapter 20 to the Round Table, chivalry, and champions of romance, but in *A Legend of Montrose* our search for medieval echoes comes sooner to a close. We are left, finally, with the question of how Captain Dalgetty fits into all this. Even if he owes nothing to Chaucer's Knight, he is as carefully drawn and as delightfully ambiguous as some of Chaucer's very best characters; if he has no exact prototype in Chaucer, he is still genuinely and profoundly Chaucerian. We remember Dugald Dalgetty long after we have forgotten the rest of the novel and its more obvious connections with medieval romance.

Ivanhoe (1819)

The background to *Ivanhoe*,* Scott's most famous novel, has already been admirably discussed by Roland Abramczyk in one of the finest German dissertations from its period that I have ever examined.[14] Abramczyk goes into the historical as well as the literary background, and in his hunt for literary sources he casts a wide net; in addition to parallels in Chaucer and

---

*The reader should be warned that the numbering of the chapters in the 48-volume Border Edition is faulty. The chapter (in the first volume) which should be chapter 7 is mistakenly numbered 8, and thus all the remaining chapters are off by one. My references to chapters of the novel reflect the correct numbering found in other editions.

medieval romance he is interested in the influence of ballads, especially the Robin Hood ballads, and of later writers such as Goethe, "Monk" Lewis, and Samuel Richardson. As elsewhere in my own study I am primarily concerned with Scott's indebtedness to Chaucer and medieval romance, and in concentrating on one aspect of the broad subject I have been able to find some interesting parallels not noticed by Abramczyk as well as to bring into sharper focus here and there what he already has said.

After a long absence, Ivanhoe, disguised as a palmer, appears at Rotherwood, the home of his father Cedric the Saxon. Cedric is unfriendly to his son because of Ivanhoe's loyalty to Richard the Lion-Hearted (a Norman) and his love for Cedric's blue-blooded ward Rowena, whom Cedric has intended for Athelstane the Unready, last scion of Saxon royalty. That night at supper Cedric extends his hospitality to a group of Normans, including Prior Aymer and Brian de Bois-Guilbert, and to Isaac of York, whom our hero in disguise treats kindly after the elderly Jew has been given the cold shoulder by everyone else in the hall. During the conversation at supper the palmer speaks up in behalf of the Saxon knights fighting in Palestine. In naming those who distinguished themselves in a tournament at Acre, he seems to have forgotten one (himself) whom Brian names for him: "It was the Knight of Ivanhoe." Before retiring to bed the palmer meets in private, at her request, with the Lady Rowena, who is anxious to find out more about the Knight of Ivanhoe.

These familiar events of chapters 5 and 6 have numerous parallels in medieval romance. For the hero to be disguised as a palmer is a commonplace: one need only think of Richard the Lion-Hearted, in his own romance, just before his imprisonment by the King of Almain; of Bevis of Hampton (and of Terri, son of the faithful steward Saber, when he travels far and wide searching for Bevis); of Guy of Warwick, of Wolfdietrich (in the *Heldenbuch*), and of St. George (in *The Seven Champions*). After an absence (imprisonment) of seven years Bevis appears in Mombrant, disguised as a palmer and in the company of other palmers. His beloved Josian, who is still faithful to him (although now married to King Yvor), does not immediately recognize him:

> And whan þe maide seȝ him þar,
> Of Beues ȝhe nas noþing war;
> "þe semest," queþ ȝhe, "man of anour,
> þow schelt þis dai be priour
> And be-ginne oure deis:
> þe semest hende and corteis." [2119-24][15]

She then asks the palmers whether they know anything about Bevis, and the plot begins to unravel:

> "Herde euer eni of ȝow telle
> In eni lede or eni spelle,
> Or in feld oþer in toun,
> Of a kniȝt, Beues of Hamtoun?"
> "Nai!" queþ al, þat þar ware.
> "What þow?" ȝhe seide, "niwe palmare?"
> þanne seide Beues and louȝ:
> "þat kniȝt ich knowe wel inouȝ!" [2129-36]

Shortly afterwards she recognizes him, as does his horse Arondel.

There is similar material in *Guy of Warwick*, but with no recognition. Not long after marrying Phyllis, Guy decides to go on a pilgrimage to the Holy Land out of remorse for all the men he has killed "for the love of a woman." The story continues as follows in an old prose version:

> So with abundance of Tears betwixt them, he takes his journey, only with a Staff in his Hand, to the *Holy Land*, and she as a pensive Widow, remains at home, giving Alms at her Door to all Pilgrims for his sake, enquiring of them evermore, if they could tell her any news of him; but he not making himself known to any of them in all his travels, they could relate nothing of him to her.
>
> Many times when he returned from the *Holy Land*, he hath received Alms from her own Hands; and she not knowing of him, he hath departed with Tears in his Eyes to his Cave, where he liv'd and died, as you shall understand hereafter.[16]

An equally old version in couplets is more detailed and more interesting in relation to the novel. The following lines occur just after Guy, having returned from the Holy Land, has killed the terrible giant Colbron and has revealed himself to King Athelstone:

> This said, *Guy* goes with humble leave most meek
> Some solitary Den or Cave to seek,
> And so live poorly in the hollow Ground,
> Making his Meat of Herbs, and Roots he found.
> Sometimes for Alms unto his Spouse he'd go,
> Who unto Pilgrims did most Bounty show;
> And she wou'd ask all Palmers that came there,
> If at the *Holy Land* they never were;
> Or if an *English* Lord they had not seen,
> Who many Years away from thence had been,
> A Knight ne'r Conquer'd; only she did fear
> The Tyrant Death, that Conquers every where;
> But Gracious Heav'n grant, if he be dead,
> Upon the Earth I may no longer tread.
> This oft he heard his Wife with Tears enquire,
> Yet Comfort he gave not to her desire;

> But look'd upon her as his Heart wou'd break,
> Then turn'd away for fear his Tongue shou'd speak;
> And so departs with weeping to his Den.

Of course the motif of a lover or husband returning home after long absence and talking in disguise with his ladylove or wife was nothing new in medieval romance; it is in the *Odyssey*.

The disguised Ivanhoe's reluctance to name himself when he tells about the tournament has parallels in *Tirant lo Blanch*, a romance that owes much to the story of Guy of Warwick. When young Tirant arrives in England from Brittany, he encounters a hermit (actually William of Warwick). "When asked [by Tirant] who were the best knights of England at that very time, he mentioned the names of the good knight Muntanyanegre, the Duke of Exeter, and Sir John Stuart. Tirant, disappointed at this answer, asked why he did not make mention of the Earl William of Warwick. . . . The hermit replied that he had heard of William of Warwick, but having never seen him he did not mention his name." A little later, in a repetition of this episode, the characters have reversed roles:

The hermit had already twice asked who had been declared the best and greatest knight among the victors. But Tirant seemed to pay no attention to his questions. And finally the hermit said: "But, Tirant, why do you not answer my question?" Then arose one of the company and his name was Diaphebus. He drew forth a parchment saying that the document in his hands would answer the question. This he read to the hermit, who was delighted when he heard that it was a proclamation to the world that the noble and valiant Tirant lo Blanch was declared the best knight of all those that had taken part in the exercises of arms at the festivities connected with the General Court.[17]

Before leaving the hall at Rotherwood we should note that the very unfriendly reception of Isaac the Jew also has a parallel in medieval romance. When at the court of the Emperor of Rome, Robert the Devil, although repentant for his past sins and now undergoing a strict penance imposed on him by the Pope, is not above playing a crude practical joke on a Jew who is a guest at the emperor's table:

> Muche myrth and sporte he made euer amonge
> And as the Emperoure was at dyner on a daye
> A Jue sate at the borde, that great rowme longe
> In that house beare, and was receyued all waye
> Than Roberte hys dogge toke in hys armes in faye
> And touched the Jue and he ouer hys sholder loked backe
> Robert set the dogges ars to hys mowth without naye
> Full soore the Emperoure loughe when he sawe that.[18]

This episode is not in the kindred romance about Sir Gowther.

The next big scene is the tournament at Ashby, which gets under way in chapter 7. The lines from *Palamon and Arcite* that stand as the chapter's motto are clear indication that the Knight's Tale, in Dryden's "translation," was very much on Scott's mind. Another quotation from *Palamon and Arcite* serves as the motto to chapter 8, in which the first day of the tournament is described, while a quotation from Chaucer's original, the striking alliterative passage of Part IV—"Ther shyveren shaftes upon sheeldes thikke. . . . Out brest the blood with stierne stremes rede"—sets the tone for chapter 12 and Scott's vivid account of the tournament's second day. The third day involves sports and games of a more popular nature, including the archery contest in which Locksley distinguishes himself. Three-day tournaments are frequent in medieval romance; one can find them in *Ipomadon, Roswall and Lillian, Sir Degrevant, Sir Triamour,* and *Le Petit Jehan de Saintré*, to name a few romances that spring immediately to mind. The tournament in the Knight's Tale is not of the three-day variety, but this hard-fought battle between Palamon and Arcite and their forces was Scott's primary source of inspiration for his second day, when there is a general tournament, all knights fighting at once. As in Chaucer it is conducted with a respect for human life: the dagger is forbidden; and once a knight is overcome, he is considered vanquished and is not to engage further in combat. Like Palamon, the Disinherited Knight (Ivanhoe) finds himself beset by several formidable adversaries—by Brian de Bois-Guilbert, Front-de-Bœuf, and Athelstane—but, more fortunate than Palamon, he receives effective help from a mysterious Black Knight (Richard), who easily topples Front-de-Bœuf and Athelstane, leaving Bois-Guilbert for the Disinherited Knight, and afterwards rides off into the forest. Abramczyk and others have pointed out that Scott is indebted here to an episode in *Richard Coer de Lyon,* in which Richard, formidable in appearance and disguised in black, easily defeats several adversaries and then rides away into a forest. When Prince John sees that the Disinherited Knight has gotten the better of Bois-Guilbert, he stops the tournament. Chaucer's Theseus stops the tournament in Athens when Palamon has been decisively overcome.

Indeed, the stopping of a tournament by a monarch is quite frequent in romance. Tirant lo Blanch's fight with the Scottish knight Villa Fermosa is stopped by the Queen of Scotland "before either of the knights had come to grief."[19] There are further parallels in Malory,[20] in *Palmerin of England,*[21] and in *Le Petit Jehan de Saintré*. On two occasions during the course of the tournament at Barcelona, the King of Aragon calls a halt to the fighting between Saintré and Sir Enguerrant. On the third and final day, "when Sir Enguerrant found himself without an axe, he advanced all suddenly like one possessed, and came and laid hold on Saintré by the body, and Saintré on him by one arm, for with the other he held his axe. Now when the King saw Sir Enguerrant's axe upon the ground and their two bodies at grips, he straightway threw down his wand, like a just prince and judge, crying out: 'Hold, hold!' Then were the combatants parted by the men-at-arms."[22] Author Antoine de la Sale's elaborate description of the dress and pageantry and general atmosphere at Barcelona may also have had some influence on the author of *Ivanhoe*, although to pin Scott down to particulars would be difficult. We have the sounding of trumpets, and there is jousting on horseback and the bursting of lances, and the spectators become much involved in what is going on. Unlike Ivanhoe and Bois-Guilbert, however, Saintré and Sir Enguerrant try to outdo each other in courteous behavior towards one another.

Probably enough has been said in other places about Richard's visit with Friar Tuck (chaps. 16-17). As indicated in the discussion of *The Lady of the Lake* (Chapter 2), a lot of stories have come down to us involving a king in disguise who is given hospitality by a lowly subject.[23] In the introduction of 1830 Scott mentions *John the Reeve, The King and the Tanner of Tamworth, The King and the Miller of Mansfield,* and *Rauf Coilyear;* he also discusses in some detail *The Kyng and the Hermite,* which was his immediate inspiration. Scott adds to the story the motif of the exchanging of blows. Some time after Richard's visit with the friar, indeed after the fall of Torquilstone, he and the friar test their bodily strength. Richard holds up under the friar's hardest cuff, but the friar falls "head over heels" when Richard strikes him (see chap. 32). Scott himself tells us in a note that this incident was inspired by a passage in *Richard Coer de Lyon.* When Richard is in the prison of the King of Almain, the king's son Ardour suggests to Richard that they exchange buffets. Richard staggers under the young man's blow but recovers himself. When Ardour's time comes to receive a buffet in return, Richard strikes him so hard that he is killed.[24] In the novel, when Richard reveals who he is (chap. 40), the friar is mortified not only because of his crusty behavior when he was the king's host (such is typical of the king-in-disguise stories) but also because he has actually struck at anointed royalty. This bringing together of two radically different worlds, so well illustrated in *Rauf Coilyear* and the other stories, is a recurrent theme in Scott; and this novel it is even more forcefully presented in the conflict between Norman and Saxon (with Ivanhoe having divided loyalties and thus caught in the middle) and between Christians and Jews (with Rebecca caught in the middle).

Other motifs include the unwanted marriage: Rowena has no interest in Athelstane the Unready, and she abhors the thought of a forced marriage to Maurice de Bracy; Rebecca has her problems too, in that she is adamantly opposed to any sort of relationship with Brian de Bois-Guilbert. Since both girls love Ivanhoe, and both are eminently worthy, we have another variation of the Knight's Tale story-pattern. And the list of motifs goes on and on. Wamba's blowing of a horn for help, in chapter 40, when the Black Knight is attacked by several adversaries at once, has its inspiration in medieval literature, as all readers of *The Song of Roland* will realize. Helyas, the Knight of the Swan, also has a horn, given to him by his father King Oriant, which will keep him from harm; and it is this horn which he blows loudly when, in a swan-drawn ship, he approaches the city Nymaie to offer his help to the Duchess of Boulyon, who has been accused falsely of murder. The important roles played by Wamba, Cedric's jester, and by his friend Gurth, the swineherd, are in the best tradition of the "matter of England" romances, in which characters of lowly birth exhibit strikingly worthy qualities. Wamba and Gurth are indeed often "nobler" than their betters, as is Higg, the son of Snell, a "poor peasant, a Saxon by birth," who testifies at Rebecca's trial and carries a message from her to her father. A probable source for Athelstane's resuscitation, as Abramczyk has pointed out, is an episode in Lewis's *The Monk*, but it may owe something too to the revival of Guy of Warwick's friend Heraud, who in the Auchinleck version is so grievously wounded by Lombard assailants that he is taken for dead by Guy himself, who entrusts the supposed corpse to monks at a nearby abbey for decent burial and who is later overjoyed to find out that Heraud still lives (see Abramczyk, pp. 104-6). Resuscitation of the dead is also a motif in Celtic literature, as for example the story of "Branwen Daughter of Llŷr," in *The Mabinogion*, in which dead warriors are put into a magic cauldron; the next day they are alive and can fight (but cannot speak).[25] Scott has an impressive array of precedents, then, for this not-so-celebrated incident of the novel. He does not answer his critics as well as he might when he says (in a note), "It was a *tour-de-force* to which the author was compelled to have recourse, by the vehement entreaties of his friend and printer, who was inconsolable on the Saxon being conveyed to the tomb."

There are of course many analogues in medieval romance to the trial of Rebecca, who is accused falsely of witchcraft. If she cannot find a champion to fight for her against Bois-Guilbert, she will be considered guilty and will be burned at the stake. In the Man of Law's Tale, Constance is falsely accused of having murdered Dame Hermengyld. At her trial the judgment of God is appealed to, and a voice from Heaven declares her innocence. There are judicial combats in *The Earl of Toulous*, when the Earl's ladylove is accused falsely of adultery—the Earl fighting against the two evil stewards, her accusers, once he is convinced of her innocence; in *Amadis of Gaul* (Book III in Rose's version), when "an insolent but puissant knight" named Dardan quarrels unjustly with the lady Lycena over her "fiefs and wide domain"—Amadis arriving just in time to take up Lycena's cause against Dardan and to defeat him; in the *Morte Darthur* (Book XVIII in Caxton editions), when Guenever is accused falsely by Sir Mador de la Porte of having poisoned his cousin Sir Patrise—the Queen's cause being taken by Sir Launcelot, who defeats Sir Mador and saves Guenever from the flames;[26] in the *Chevalere Assigne* (and its prose counterpart, *The Knight of the Swan*), when the hero's mother is accused falsely by her mother-in-law of having copulated with a dog, and is saved when a young unlikely-looking champion (her long-lost son) appears and defeats the evil mother-in-law's knight—winning miraculously in the poetical version and thereby saving his mother from being burned at the stake. There are long notes in Rose's version of *Amadis of Gaul* and in Way's *Fables* on judicial combat, a subject that interested Scott immensely. Bois-Guilbert's death recalls vaguely the fate of Arcite: "That champion, to the astonishment of all who beheld it, reeled in his saddle, lost his stirrups, and fell in the lists" (chap. 43)—but all other circumstances are quite different.

In the unspoken affection that gradually develops between Ivanhoe and Rebecca, Scott gives us his finest example of the love between a Christian and a non-Christian, another motif borrowed from medieval romance. I think first of *Floris and Blancheflur,* a story that almost rivals Scott's in emotional intensity; in this case the man is Mohammedan and the girl is Christian. Closer to Scott at least superficially are the stories of Aucassin and the beautiful paynim girl Nicolette; Otuit and the daughter of the King of Syria, in the *Heldenbuch;* Bevis and his paynim ladylove Josian, who readily renounces her religion for his sake; Florens (brother of Octavian) and the Saracen princess Marsibelle, who gives up her faith and is baptized; St. George of England and Sabra, the King of Egypt's daughter, in *The Seven Champions of Christendom;* and St. James of Spain (another of the seven champions) and the fair Jewess, Celestine, daughter of the King of Jerusalem, who goes against the wishes of her father and her people in saving her lover. There is no happy ending in Scott; Rebecca's love for Ivanhoe must go unrequited. Unlike Josian and Marsibelle, she could never have given up her own religion, and besides Ivanhoe is already spoken for. Moreover, their different ways of thinking would have proved ultimately an insurmountable problem, as is obvious from the discussion (wonderfully ironic on Scott's part) which they get into about chivalry during the storming of Torquilstone (chap. 29). Scott has taken over an old motif from medieval romance, but he has varied, refined, and deepened it into something genuinely touching and beautiful.

Rebecca is Scott's most memorable dark-lady type. She is also his most memorable female physician, Scott apparently having taken to heart one of the notes to *Aucassin and Nicolette* in Way's *Fables:*

Some degree of chirurgical and medical knowledge was considered, during the middle ages, as a very necessary female accomplishment; and, while the occupations and amusements of men naturally led to bruises and broken bones, it was likely that ladies would acquire sufficient experience by the casualties that occurred in their own families. It accordingly appears from the Romances that many women of high birth were consulted in preference to the most learned professors, and it is probable that their attentive and compassionate solicitude may have frequently proved more efficacious than the nostrums of the faculty.

The note goes on to describe the place of Jews in medieval medicine. The famous scene in which Rebecca observes from a window the storming of Torquilstone and relates to her bedridden patient what is happening (chap. 29) owes much, as Abramczyk has shown, to a scene in *Götz von Berlichingen*, which Scott had translated as a young man. It may also owe a little to an episode in *Le Bone Florence of Rome*, in which Florence observes from a tower the preparations for storming the castle:

> The maydyn mylde up sche rase,
> With knyghtes and ladyes feyre of face,
>   And wente unto a towre.
> There sche sawe ryght in the feldys
> Baners brode and bryght scheldys
>   Of chevalry the flowre,
> They nowmberde them forty thousand men,
> And a hundurd moo then hur fadur had then,
>   That were ryght styffe in stowre.
>
> Allas! seyde that maydyn clere,
> Whedur all the yonde folke and there
>   Schoulde dye for my sake,
> And y but a sympull woman!
> The terys on hur chekys ranne,
>   Hur ble beganne to blake.
>   [Ritson's text, lines 565-79]

The situation in *Ivanhoe* is of course more dramatic: the girl sees the actual fighting and reports it to someone else as it is taking place. The probable source for the equally famous scene, in which Rebecca goes to the window and threatens to jump to escape from Bois-Guilbert (chap. 24), is, as Abramczyk reminds us, a passage in Richardson's *Clarissa*, "in which Clarissa," to quote Scott himself, "awes Lovelace by a similar menace of suicide." It may also owe something in a topsy-turvy way to a strange episode in the *Morte Darthur* in which Sir Bors, in his quest for the Holy Grail, encounters a lady who threatens to jump from a high tower, together with her twelve gentlewomen, if he will *not* make love to her.[27]

Although Rebecca is a Jewess in a novel about the Middle Ages, she is respected by everyone—she is put on a pedestal as if she were a heroine of courtly romance; but Rowena, our light-lady type with her blue eyes and fair complexion, is the more conventional heroine, and not only in physical appearance. She is Ivanhoe's inspiration—the source of all his better actions. She is somewhat above him in social hierarchy, inasmuch as she is a descendant of King Alfred. She is not easily won by him because of Cedric's determination to marry her off to Athelstane. If absences have a salutary effect on love affairs, as Andreas Capellanus suggests, theirs must indeed be in order, for she and Ivanhoe do not see very much of each other either before or during the time of the novel. Like many a lady in courtly love stories, she has a lady-in-waiting, the rather colorless Elgitha.

If Ivanhoe, like Malory's Balin, feels sometimes that he is "destined to bring ruin on whomsoever hath shown kindness" to him (chap. 25), Richard has better luck, at least on the surface. Maurice de Bracy avers "that neither Tristram nor Lancelot would have been match, hand to hand, for Richard Plantagenet," while Waldemar Fitzurse, in less complimentary but perhaps more realistic terms, considers him "a true knight-errant"—one who "will wander in wild adventure, trusting the prowess of his single arm, like any Sir Guy or Sir Bevis, while the weighty affairs of his kingdom slumber, and his own safety is endangered" (chap. 34). Richard's carelessness almost leads to disaster when he is attacked by Fitzurse and others (in chap. 40), but Wamba blows his horn, as we have seen, and the fight between the Black Knight and the Blue Knight (the colors recalling Malory's *Tale of Sir Gareth*) ends in victory for the Black Knight. He is a "verray paragon" of medieval knighthood.

There are at least two specific references to King Arthur. In the archery contest of chapter 13, Locksley complains that the targets are too large: "For his own part . . . and in the land where he was bred, men would as soon take for their mark King Arthur's round-table, which held sixty knights around it." And in chapter 15, Fitzurse, musing upon the possible return of Richard, notes that "these are not the days of King Arthur, when a champion could encounter an army. If Richard indeed comes back, it must be alone,—unfollowed—unfriended." Both allusions contribute in a small way to the novel's medieval atmosphere, as does the spirited conversation about hunting between Cedric and Prior Aymer at Rotherwood (chap. 5). The first editor of *Sir Tristrem* must have enjoyed writing this dialogue:

"I marvel, worthy Cedric," said the Abbot, as their discourse proceeded, "that, great as your predilection is for your own manly language, you do not receive the Norman-French into your favour, so far at least as the mystery of wood-craft and hunting is concerned. Surely no tongue is so rich in the various phrases which the field-sports demand, or furnishes means to the experienced woodman so well to express his jovial art."

"Good Father Aymer," said the Saxon, "be it known to you, I care not for those over-sea refinements, without which I can well enough take my pleasure in the woods. I can wind my horn, though I call not the blast either a *recheate* or a *morte*—I can cheer my dogs on the prey, and I can flay and quarter the animal when it is brought down, without using the newfangled jargon of *curée, arbor, nombles*, and all the babble of the fabulous Sir Tristrem.

This passage not only is humorous, but it contributes to Scott's fine characterization of the doughty old Saxon.

Allusions to Chaucer are frequent, as already indicated. Moreover, Prior Aymer is compared explicitly with the Monk, as is clear from the motto to chapter 2, a quotation from Chaucer's description of the "outrydere" in the General Prologue. Like his counterpart, the prior loves hunting; moreover, his sleeves are lined with fur, and his horse's bridle is ornamented with little bells. Before proceeding to Rotherwood to seek hospitality, Bois-Guilbert hypocritically promises Prior Aymer that he will deport himself "as meekly as a maiden" (Chaucer's phrase describing his Knight); in fact, the Knight Templar is very *un*like Chaucer's Knight as Scott conceived of him. At the Preceptory of Templestowe we find a young squire who no doubt owes his name, Damian, to the squire of the Merchant's Tale. And at Athelstane's funeral we find more than one damsel who is "more interested in endeavouring to find out how her mourning-robe became her, than in the dismal ceremony" at hand, while "the appearance of two strange knights" occasions "some looking up, peeping, and whispering" (chap. 42)—all this recalling the thoughts of the Wife of Bath at her fourth husband's funeral.

A few other names deserve comments. Scott himself tells us that he got the name Front-de-Bœuf from a "roll of Norman warriors" in the Auchinleck MS. Swineherd Gurth is the "son of Beowulph," Scott certainly knowing *of* the Old English masterpiece, which had been printed for the first time ever in 1815 in the edition by the Danish scholar Thorkelin— "the learned Thorkelin," as Scott calls him in his abstract of the *Eyrbiggia-Saga* (included in Weber's *Illustrations of Northern Antiquities*). Athelstane the Unready does not owe his Christian name to the romance *Athelston*, which Scott did not know, but probably to the King Athelstone of *Guy of Warwick* or the King Athelstan of history; he probably owes his epithet to Ethelred the Unready of history. The name Rowena was probably suggested by Geoffrey of Monmouth's Renwein, the beautiful daughter of Hengist who marries Vortigern, King of the Britons. In his final temptation of Rebecca, Bois-Gulbert urges her to mount behind him on his steed, "on Zamor, the gallant horse," which he "won . . . from the Soldan of Trebizond"—the exotic name *Trebizond* occurring, as we have already seen, in the Amadis cycle of romances.[28]

Unlike the novels we have examined up to this point, *Ivanhoe* does not belong to the fairly recent or not too remote past, and its setting is not Scotland; hence, perhaps, its very noticeable dependence on a realm of literature that Scott knew so well. In *The Heart of Mid-Lothian* Scott used deep-lying motifs from medieval romance; in *Rob Roy* he prefers to use allusions. In *Ivanhoe* he uses both. Of all the novels examined so far, *Ivanhoe* is easily the most heavily indebted to Chaucer and medieval romance.

5

NOVELS OF THE HIGH-NOON PERIOD 1820-1825

THESE ARE the novels which Scott wrote between his recovery from illness and his financial ruin. It was a period of restless activity, producing eleven novels. It was a period of experimentation—with the unabashed supernatural in *The Monastery*, with sixteenth- and seventeenth-century English settings in *Kenilworth* and *The Fortunes of Nigel*, with contemporary material in *St. Ronan's Well*, and with a bold leap from the British Isles to medieval France in *Quentin Durward*. It was also a period in which Scott explored the confict of *Old Mortality* between Puritan and Cavalier on new *English* ground, in *Peveril of the Peak*. And at the end of the period Scott returned to home ground, the not too distant Scottish past, in *Redgauntlet*, and to the now familiar century of *Ivanhoe* for *The Talisman* and *The Betrothed*. If the high-noon novels do not quite measure up to the highest quality of his earlier achievements, still, we would not want to be without *Kenilworth*, *The Fortunes of Nigel*, *Quentin Durward*, and *Redgauntlet*, which fall just below his very best work. The influence of medieval romance continues.

The Monastery (1820)

Scott has turned again to Chaucer's Knight's Tale for the underlying story-pattern of two worthy young men in love with the same girl—in this case two brothers, Halbert and Edward Glendinning, vying for the favor of Mary Avenel, daughter of the recently deceased Lady of Avenel and niece of Julian Avenel, who has usurped her rights by taking over the castle which should be hers. Thus Mary, like most heroines in stories of courtly love, belongs to a higher social sphere than that of Halbert and Edward, sons of Dame Elspeth Glendinning of Glendearg, as Father Eustace reminds Edward very late in the story when Edward admits his "love of Mary Avenel." " 'Of Mary Avenel!' said the priest—'of a lady so high above either of you in name and in rank? How dared Halbert—how dared you, to presume to lift your eye to her but in honour and respect, as a superior of another degree from yours?' " (chap. 32). Interestingly, Scott describes the brothers from the very outset (chap. 2) in terms that recall his famous dark and light ladies:

Halbert Glendinning, the elder of the two, had hair as dark as the raven's plumage, black eyes, large, bold, and sparkling, that glittered under eyebrows of the same complexion; a skin deep embrowned, though it could not be termed swarthy, and an air of activity, frankness, and determination, far beyond his age. On the other hand, Edward, the younger brother, was light-haired, blue-eyed, and of fairer complexion, in countenance rather pale, and not exhibiting that rosy hue which colours the sanguine cheek of robust health. Yet the boy had nothing sickly or ill-conditioned in his look, but was, on the contrary, a fair and handsome child, with a smiling face, and mild, yet cheerful eye.

This is the way in which Scott has varied the familiar Knight's Tale story-pattern. Not surprisingly, but unlike her counterpart in Chaucer, Mary Avenel gradually begins to show a decided preference—for the more romantic Halbert; but like Emily she is a colorless heroine: the only time she shows any emotion is when she fears that Halbert has been killed by the long-winded Euphuist, Sir Piercie Shafton.

For the concept of the White Lady, Scott depended primarily on fairy lore, the "theory of astral spirits," and Fouqué's *Undine*, as he explains in the introduction of 1830, but her appearance when someone in the Avenel family is going to die recalls also the legends that grew up about Melusine, who is said to have appeared "whenever one of her descendants, or a king of France, was about to die."[1] Like some Breton lais, the medieval romance about Melusine involves a taboo: her husband Raymond must never look in on her on Saturdays (when she turns into a serpent from the waist downward); if he should do so, their relationship will end. Early in *The Monastery* we learn of a taboo-like superstition regarding the fairies of the Border Country locality where the story takes place: "It was deemed highly imprudent to speak of the fairies either by their title of *good neighbours* or by any other, especially when about to pass the places which they were supposed to haunt" (chap. 3). The lonely glen of Corri-nan-shian with its fountain and wild holly tree, where Halbert twice summons the White Lady—

> Thrice to the holly brake—
> Thrice to the well:—

> I bid thee awake,
> White Maid of Avenel!
>
> Noon gleams on the lake—
> Noon glows on the fell—
> Wake thee, O wake,
> White Maid of Avenel!—

vaguely recalls other Celtic stories. The obvious importance attached to the noontide hour has a parallel in the Middle English lai of *Sir Orfeo*, in which Heurodis unwittingly puts herself under the control of spirits from the Otherworld by sitting under an ympe tree at the hour of noon. Halbert and later Edward both encounter the White Lady at times when troubles and cares are weighing heavily on them—when they are in "obstructive circumstances," to quote a phrase used by G.V. Smithers.[2] The point of this discussion simply is that if Scott was drawing primarily from fairy lore and superstition in his conception of the White Lady, he was also dealing with material that is part and parcel of medieval romance, especially the Breton lais. The White Lady has an aura of romance about her.

Some of Sir Piercie's escapades have vague parallels in medieval romance. Like Hughdietrich of the *Heldenbuch* he once disguises himself as a female, not to help him get to an imprisoned ladylove but so that he can escape, with the aid of the miller's daughter, Mysie Happer, from a not so close confinement at Glendearg. Shortly afterwards this "Maid of the Mill" disguises herself as a page—like St. Anthony's ladylove in *The Seven Champions of Christendom*—so that she can follow her friend and be of service to him. "The romance of the situation flattered [Sir Piercie's] vanity and elevated his imagination, as placing him in the situations of one of those romantic heroes of whom he had read in the histories, where similar transformations made a distinguished figure" (chap. 29). But despite Scott's contention that Sir Piercie "preserved still the decaying spirit of chivalry, which inspired of yore the very gentle Knight of Chaucer, 'Who in his port was modest as a maid' " (chap. 29); and despite his assurance, in the introduction of 1830, that in the Elizabethan period "the language of the lovers to their ladies was still in the exalted terms which Amadis would have addressed to Oriana, before encountering a dragon for her sake"; and despite indeed Sir Piercie's knowledge of the romance about Richard Cœur-de-Lion, who "ate up the head of a Moor carbonadoed" (chap. 16), and his occasional use of sentence structure ("Woe worth the hour," and the like) that might have been copied from Chaucer's Pandarus—despite these trappings he is clearly no hero of romance, as Halbert realizes in his meditation on the night before his duel with him: "Were Sir Piercie Shafton generous, noble, and benevolent, as the champions of whom we hear in romance, I might indeed gain his ear, and, without demeaning myself, escape from the situation in which I am placed. But as he is, or at least seems to be, self-conceited, arrogant, vain, and presumptuous—I should but humble myself in vain—and I will not humble myself!" (chap. 20).

There are other aspects of the novel which hark back to medieval literature. The trouble that the Monks of St. Mary's have with the feisty keeper of the drawbridge over the Tweed is a motif from romance, and we are reminded too of Hagen's trouble with an insolent ferryman when the Nibelungs journey to Hungary. The pilgrim Henry Warden's invitation to Halbert to tell him his sorrows—"My son, it has been said that sorrow must speak or die—Why art thou so much cast down?—Tell me thy unhappy tale, and it may be that my grey head may devise counsel and aid for your young life" (chap. 23)—recalls situations in medieval literature involving an older man's attempt to get a young man to unburden himself so that his sorrows may be eased; Pandarus and Troilus in Book I of *Troilus and Criseyde* come immediately to mind (as do the Old Man and Thomas Hoccleve in the Prologue to the *Regement of Princes*, which Scott apparently did not know). When Warden, who turns out to be a Protestant Minister, and Father Eustace argue over the question of proper religious faith, we have something resembling a popular medieval literary genre, namely, the debate. Scott compares Hob the Miller with Chaucer's Miller as to "manly make," and like Symkyn, the miller of the Reeve's Tale, he has a daughter, Mysie Happer; but Mysie obviously has higher moral values than the camus-nosed, broad-buttocked wench who is "swyved" three times in one night by Aleyn, the young Cambridge student. Scott uses a favorite proverb of Symkyn's when he tells of Father Eustace's blindness to Edward's budding romantic interest in Mary Avenel: "The greatest clerks are not the wisest men" (chap. 11). Like many a medieval romance *The Monastery* ends with two marriages: Halbert Glendinning weds Mary Avenel, and Sir Piercie Shafton, who turns out to be not so blue-blooded after all, weds Mysie Happer.

In the introduction of 1830 Scott attributed the failure of *The Monastery* to the White Lady and to the Euphuist. Indeed, Scott does not handle the romantic, supernatural element in an especially imaginative or subtle way; and Sir Piercie, besides being no hero of romance, is undoubtedly the biggest bore in all the Waverley Novels.

The Abbot (1820)

In this successful sequel to *The Monastery*, Scott uses again the motif of the fair unknown. When Roland Græme, the hero, is introduced as a boy, having been saved from drowning near the Castle of Avenel by a household dog (so like Amadis of Gaul he is, in a sense, a child of the sea), he does not know who he is; but from what he has been told darkly by the aged pilgrim woman who has brought him up, he believes and feels that he is of nobler birth than he seems. This "wild" and "singular" old wanderer is Magdalen Græme, who is remarkable for her "zeal," her "ecstatic devotion," and her "high strain of enthusiasm" on behalf of Mary, Queen of Scots, and the Church of Rome. She resembles Meg Merrilies in many ways, and like Meg (and like older women in medieval romance) she holds the key to the hero's identity. There are hints along the way—the reader pretty much knows who Roland is before he himself does—but Roland does not find out and the reader does not know for certain until the very end, when Roland turns out to be the long-lost son of Julian Avenel and the unfortunate woman who, in *The Monastery*, we thought was his mistress but who was actually his lawful wife, Catherine Græme, daughter of Magdalen Græme. (Both father and mother lost their lives shortly after Roland's birth, as is related in a closing chapter of *The Monastery*.) Roland is thus the first cousin of the Lady of Avenel, Halbert Glendinning's wife, who takes Roland into her household as a page after he is rescued from drowning—and who spoils him rotten.

Roland is a thoroughly obnoxious young man at the outset, and he incurs the enmity of almost everyone at the Castle of Avenel. We are not told that as a baby he bit the breasts of his nurses so hard that they died, and he does not go out killing ecclesiastics for the sport of it, but we are reminded more than once of Sir Gowther and Robert the Devil, who were sired by devils. On a couple of occasions he almost does run Adam Woodcock, the falconer, through with ten inches of steel—and ironically, Adam is one of the very few people who can abide him.

"Will you be pleased to tell me one thing, Master Roland Græme, and that is, whether there be a devil incarnate in you or no?"

"Truly, Master Adam Woodcock," answered the page, "I would fain hope there is not." [Chap. 17]

Such a possibility comes up again in the remarkable scene in which Adam must part company with him:

May I never hood hawk again . . . if I am not as sorry to part with you as if you were a child of mine own, craving pardon for the freedom—I cannot tell what makes me love you so much, unless it be for the reason that I loved the vicious devil of a brown galloway-nag, whom my master the Knight called Satan. . . . I loved that nag over every other horse in the stable—There was no sleeping on his back—he was for ever fidgeting, bolting, rearing, biting, kicking, and giving you work to do, and may be the measure of your back on the heather to the boot of it all. And I think I love you better than any lad in the castle, for the self-same qualities." [Chap. 20]

Like the authors of *Sir Gowther* and *Roberte the Deuyll*, Scott had the difficult task of making his readers change their opinions about a spoiled brat of a hero, and Adam's touching farewell speech, more than anything else, turns the tables in Roland's favor. No penance is imposed upon him by the Pope, but his selfless and dedicated service to Queen Mary, in captivity at Lochleven, brings out the best in him. At the end of the story he has become a thoroughly sympathetic young man, even though his father, Julian Avenel, had been indeed little better than a devil incarnate. In varying his pattern, Scott has grafted material reminiscent of Sir Gowther and Robert the Devil onto the basic story about a fair unknown.

A medieval atmosphere prevails in the village of Kinross when Roland is sent there for a day from the confines of Lochleven. A carnival or fair is in full swing. An "itinerant minstrel" is reciting the old romance of *Roswall and Lillian*, to the accompaniment of his "three-stringed fiddle, or rebeck," but his audience leaves him when a play begins. One of the characters in the play is a pardoner, who like Chaucer's Pardoner "[exhibits] pig's bones for relics," and he "[boasts] the virtues of small tin crosses, which had been shaken in the holy porringer at Loretto, and of cockleshells, which had been brought from the shrine of Saint James of Compostella"—the latter being a place once visited by the Wife of Bath. He also has "a small phial of clear water" by which a woman's fidelity can be tested. It comes supposedly from the stream in which the chaste Susanna bathed herself. If a woman has "stepped aside," she will sneeze when the phial is placed under her nose. This motif is kin to the drinking horn in Arthurian romance, as Scott says—specifically, in the Tristram section of Malory's *Morte Darthur* (Book VIII, chap. 34, in Caxton editions). One young woman is displeased with being the subject of the ludicrous test—she knocks down a clown who has presented her with the phial—and Roland thinks she is Catherine Seyton, whom he had left behind at Lochleven. "Were the tales of enchantment which he had read in romances realized in this extraordinary girl? Could she transport herself from the walled and guarded Castle of Lochleven, moated with its broad lake . . . and watched with such scrupulous care as the safety of a nation demanded—Could she surmount all these obstacles, and make such careless and dangerous use of her liberty, as to engage herself publicly in a quarrel in a village fair?" Later, when asked by the supposed damsel how he would "face a fiery dragon, with an enchantress mounted on its back," Roland replies proudly, showing his knowledge of medieval romance,

"Like Sir Eger, Sir Grime, or Sir Greysteil." Roland finds out much later that the "damsel" was actually Henry Seyton, Catherine's twin brother, in disguise. Indeed, disguises are used so frequently in the story that Roland once exclaims in frustration, "A land of enchantment have I been led into, and spells have been cast around me—every one has met me in disguise—every one has spoken to me in parables—I have been like one who walks in a weary and bewildering dream" (chap. 28).

Very consciously, and throughout the novel, Scott has used medieval romance as a frame of reference in delineating his hero, whose Christian name conjures up the most renowned of Charlemagne's paladins. Ironically, Roland feels "as if [he] were the most faithless spy since the days of Ganelon" during the early part of his stay at Lochleven, before he has gained the confidence of the queen and her party. In chapter 4 a question arises as to Roland's parentage, Scott preparing the reader by an allusion in the motto to Valentine:

> Amid their cups that freely flow'd,
> Their revelry and mirth,
> A youthful lord tax'd Valentine
> With base and doubtful birth.

The stanza quoted thus by Scott appears near the beginning of the second part of Percy's ballad "Valentine and Ursine." Like Roland, Valentine does not know who he really is, and hurt by the "foul reproach" he vows never to rest until he has found his parents. Catherine Seyton archly compares Roland to still another renowned hero when, in exploring the ground floor of the ruined nunnery to which Magdalen Græme has taken him, he is startled by the lowing of a cow and still more surprised to encounter Catherine: " 'Good even to you, valiant champion!' said she; 'since the days of Guy of Warwick, never was one more worthy to encounter a dun cow' " (chap. 12).

Before beginning his assignment at the Castle of Lochleven, Roland, like many a hero of romance, is strangely presented with a special sword—named Caliburn—which he is told not to unsheathe until commanded to do so by his "lawful Sovereign." The person giving him the weapon he thinks is Catherine Seyton, but it is her brother Henry, and only later does he understand the mysterious admonition. Just before Roland's departure Lord Murray, the Regent, gives him an important ring which, if he should notice anything suspicious at Lochleven, will be his "warrant to order horse and man" to send to Murray to report it. Upon returning to Lochleven after the visit to Kinross, Roland gets locked out of the castle and must spend the night in the adjoining garden. There he falls "fast asleep" ("Dare I confess the fact," Scott writes, "without injuring his character for ever as a hero of romance?")—provoking Catherine's acid comparison of him, when the queen's first attempt to escape fails, with "some moon-stricken knight in a Spanish romance" (chap. 31). In later repartee Catherine exclaims "Ay! . . . there spoke the doughty knight of romance, that will cut his way to the imprisoned princess, through fiends and fiery dragons!" (chap. 34). But it is Roland who comes up with the plan of forging a set of keys that will resemble those of the Lady of Lochleven and will be swapped for the real keys—a motif that Scott perhaps adapted from a French prose version of the Tristan-story: Tristan helps his brother-in-law Runalen forge a set of false keys that enable him "to enter the castle of a knight with whose lady he was enamoured" (Dunlop, 1:266). When the husband returns unexpectedly, Tristan and Runalen escape from the castle, but they are pursued; Runalen is killed, and Tristan receives the wound from a poisoned weapon from which he ultimately dies. Perhaps we are to take the false-key motif as a subtle hint on Scott's part that Mary's success will be short-lived.

The Tristan-story seems to be reflected in another way too in the exciting closing chapters of this novel. I have observed (see Chapter 2) that Scott was intrigued by "curious evasive shifts" such as those that Tristan and Iseult use to get out of a difficult situation. Near the end of *The Abbot* we find something remarkably similar. Abbot Ambrosius (Edward Glendinning) has arrived at Lochleven, disguised as a man-at-arms, with the purpose of aiding in Queen Mary's escape. By skillfully answering the questions of Mary's Protestant keeper, the Lady of Lochleven, he makes her think he is on her side. "You hold, unquestionably, the true faith?" she asks. "Do not doubt of it, madam," responds the disguised abbot. A few lines later the lady, still in the presence of Queen Mary, asks him whether he fears the night air; and he replies: "In the cause of the lady before whom I stand, I fear nothing, madam" (chap. 35). A bit later, when Roland Græme (who has recognized the abbot all along) tells Mary who he is, she muses: "But marked you not how astuciously the good father . . . eluded the questions of the woman Lochleven, telling her the very truth, which yet she received not as such?" Roland's thoughts about such shifts are very much like Scott's with regard to Ysonde's equivocal oath at Westminster: he "thought in his heart, that when the truth was spoken for the purpose of deceiving, it was little better than a lie in disguise" (chap. 35).

Further allusions to romance come in scattered places. When Halbert Glendinning stops the hubbub at St. Mary's arising from the confrontation between the monks and the Abbot of Unreason's revellers, he is offered by his brother, Father Ambrosius, "such a meal as a hermit in romance can offer to a wandering knight" (chap. 15). When plans are under way in earnest for the queen's escape, she observes that "with Henry [Seyton] for my knight, and Roland Græme for my trusty squire, methinks I am like a princess of romance, who may shortly set at defiance the dungeons and the weapons of all wicked sorcerers" (chap. 34). Shortly before the abdication scene Lord Lindesay contrasts his own blunt speech with that of "gallants" who are well versed in *Amadis of Gaul*. Another man who, with Lindesay, forces Mary to sign the abdication paper is Lord Ruthven, whose "martial cast of . . . form and features procured him the popular epithet of Greysteil . . . after the hero of a metrical romance then generally known"—and well known, as we have just seen, to Roland Græme. The "heavy-headed knave" who is on watch on the night of Mary's escape is named Hildebrand, humorously, after the hero of German romance.

In sum, medieval romance lurks almost everywhere in *The Abbot*. It provides the underlying story-pattern of the fair unknown, and it forms a backdrop adding depth and universality to much of what Scott has written in this exciting romance of later times.

Kenilworth (1821)

It is the privilege of tale-tellers to open their story in an inn, the free rendezvous of all travellers, and where the humour of each displays itself, without ceremony or restraint. This is especially suitable when the scene is laid during the old days of merry England, when the guests were in some sort not merely the inmates, but the messmates and temporary companions of mine Host, who was usually a personage of privileged freedom, comely presence, and good-humour. Patronised by him, the characters of the company were placed in ready contrast; and they seldom failed, during the emptying of a six-hooped pot, to throw off reserve, and present themselves to each other, and to their landlord, with the freedom of old acquaintance.

The opening paragraph of this famous novel, with its description of the Black Bear Inn in the village of Cumnor, makes one think of Chaucer's Tabard Inn, and in the very next paragraph Scott explicitly compares the proprietor, Giles Gosling, with Harry Bailey. Gosling is not a carbon copy of his illustrious predecessor, but like Bailey he has problems with women, as Edmund Tressilian finds out when he asks him for more information about the people at Cumnor Hall and receives instead a "declamation against the wiles of the fair sex, in which [Gosling] brought, at full length, the whole wisdom of Solomon to reinforce his own" (chap. 2). Gosling's nephew Michael Lambourne, who appears at Cumnor after long absence, had been noted for his "juvenile wildness"—Scott introducing here the frequent medieval topic of misspent youth. Among other escapades Michael had robbed an abbot's orchard, like St. Augustine and John

Lydgate before him, but we soon learn that he has not outgrown his youthful ways.

The references to Chaucer continue. During the course of the confrontation at Greenwich Palace, Queen Elizabeth says to Tressilian, "Your true affection . . . hath been, it seems, but ill requited; but you have scholarship, and you know there have been false Cressidas to be found, from the Trojan war downwards" (chap. 16). Of course this allusion, like Lambourne's later comparison of Richard Varney with "Sir Pandarus of Troy" (chap. 32), could have come just as readily from Shakespeare (indeed the spelling *Cressida* suggests that it does), but Chaucer's poem, which Scott knew, lies behind the Shakespeare play. The ninth chapter, in which Wayland Smith tells Tressilian his life story, is introduced by a few lines from the Canon's Yeoman's Prologue (VIII, 620-26). The motto is apt in that Wayland, like the Yeoman, has learned a lot about astrology and alchemy from a master whom he forsakes. When Wayland and Amy Robsart are riding toward Kenilworth, not long after Amy's escape from Cumnor Hall, Wayland sees Richard Varney approaching. " 'Draw your sword,' answered the lady, 'and pierce my bosom with it, rather than I should fall into his hands!' " (chap. 24). This emotional outburst recalls Chaucer's Physician's Tale, in which a beautiful young lady requests that her father slay her rather than let her fall into the hands of an evil man— "Yif me my deeth, er that I have a shame" (VI, 249)—and the father draws his sword and cuts off her head. Like the false-key motif in *The Abbot*, the disturbing connotations resonating from Amy's heartrending exclamation may be a subtle hint on Scott's part that the story will end tragically; but for the time being Wayland and Amy manage to mingle with a party of actors who are on their way to Kenilworth and thus to escape Varney's detection.

That Chaucer was on Scott's mind is clear when Amy falls into a one-sided conversation with a garrulous middle-aged woman who "might have been the very emblem of the Wife of Bath": "And yet, Lord help me," the woman says, "I have seen the day I would have tramped five leagues of lealand, and turned on my toe the whole evening after, as a juggler spins a pewter platter on the point of a needle. But age has clawed me somewhat in his clutch, as the song says; though, if I like the tune and like my partner, I'll dance the hays yet with any merry lass in Warwickshire, that writes that unhappy figure four with a round O after it" (chap. 24). Scott was obviously inspired here by a much talked-about passage in the Wife of Bath's Prologue:

> But, Lord Crist! whan that it remembreth me
> Upon my yowthe, and on my jolitee,
> It tikleth me aboute myn herte roote.

> Unto this day it dooth myn herte boote
> That I have had my world as in my tyme.
> But age, allas! that al wole envenyme,
> Hath me biraft my beautee and my pith.
> Lat go, farewel! the devel go therwith!
> The flour is goon, ther is namoore to telle;
> The bren, as I best kan, now moste I selle;
> But yet to be right myrie wol I fonde. [III, 469-79]

At Kenilworth the Queen shows her knowledge of Chaucer when she says with regard to Tressilian, but not knowing how things really stand, that he "may be one of those of whom Geoffrey Chaucer says wittily, the wisest clerks are not the wisest men" (chap. 31)—the same proverb from the Reeve's Tale that Scott used in *The Monastery* with respect to Father Eustace.

We find a cluster of references to medieval romance in connection with the festivities and pageantry at Kenilworth. "Upon the battlements were placed gigantic warders, with clubs, battle-axes, and other implements of ancient warfare, designed to represent soldiers of King Arthur." There is "the gigantic porter who waited at the gate," so large that he could "enact Colbrand, Ascapart, or any other giant of romance. . . . In fine, he represented excellently one of those giants of popular romance, who figure in every fairy tale, or legend of knight-errantry" (chap. 26). The Lady of the Lake appears in the pageantry enacted at the queen's arrival (chap. 30). One reference to Arthurian romance is not a part of the pageantry: having been thwarted in his lascivious designs on Amy by the jailor Lawrence Staples, with whom he fights, Michael Lambourne says of Staples that "that filthy paunch of his devours as many distressed damsels and oppressed orphans, as e'er a giant in King Arthur's history" (chap. 33). The masque presented for the queen's amusement includes Merlin (chap. 37); and we read that Captain Coxe, "that celebrated humorist of Coventry," had read about Amadis, Belianis,[3] Bevis, and Guy of Warwick "in an abridged form" (chap. 39)—these renowned heroes of old inspiring his memorable actions in the mock battle between Saxons and Danes. The gusto with which Scott describes all the pageantry connected with the royal visit is in the manner of medieval romance, as he would have known from *Sir Eglamour of Artois*.

What about the Tristan-story? Father Ambrosius's evasive shifts near the end of *The Abbot* are topped by one in *Kenilworth* that comes at a dramatic moment in the confrontation at Greenwich Palace (chap. 16). Queen Elizabeth is listening to Edmund Tressilian's complaint, in the presence of the rival Earls of Sussex and Leicester, that Richard Varney, Leicester's right-hand man, has seduced Amy Robsart. When Varney retorts that he has *married* Amy, the Queen asks: "My Lord of Leicester, will you warrant with your honour,—that is, to the best of your belief,— that your servant speaks truth in saying that he hath married this Amy Robsart?" Leicester is in a most embarrassing and even dangerous predicament. He himself, not Varney, is married to Amy Robsart, and he must keep his marriage a secret from the queen, since she has a romantic interest in him which, if cultivated, might lead him to the throne of England. In this very tense situation he replies, "after a moment's hesitation," with a splendid evasive shift: "To the best of my belief—indeed on my certain knowledge—she is a wedded wife." Although Scott does not mention Tristan and Iseult in either *The Abbot* or *Kenilworth*, I would contend that the evasive shifts in both novels were inspired by the Tristan-story. Another trace of Tristan, this time from the prose tradition only, comes in chapter 22. Tony Foster forcibly takes a flask from his daughter Janet's hand when she is about to drink from it; he knows it contains a potion intended to make Amy Robsart sick. This incident recalls the scene in Malory's *Tristram* when King Melyodus is about to drink from a vessel that contains poison which his queen has prepared for Tristram: "And as he wolde have drunken thereof the quene aspyed him and ran unto hym and pulde the pyse [i.e., vessel] from hym sodeynly."[4]

Like other Scott novels, *Kenilworth* has its share of unspecific references and parallels to romance, as in a conversation at the Black Bear about the inhabitants of Cumnor Hall. "What adventurous knight," asks Lambourne, "ever thought of the lady's terror, when he went to thwack giant, dragon, or magician, in her presence, and for her deliverance?" Goldthred replies, "Yonder is the enchanted manor, and the dragon, and the lady, all at thy service, if thou darest venture on them." When Lambourne wonders why Tressilian wants to accompany him to Cumnor Hall, Tressilian continues with the imagery: "I am a traveller, who seeks for strange rencounters and uncommon passages, as the knights of yore did after adventures and feats of arms" (chap. 2). Giles Gosling must remember this conversation when he tells Tressilian, after the unsatisfying visit at Cumnor Hall, "I see not why you should play the champion of a wench that will none of you, and incur the resentment of a favourite's favourite [i.e., Varney], as dangerous a monster as ever a knight adventurer encountered in the old story books" (chap. 8). Amy's ominous dream during the one night she spends at Kenilworth (see chap. 33) has analogues in medieval romance, while Varney's success in convincing Leicester that Amy has a lover (chap. 36) is very obviously inspired by the "temptation scene" in *Othello*, which itself has an analogue in the opening chapters of *Valentine and Orson*, in which the evil archbishop convinces the Emperor of Constantinople that his wife Bellyssant is an adulteress, the archibishop (like

Varney) having been rebuffed by the lady when he himself had made overtures to her.

Throughout the novel there is the motif of the undesired marriage but with a striking variation: instead of a lady being forced into a marriage she does not want, the Earl of Leicester finds his marriage to Amy undesirable because it stands in the way of his ambition. There is also the motif of two young men (Tressilian and Leicester) in love with the same girl (Amy), but this girl has already decided in favor of one of the rivals—a necessary variation, since Tressilian is from Cornwall, where the knights in medieval romance (especially in Malory) are usually inferior to English knights. And the variations continue. Instead of the one big emotional scene of recognition and reunion so typical of romance, we have recognitions on a smaller scale—Gosling finally recognizes his nephew Michael Lambourne; a Jewish apothecary recognizes Wayland Smith in London; Dickie Sludge recognizes Wayland at Kenilworth—and we have false recognitions: on different occasions Amy momentarily mistakes Tressilian, Varney, and even Lambourne for the Earl of Leicester, these incidents preparing us for the tragic mistake, at the end, that leads her to her death.

Although the time of the story is 1575, *Kenilworth* obviously contains elements from medieval romance or variations thereof. As in *The Abbot*, they help to enhance and deepen the tragedy that unfolds.

The Pirate (1821)

This story takes place on the Orkney and Shetland Islands and reflects Scott's trip to that region in 1814. It is permeated with references to Old Norse lore, as might be expected, inasmuch as Scott's purpose is to show the effects of the encroachment of outside forces, around 1700, on a society that was originally Scandinavian and still owed much to Scandinavian culture. As a boy the novel's hero, Mordaunt Mertoun, hears from the lips of Swertha, his father's housekeeper, the "old Norwegian ballads, and dismal tales concerning the Trows or Drows, (the dwarfs of the Scalds,) with whom superstitious eld had peopled many a lonely cavern and brown dale in Dunrossness, as in every other district of Zetland." As he grows older he feels that "the classic fables of antiquity were rivalled at least, if not excelled . . . by the strange legends of Berserkars, of Sea-kings, of dwarfs, giants, and sorcerers" (chap. 2). So throughout the novel there are references to Sea-kings, to Champions, to Odin and Thor, to Valhalla, to dwarfs, and to other creatures and places, gods and demigods, of Scandinavian sagas and balladry. Perhaps the most striking use Scott makes of the Germanic mythology is in chapter 10, when old Norna suddenly appears to Mordaunt Mertoun in a quiet natural setting and at a time when he is depressed because he has apparently fallen out of favor with Magnus Troil and his two daughters. The "mysterious female" is "standing on a sudden so close beside him, and looking upon him with such sad and severe eyes," that she invites comparison to a Valkyrie maiden come to announce his imminent death.

This mysterious personage—known as Norna of the Fitful-head, although her real name is Ulla Troil and she is a cousin of Magnus Troil—is one of Scott's many old sibyls, one of his spaewomen; she believes that she can control the elements and foresee and direct future events. She appears and disappears as suddenly and mysteriously as does Meg Merrilies, to whom critics often compare her; and she recalls, even more than does Meg, the old sibyl of the Amadis cycle, Urganda the Unknown. Other characters also seem copied to some extent from earlier novels: the misanthropic elder Mertoun recalls the Black Dwarf; the dark-haired, melancholy Minna Troil is reminiscent of Flora MacIvor; the pirate, Clement Cleveland, is not much different from George Staunton, alias Robertson; and Magnus Troil, the Udaller, the worthy descendant of the Sea-kings and upholder of the Scandinavian culture, is of the same cast as Cedric the Saxon. Norna's resemblance to Meg Merrilies, however, seems to have received the most attention from Scott's readers, who seem on the other hand not to have noticed a chain of events in her past life that recalls *The Heart of Mid-Lothian* and medieval romance: as a young woman, Norna is seduced by one Vaughan (whom we first meet as the elder Mertoun); she becomes pregnant; her pregnancy must be concealed; a male child is born in mysterious circumstances; the infant disappears, the mother not knowing what has become of him. Of course there are differences. Norna actually does (unintentionally) bring about the death of her father, while Effie only feared that she had killed David Deans when he fainted in the courtroom; and Norna's child is looked after by her lover for a number of years, both of them making a mark as pirates before becoming separated, whereas neither Effie nor George Robertson knew what became of their child. There is no scene like the one in *Mid-Lothian* in which father and son do battle, unknown to each other, but a son does fight with his half-brother, neither knowing the true identity of the other—the pirate son (whom we know as Captain Cleveland) severely wounding his opponent (Mordaunt Mertoun, Vaughan's son by another woman).

The encounter takes place by night at Burgh-Westra, Magnus Troil's home, on the lawn just outside the bedchamber of Minna and Brenda (in chap. 23). At first Minna hears Cleveland, her friend, singing at the window, but she cannot go to the window without extricating herself from her sleeping sister's embrace and thereby awakening her. A little later she hears heated words, presumably between Cleveland and Mordaunt. Then they fight, and one of them falls with a groan, perhaps wounded mortally. At this, Minna does disengage herself from Brenda. Scantily dressed and barefooted, she jumps from the window, which is eight feet above the ground, and tries to follow the pair—one of whom is carrying the other—but they disappear. After a conversation with the minstrel Claud Halcro, Minna returns to her room. The next morning Brenda notices blood on her sister's feet and thinks that Minna has been injured, but it is blood she stepped in after she had jumped from the window. Minna is distraught, and an emotional illness ensues.

This passage is not inspired, as one might think, by Scandinavian lore, but rather by Marie de France's *Lai of Yonec*. In this story an elderly, jealous husband keeps his young wife in close confinement in a tower, where after seven years she is visited by a handsome lover who comes to her as a hawk—changing into his proper person after he enters the tower room through the window. Having discovered the liaison (with the help of his sister), the husband affixes razor-sharp iron spears to the window sill, and when the hawk comes the next time it is mortally injured. After a melancholy conversation with the lady in his proper person, in which he tells her he will die, he changes into a hawk once more and flies away. The distraught lady jumps from the tower window and follows her lover's drops of blood, eventually finding him dying in his castle.

Whatever their differences, the following similarities in the two stories are noteworthy:

Scott: An agitated young lady jumps from a window eight feet above the ground.
Marie: An agitated lady jumps from a window twenty feet above the ground.
Scott: The lady is scantily clad and barefooted.
Marie: The lady is clad only in her nightshirt.
Scott: The lady tries to follow her lover, who she thinks has mortally wounded another man.
Marie: The lady follows her lover, whom she knows to be mortally wounded.
Scott: The lady steps in blood, as is noticed the next morning.
Marie: The lady follows drops of blood from her wounded lover, and before she finds him she crosses a meadow in which the grass is damp with blood.

Knowing how Scott's mind works, and having observed that he attempts to escape detection by altering his source material, I think that the comparisons listed speak for themselves; they can hardly be coincidental.

One reason the two men fight is that Cleveland thinks (mistakenly) that Mordaunt is a rival for the affection of Minna—again a variation on the story-pattern of the Knight's Tale. Earlier in the novel we had one young man and two young women—the Knight's Tale turned topsy-turvy—but

Minna and Brenda were not *vying* for the attention of Mordaunt Mertoun: it simply took him a while to make up his mind that he preferred Brenda. The strange, ominous dreams that Minna and Brenda have in chapter 19, just before they are aware of Norna in their bedchamber, recall medieval romance in a general manner. Norna's dwarfish servant, however, is *specifically* likened again and again to the Pacolet of medieval romance. He even has the nickname: Minna and Brenda are introduced to him by their father as "Nick Strumpfer, maidens, whom his mistress calls Pacolet, being a light-limbed dwarf, as you see, like him that wont to fly about, like a *Scourie,* on his wooden hobbyhorse, in the old story-book of Valentine and Orson, that you, Minna, used to read whilst you were a child" (chap. 27). So an old sibyl who recalls Urganda the Unknown, from the Amadis cycle, has in her service a dwarf borrowed from *Valentine and Orson.*

Norna brings to mind the old beldam in the Wife of Bath's Tale when she converses with the elder Mertoun at the ruins of the haunted Roman Catholic Kirk of Saint Ringan's, *whispering* a word in his ear which she tells him beforehand "shall touch the nearest secret of [his] life" (chap. 25). Just as the reader of the Wife's tale must wait until later to learn what the "pistel" was which the beldam "rowned" in the knight's ear (namely, the answer to the question "What do women most desire?"), so too must the reader of *The Pirate* wait until later, not to be told, but to infer that this word must have been "Ulla," Norna's real name—Mertoun not having known until then who she was. Scott refers specifically to another Canterbury pilgrim in the last chapter when he tells us that Norna's "study, like that of Chaucer's physician, had been 'but little in the Bible.' " Early in the novel Scott makes one of his few allusions to *Piers Plowman:* the pedantic agriculturist Triptolemus Yellowley, he says, had read little vernacular poetry in his youth except Thomas Tusser's *Hundreth Good Pointes of Husbandrie* "and . . . Piers Ploughman's Vision, which, charmed with the title, he bought with avidity from a packman, but after reading the two first pages, flung it into the fire as an impudent and misnamed political libel" (chap. 4). Scott thus expresses his own attitude toward Langland's magnum opus, which he apparently did not like any better than he liked the *Divine Comedy.*

Halfway through the story, Brenda tries to bring Minna down from her romantic cloud of fantasy (as regards Captain Cleveland) with a telling reference to *Don Quixote*: "You remember the Spanish story which you took from me long since, because I said, in your admiration of the chivalry of the olden times of Scandinavia, you rivalled the extravagance of the hero.—Ah, Minna, your colour shews that your conscience checks you, and reminds you of the book I mean;—is it more wise, think you, to mistake a windmill for a giant, or the commander of a paltry corsair for a Kiempe, or a

Vi–king?" (chap. 20). The warning had come even earlier, when an elderly, very minor character named Haagen was reminiscing, during the St. John's Eve festivities at Burgh-Westra, about his service in the unlucky Earl of Montrose's last campaign.

"And Montrose," said the soft voice of the graceful Minna; "what became of Montrose, or how looked he?"
"Like a lion with the hunters before him," answered the old gentleman; "but I looked not twice his way, for my own lay right over the hill."
"And so you left him?" said Minna, in a tone of the deepest contempt.
"It was no fault of mine, Mistress Minna," answered the old man, somewhat out of countenance; "but I was there with no choice of my own; and, besides, what good could I have done?—all the rest were running like sheep, and why should I have staid?"
"You might have died with him," said Minna.
"And lived with him to all eternity, in immortal verse!" added Claud Halcro.
"I thank you, Mistress Minna," replied the plain-dealing Zetlander; "and I thank you, my old friend Claud;—but I would rather drink both your healths in this good bicker of ale, like a living man as I am, than that you should be making songs in my honour, for having died forty or fifty years agone." [Chap. 15]

Scott has played a joke on us here, because the old man has little resemblance to his cold-blooded, ruthless, courageous namesake from medieval Germanic romance. In his clearly unchivalric and antiromantic but eminently wise attitude, he more nearly resembles Malory's unforgettable Sir Dynadan, who tries (and fails) to deflate Sir Tristram's romantic notions and bring him to the world of reality. Like Sir Dynadan, both Haagen and Brenda fail to have any effect on Minna, who must learn hard lessons for herself.

The Fortunes of Nigel (1822)

This carefully wrought novel takes place in London in the early seventeenth century and is mainly indebted to history, to Elizabethan and Jacobean drama (especially Ben Jonson), and, for the colorful chapters that take place in the Whitefriars district (Alsatia), to Thomas Shadwell's famous Restoration play, *The Squire of Alsatia*. Scott has acknowledged his indebtedness in the introduction of 1831, the explanatory notes, and the mottos to some of the chapters. His sources were looked at with some care by Paul Müller long ago, but Müller did not see fit to mention medieval romance—which, in fact, is less prominent here than in other Waverley novels.[5]

There are a few specific references, sometimes in a humorous vein and sometimes not. Early in the novel George Heriot, King James I's

Scottish goldsmith, guesses that Nigel's servant Richie Moniplies is "a son of old Mungo Moniplies, the flesher, at the West-Port [of Edinburgh]." When he asks Richie why he pretended to be of noble birth, Richie's reply is typical of his way of thinking: "I hear muckle of an Earl of Warwick in these southern parts,—Guy, I think his name was,—and he has great reputation here for slaying dun cows, and boars, and such like; and I am sure my father has killed more cows, and boars, not to mention bulls, calves, sheep, ewes, lambs, and pigs, than the haill Baronage of England" (chap. 2). In telling Margaret Ramsay her life story, Lady Hermione says of her Scottish mother's objections to her suitor: "I had been educated with different feelings, and the traditions of the feuds and quarrels of my mother's family in Scotland, which were to her monuments and chronicles, seemed to me as insignificant and unmeaning as the actions and fantasies of Don Quixote" (chap. 20). When Nigel is conducted to the Tower of London and must enter it through the Traitor's Gate, Scott compares the "dark and low arch" to "entrance to Dante's Hell," because it seemed to forbid hope of regress" (chap. 28). George Heriot visits Nigel in prison, and is doubly angry when he discovers that the supposed young man in the room with Nigel is actually his goddaughter, Margaret Ramsay. Nigel says that if he were free, he would know how to protect Margaret's reputation, and Heriot replies sarcastically, "Upon my word, a perfect Amadis and Oriana! . . . I should soon get my throat cut betwixt the knight and the princess, I suppose, but that the beef-eaters are happily within halloo" (chap. 29). Scott's humorous contrasting of Dame Ursula Suddlechop to "the lovely Lady Cristabelle" on the evening when the old matchmaker visits Margaret Ramsay is with respect to the lovely lady of Coleridge's poem rather than to the lovely mistress and later wife of Sir Eglamour of Artois; and when Nigel accosts his false friend, Lord Dalgarno, in St. James's Park—Dalgarno letting Nigel know that he erred in assuming their relationship had been like that of Pylades and Orestes, Damon and Pythias, and Theseus and Pirothoüs—the reference in the last-named pair of friends is probably to classical literature rather than Chaucer's Knight's Tale.

There are several possible echoes of medieval literature, including Scott's use of the medieval *topos* of youth versus age, seen here most strikingly in the contrast between the old Scottish Earl of Huntinglen (who is friendly to Nigel) and his hypocritical and unprincipled twenty-five-year-old son, Lord Dalgarno; and including Dame Suddlechop's tête-à-tête with Margaret Ramsay, in which the older woman gets young Margaret to confide in her the cause of her distress—namely, her fancy for Nigel—which brings to mind the long, amusing interview in Book I of *Troilus and Criseyde*, in which Pandarus finally gets Troilus to name the young lady who is the cause of his sorrow. Dame Suddlechop thinks that "romances have cracked [Margaret's] brain" (chap. 7), and later Margaret does play the role of a damsel from romance when she disguises herself as a boy with the intention of helping Nigel in his plight, ending up in the Tower with him and provoking Heriot's sarcastic remark (quoted above). Nigel must feel like Malory's ill-fated Balin, the knight with two swords, when he says, "I am an unhappy, a most unhappy being . . . nothing approaches me but shares my own bad fate!" (chap. 28). But things are not so bad as they seem. Like many a romance the novel ends with two weddings: Nigel marries Margaret Ramsay, and Richie Moniplies marries Martha Trapbois, the homely but high-minded daughter of the wealthy old usurer who was murdered in Alsatia.

Scott has "[cleared] the floor for a blithe bridal" by shipping one memorable character, Jenkin Vincent, off to Paris. Jenkin, or Jin Vin as he is usually called, is an apprentice to Margaret's father, David Ramsay the watchmaker, and he is in love with Margaret. But never, as in the Knight's Tale, do two attractive and equally qualified young men vie for the hand of one girl, because Nigel does not have any inkling until almost the end of the novel that Margaret loves him, and she never seriously considers Jenkin as a suitor; although very attractive in his own way, he cannot compare in her mind with the noble hero. The main plot concerns Nigel's efforts, finally successful, to keep from losing his paternal estate in Scotland. There is thus a certain similarity to the plot of *Guy Mannering*. But Nigel Olifaunt, the young Lord of Glenvarloch, is no fair unknown—he knows all along who he is, and so does everybody else—nor has he returned from exile. So the familiar motifs from medieval romance that Scott has used elsewhere are not to be found here.

There are a few verbal borrowings from Chaucer and medieval romance (cited in Chapter 7), but it should be clear by now that Scott's brilliant story of intrigue dominated by two very *un*romantic characters, King James I and Richie Moniplies, does not owe very much to romance except by way of contrast. When Jenkin complains to Dame Suddlechop that she has made a fool and a rogue of him, she replies, "Tut, man, it was only in the time of King Arthur or King Lud, that a gentleman was held to blemish his scutcheon by a leap over the line of reason or honesty—It is the old look, the ready hand, the fine clothes, the brisk oath, and the wild brain, that makes the gallant now-a-days" (chap. 21). As Scott well knew, Ben Jonson's London was not the land of romance.

Peveril of the Peak (1823)

During the course of the chapters whose action takes place on the Isle of Man, Julian Peveril's friend, the foppish Earl of Derby, offends his mother the countess by thoughtlessly pretending he has given his late father's signet to a monkey to play with. When he sees that her feelings are hurt he says, "But believe me, though to be an absolute Palmerin of England is not in my nature, no son ever loved a mother more dearly, or would do more to oblige her" (chap. 15). The young earl is certainly no Palmerin, and if his remark leads readers to suspect that medieval romance looms no larger in *Peveril of the Peak* than in *The Fortunes of Nigel*, they would be mistaken.

The mutual affection that grows up between Julian Peveril and Alice Bridgenorth from the time they are very small children has analogues in medieval romance. One need only recall young Valentine's friendship for Eglantine, the daughter of King Pepyn; or the esteem of young Amadis, son of King Perion of Gaul, for Oriana, daughter of King Lisvard of Britain. Amadis vows fealty to Oriana at a very early stage in the story:

> It chanc'd, one day the beauteous children came
> Together to salute the royal dame.
> The queen, as they approach'd to pay their court,
> Pointed to Perion's boy, and cried in sport:
> "Receive this servant, royal maid! and thou,
> Child of the Sea, thy future duty vow!"
> With joyous air the boy his homage paid,
> And humbly vow'd his service to the maid:
> And from that hour her every look observ'd,
> Nor after from his fond allegiance swerv'd.[6]

Young Julian's allegiance to Alice is most vividly dramatized early in the novel when the Countess of Derby, still dressed in mourning for her husband, suddenly appears in the gilded chamber where the children are playing and startles them. Julian refuses to leave Alice's side. Their relationship, like that of Amadis and Oriana, continues to develop despite formidable obstacles; neither of them can conceive of marrying someone else.

The Roman Catholic countess's supposedly deaf and dumb servant, known as Fenella, thinks she is the daughter of the martyred Puritan William Christian, but she is actually the illegitimate daughter of his wily and unprincipled brother, Edward, who throughout the novel schemes revenge on the countess for having executed William after the Restoration. Fenella has often been compared with Goethe's Mignon, from *Wilhelm Meisters Lehrjahre*;[7] I think that the Middle English romance *Sir Gowther* is also in the background. Gowther pretends (like Fenella) that he cannot speak—such being part of the penance imposed on him by the Pope because of his past sins. While visiting in disguise at the court of the Emperor of Almayne, he finds that the emperor has a daughter who has been dumb from birth, and the two fall in love. When the Sowdan of Percé (Persia) demands the girl's hand in marriage, her father refuses and fights against the Saracens. He is given strong support by Gowther, who fights bravely but in other disguises. The girl, watching the struggle from a tower, recognizes the stranger all along, and when she sees him sorely wounded in the third encounter with the enemy, she swoons and falls from the tower. When after several days she finally revives, she can speak, and she informs her father that it was the good stranger who had fought so bravely in his behalf. The Pope, who had come to Almayne for the girl's funeral, recognizes the stranger as Gowther and releases him from his penance. The emperor's daughter, unlike Fenella, really is dumb—she is not just pretending—and she gains speech as a result of a moment of intense excitement. Fenella gives away her long-kept secret in the last chapter when King Charles, suspecting that she is not deaf and dumb, plays a trick on her by announcing to the assembled company that Julian Peveril, whom she loves, has been stabbed. In this moment of intense agony, hearing the king's false report and thinking that her loved one has been severely wounded or killed, she loses control over herself, first screaming and then speaking. I am not arguing that *Sir Gowther* is a source for *Peveril of the Peak;* nevertheless, like Gowther, Fenella pretends to be dumb; and like the emperor's daughter, she speaks after a great shock. Scott's Fenella is the stuff of which at least two medieval romances, *Sir Gowther* and *Robert the Devil*, are made. Moreover she is a "dark ladye" and thus in contrast with Alice Bridgenorth, who has had the hero's heart from the beginning and does not need to fear any competition, however attractive and skilled.

When Julian is sharing a cell at Newgate with the dwarf Geoffrey Hudson, he is presented by his little companion with a book that proves to be one of the "now forgotten romances" of Madeleine de Scudéry—romances, Scott tells us, that "contrive to unite in their immense folios all the improbabilities and absurdities of the old romances of chivalry, without that tone of imagination which pervades them, and all the metaphysical absurdities which Cowley and the poets of the age had heaped upon the passion of love, like so many load of small-coal upon a slender fire, which it smothers instead of aiding" (chap. 35). Scudéry's romances nevertheless are much admired by little "Sir" Geoffrey, who himself is part of the stuff romance is made of, though not in the way the reader might first think. He tells Julian that "in the history of all ages, the clean, tight, dapper little fellow hath proved an overmatch for his bulky antagonist," citing among his examples Bevis and Ascaparte, Guy and Colbrand, and King Arthur and the giant Hoel. Scott compares him "paining himself to stand a-tiptoe" with Chaucer's "gallant Sir Chaunticlere"; this is the trial scene of chapter 41 in which he, Julian Peveril, and Julian's father Sir Geoffrey are acquitted. A bit later Scott compares him to none other than Little John of Saintré, or so the motto to chapter 46 would imply. There is a "strain of romance" in the dwarf's account of the conspiracy contemplated by the Duke of Buckingham—this is owing to his strange encounter with Fenella—and the king himself says of him, "For wielding his sword and keeping his word, he is a perfect Don Quixote in decimo-octavo" (chap. 46).

Somewhat earlier in the novel I think it not unlikely that Scott has borrowed and adapted from the Tristan-story the motif of the white and black sails. While imprisoned at Newgate, Julian is given a chance to escape if he will renounce his beloved Alice Bridgenorth. If he agrees, he is to wear a white ribbon on his cap while he is being transported by boat from Newgate to the Tower; this will be the signal to those in another boat who will then intercept his boat and free him. But Julian will not buy his freedom at this price; he deliberately wears a piece of black crape, which causes the men on the other boat to "[alter] their course." If I am correct in my hunch, Scott has done a very good job of covering his tracks. Not even Chief Justice Scroggs, who presides at the trial of the Peverils and other alleged Papists during the Popish Plot scare, would have been able to sentence him for plagiarism on the basis of such evidence. Of course, this motif occurs also in the classical story of Theseus, which Scott would have known; but in view of his deep involvement with the Tristan-story, it seems safe to say that the medieval romance was the primary influence—although the ultimate source may indeed be the story of Theseus, since some scholars think that it lies behind the famous episode in the Tristan-story.

Besides the underlying motifs there are unmistakable allusions to medieval literature throughout this very long novel, often in the dialogue. The Countess of Derby (and Queen in Man) is like an "enchanted queen" when young Julian first sees her in the gilded chamber at Martindale Castle. She cites the *Morte Darthur* when she labels Major Bridgenorth as "this discourteous faitour" (chap. 6). Later, at Holm-Peel Castle on the Isle of Man, she remarks to Julian: "The wheel appears to be again revolving; and the present period is not unlikely to bring back such scenes as my younger years witnessed" (chap. 18). (The idea of the wheel of fortune is certainly medieval; it in fact occurs near the end of the *Morte Darthur*, in Arthur's ominous dream before the final disaster.) Her son teases Julian about his activities on the island in the language of Arthurian romance: "Thrice welcome, Sir Knight of Dames . . . here you rove gallantly, and at free will, through our dominions, fulfilling of appointments, and achieving amorous adventures; while we are condemned to sit in our royal halls, as dull and as immovable as if our Majesty was carved on the stern of some Manx smuggling dogger, and christened the King Arthur of Ramsey" (*ibid.*). But things are not so rosy for Julian. Like many a hero of romance he has formidable difficulties in his clandestine love affair with an enemy's daughter; and he later experiences the caprices of Dame Fortune when Martindale Castle is surprised, his father is arrested for alleged conspiracy in the Popish Plot, and he himself is a prisoner of his truelove's father, Major Bridgenorth, to whom he says resignedly that "those who have stood high on Fortune's wheel, must abide by the consequence of its revolutions" (chap. 23). The despicable opportunist Edward Christian quotes freely from the Miller's Tale and the Knight's Tale in conversation with Julian at the Cat and Fiddle Inn (chap. 21), his erudition being an important facet of his villainy. Even the unlearned turnkey at Newgate, Jem Clink, refers (unwittingly) to medieval romance when he tells Julian, who has just asked to be transferred to the Tower in order to be with his father, that "the Tower is for lords and knights, and not for squires of low degree" (chap. 33). This remark calls attention to itself because it looks forward to Scott's next novel, *Quentin Durward*, which is much inspired by *The Squyr of Lowe Degre*.

Near the end of the novel the King says, "Here is a plot [i.e., Buckingham's conspiracy] without a drop of blood; and all the elements of a romance, without its conclusion. Here we have a wandering island princess, (I pray my Lady of Derby's pardon,) a dwarf [Geoffrey Hudson], a Moorish Sorceress [Fenella], an impenitent rogue [Edward Christian], and a repentant man of rank [the Duke of Buckingham], and yet all ends without either hanging or marriage." But Old Rowley is wrong, as the countess is quick to tell him: everything will indeed end in a marriage—of Julian Peveril and Alice Bridgenorth.

Quentin Durward (1823)

Scott has a lot to say about King Louis XI in his introduction of 1831. "The selection of this remarkable person as the principal character in the romance—for it will be easily comprehended that the little love intrigue of Quentin is only employed as the means of bringing out the story—afforded considerable facilities to the author." Louis XI is indeed a fine historical portrait, perhaps Scott's very best, but there is more to "the little love intrigue of Quentin" than he would have us believe. Before the time of the novel the hero was an avid reader of romances—"those prudent instructors," which "had taught his youth, that if damsels were shy, they were yet neither void of interest nor of curiosity in their neighbours' affairs" (chap. 4). These are his thoughts after he has seen the mysterious beauty (Isabelle of Croye) at a window in the Fleur-de-lys Inn, and after he has heard her song about County Guy—which was perhaps suggested (and only suggested) by the "strain" ending "Ah! County Guy! / For love of thee my smiles and solace fly!" which is "breath'd" by Alexander's Indian mistress in G. L. Way's "Lay of Aristotle" (Way, 2:56). When Quentin first encounters gypsies, after having cut down one who had recently been hanged (and getting into a lot of trouble for doing so), he thinks that they are Saracens—"those 'heathen hounds,' who were the opponents of gentle knights and Christian monarchs, in all the romances which he had heard or read" (chap 6). As his fortunes begin to unfold, he thinks of himself as a knight of romance; but his self-image is constantly being threatened by reality. His fantasizing about the mysterious beauty is brought to a halt, temporarily at least, during the meeting with his uncle, Ludovic Lesly, a singularly unromantic Archer of the Scottish Guard, who opens to him "a page of the real history of life" (chap. 5).

Much later in the story, after Quentin, like a true knight, has safely conducted Isabelle and her aunt (Lady Hameline) to Liège and has rescued Isabelle from the clutches of William de la Marck and has surrendered her to the protection of the Count of Crèvecœur, he is abruptly brought back to the world of reality when the count, who has noticed the budding little love intrigue, says to him, "You have had, I imagine, a happy journey through Fairy-land—all full of heroic adventure, and high hope and wild minstrel-like delusion, like the gardens of Morgaine la Fée. Forget it all, young soldier . . . remember yonder lady only as the honoured Countess of Croye—forget her as a wandering and adventurous damsel" (chap. 24). When Quentin expresses anger and indignation, the Count replies with a sarcastic allusion to romance: "Heyday! . . . I have come between Amadis and Oriana . . . " Crèvecœur goes on to say, "I can allow thee, like a youth who hath listened to romances till he fancied himself a Paladin, to form pretty dreams for some time; but thou must not be angry at a well-meaning friend, though he shake thee something roughly by the shoulders to awake thee."

One romance that has a profound effect on Quentin is *The Squyr of Lowe Degre,* which he first becomes acquainted with just after he has brought Isabelle and Hameline safely to Schonwaldt, the palace of the ill-fated Bishop of Liège. The volume that catches Quentin's attention, Scott tells us, is a black-letter edition recently printed in Strasbourg; but this is pure fiction. The two earliest printed editions are by Wynkyn de Worde (c. 1520) and William Copland (c. 1560), which were done in London in English; there existed no French (or German) original printed in Strasbourg or anywhere else at the time of our story, 1470.[8] We must allow Scott a little poetic licence here. What is important is the parallel that

Quentin sees between himself and the squire, who, though "a gentleman void of land and living," finally managed to win the hand of his truelove, "the King's daughter of Hongarie," with the help of the king himself. Both the squire and Quentin have to prove their worthiness. Fortunately for Quentin, he sees the girl of his dreams and wins her within a period of six months, instead of the fourteen years between first sight and marriage in the old romance.

Quentin's identity is known to everyone from the very beginning, so this is not a story about a fair unknown who either does not know or deliberately conceals his parentage. In some ways, however, Scott's story does recall Malory's *Tale of Sir Gareth*. Both Quentin and Gareth are attractive young men who must prove themselves worthy. Early in the novel, as Quentin and Maître Pierre (King Louis XI) approach the castle Plessis-les-Tours, Quentin is disturbed at the sight of the body of a man who has been hanged from a nearby tree. Maître Pierre explains that the man was a traitor, but Quentin is still noticeably shaken, as is Sir Gareth when he and Dame Lyonette see the bodies of forty knights who have been hanged from trees by the pitiless Rede Knyght of the Rede Laundes, with whom Gareth must fight on behalf of Lyonette's sister, Dame Lyonesse.[9] Quentin falls in love with Isabelle at first sight at the Fleur-de-lys Inn, as does Gareth with Dame Lyonesse when he first sees her at the window of her castle. Both the novel and the romance are stories of true love in its finest sense. When, under Quentin's protection, Isabelle and Lady Hameline begin their journey from Plessis-les-Tours to Liège, Hameline's uneasiness about Quentin's youth and inexperience recalls Dame Lyonette's initial disappointment in having young Gareth, an unproven knight, assigned to the task of rescuing her sister. But never does Hameline upbraid Quentin in the way Dame Lyonette does Sir Gareth, whom she considers a "stynkyng kychyn knave" until he has proved his worth many times over. Early in the journey Quentin shows his valor by fighting decisively against two of France's best knights, the Duke of Orleans and the Count of Dunois. Later, when the king is a virtual prisoner at Peronne, he asks Ludovic Lesly if he has perhaps "heard from that wandering Paladin, your nephew? . . . for he hath been lost to us, since, like a young knight who had set out upon his first adventures, he sent us home two prisoners, as the first-fruits of his chivalry" (chap. 26). The king may well have had the *Tale of Sir Gareth* (or something like it) in mind, inasmuch as Gareth sends back to King Arthur's court all the knights whom he has conquered during the course of his mission.

I have already hinted at some of the other motifs from medieval romance in *Quentin Durward*. A king in disguise—Louis XI as a wealthy silk-merchant—is a motif exemplified in a number of ballads and most notably in the romance *Rauf Coilyear*. As is typical of these stories, Quentin is very much surprised when he finds out who Maître Pierre really is—so surprised that he almost drops his weapon. "Singular suspicions respecting the real rank of this person had at different times crossed his thoughts; but this, the proved reality, was wilder than his wildest conjecture" (chap. 8); later he apologizes to the king for his "rustic boldness" when he was unaware how things really stood. The journey from Plessis-les-Tours to Liège is like the typical perilous journey, and it proves to be even more perilous than Quentin foresaw at the outset. Moreover, the hero has not only his own welfare to think about but also that of the two ladies under his protection. Quentin's rescue of Isabelle from Schonwaldt and William de la Marck, the Wild Boar of Ardennes, is again in the manner of medieval romance; it is a rescue in the nick of time, for the drunken man who did not hesitate to order the murder of the bishop before everyone present in the castle-hall would hardly have respected Isabelle's sex. The reason Isabelle fled from Burgundy to France in the first place was that she did not want to marry Campo-Basso, the nobleman whom her liege lord the Duke of Burgundy, Charles the Bold, had determined for her—so we have the motif of the undesired marriage. When Charles changes his mind in favor of the Duke of Orleans, she is equally unenthusiastic, for she is now in love with Quentin. The king does not desire this marriage either, because it ruins his long-standing plans for a marriage between his daughter Princess Joan and the duke; but this too is an undesired marriage—undesired by the duke because Joan is so homely.

Other echoes from and allusions to medieval literature contribute in smaller ways to the novel's medieval atmosphere. As antifeminist as any medieval monk, Maître Pierre says to Jacqueline (Isabelle) at the Fleur-de-lys Inn that she will one day be "a false and treacherous thing, like the rest of [her] giddy sex" (chap. 4)—a note informing us that Louis "entertained a great contempt for the understanding, and not less for the character, of the fair sex." A considerably higher opinion of her is expressed by Johnny Guthrie, one of the Scottish Archers at Plessis-les-Tours, who compares her "singing to the lute" with "music of the Fairy Melusina's making" (chap. 7). After having been soundly defeated by Quentin when he was trying to waylay Isabelle, the Duke of Orleans declines to surrender his valuable sword to the authorities who break up the melee; instead, he melodramatically throws it into a nearby lake—and although no hand rises from the lake to grasp the sword, the reader of course thinks of Excalibur and the closing pages of the *Morte Darthur*. When Hayraddin Maugrabin realizes his mistake in thinking that Quentin is romantically interested in the thirty-five-year-old Hameline rather than her young niece, he says to Hameline rather ungallantly that "the youth prefers veal to beef" (chap. 20), echoing Chaucer's January, in the Merchant's Tale, who believes that "bet than old boef is the tendre veel" (IV, 1420). He then informs Hameline that if she should refuse to follow him, he is one "who would care little to strip [her] naked, and bind [her] to a tree, and leave [her] to [her] fortune"—which is more or less what does happen to Florence, in *Le Bone Florence of Rome*, at the hands of her wicked brother-in-law (and to Jereslaus's wife in the similar story in verse by Hoccleve, which Scott might have known not from Hoccleve but from Hoccleve's source, the Latin prose version in the *Gesta Romanorum*).

While Quentin and Isabelle discuss last-minute strategy in preparation for his daring rescue of her from Schonwaldt, she says to him, "Plunge your dagger in my heart . . . rather than leave me captive in the hands of these monsters." Like Amy Robsart's similar remark to Wayland Smith in *Kenilworth*, this heartfelt exclamation has an analogue in Chaucer's Physician's pathetic tale about the beautiful Virginia, who, having made the same request of her father, dies at his hands rather than be shamed by the lascivious judge. Near the end of the novel the gypsy Hayraddin Maugrabin, one of Scott's most intriguing characters, is put to death at the king's orders, so that he cannot reveal information that would be embarrassing to Louis and damaging to the delicate truce between France and Burgundy. This too has an analogue in medieval literature, namely, in *Valentine and Orson*. On one occasion Orson is falsely accused of treason and must fight against two adversaries; he kills Florent and fells Garnyere. When Haufray, a son of King Pepyn and one of the conspirators, hears Garnyere say "I haue done the treason and put a knyfe in the kinges bed" (chap. 60), he draws his sword and kills him, to keep him from talking further about the treason and implicating Haufray and his evil brother Henry. Finally, one very minor point deserves mentioning. The French battlecry *Dennis Montjoye* of the novel is eminently authentic; it can be found in *Valentine and Orson*, in *Le Petit Jehan de Saintré*, and in William Stewart Rose's *Partenopex de Blois*.

One finds throughout the novel the conflict between romance and reality, between chivalry and Machiavellianism. Readers are curiously reminded of the Tristan-story every time King Louis's unscrupulous Provost-Marshal, Tristan l'Hermite, appears on the scene. Such was the man's name, according to history; but how ironic that he, of all people, should have had the name of the famous hero of medieval romance! and what a striking way for Scott to have pointed up the demise of chivalry at the court of Louis XI! Fortunately, the forces of romance and chivalry win out. When Isabelle indicates that she will not have the Duke of Orleans for a husband, Duke Charles of Burgundy decrees that whoever brings to him the head of William de la Marck shall have her, according to the laws of chivalry. As things turn out, Ludovic Lesly kills and beheads William and thus is entitled to the prize; however, he graciously gives up the lady in favor of his nephew Quentin, who fought long and hard against William before having to leave the battle to rescue a damsel in distress. This grand event may also owe something in a topsy-turvy way to the Tristan-story. Sir Tristrem kills the dragon in Ireland and thereby is entitled to the hand of Ysonde, but he announces to the Irish court that he will give her over to King Mark, his uncle. She does not seem to care one way or the other in the Middle English poem, but in some versions of the story she is understandably disappointed.

Medieval romance is full of instances of knights winning brides by fighting against formidable adversaries, and Scott prepares from the beginning for the event that brings the novel to an end. On two occasions Lady Hameline reminds Isabelle of how the hand of her great-grandmother was won by Rhinegrave Godfrey, the "best son of chivalry," at a tournament in Strasbourg. And twice Ludovic Lesly says it has been foretold to him that he will "make the fortune of [his] house by marriage." Quentin is disappointed upon first meeting his unromantic, unchivalric uncle because he had aways imagined him to be like "some of the champions and knights-errant of whom minstrels sang, and who won crowns and kings' daughters by dint of sword and lance" (chap. 6); ironically, Ludovic Lesly, if not as Quentin had imagined him, in fact does win the hand of a fair countess by dint of arms, and it is in the best spirit of chivalry that he surrenders his claim. The Count of Crèvecœur, who tried to bring Quentin down from his cloud of romantic fantasy, accepts the fact at the end that romance and chivalry have won the day. "But why should I grudge the youth his preferment? since, after all, it is sense, firmness, and gallantry, which have put him in possession of WEALTH, RANK, and BEAUTY!"

St. Ronan's Well (1823)

In the introduction of 1832 Scott tells us that this most contemporary of all his novels (the period of 1804) is "entirely modern." I would agree that the novel's most memorable character, crabby old Meg Dods, hostess of the Cleikum Inn in the old town of St. Ronan's, is more or less modern, as are the frivolous, superficial people that reside at the new spa—Lady Penelope Penfeather, Sir Bingo and Lady Binks, the Reverend Mr. Chatterly, Dr. Quentin Quackleben, Philip Winterblossom, and all the rest—whom Scott satirizes without mercy. But is the story "entirely modern"? Well, not quite. It is true that the Reverend Josiah Cargill has long gotten over his unfulfilled affair of the heart with his patron's daughter, Augusta Bidmore, and thus he is not "like Beltenebros in the desert" (this being a name assumed by Amadis of Gaul in the wilderness at a time when he was in disgrace with Oriana); but the absent-minded clergyman as a young man certainly felt the pangs of love very intensely, maybe as intensely as did Amadis, and he became physically and emotionally ill when he heard the news that Augusta had married someone else. He is gradually able to redirect his energies into the study of medieval history, especially the Crusades; Saladin and Conrade of Montserrat, these luminaries of both history and romance, occupy his mind as much as do the people about him (as indeed they must have occupied Scott's mind, for they were about to appear as important characters in *The Talisman*).

Even so decidedly unromantic a personage as Cargill's new friend Peregrine Touchwood shows some knowledge of medieval history when he tells Mrs. Dods that upon visiting at the spa he heard so much about Frank Tyrrel, the book's hero, that he became "almost as sick of Tyrrel as William Rufus was" (chap. 15), and in the same breath he alludes also to Don Quixote. Tyrrel's half-brother, formerly known as Valentine Bulmer and now the titular Earl of Etherington, is our villain. How ironic that his Christian name should be Valentine, for he is no more like the Valentine of romance than Tristan l'Hermite, of *Quentin Durward*, is like the Tristan of romance. Apparently he knows for whom he was named, because on one awkward occasion he deceptively tells Mr. Cargill, who has recognized him as the mysterious bridegroom of seven years before, that he is "neither Valentine nor Orson" (chap. 21). So we are reminded of olden times and the world of romance sometimes if only by contrast.

Lady Penelope refers to the heroine, Clara Mowbray, as "the Dark Lady," and although Coleridge's fragmentary poem was foremost in Scott's mind (as a note indicates), Clara does resemble in a general way the dark ladies of romance. We learn from Dr. Quackleben that "what education she got was at her own hand—what reading she read was in a library full of old romances" (chap. 7). This statement is corroborated by her own discourse: "I would I had the fairy prince's quarters of mutton to toss among them if they should break out—He, I mean, who fetched water from the Fountain of Lions" (chap. 7, in reference to "The Story of Prince Ahmed and the Fairy Pari Banou," from the *Arabian Nights*); and by what we learn much later from Hannah Irwin, her former confidante: "We read these follies together, until we had fashioned out for ourselves a little world of romance, and prepared ourselves for a maze of adventures" (chap. 32). As we have seen, quite a few of Scott's interesting characters (Lucy Ashton and Waverley come immediately to mind) have difficulty coping with real life because of their over-immersion, during their formative years, in the world of romance; they are usually not so fortunate as Quentin Durward, who was also an avid reader of romance.

It was partly owing to the influence of romance that Clara, before the time of the story, was led into a secret love affair with Frank Tyrrel ("Saint" Francis, as Valentine sarcastically refers to him in a letter to his friend Captain Jekyl). What neither she nor Tyrrel knew was that Valentine, for his own reasons, was interested in her too—again, a variation of the Knight's Tale story-pattern. Tyrrel and Clara were to become man and wife in a secret marriage, but Valentine substituted himself for the bridegroom—the treachery not being noticed in the darkness of the church and because of disguises—and he and Clara were married (by the Reverend Mr. Cargill). The mistake was discovered, but too late—and in Scott's original version, which James Ballantyne insisted that he rewrite, not until the marriage had been consummated.[10] In the aftermath of this love affair gone sour, both Tyrrel and Valentine agreed to distance themselves from Clara Mowbray and leave her in peace. But when the novel begins, seven years later, both Tyrrel and Valentine are again at St. Ronan's, Valentine (as Lord Etherington) intending to pursue his claim on Clara, Tyrrel determined to keep him away from her. They even engage in an impromptu duel when they meet unexpectedly in the forest near St. Ronan's. Once again, Scott seems to have the Knight's Tale in mind, and his use of *occupatio* in chapter 20, where he tells us at great length about the preparations for the festivities at Shaws Castle while pretending to pass over them, is clearly in the manner of the Knight's account of Arcite's funeral. But the deep-seated hatred and the bitterness between the half-brothers make them seem more like Polyneices and Eteocles than Palamon and Arcite, and Scott suggests as much in a conversation involving Lady Penelope, the Reverend Mr. Chatterly, and Touchwood at the spa (in chap. 31), just before Tyrrel and Valentine meet for the first time after the shooting incident.

A few more words about the secret marriage are in order. Clara Mowbray was deceived and was married to a man she thought to be someone else. I cannot find an exact parallel in medieval romance, but this all-important incident prior to the time of the novel does recall the opening pages of the *Morte Darthur*, in which Uther Pendragon comes to the Castle of Tyntagil disguised (with the help of Merlin) as the Duke of Cornwall and makes love to the Duke's wife, Igrayne. It also has some similarity to an episode in *Florisel de Niquea*, in which "Sidonia, the queen of this country [the isle of Guinday], proposed to marry Falanges [a Greek knight]; but, as he was scrupulous in maintaining his fidelity to Alastraxare [his Amazon wife], Florisel [son of Niquea and Amadis of Greece] agreed to substitute himself in the place of his friend, and accordingly espoused her majesty under the feigned name of Moraizel. He soon after abandoned his bride" (Dunlop, 2:38). Sidonia, like Clara, did not know whom she was marrying, but apparently she did not mistake the bridegroom for his friend Falanges. Like Clara she later "conceived the most bitter resentment" against her husband—not so much, because he had deceived her, however, but because he had abandoned her. One will recall too that Sir Lancelot sleeps on a couple of occasions with Elaine (who will be the mother of his son, Sir Galahad), thinking that she is the queen and not realizing his error until later. King Mark never does realize that his sex partner on the night of his marriage was not Iseult (no longer a virgin, thanks to Tristan) but rather Brangien. Whether a closer parallel turns up or not, we are dealing here with material that has more than a passing resemblance to medieval romance.

Underlying the entire novel is the obvious motif of the undesired marriage, in a double sense. Clara's original marriage to Valentine Bulmer was wholly undesired on her part. When as the Earl of Etherington he returns to St. Ronan's after seven years and proposes either recognition of the previous marriage or a new marriage, Clara finds herself in a highly undesirable predicament. Her mind, partly unhinged by the previous betrayal, gives way when her brother brutally commands her to marry Etherington so that the dwindling fortunes of the Mowbray family may be repaired; and the tragic catastrophe ending in her death is soon at hand. Scott must have enjoyed pretending that his story was "entirely modern." He more than anyone else was fully aware that what really counts so far as emotion is concerned comes right out of the pages of medieval romance.

Redgauntlet (1824)

This much admired novel, much of it in epistolary form, is the story of two friends: Darsie Latimer, a wealthy young man who does not know his parentage and who is all too prone to flights of fancy, and the more down-to-earth Alan Fairford, a young untried barrister, son of the Edinburgh lawyer Saunders Fairford. Darsie's romantic temperament is attested by numerous allusions on his part, and Alan's, to romance. At the beginning of the story Darsie leaves Edinburgh for an excursion to the southwest of Scotland—a "wildfire chase of romantic situation and adventure," in the words of Alan, who in the same letter tries to give Darsie some plain, down-to-earth advice: "Do not think you will meet a gallant Valentine in every English rider, or an Orson in every Highland drover. View things as they are, and not as they may be magnified through thy teeming fancy" (letter 2). Later, Alan addresses his friend as "my dear Amadis" and advises him to return home. "We will beat about together," he continues, "in search of this Urganda, the Unknown She of the Green Mantle" (letter 8)—this with reference to the beautiful girl whom Darsie has encountered on one of his adventures (and who turns out to be his sister Lilias). Darsie teases Alan about the "wandering damoselle" who had come to Alan in Edinburgh to warn him of danger in store for his friend. The girl of his own life (and fantasy) is "like a princess gracing a squire of low degree"—and of course Darsie does not realize at this point in the story that the young ladies are one and the same.

Don Quixote is a favorite frame of reference for both young men. "See not a Dulcinea," Alan advises, "in every slipshod girl, who, with blue eyes, fair hair, a tattered plaid, and a willow-wand in her gripe, drives out the village cows to the loaning" (letter 2). After Darsie first sees the mystery girl, he writes, "Now, if thou expectest a fine description of this young woman, Alan Fairford, in order to entitle thee to taunt me with having found a Dulcinea in the inhabitant of a fisherman's cottage on the Solway Frith, thou shalt be disappointed" (letter 4). In another letter he alludes to "Sancho's doctor, Tirtea Fuera," in connection with the Quaker Joshua Geddes. Alan warns Darsie not to get involved in Joshua's dispute with the Laird of the Solway Lochs (who turns out to be Edward Hugh Redgauntlet, uncle of Darsie and Lilias) regarding the right way of fishing: "If you are Don Quixote enough to lay lance in rest in defence of those of the stake-net and of the sad-coloured garment, I pronounce you but a lost knight. . . . Come back, and I will be your faithful Sancho Panza upon a more hopeful quest" (letter 8). Darsie replies assuringly, "If the Tritons of the Solway shall proceed to pull down honest Joshua's tide-nets, I am neither Quixote enough in disposition, nor Goliath enough in person, to attempt their protection" (letter 10). Much later he compares a steel mask he must wear to "Quixote's visor" (chap. 9).

It is often said that Darsie epitomizes the romantic, imaginative side of Scott's own personality, while Alan represents the side of reason and good sense. So we have *Waverley* all over again, in a different mode, and the Knight's Tale with its analogous conflict between the romantic and the realistic, between passion and reason. But Chaucer's tale is more visible in other ways. *Redgauntlet* is a story about two young men equally attractive and equally worthy who are fascinated by the same girl. Unlike Chaucer, however, Scott gives his lovers quite different personalities. Moreover, it is unlikely that they would ever have fought a duel over the girl, even if she had not been Darsie's sister, for Darsie makes plain that his love for Alan "surpasses the love of woman" (letter 12). When Darsie is in captivity in England, he makes no attempt to escape, partly because he senses that the mysterious lady is "under the same roof," and it is not long before he sees her from his prison window "at the early hour of daybreak . . . in the court of the farm" (chap. 9)—this incident no doubt being inspired by the similar experience of Palamon and Arcite while they are Theseus's prisoners in

Athens. The remarkable conversation about free will and destiny that Darsie gets into with his captor, whom he knows at this point (chap. 8) not as his uncle but as Mr. Herries of Birrenswork, is clearly Boethian, as is the philosophical underpinning of much of the Knight's Tale. Finally, Scott's mildly satirical attitude toward love, in connection with Darsie's feelings toward Lilias (when, still not knowing she is his sister, he feels that she is too forward in her demeanor to him), is in the general spirit of the Knight's Tale.

The relationship between Darsie and Alan is one of perfect friendship. Darsie argues that because he and Alan can write to each other they even "have an advantage over the dear friends of old, every pair of them"; he cites David and Jonathan, Orestes and Pylades, and Damon and Pythias. He might also have included the medieval romances *Amis and Amiloun* and *Eger and Grime*. Scott knew the latter in the early printed version usually entitled *Sir Eger, Sir Grahame, and Sir Gray-Steel*, in which, interestingly, the fair lady who kindly cares for both Eger and Grahame when they are wounded and who marries first Grahame and later Eger (after Grahame's death) is named Lilias. It would be hard to imagine a more perfect friendship. "The young men were united," Scott writes, "by the closest bonds of intimacy; and the more so, that neither of them sought nor desired to admit any others into their society. Alan Fairford was averse to general company, from a disposition naturally reserved, and Darsie Latimer from a painful sense of his unknown origin. . . . The young men were all in all to each other" (chap. 1).

Like Roland Græme of *The Abbot*, and like Libeaus Desconus from medieval romance, Darsie Latimer is a fair unknown even to himself: "I am here," he writes to Alan, "and this much I know; but where I have sprung from, or whither my course of life is like to tend, who shall tell me?" (letter 7). The entire novel deals with Darsie's quest for a proper identity. As we approach the end, we learn that Darsie is the only son of Sir Henry Redgauntlet, who fought for Prince Charles Edward and was executed after the uprising of 1745 had been put down. Darsie's English mother, fearing that Henry's fanatical Jacobite brother Edward Hugh might have plans for her son, tries desperately to keep him away from his uncle, especially after Darsie's younger sister is abducted. She takes her son to Scotland, where he will be safer, and after her early death he grows up in the household of Saunders Fairford, Alan's father. Partly owing to his own free will but mainly to the force of destiny, he falls while on his "wildfire chase of romantic situation and adventure" into the hands of his uncle, who abducts and confines him and tries to win him over to the Jacobite cause in the long-planned conspiracy, fortunately abortive. The novel has a happy, romantic ending, with Alan to marry Lilias.

Other motifs as well are inspired, or seem inspired, by medieval literature and lore. The communication with Wandering Willie, by means of song and music, that Darsie achieves while in confinement has an obvious parallel from the Middle Ages: "The history of Richard Cœur de Lion and his minstrel, Blondel, rushed, at the same time, on my mind," Darsie writes in his journal (chap. 9). The stance of guardian ("captor" would be a better word) that the Laird of the Solway Lochs alias Mr. Herries of Birrenswork, actually Edward Hugh Redgauntlet, assumes toward his nephew Darsie makes him resemble some of the imperious hosts of medieval romance. When Edward Hugh moves Darsie to Joe Crackenthorp's pub toward the end of the novel, he insists that Darsie disguise himself as a young lady—so as in a number of medieval romances the hero is dressed temporarily in female attire. Earlier, when Alan Fairford receives word that Darsie has disappeared, he drops all his duties to go out and search for his friend. The Quaker Joshua Geddes does likewise. So there are two characters in search of the hero—this being a story-pattern that has a multitude of analogues in romance. One thinks immediately of the faithful Rohand, who looks far and wide for Sir Tristrem after he has been abducted by seamen, finally finding him at the court of King Mark; or of the faithful steward Heraud and his son, who search for years for Guy of Warwick's son Reinbrun after he has been abducted by merchants; or of Sir Bors, Sir Ector, and Sir Lyonell, who ride "frome contrey to contrey, in forestes and in wyldirnessys and in wastys" in search of Sir Launcelot after he has run forth insane owing to Queen Gwenyver's displeasure with him over Elaine, and has disappeared.[11]

Having mentioned Wandering Willie, I must not conclude without saying something about his haunting tale (in letter 11). Parallels between it and certain material in the *Minstrelsy of the Scottish Border* have already been pointed out.[12] Steenie Steenson's encounter in the dark woods with the strange horseman is really an encounter with the devil, and such encounters have literary analogues from Chaucer's Friar's Tale about an evil summoner and the devil to Nathaniel Hawthorne's "Young Goodman Brown." Steenie is told that the "auld Laird is disturbed in his grave by [his] curses, and the wailing of [his] family," and a long note informs us that "the belief was general throughout Scotland, that the excessive lamentation over the loss of friends disturbed the repose of the dead, and broke even the rest of the grave." Scott cites no medieval examples, but one he certainly would have known is Ovid's story of Ceyx and Alcione, as told by Gower, or by Chaucer in the *Book of the Duchess*—Alcione's lamentation over Ceyx's disappearance and probable death causing him to appear mysteriously at her bedside to urge her to accept the irreversible fact of his death and to grieve no more. Steenie's encounter in the land of the dead with the late Sir Robert Redgauntlet and his ghastly companions brings vaguely to mind Sir Orfeo's encounter, in the Middle English poem, with the King of the Celtic Otherworld and his beholding the ghastly company there who are still in the postures in which they were taken from life—somewhat like the Claverhouse in Steenie's story, who has "his left hand always on his right spule-blade, to hide the wound that the silver bullet had made." But there are no really close parallels between Wandering Willie's Tale and medieval romance, only echoes—which do, however, contribute to the wonderfully uncanny atmosphere of this unforgettable story within a story, in all ways one of Scott's finest achievements.

Just as Steenie must confront the forces of darkness before he can succeed in obtaining the all-important receipt which is his due, thereby saving himself and his family from ruin, so too must Darsie Latimer overcome the dark forces that have conspired against him: his uncle is determined to win him over to the Jacobite cause, which by the time of the novel has lost whatever luster it once had and can only lead to defeat and death. If Steenie had erred on his quest—if he had been willing to play the bagpipes which are offered him (the chanter is of white-hot steel!), if he had accepted food and drink from the ghastly company, if he had agreed to return in a year and a day to pay homage to the shade of Sir Robert—he would have been lost irrevocably. Darsie's quest begins as a madcap excursion, but it soon turns into a quest fraught with the utmost peril, like that of a knightly hero of romance, in which one false step could have destroyed him. And it is more than a quest to find out his parentage: he must find out who he is in a deeper sense—he must learn to know himself and to understand how he relates to his family, his society, and the dangerous political situation at hand. Like Steenie, Darsie Latimer emerges from his quest—his descent, if you will—a stronger person. He has proven that he is worthy of the name Redgauntlet, although not in the way his uncle had envisaged. This is a complex novel, and one might say that it is the last truly great Waverley Novel. Darsie's quest for his identity is an age-old quest. The references to medieval literature and the motifs from medieval romance give the work an added depth and dimension suggesting the timelessness of what Scott is saying.

The Betrothed (1825)

This somewhat neglected Waverley Novel, which takes place in the late twelfth century along the Welsh border, is highly indebted to medieval romance, especially the Tristan-story. The novel's young hero, Damian, out of a sense of duty, helps his forty-five-year-old uncle, Hugo de Lacy, woo the heroine, Eveline Berenger. As the reader soon realizes, however,

Damian is in love with her himself and she with him. In case the reader is not perceptive enough to see the basic similarity between the story of the novel and the Tristan-story, Scott gives a delightfully blunt hint in chapter 15: the name of Eveline's horse is Yseulte! In the next chapter, just before Eveline's betrothal to Hugo, Damian becomes ill, displaying all the usual symptoms of an ill-starred courtly lover—and in the same chapter we learn that Eveline (like Iseult) knows something about the art of healing. When Damian arrives at the betrothal, in chapter 17, he is visibly ill. "Your cheek is pale, my lord, your eye is bloodshot," old Raoul tells him—and Raoul likes the young man because he has heard that he "was a second Sir Tristrem in silvan sports by wood and river."

In chapter 20 the supposed minstrel Vidal sings to Hugo a "lay" about Ysolte, Sir Tristrem, and King Mark. "This was not the lay of love and fidelity which De Lacy would have chosen; but a feeling like shame prevented his interrupting it, perhaps because he was unwilling to yield to or acknowledge the unpleasing sensations excited by the tenor of the tale." That night in his dreams he has "some confused idea of being identified with the unlucky Mark of Cornwall" (chap. 21). Scott may have gotten from the prose Tristan the idea of having one character disturb another by singing a lay. Near the end of Malory's chapter on King Mark,[13] Sir Dynadan "makes" a highly uncomplimentary lay about Mark and teaches it to harpers, who go to Wales and Cornwall to sing it. One of the harpers sings it in the presence of Mark, who is "wondirly wrothe." In a similar situation, Scott's Hugo de Lacy is upset rather than angry; indeed the parallel between the two men goes just so far. Throughout the novel Hugo is depicted as a wiser and kindlier man than Mark, and at the end of the story he graciously resigns his claim on Eveline in favor of Damian, who, conspicuously unlike Sir Tristrem, has been totally faithful to the older man, all malicious rumors to the contrary notwithstanding. *The Betrothed* is a Tristan-and-Iseult love story with a happy ending.

Near the beginning of the story the castle of Sir Raymond de Berenger, a much respected Norman knight, is besieged by the powerful Welsh prince Gwenwyn, who is angry because his request for the hand of Raymond's daughter Eveline has been rejected. This of course is a stock situation in medieval romance. In *Sir Eglamour of Artois* a heathen giant named Marras besieges a city belonging to King Edmond in order to win the hand of his daughter Organata. Sir Eglamour comes to the rescue and slays the giant. In *Valentine and Orson* an evil "grene knyght" makes war on Duke Sauary of Acquytayne because he wants the Duke's daughter Fezonne for his wife. He gives the Duke six months to find a champion to fight against him; if he fells the champion, he is to be given Fezonne's hand in marriage. Valentine and Orson deal decisively with the challenger, and

Orson is "handfest," or betrothed, to Fezonne. In another interesting parallel with Scott's novel, however, the wedding is postponed when Valentine tells Fezonne's father that "he and Orson had vowed and promysed for to go vnto Iherusalem afore they dyde ony other thinge, after that they hadde conquered the grene knyght" (chap. 24).

At the beginning of *Le Bone Florence of Rome*, the Emperor of Constantinople, named Garcy, makes war on Otes, Emperor of Rome, because his request for the hand of Otes's daughter Florence has been rejected. Esmere and Mylys, sons of the King of Hungary, come to Rome to help out. Otes urges them not to fight with the enemy on the field:

> Syr Mylys seyde the emperowre too,
> And ye wolde at my councell doo,
>   Ye schoulde not fyght in fylde,
> But close the yatys, and the brygges up drawe,
> And kepe us clene owt of ther awe,
>   And owre wepons wyghtly welde:
> And kepe the town bothe nyght and day,
> Tyl they be wery and wende away:
>   Syr Emere hym behelde.
>
> Emere seyde Mylys unto,
> So myght a sympull grome do,
>   Kepe an holde wythynne;
> But we wyll manly to the felde,
> And syr Garcy batell yelde,
>   To morne or that we blynne.
>   [Ritson's text, lines 529-43]

As in *The Betrothed*, this chivalric encounter leads to disaster, and to the death of Otes. Scott's story differs in that it is the heroine's father, Raymond de Berenger, who wants to fight the enemy in chivalric fashion on the plain and who is killed there by the rejected suitor. Vaguer parallels are evident too when Esmere eventually marries Florence and becomes Emperor of Rome, but she will not let their marriage be consummated until he has avenged her father's death by killing Garcy. While Esmere is away, Mylys falsely accuses Florence of adultery. The postponement of real marriage and the false accusation are apropos, but the rest of the story-material in *Le Bone Florence of Rome* is completely different from *The Betrothed*.

Raymond de Berenger insists on fighting the Welsh on the plain, even though the odds are very much against him, because he once promised Gwenwyn that if "a prince of the Cymry shall again come in hostile fashion before the Garde Doloureuse, let him pitch his standard down in yonder plain by the bridge, and, by the word of a good knight and the faith of a Christian man, Raymond Berenger will meet him as willingly, be he many or be he few, as ever Welshman was met withal" (chap. 3). As Raymond himself realizes, this was a rash promise, but he feels honor-bound to abide by it. The rash promise, a motif common in medieval literature, leads here into the novel's philosophical content: namely, the conflict between the chivalric and the practical, which occurs in one form or another in several Waverley Novels. Raymond's strict adherence to a promise brings about not only his own death but also the deaths of many loyal followers; he could have won if he and his men had remained within the walls of the castle until help arrived. Yet, although everyone realizes the hopelessness of the situation, no one finds fault with Raymond's decision. In fact, his loyal squire Dennis Morolt pleads with Raymond to reverse an order that he stay behind in the castle and to allow him to fight along with the others. Larry Benson reminds us that King John of France lost the battle of Poitiers and James IV lost at Flodden Field because of their adherence to principles of chivalry, for which they were *praised* by their contemporaries.[14] And Scott never says that what Raymond did was not right.

While the castle is under siege Eveline de Berenger makes a solemn promise to the Virgin Mary that she will honor the wishes of the leader who frees her from this peril, even if he should request her hand in marriage. In a sense this too is a rash promise. Not only is Hugo de Lacy old enough to be her father, but his personal appearance is not attractive enough to captivate the fancy of a young lady. Nevertheless, when she learns that Hugo wants the marriage and that it was the wish of her father as well, Eveline feels honor-bound to comply, even though it brings almost unbearable psychological pressure upon herself and Damian. A strange feeling gradually comes over Eveline, like Malory's Balin, that whenever she tries to do good it turns out badly, that she brings sorrow to everyone with whom she comes in contact. The name of the castle is the Garde Doloureuse, which is suggested partly by Malory's Joyus Garde and partly by the *dolorous* stroke smitten unwittingly by Balin when he was trying to do good. Merlin prophesies correctly that Balin will kill the person whom he loves most in the whole world, and things come dangerously close to tragedy in *The Betrothed*. After her frightening encounter in the haunted chamber at Baldringham with the Bahr-Geist, whose discomforting prophecy weighs heavily on her mind, Eveline is fearful of the worst.[15]

Some of the characters' names also have an aura of romance about them. The name Raymond recalls the honorable Raymond de Lusignan of the Melusine story. Raymond de Berenger's squire is Dennis Morolt, whose family name might have come from the pages of the Tristan-story; but what a contrast between the faithful Dennis and the Morolt whom

Tristan kills! The name of our young hero recalls the Damian of Chaucer's Merchant's Tale—who is squire to the old knight January and falls in love with January's beautiful young wife May, undergoing the sickness experienced by most men in stories of courtly love. Further evidence that the Merchant's Tale was on Scott's mind can be seen in the relationship of the old huntsman Raoul, who is likened to January, and his flirtatious wife Gillian, who is considerably younger, yet "past the delicate bloom of youthful May" (chap. 17).[16] But again, what a contrast between Damian de Lacy and Chaucer's Damian, who is not prevented by conscience or honor from having sex with May in a pear tree! Damian de Lacy's code of honor prevents him from expressing his love for Eveline; it locks him into a pattern of action that brings on psychological harm and even physical illness. Yet if he had *not* acted in a chivalric manner, Scott implies, things assuredly would have been worse.

The other side in the conflict between the chivalric and the practical is best represented by the Flemings Wilkin Flammock and his daughter Rose. As Eveline's best friend and lady-in-waiting, Rose tries from time to time to get her mistress to abandon her high-flown principles and look at her situation realistically. Wilkin Flammock runs a fulling-mill near the Garde Doloureuse, and he has the task of defending the castle after the defeat and death of Raymond de Berenger. A man of enviable ability and good common sense, he is as brave as Raymond de Berenger and Dennis Morolt but not one to throw his life away in a hopeless cause. In one conversation Flammock does show a passing knowledge of medieval romance—mentioning specifically Charlemagne, King Arthur, the Knight of the Swan, and the Castle Tintagel—but he is incurably skeptical of the chivalric code. He declines Hugo's proposal that he be Eveline's guardian while Hugo is off in the Holy Land: "I would not undertake to be guardian to the chaste Susannah, though she lived in an enchanted castle which no living thing could approach" (chap. 21).

Hugo de Lacy, the novel's most prominent character, is an interesting mixture of the chivalric and the practical. Before the time of the story Hugo distinguished himself in a great tournament at Chester, where he is constable, and assigned the prize he won to Eveline because of her beauty—in true chivalric fashion. And after his decision to go to Palestine, "Hugo de Lacy, hitherto rather an unimpassioned lover, stood in [Eveline's] presence with feelings as if all the exaggerations of romance were realised, and his mistress were a being of a higher sphere, from whose doom he was to receive happiness or misery, life or death" (chap. 19). When he returns to England after three years in the Holy Land, he finds his nephew imprisoned, his betrothed suspected of adultery, and his affairs in shambles. Like many a hero of romance he must strive to gain back what is rightfully his; in doing so he assumes the conventional disguise of a pilgrim in order to test (like Sir Orfeo) the fidelity of various people, first of Raoul and Gillian and finally of Damian. The practical side of his personality comes out most memorably in his debate with Archbishop Baldwin over whether he must indeed go on the crusade (chap. 18). Scott's story material here was partly inspired, I think, by an eighty-eight-line poetic fragment entitled "The Crusaders," translated from "Les Croisades" (Le Grand, 2:163-70) and ultimately from a poem by Rutebeuf (see Way, appendix to vol. 2), which is essentially a debate between a crusader and a noncrusader over the merits and demerits of crusades. Hugo is understandably reluctant to be separated from his newly betrothed; he is like the poem's noncrusader in his hesitance to leave his family and possessions unprotected, in his dissatisfaction at being told that an immortal soul is reward enough for his labor, and in his suspicion that ecclesiastics reap the tangible rewards of the crusaders' brave efforts.

Obviously, there is much more medieval literature in the background to *The Betrothed* than Scott's introduction of 1832, with its emphasis on the ballad about the Noble Moringer (with liberal quotations from Scott's own translation), would lead us to believe. The Welsh episodes in Froissart's *Meliador* have similar story material, with Meliador coming to the rescue of ladies living in the march area who are desperately trying to defend their estates and inheritance against Welsh invaders, who do not understand the principles of chivalry; but I have found no evidence that Scott knew this long verse romance by the chronicler whom he so much admired.

The Talisman (1825)

The second of Scott's popular Tales of the Crusaders owes much to historical accounts of the Third Crusade but also to medieval romance. *Richard Coer de Lyon* engages one's attention first, since Scott cites it in his introduction of 1832 and since much of it deals directly with Richard's feats in the Holy Land.[17] As in the novel, Richard falls sick of a fever; but instead of being treated by the Saracen physician El Hakim (who is Saladin in disguise), he eats a roasted Saracen's head, thinking it is pork, and drinks the broth from it. In both romance and novel he falls into a deep sleep thereafter and is well again when he awakens. Scott's Thomas de Vaux, a blunt soldier absolutely loyal to Richard, is the same man as the Thomas de Multon of the romance, who accompanies Richard to Palestine and is always "noticed with distinction." Richard's distrust of Conrade of Montserrat has a parallel in the romance, as does his enmity toward King Philip of France, whom he considers devious and cowardly. The trouble with the Duke of Austria over a banner also has a parallel in the romance, but the circumstances are quite different: Richard has a run-in with the Duke when he refuses to help in the rebuilding of the walls of the town Chaloyn. Richard insists that he "remove his banner from the wall," and when he declines to do so Richard knocks him prostrate on the ground, accuses him of being a lazy glutton, and tells him he will "destroy [his] vile banner, / and cast it in the foul river."[18] Richard's proposal to Saladin at the end of the novel that they fight in single combat to decide once and for all the fate of Palestine is suggested by an encounter between the two leaders in the romance. Besides providing an account other than the romance's of how Richard is cured, Scott omits altogether the notorious episode in which Richard serves stewed Saracen heads to Saladin's ambassadors and is amused at their reaction; however, both cannibalistic passages are quoted at length (from Ellis) in an appendix.

The novel's heroine, Edith Plantagenet, kinswoman to Richard, is not an historical personage, but Scott no doubt was thinking of Richard's sister Joanna, widow of the King of Sicily. The plan for her to marry Saladin's brother Malek-Adel, to which she vigorously objected, lies behind the abortive negotiation in the novel for Edith to marry Saladin. The idea of a Christian princess on the verge of marrying a sultan can be found in romance. On one occasion in *Tirant lo Blanch* when the Turks are victorious, they propose a marriage between their sultan and Carmesina, daughter of the aged Emperor of Constantinople and ladylove of Tirant. Fortunately for the lovers, the Emperor rejects the proposal, saying "that he would not give his daughter in marriage to a man who was not of the Christian faith."[19] In the Man of Law's Tale the Emperor of Rome actually does marry his daughter off to a sultan, who accepts the Christian faith and is baptized—as the proposers of Edith's marriage to Saladin expected of him—but readers of Chaucer will recall that the sultan's mother was not very happy about either the marriage or the change of religion, and much trouble ensued. The plans for Edith are in a sense a variation of the motif of the undesired marriage: Edith certainly does not want it, nor does Sir Kenneth.

Sir Kenneth, the Knight of the Leopard, is the novel's romantic hero (although it can be argued that Saladin is the real hero); at the end he is revealed as David, Earl of Huntingdon, the heir presumptive to the crown of Scotland—who in the annals of history was already married before he joined the crusade. Most of what Scott says about him is fictitious. At first we are teased into believing that he is a "squire of low degree," but as the plot thickens, we see him playing the traditional role of the fair unknown. Like Sir Gareth he deliberately conceals his identity and seeks to prove on his own that he is worthy of his rank. The motif of enmity and reconciliation is at play here as well: Sir Kenneth incurs the enmity of King Richard when the English banner disappears that he had been ordered to guard. Kenneth must then undergo a period of probation, during which he manages to reinstate himself and to prove that he is indeed worthy of Richard's esteem. Much of this time he is in Richard's camp disguised as a black Nubian slave, because Richard, having turned him over to El Hakim, has forbidden him ever to return. The motif of a hero disguising himself as a black person and returning to a forbidden place can be found in the account of St. James of Spain, in *The Seven Champions* (chap. 5); but Kenneth's reasons for doing so are more complicated: he wants to prove his worth to Richard as well as see his ladylove. His relationship with Edith is in some ways typical of a courtly love relationship. Edith is the source of all his most noble thoughts and deeds, and she is not easily won. Pretending all along that he is only a humble knight, Kenneth puts her on a pedestal, worshipping her usually from afar and always with the utmost respect. He gets into trouble when what appears to be a whimsical wish on her part conflicts with his bounden duty to guard the English banner. Returning to Saint George's Mount after having been lured to the tent of the females, he finds the banner gone and his faithful dog wounded almost to death.

This remarkable dog, this "large stag greyhound," this "sagacious animal"—who is named Roswal after the hero of the romance *Roswall and Lillian*—plays a major part in the action. In some ways he is reminiscent of the lion that is the inseparable companion of Sir Ywain; in his ability to go out hunting on his own for his master, he recalls Sir Tristrem's faithful dog Hodain. His big moment comes when he recognizes Conrade of Montserrat as the culprit who wounded him and stole the English banner: "Roswal, the noble hound, uttering a furious and savage yell, sprang forward. The Nubian [Sir Kenneth in disguise], at the same time, slipped the leash, and the hound, rushing on, leapt upon Conrade's noble charger, and, seizing the Marquis by the throat, pulled him down from the saddle. The plumed rider lay rolling on the sand" (chap. 24). In *Sir Triamour* a faithful greyhound recognizes after several years the man who had attempted to seduce the queen and who had killed his master; he seizes the villain by the throat when he is at the dinner table and kills him. Even closer to Scott is the seventy-eighth tale in the *Gesta Romanorum*, which involves a greyhound recognizing at dinner the man who had killed his master and pouncing on him; this remarkable occurrence leads to a solemn trial by combat between the villain (whose name is Macharie) *and the dog,* who grabs Macharie's staff with his teeth, pulls him down from his horse to the ground, and holds him tightly by the throat until Macharie cries out for mercy. Not only does Scott's story involve a dog who recognizes a villain and pulls him off his horse, but there is a trial by combat between the villain and the dog's master: Sir Kenneth soundly defeats Conrade in the lists at the Diamond of the Desert, before thousands of spectators both Christian and Saracen.[20]

The fight in the opening chapter between Sir Kenneth and Sheerkohf (*alias* El Hakim, actually Saladin) ends in a manner typical of Malory, with the combatants ceasing hostilities and assuming a friendly attitude toward each other. "It is not worthwhile preserving any permanent enmity against a foe," Scott explains in the next chapter, "whom a champion has fought with to-day, and may again stand in bloody opposition to on the next morning. The time and situation afforded so much room for the ebullition of violent passions, that men, unless when peculiarly opposed to each other, or provoked by the recollection of private and individual wrongs, cheerfully enjoyed in each other's society the brief intervals of pacific intercourse which a warlike life admitted."

There are several specific references to the Arthurian stories. The female dwarf who appears to Kenneth in the chapel of Engaddi is named Guenevra, and she pretends that her male companion, Nectabanus, is "King Arthur of Britain, whom the fairies stole away from the field of Avalon" (chap. 5). In fact, however, he is like many a mischievous dwarf in the *Morte Darthur* and other romances, and he is named after the father of Alexander the Great in medieval romances and stories about Alexander. Near the end of the novel, when Richard is in good spirits owing to the arrival of Blondel, his favorite minstrel, De Vaux decides to remain in the King's presence and hear Blondel's glee, although he really does not care much for this sort of entertainment. "To see your Majesty in such a cheerful mood . . . by my faith, I could remain till Blondel had achieved the great Romance of King Arthur, which lasts for three days." Richard replies, "We will not tax your patience so deeply" (chap. 26). In the very next chapter, after severing a thick steel mace with one blow of his broadsword,[21] Richard is asked by Saladin whether he could sever a cushion with the same sword. "No, surely," he responds. "No sword on earth, were it the Excalibar of King Arthur, can cut that which opposes no steady resistance to the blow." Saladin then proceeds to perform the feat with his scimitar.

Although Scott has no specific references to Chaucer in *The Talisman*, one cannot help thinking of the framework of the *Canterbury Tales* when the supposed physician El Hakim and his entourage, including the disgraced Sir Kenneth, are entertained by the story teller Hassan while they are all riding away from the Christian camp on their horses and camels. "At another time, notwithstanding his imperfect knowledge of the language, Sir Kenneth might have been interested in the recitation, which, though dictated by a more extravagant imagination and expressed in more inflated and metaphorical language, bore yet a strong resemblance to the romances of chivalry, then so fashionable in Europe" (chap. 22). In this observation Scott shows his knowledge of the relationship between the romances from the Middle East and those of Europe—a subject that still commands attention at conferences of medievalists. In the final chapter it is hard not to think of Chaucer's Pardoner when the wicked Grand Master of the Templars says to Conrade of Montserrat, after having insisted that *he* rather than the Hermit of Engaddi should be hearing Conrade's confession, "The absolution of the wicked priest is as effectual as if he were himself a saint." I have already commented on the similarity in story material between the opening stanzas of the Man of Law's Tale and the plans for a marriage between Edith and Saladin, but Scott makes no reference to the story of Constance.

Among other possible echoes from medieval literature, Scott's very striking opening description of the Dead Sea and its environs has a parallel in the Middle English poem *Cleanness* (or *Purity*), which I have no evidence that he knew; but he probably was familiar with a similar description in the *Travels* of John Mandeville, whom he mentions in the introduction to *The Betrothed*. The dreamlike atmosphere in the description of the Hermit of Engaddi's cave and chapel vaguely recalls some medieval dream poems, like the *House of Fame* and Lydgate's *Temple of Glas*; and the beautiful service Sir Kenneth witnesses may owe something, again in a vague way, to medieval stories about the Holy Grail.[22] Edith cites medieval lore in a heated altercation with Richard when she says that "the spotless virgin fears not the raging lion" (chap. 17). And the pleading on the part of virtually everyone that Sir Kenneth's life be spared impels Richard to exclaim: "By Saint Louis, it reminds me of Blondel's tale of an enchanted castle, where the destined knight was withstood successively in his purpose of entrance by forms and figures the most dissimilar, but all hostile to his undertaking! No sooner one sank than another appeared! Wife, kinswoman, hermit, Hakim, each appears in the lists as soon as the other is defeated! Why, this is a single knight fighting against the whole mêlée of the tournament—ha! ha! ha!" (chap. 18). Throughout the novel Scott stresses the magnanimity and chivalry of Saladin, who puts the Christians to shame with their endless quarreling and bickering among themselves. Scott may have been influenced by the poem "The Order of Knighthood" (Way, vol. 1), which is concerned with Saladin's magnanimity towards his captive Sir Hugh of Tabaria, but a charitable attitude toward Saracens is not infrequently expressed by medieval writers, even Langland. In the last chapter the evil Templar murders Conrade of Montserrat (after Conrade has been defeated in judicial combat by Sir Kenneth) so that he will not be able to tell on his deathbed about their conspiracy. This dastardly act has an obvious analogue in *Valentine and Orson* when the false Garnyere, having been vanquished in judicial combat by Orson, admits his treason and is suddenly killed by Pepyn's son Haufray, his fellow-conspirator (see the discussion of the execution of Hayraddin Maugrabin in *Quentin Durward*, above).

With the two Tales of the Crusaders we come to the end of the novels of Scott's high-noon period. Both are heavily indebted to medieval romance, and they invite comparison with each other and with *Ivanhoe*. Although *The Talisman* has been from the outset more popular, I prefer *The Betrothed* because of the subtlety with which Scott has portrayed the dilemma caused by overly zealous adherence to the chivalric code—which, we are told in *The Talisman*, "proposed objects and courses of action inconsistent with the frailties and imperfections of man" (chap. 12). Both books fall short of Scott's achievement in *Ivanhoe*, partly because they lack the vivid characters which Scott gave us in the earlier novel. Eveline de Berenger and Edith Plantagenet may be as interesting as Lady Rowena, but they are nothing beside Rebecca; and Hugo de Lacy, perhaps the most carefully drawn character in the Crusader novels, does not captivate the reader's imagination in the way Brian de Bois-Guilbert does. The medieval material that worked so wondrously well in *Ivanhoe* has worked again, certainly, but in *The Betrothed* and *The Talisman* one misses the luster, the freshness, the zest, the imagination, and the psychological truth of the earlier great novel. Perhaps one can say the same in general about other novels of the high-noon period in comparison with Scott's best earlier novels.

It comes as no great surprise that Scott is highly indebted to Chaucer and medieval romance in his novels that are set in the Middle Ages. What does surprise, and is especially worthy of comment, is that with the important exception of *The Fortunes of Nigel* the medieval influence is almost equally prominent in the novels set long afterwards. This observation applies also to the early novels and those of the broken years—and, as we shall see, to the novels of the dark days and servitude.

6

NOVELS OF THE DARK DAYS AND SERVITUDE
1826-1832

MUCH OF the work that Scott did after his financial collapse has genuine merit, despite the feverish haste with which he was writing in a gallant attempt to pay off his enormous debt. Moreover, in these last seven years he endured the personal sorrow of the death of his wife and then suffered a series of strokes, making one wonder all the more at his impressive achievement. In *Woodstock* he returned to the conflict between Cavaliers and Roundheads, which he had already treated in *Old Mortality* and *Peveril of the Peak*, but set the story in a somewhat earlier period. Almost everything else is set in the Middle Ages: medieval Scotland (in *The Fair Maid of Perth* and *Castle Dangerous*), fifteenth-century Burgundy and Switzerland (in *Anne of Geierstein*), and eleventh-century Constantinople (in *Count Robert of Paris*). The exceptions here are the first Chronicles of the Canongate—comprising "The Highland Widow," "The Two Drovers," and *The Surgeon's Daughter*—and his final, still unpublished novel, *The Siege of Malta*, which takes place in the second half of the sixteenth century. Whether set in medieval times or not, however, most of these works of Scott's last period owe much to the literature of the Middle Ages.

Woodstock (1826)

On the title page of this novel's first edition there is an often quoted verse from Chaucer's description of the Knight in the General Prologue; it is spelled in Modern English: "He was a very perfect gentle Knight." This refers to Sir Henry Lee, the loyal old Cavalier who is one of the story's principal characters. It has special significance inasmuch as Scott, as Edgar Johnson has shown,[1] has put something of himself into the old loyalist, who fears he will be driven forth from his home at Woodstock, just as Scott himself feared, at the beginning of this most trying time of his life, that he might lose Abbotsford. Another reference to the General Prologue comes in the church scene of the opening chapter, when Scott describes the "pretty daughters" attending the Presbyterian service, "whose study, like that of Chaucer's physician, was not always in the Bible." Later, when the strange happenings at Woodstock are in full swing, Joshua Bletson, one of Cromwell's commissioners, tries to explain them away as dreams. In doing so he quotes Chaucer, who "lays the whole blame of our nocturnal disturbance on superfluity of humours"; the "humour of Melancholy," for example,

> Causeth many a man in sleep to cry
> For fear of great bulls and bears black,
> And others that black devils will them take.

Pertelote speaks these lines to Chauntecleer in the Nun's Priest's Tale, just after he has told her of his disturbing dream about the fox. Bletson does not quote Chaucer very precisely—or very persuasively, either, since "his pale face and shaking limbs, belied the assumed courage with which he spoke" (chap. 16).

The novel is full of medieval touches of one sort or another. We are told in chapter 29 that Joseph Tomkins, the zealous Independent who seizes the pulpit from the Rev. Nehemiah Holdenough in the opening scene at church, was a quite different sort of man in earlier years, with his "deer-stealing, orchard-robbing, drunken gambols, and desperate affrays" (Scott playing here with the familiar medieval *topos* of misspent youth); now, however, he has assumed a righteous character, even feeling obliged on one occasion to criticize Shakespeare's plays: "Seeks a wife a foul example for adultery, here she shall find it—Would a man know how to train his fellow to be a murderer, here shall he find tutoring— . . . Would you be drunk, Shakespeare will cheer you with a cup—Would you plunge in sensual pleasures, he will soothe you to indulgence" (chap. 3)—the invective being very reminiscent of Roger Ascham's famous condemnation of Malory for too much "open manslaughter and bold bawdry." When the clergyman upbraids the Mayor of Woodstock for not having "striven a little more" to oust Tomkins from the usurped pulpit, the mayor replies with an allusion to two famous heroes from medieval romance: "Guy of Warwick, or Bevis of Hampton, might do something with this generation; but truly, they are too many and too strong for the Mayor of Woodstock" (chap. 10). Bevis, moreover, is the name of Sir Henry's loyal wolfdog, a prized animal that plays almost as important a role in *Woodstock* as Roswal does in *The*

Talisman. He is "tawny-coloured like a lion," Scott writes, reminding us of Sir Ywain's faithful lion and other animal companions of medieval romance.

If one must pick a hero, I suppose it is Colonel Markham Everard, Sir Henry Lee's nephew, who is in love with Alice Lee, Sir Henry's daughter. Because he is a follower of Oliver Cromwell, we have the usual complication in Scott of a hero with divided loyalties. One morning he looks out at an area formerly well kept but now conspicuous with "untrimmed hedges and neglected walks":

This had been a favourite scene of Markham's sports when a boy. He could still distinguish, though now grown out of shape, the verdant battlements of a Gothic castle, all created by the gardener's shears, at which he was accustomed to shoot his arrows; or, stalking before it like the knight-errants of whom he read, was wont to blow his horn, and bid defiance to the supposed giant or Paynim knight by whom it was garrisoned. He remembered how he used to train his cousin, though several years younger than himself, to bear a part in these revels of his boyish fancy, and to play the character of an elfin page, of a fairy, or an enchanted princess. He remembered, too, many particulars of their later acquaintance, from which he had been almost necessarily led to the conclusion, that from an early period their parents had entertained some idea that there might be a well-fitted match betwixt his fair cousin and himself. [Chap. 6]

The passage shows that Markham Everard and Alice Lee were destined for each other even in childhood—like Julian Peveril and Alice Bridgenorth, Amadis and Oriana, and other lovers from romance. But now, although Everard still hopes somehow to marry Alice Lee, he has tried to cast off "the wild spirit of romantic chivalry"—which is a major component of both his uncle's personality and that of his friend Roger Wildrave, also a passionate Royalist albeit somewhat dissipated—and to accept the events of history that have put Cromwell at England's helm, believing that to do so is the only safe way to prevent further spilling of English blood.

In a sense the novel is a medley of motifs typical of medieval romance. When Albert Lee returns to Woodstock in chapter 19, his father Sir Henry, thinking he is an intruder, makes a pass at him with his rapier. Albert is not hurt, but when Joceline Joliffe, a loyal forester in Sir Henry's service, exclaims, "Lord in Heaven, he has slain his own son!" Sir Henry falls into a swoon and for a moment is feared to be dead. It is a variation of the father-and-son fight, in this case the father not recognizing the son. In the preceding chapter Alice goes out alone from the castle to get a pitcher of water from Rosamond's well. (There are many allusions to the amours of King Henry II and fair Rosamond, whom he kept at Woodstock.) She encounters there an ugly, gypsy-looking woman who frightens her—and who turns out, we learn later, to be young King Charles, who is trying to elude his pursuers in the aftermath of the defeat of the Royalist forces at Worcester (in 1651). For a hero to be dressed as a woman is a motif common enough in medieval romance; and Alice's meeting with a grotesque figure at a lonely well is virtually a parody of the situation in romance in which a human being, usually a man, alone and in "obstructive circumstances," encounters a fairylike female creature. Here the mortal is female and the strange creature is the one who is in obstructive circumstances. Although there is no *rescue* in the nick of time, the king does *escape* just in time from Woodstock, when word comes that Cromwell and his men are in the vicinity.

I do not know to what extent Scott was familiar with the *De Regimine Principum* literature of the Middle Ages. He seems not to have known Hoccleve's *Regement of Princes* (although a manuscript was available to him), and he never alludes specifically to the instruction for princes in Book VII of Gower's *Confessio Amantis*. But just as Lydgate in the *Siege of Thebes* gives advice to kings and princes indirectly in his depiction of his hero, Tydeus, who has all the qualities a good prince should have (and which are conspicuously lacking in Polyneices and Eteocles), so too does Scott express his ideas about kingship in the remarks especially of Albert and Alice Lee. When asked "for some account of his Majesty's character" (chap. 22), Albert, who knows all along that the supposed young page Louis Kerneguy is really Charles Stuart, says guardedly to his father and sister, in Kerneguy's presence: "If the King had not possessed enterprise and military skill, he never would have attempted the expedition to Worcester;—had he not had personal courage, he had not so long disputed the battle that Cromwell almost judged it lost. That he possesses prudence and patience must be argued from the circumstances attending his flight; and that he has the love of his subjects is evident, since, necessarily known to many, he has been betrayed by none."

Alice, not knowing at this point that Charles is in their midst, goes further than her brother when she tells how she imagines the king to be: "He shall have all the chivalrous courage, all the warlike skill, of Henry of France, his grandfather, in order to place him on the throne;—all his benevolence, love of his people, patience even of unpleasing advice, sacrifice of his own wishes and pleasures to the commonweal, that, seated there, he may be blest while living, and so long remembered when dead, that for ages after it shall be thought sacrilege to breathe an aspersion against the throne which he has occupied!" She wishes him, furthermore, to be like his late father—"temperate, wise, and frugal, yet munificent in rewarding merit—a friend to letters and the muses, but a severe discourager of the misuse of such gifts—a worthy gentleman—a kind master—the best friend, the best father, the best Christian." She learns otherwise of him in chapter 26, when he reveals his identity and true colors and attempts to seduce her. Maintaining her composure and dignity, she takes the occasion to give him a lot of good, wholesome advice.

Charles does have a better side. His magnanimity comes out in chapter 28 when he reveals himself to Markham Everard—a Roundhead—in order to prevent a breakup of Everard's relationship with Alice, which Charles has now learned to appreciate. He knows his friends will laugh at him, "but, oddsfish! let them laugh as they will, there is something at my heart which tells me that for once in my life I have acted well." Charles Stuart is a better man because of his experiences at Woodstock, and he has had the schooling to be a better king. In a special sense, then, Scott's *Woodstock* belongs to a tradition in literature that goes back to the Middle Ages and even earlier; like Lydgate's *Siege of Thebes* it presents indirectly and unobtrusively a concept of what proper kingship should be; it is Scott's *De Regimine Principum*.

Chronicles of the Canongate, First Series (1827)

The important works in this collection are "The Highland Widow," "The Two Drovers," and the short novel *The Surgeon's Daughter*; they are held very loosely together by a framework (rather unlike that of the *Canterbury Tales* and other medieval collections) in which Chrystal Croftangry, a crusty old bachelor and antiquary, is the principal personage. In his youth Croftangry behaved like many a young man from the pages of medieval literature in that he "devoured his patrimony," wasted his time with "reiving companions," and "wrecked a dainty estate, and brought harlots to the door-cheek of his father's house, till he made it nae residence for his mother." So says his mother's former servant, Christie Steele, whom the reformed and older Croftangry visits incognito, only to find that she still bears a relentless grudge against him because of his misspent youth. The interview is a virtual parody of the stock situation in romance in which the faithful servant tearfully embraces the returning master. Croftangry then decides to settle in the Canongate, where he had hidden from creditors in his youth—"the very portion of the Canongate in which I had formerly been immured, like the errant knight, prisoner in some enchanted castle, where spells have made the ambient air impervious to the unhappy captive, although the organs of sight encountered no obstacle to his free passage."

Croftangry tells us that he got the story of "The Highland Widow" from a Mrs. Bethune Baliol—who, in her introductory chapter, tries to enhance what she is about to tell by allusions to medieval romance and history and to classical legends. Her guide in the Highlands chooses "such halting-places as Le Sage or Cervantes would have described"; the mountain Cruachan Ben reminds her of Robert Bruce's near annihilation of "the warlike clan of MacDougal of Lorn"; and she tells us that Elspat MacTavish, the Highland Widow, is looked on by the Highlanders as the Greeks regarded Orestes and Oedipus and people pursued by the Furies: that is, "as being the less voluntary perpetrators of their crimes than as the passive instruments by which the terrible decrees of Destiny had been accomplished."

The story of Elspat MacTavish is of a mother's scheme, tragically successful, to prevent her son Hamish from joining the military unit in which he has just enlisted; the result is his killing of the leader of the soldiers who come to get him, followed by his capture and inevitable execution. As Hamish approaches his mother's hut to bid her a last farewell, he is met by a strange man dressed like himself in Highland fashion who warns him by gestures not to return to his mother but to depart at once. The person then vanishes, apparently, and Hamish is convinced that he has seen the ghost of his father, MacTavish Mhor—who thus is like the warning apparitions so often to be found in medieval and earlier literature. The means by which Elspat accomplishes her design is a sleeping potion, one of several sorts of potions that figure prominently in medieval romance. When Hamish awakens and becomes aware of what has happened, Elspat tries to persuade him with "energy of language somewhat allied to hyperbole" to flee with her far northward, where things will be much better for both of them; and near the end of the story, when she finds out from a Protestant clergyman that Hamish is dead, she curses him in equally energetic and rhetorical language—both passages resembling the inpassioned set speeches of medieval and early sixteenth-century prose romances and helping to give the story resonance beyond its immediate time and place.

The next story, "The Two Drovers," told by Chrystal Croftangry himself, is one of Scott's finest achievements; nowhere does he present more concisely or more poignantly the difference between Scottish and English mentality. This splendid story shows no obvious influence of either Chaucer or medieval romance, although one might compare the opening description of Harry Wakefield, with its really important detail (his irascibility, which brings about the fatal conflict with his Scottish friend, Robin Oig) coming at the end, with Chaucer's Clerk's description of Walter, Marquis of Saluzzo. In both, the telling detail is saved for last: Harry's irascibility, and the admission that "in somme thynges" Walter "was to blame." One also finds more than a few instances in medieval romance of good friends, such as Sir Lancelot and Sir Gawain, becoming bitter enemies.

Novels of the Dark Days and Servitude

In *The Surgeon's Daughter* Scott again uses the motif of two friends—Adam Hartley and Richard Middlemas, young apprentices to Dr. Gideon Gray, the surgeon in Middlemas—falling out and becoming enemies; but here a girl is involved, the surgeon's rather colorless daughter, Menie, so again we have the Knight's Tale story-pattern of two young men in love with the same uninteresting girl. The two youths are hardly equally attractive, however, and the girl unwisely chooses the unattractive suitor, who has been part of the surgeon's household from infancy and has grown up with the daughter. Thus Scott sets the stage for an ideal romantic relationship from childhood, like that of Amadis and Oriana, but then he surprises us by depicting the man as totally unworthy of his ladylove. Even if Menie had not been on the scene, Adam and Richard would no doubt eventually have fallen out with each other because Richard is arrogant, ungrateful, greedy, abrasive, and downright mean. The conflict between Adam and Richard is one of reason and decency and good common sense against romanticism gone bad—again a variation of one of Scott's favorite themes.

The circumstances of Richard's birth fit the story-pattern of a male child who is born in mysterious circumstances, is separated from his parents at a very early age, and grows up not knowing who he really is. An unknown man of wealth and his consort appear suddenly in Middlemas, the lady about to go into labor. She gives birth to a male child at the home of Dr. Gray. The child's father then departs, promising to return in ten days but not doing so. The lady's irate father, a wealthy Jew, then arrives on the scene and takes her away with him, leaving the child with Dr. Gray and sending money from time to time but stipulating that his grandson should never try to make contact with him. Richard eventually does find his parents, almost by coincidence, but the climax in chapter 8 is hardly the happy recognition and reunion scene of romance: his mother is so emotionally upset that she dies; his father flies into uncontrolled rage and banishes his son from his sight. Since his parents were not properly married at the time of his birth, Richard has no legal claim on any inheritance, which will pass on to the two legitimate children.

The scene then shifts to India, where Richard seeks a fast fortune and Adam is practicing medicine. Richard entices Menie Gray (her father having died) into coming to India; he makes her think that he will marry her but actually plans to place her in the harem of the Indian prince Tippo Saib, hoping to gain Tippo's trust so that he can more readily betray him to the British and thereby regain lost favor and rank. This is the old motif of a Christian girl in need of rescue from marriage or worse with an infidel. "A lover of romance might have meditated some means of effecting her release by force or address," Scott writes in the final chapter, "but Hartley, though a man of courage, had no spirit of adventure, and would have regarded as desperate any attempt of the kind." Fortunately, Adam procures the help of Tippo's father, Hyder Ali, the Rajah of Mysore, who arrives at a timely moment, thwarts his son's plans, and assumes absolute control of the situation. The rajah appears to be honoring his son's promises to Richard. A throng of people are present in this exciting scene at Bangalore, including many of the novel's important characters: Tippo, Hyder Ali, Adela de Montreville (Richard's mistress), Menie Gray, and of course the rival lovers Adam and Richard. At this point "a horse [is] led forward, as the Prince's gift" to Richard. Readers familiar with Scott's indebtedness to the Knight's Tale no doubt expect Richard to mount and the horse to rear up and give him (like Arcite) a fatal fall. As he does so often, however, Scott introduces the unexpected. An elephant is paraded before the watching crowd—another present for Richard—but instead of kneeling so that Richard can mount him, the animal responds to a different command from Hyder Ali: "Curling his long trunk around the neck of the ill-fated European, the monster suddenly threw the wretch prostrate before him, and stamping his huge shapeless foot upon his breast, put an end at once to his life and to his crimes." So much for Richard. The stage is thus clear for a marriage between Menie Gray and Adam Hartley, but it does not occur: Adam dies two years later, and Menie returns unmarried to Britain. Thus a novel which began like a medieval romance ends in hard reality. Its chief interest lies in the finely wrought psychological portrait of Richard Middlemas, a bastard only less memorable than Edmund of *King Lear*.

Two more short tales—"My Aunt Margaret's Mirror" and "The Tapestried Chamber"—and the sketch ("this trifle") entitled "Death of the Laird's Jock" were originally intended for the Chronicles of the Canongate, but as things worked out they were published first in *The Keepsake* for 1828, a beautifully illustrated annual. They appear also in later editions of the Chronicles. The action of the first tale revolves around a strange mirror which can show what is taking place or has just taken place. Its animated image can last only seven minutes, and those who behold it must remain quiet during this time; if they do not, it will vanish and harm may befall them. Lady Forester and her sister, Lady Bothwell, look into this mirror to try to find out something about Lady Forester's husband, Sir Philip, who has been away on the Continent for a long time. They are shown that he is about to marry a young lady, but the marriage ceremony is broken up by an intruder—and then the vision ends. The idea of a mirror with strange virtues is nothing new on Scott's part. In the Squire's Tale there is a mirror that can reveal to the beholder who his friends and enemies are,

> And over al this, if any lady bright
> Hath set hire herte on any maner wight,

> If he be fals, she shal his tresoun see,
> His newe love, and al his subtiltee,
> So openly that ther shal no thyng hyde. [V, 137-41]

And there are numerous other magical mirrors in folklore and romance.[2] "The Tapestried Chamber; or, The Lady in the Sacque" involves a brave general, Richard Browne, who stays for a night in an ancient chamber of the castle of his friend Lord Woodville and is terribly frightened when he sees, or thinks he sees, an old woman with a diabolical face. He recognizes his nocturnal visitor the next day while walking with his host through the family portrait gallery. The tale recalls immediately the haunted-chamber chapter of *The Betrothed*, in which Eveline de Berenger sees the Bahr-Geist. Both of Scott's endeavors may have been inspired by the somewhat similar ghost story in *Ysaie le Triste*.[3]

The main event of the "Death of the Laird's Jock," Scott tells us, occurred in "the latter years of Queen Elizabeth's reign," but it closely resembles a combat between two knights in a medieval tournament. Young Armstrong, son of John Armstrong (known as the Laird's Jock), fights against an Englishman named Foster, who has sent "a challenge to the best swordsman in Liddesdale." Young Armstrong uses for the first time his father's huge two-handed sword, which "was as dear" to the elder Armstrong "as Durindana or Fushberta to their respective masters" (the swords of Orlando and of Rinaldo, in Boiardo's *Orlando Innamorato* and Ariosto's *Orlando Furioso*). The stakes are for keeps, and when young Armstrong loses, the elder Armstrong utters "a cry of indignation, horror, and despair"—not at the death of his son but because of the shame brought upon his clan and country: the "awful" sword that few others could even lift and that had won for him his "reputation of the best swordsman on the Border side" is now in the possession of an Englishman. Three days later the Laird's Jock dies. The resemblances to medieval romance are obvious, and the eventful combat looks forward to the material of Scott's next novel.

The Fair Maid of Perth (1828)

The bloody combat between Clan Chattan and Clan Quhele, in which thirty warriors from each clan fight in tournament fashion outside the city of Perth with King Robert III looking on, is the most memorable event of this fine novel of intrigue and violence, which constitutes the entire second series of the Chronicles of the Canongate; it is also an event of history—Scott quoting Wyntoun and the Scoti-Chronicon and mentioning Hector Boece, Leslie, and Buchanan in the preface of 1831, and quoting from Boece (in Bellenden's translation) in a note to the chapter in which the event is described.[4] Torquil of the Oak, who belongs to the Clan

Quhele and valiantly defends its young chief Eachin MacIan, seems "more like the giants in romaunts than a man of mould" to Simon Glover, the Fair Maid's father. Unlike the grand tournament in Chaucer's Knight's Tale, which is conducted without loss of life, the combat at Perth results in great slaughter on both sides, with only a handful of men left alive. The affair occurs, ironically, on Palm Sunday, with hundreds of good Christians watching the carnage as if it were a sport. The outcome is all the more horrible in contrast with Scott's account in chapter 7 of an encounter many years earlier between Scottish warriors led by Sir William Wallace, and a band of pirates led by Thomas de Longueville, who is an ancestor of Sir Patrick Charteris, the provost of Perth at the time of the novel: "Wallace himself rushed on the pirate captain, and a dreadful strife began betwixt them, with such fury that the others suspended their own battle to look on, and seemed by common consent to refer the issue of the strife to the fate of the combat between the two chiefs." In this romance-like situation Wallace wins, the pirates surrender to the Scots, and Thomas de Longueville eventually joins up with Wallace. No one is killed.

In the story proper, the murder of Oliver Proudfute leads into a solemn trial by combat in which Henry Smith, who is Catharine Glover's favored suitor, takes up the cause of Proudfute's widow and fights against Anthony Bonthron, the hired assassin who did the deed. Catharine views such ordeals of battle "as an insult to religion," but in this case right prevails: Smith defeats Bonthron, who publicly admits his crime but escapes execution through the machinations of his friends. Bonthron could have chosen to undergo the ordeal of bier-right, as do the other followers of Sir John Ramorny who are suspected of the crime. In this ordeal a person suspected of murder approaches the body of the deceased; if the death-wound begins to bleed afresh, the suspect is declared guilty. Scott knew about bier-right from history, from balladry, and from romance. One stanza from the ballad "Earl Richard" illustrates the old belief that a victim of murder will bleed in the presence of the murderer:

> The maiden touched the clay-cauld corpse,
>   A drap it never bled;
> The ladye laid her hand on him,
>   And soon the ground was red.[5]

Scott has a long, interesting footnote keyed to this stanza and the lines that follow. He was familiar with similar material in the *Nibelungenlied*, the following passage from Weber's paraphrase (in the manner of Ellis's *Specimens*) being especially apropos:

She ordered a splendid coffin of gold and silver to be made, in which the body [of Siegfried] was carried to the cathedral. Gunter, with Haghen and his attendants, came to bewail the death of Siegfried, and pretended it had been perpetrated by robbers; but Chrimhilt bade those who knew themselves innocent go and touch the dead body.

A marvel high and strange   is seen full many a time:
When to the murdered body nighs   the man who did the crime,
Afresh the wounds will bleed: the marvel now was found,—
That Haghen felled the champion   with treason to the ground.

Ghernot and Ghiseler seemed to bewail the hero with unfeigned sorrow; and the lamentations, whether sincere or feigned, resounded through the whole court.[6]

Bonthron declines to undergo the ordeal because he is afraid that the wounds of the deceased will indeed bleed. He then chooses the alternative ordeal of combat, which he thinks will give him a sporting chance—and he is assured by his friends that if he is defeated they will save him from being executed. Before the scene at St. John's, interestingly, the corpse of Proudfute appears to bleed when Henbane Dwining, the Machiavellian physician and apothecary who was privy to the murder, enters the Proudfute home to cure a sick child; but the apparent bleeding is attributed to Dwining's having examined the body soon after Oliver's death and having thus probed the wound with medical instruments. "How could the poor dead corpse know," asks a woman in attendance, "that that was done with good purpose?" (chap. 22).

Instead of the normal Knight's Tale pattern, this novel presents *three* young men—the Duke of Rothsay (the Prince), Eachin MacIan (alias Conachar), and Henry Smith—all in love with the same girl, Catharine Glover; each man has his faults, and the girl, unlike Chaucer's Emily, has intelligence, knowledge, and personality. Although handsome and first in line to the throne of Scotland, the Duke of Rothsay is the least desirable of Catharine's admirers: "His form, though his stature was low, and his limbs extremely slight, was elegant in the extreme; and his features no less handsome. But there was on his brow a haggard paleness, which seemed the effect of care or of dissipation, or of both these wasting causes combined" (chap. 11). In short, the prince is a good example of the sort of man, so frequent in medieval literature (and in Scott), who is misspending his youth. Like Michael Lambourne of *Kenilworth*, he does not change his ways and he is murdered. Not long before his death he attempts to deceive Catharine by disguising himself as a woman, namely, as his own undesired wife Margery Douglas. Female disguises sometimes work for heroes of romance, but not for Rothsay, who finally realizes that Catharine is not to be had by foul means. He is aided in this abortive escapade by Henbane Dwining, dressed as an old woman named Griselda. This is an ironically humorous touch on Scott's part, since there could be no greater contrast between the unscrupulous Dwining and the long-suffering Griselda of Chaucer's Clerk's Tale.

The circumstances of Eachin MacIan's birth and childhood seem straight out of medieval romance. In chapter 26 Simon Glover tells Sir Patrick Charteris what he knows. Just before Eachin's birth his father, chief of the Clan Quhele, suffered a grievous defeat at the hands of the rival Clan Chattan. "Seven of his sons were slain in battle and after it, himself put to flight, and his castle taken and given to the flames. His wife . . . fled into the forest. . . . Here, in sorrow and care enough, she gave birth to a boy; and as the misery of the mother's condition rendered her little able to suckle the infant, he was nursed with the milk of a doe, which the forester who attended her contrived to take alive in a snare." The father later found his wife and child, to his great joy, but further complications ensued, and the child was given over to Simon Glover as an apprentice. He grew up under the name Conachar, until "at length, I suppose the lad either guessed the secret of his birth, or something of it was communicated to him." Upon the death of his father Eachin abandons Glover and returns to the Highlands to be the new chief of his clan. With such background, he ought to be an exemplary hero, but he has one great personal deficiency—cowardice—which he himself recognizes and even admits. "Were Catharine to look kindly on the earnest love I bear her," he tells Glover in chapter 29, "it would carry me against the front of the enemies with the mettle of a war-horse. Overwhelming as my sense of weakness is, the feeling that Catharine looked on would give me strength." In stories of courtly love the lady indeed is the inspiration for her lover's doughty deeds, but the lover-hero is never a coward to begin with. Ladies cannot love a coward, as Pertelote pointedly tells Chauntecleer in the Nun's Priest's Tale.

Henry Smith, or Gow, the armorer of Perth, is the most complicated of Catharine's three suitors. He attributes his propensity to get into a good fight, for which Catharine severely reproves him, to his exposure to ballads and romances, citing specifically Blind Harry the Minstrel: "When I hit a downright blow, it is not (so save me, Saint John!) to do any man injury, but only to strike as William Wallace struck" (chap. 6). But the old stories affect him in a positive way as well (he even tries his own hand at ballads, roundels, and carols), and his occasionally beautiful speech belies his claim to be just a "coarse ignorant borrel man." Early in the story he describes to Glover how he felt when, after a long absence, he saw Perth once more: "I promise you, father, that when I crossed the Wicks of Baiglie, and saw the bonny city lie stretched fairly before me like a fairy queen in romance, whom the knight finds asleep among a wilderness of flowers, I felt even as a bird, when it folds its wearied wings to stoop down on its own nest" (chap. 2). Or again, after a slight misunderstanding with Catharine, Henry tells her father eloquently, "It is not of her coyness, or her blushes that I speak; it is of the paleness which so soon followed the red, and chased it from her cheeks; and it is of the tears which succeeded. It was like the April shower stealing upon and obscuring the fairest dawning that ever beamed over the Tay" (chap. 5). His discourse also has allusions to "Sir Chanticleer" (chap. 3) and "Sir Pandarus of Troy" (chap. 11), and his sarcastic comment about Father Clement—"O, I comprehend!—a buxom priest, that thinks more of good living than of good life—tipples a can on Fastern's Eve, to enable him to face Lent—has a pleasant *in principio*—and confesses all the prettiest women about the town" (chap. 3)—recalls in a general way Chaucer's pilgrim Friar and the friar of the Summoner's Tale.

Henry's exposure to medieval romance is a major factor in his relationship with Catharine. He thinks of himself as "the squire of low degree, who was honoured, if song speaks truth, with the smiles of the King of Hungary's daughter" (chap. 5). His love for her is the inspiration for his better thoughts and sentiments. Like other courtly lovers, he puts his beloved on a pedestal and worships her almost as if she were a saint: "I feel myself an earthly, coarse, ferocious creature, scarce worthy to look on her." His awe of her, his purity of affection, and his becoming her Valentine recall the medieval "legend" of St. Catharine and St. Valentine, whose relationship is chaste even after they are married, according to the standard versions of the story (including that of Chaucer's Second Nun). "His sentiments towards her were certainly as exalted as if they had been fixed upon an actual angel, which made old Simon . . . think that his passion was too high and devotional to be successful with a maiden of mortal mould." Simon tells Henry that he wishes Catharine "would put off being entirely a saint till the time comes for her being canonised for St. Catharine the Second." But in her own way Catharine understands "the nature and depth of the armourer's passion," and she has "as much secret pride in the attachment of the redoubted Henry Gow, as the lady of romance may be supposed to have in the company of a tame lion, who follows to provide for and defend her" (Scott no doubt thinking here of the romance *Octavian*, and perhaps of *Ywain and Gawain*). Although Henry and Catharine are not of the nobility, their relationship is as deeply felt as that of Sir Kenneth and Lady Edith, in *The Talisman*, and it is depicted by Scott with more complexity and depth. When at the end the Earl of Douglas says of Henry, who has just refused an offer to enter his service, "A churl will savour of churl's kind," we know that he is wrong.

Douglas's expression closely resembles the lady of the manor's words to the angry friar with regard to old Thomas, of the Summoner's Tale: "A cherl hath doon a cherles dede." And there are other Chaucerian echoes, sometimes in unlikely places and connections. One of Henry Smith's apprentices is named Jankin, which is the name of the Wife of Bath's fifth husband—and of the young squire who appears briefly in the aftermath to the Summoner's Tale. When a *dey* ("or farm-woman," according to Scott) appears at Falkland near the end of the novel, I cannot help wondering whether Scott was thinking of Chaucer's "povre wydwe," who we are told was "a maner deye" (usually glossed as "a sort of dairy-woman"). Henbane Dwining speaks once of "wastel bread"—the sort of bread the Prioress feeds to her dogs; and a "Dominican monk" upbraids him on one occasion for his lack of reverence: "I know that Chaucer, the English Maker, says of you mediciners that your study is but little on the Bible" (chap. 22). It has even been argued that the detailed description in chapter 8 of the procession of Perth citizens on the road to their provost's castle was inspired by Thomas Stothard's famous painting of the Canterbury Pilgrims, a black-and-white print of which hung (and still hangs) in Scott's study at Abbotsford.[7]

When Oliver is thrown from his horse by a man who calls himself Devil's Dick, his companions see him "meet with a Rowland." Throughout the novel the cowardly Oliver contrasts humorously with Roland's brave companion-in-arms of the same name in the *Chanson de Roland* and other stories. He confides to Henry that he has in his yard "the stern-post of a dromond," which he pretends is a "soldan" and strikes at valiantly with his sword from time to time; in fact, virtually all of his warlike encounters are with his wooden soldan. Telling the provost about the mishap, Oliver refers grandiosely to his antagonist as Richard the Devil. " 'How, man? he that the rhymes and romances are made on?' said the Provost. 'I thought that smaik's name had been Robert' " (chap. 8). On the night of his murder Oliver is waylaid by revelers and is brought before their "emperor" (Rothsay in disguise), who asks him his name. " 'Oliver, may it please your honour—I mean your principality.' 'Oliver, man? nay, then thou art one of the Douze peers already' " (chap. 16). A note reminds us that the emperor is referring to "the *twelve* peers of Charlemagne, immortal in romance." And thus Scott utilizes the Charlemagne romances and *Robert the Devil* in *The Fair Maid of Perth*.

All in all, *The Fair Maid* is very heavily indebted to medieval literature. It seems strange, then, that references to Arthurian romance are few and far between. When Henry speaks disparagingly of Highlanders, Simon Glover reminds him that "there are times . . . when King Arthur and his Round Table could not make a stand against them" (chap. 6). The Duke of Rothsay suggests solving the problem between the feuding clans by having the two chiefs fight each other, like "two salvage knights, for the first time in their lives wearing breeches, and mounted on horses, as has not been heard of since the days of King Arthur" (chap. 13). Arthur is mentioned, along with Charlemagne and others, in connection with bier-right (chap. 20), and once more by Henbane Dwining, when Dwining introduces his plot to save Bonthron from execution: "I will carry him off from the very foot of the gallows into the land of faëry, like King Arthur, or Sir Huon of Bordeaux, or Ugero the Dane" (chap. 22). Scott makes much more use of Arthurian material in his next novel.

Anne of Geierstein (1829)

For this second venture on the continent Scott returned to the fifteenth century. The story is set in Burgundy, Germany, Provence, and Switzerland; and the historical portrait of Charles the Bold, which we have already seen in *Quentin Durward*, is deepened and completed here. Again we find the Knight's Tale story-pattern of two worthy young men—Arthur Philipson (or Sir Arthur de Vere) and his Swiss adversary, Rudolph Donnerhugel—in love with the same girl, in this case an intriguing girl with a strange background. It is clear from the outset that Anne of Geierstein has no romantic interest whatever in Rudolph; nevertheless, his claim on her is strong because of the esteem in which he is held by Anne's cousins and by Swiss youth in general. Like Arcite he seems more interested in war than in love, but he jealously guards what he considers his prerogative with respect to Anne, and he immediately senses a rival in Arthur. Twice the two youngsters fight. Their first encounter, like that of Palamon and Arcite, is broken up (by Arthur's father and Anne's uncle, Arnold Biederman), and like many combatants in Malory's *Morte Darthur* they quickly make up and become friends—not fast friends, however, because the rivalry over Anne leads eventually to their second encounter, in which Arthur kills Rudolph.

The name Arthur, of course, recalls the legendary king, and Philipson is frequently addressed as "King Arthur" or "Arthur of England" by Rudiger, Ernest, and Sigismund Biederman (sons of Arnold), and incessantly so by Rudolph Donnerhugel. When Rudolph alludes to "the coward knights of Cornouailles," a note tells us that "the chivalry of Cornwall are generally undervalued in the Norman-French romances"—and in Malory too, Scott might have added. "So little did Philipson relish [Rudolph's] affectation of superiority, that the poor jest, that termed him King Arthur, although quite indifferent to him when applied by any of the Biedermans, was rather offensive when Rudolph took the same liberty; so that he often found himself in the awkward condition of one who is internally irritated, without having any outward manner of testifying it with propriety" (chap. 10).

While Arthur is in all ways worthy of his name, Sigismund Biederman cuts a rather ridiculous figure in comparison with the Siegmund of Germanic romance. Unlike little Oliver of *The Fair Maid*, he is no coward—indeed, he is a brave and doughty fighter—but his sluggishness and lack of mental alacrity cause him to be looked down upon by his father and brethren, and by Rudolph, who calls him a "lazy losel"—*losel* being a good Middle English word of reprobation. When Arthur befriends him, however, he shows that he is capable of dogged loyalty as well as bravery, and he repays Arthur's kindness several times over. Like Roswall of the famous Scottish romance, Arthur finds that an act of kindness can produce a valuable friend.

Arthur and his father are Lancastrian nobility in exile, and although they are disguised as merchants until late in the story, their refinement of character and their chivalrous demeanor make other people suspect that they are not what they pretend. De Hagenbach's executioner is certain that the elder Philipson is of noble birth, because of his "free and dauntless conduct" (chap. 14), while Anne herself tells her friend and attendant, Annette Veilchen, that she is "well-nigh convinced that these Philipsons are of rank, as they are of manners and bearing, far superior to the occupation which they appear to hold" (chap. 21). We must not conclude, however, that Scott agreed with Malory and other medieval writers of romance in considering chivalry and "gentillesse" a matter solely of noble birth, for the Swiss mountaineers show true chivalry as well in their brave struggle with Charles of Burgundy.

Besides the Knight's Tale story-pattern there are other Chaucerian touches. The man who guides Arthur and his father along the way to Strasbourg, and who plans to betray them, recalls vaguely Chaucer's Pardoner—Arthur "thought, from the man's appearance, he must be one of those itinerant ecclesiastics, who travel through the country with relics, pardons, and other religious trinkets, and were in general but slightly respected, excepting by the lower orders, on whom these venders of superstitious wares were often accused of practising gross deceptions" (chap. 17)—though his physical features do not resemble in any way those of the Canterbury pilgrim. When the elder Philipson spends the night at a German inn, he encounters a friar who ingratiates himself in hopes of receiving alms and who thus is somewhat reminiscent of Chaucer's Friar; but the ill-tempered host John Mengs is no Harry Bailey, and the mood at the Golden Fleece is quite different from the genial atmosphere of the Tabard Inn. Earlier, when Arthur is on watch at the Castle of Graffs-lust and contemplating the way Anne has glanced at him that evening, Scott compares him explicitly with another Canterbury pilgrim: "Young Philipson, who, like Chaucer's Squire, was 'as modest as a maid,' almost trembled to give to that look the favourable interpretation which a more self-satisfied gallant would have applied to it without scruple" (chap. 9). Here

Scott's memory has played him false: it is the Knight who is said to be "as meeke as is a mayde"; his son the Squire is a "lusty bacheler."

Arthur is amazed when he suddenly beholds the object of his contemplation leave the ruins of Graffs-lust and move across a plain toward the forest. "He asked himself in vain with what purpose that modest young maiden, whose manners were frank, but whose conduct had always seemed so delicate and reserved, could sally forth at midnight like a damsel-errant in romance, when she was in a strange country and suspicious neighbourhood" (chap. x). Like many a lady in stories of courtly love, she is not easily won. Later, Annette Veilchen plays the role of lady-in-waiting in arranging a meeting between Anne and Arthur, but when Anne tells her that Arthur must leave the castle, Annette falls out of her role, replying saucily, "It may be very fit for a lady of high birth to send such a message, which, indeed, I have heard the Minne-singers tell in their romances; but I am sure it is not a meet one for me, or any frank-hearted Swiss girl, to carry" (chap. 21). Passages of this sort, whether serious or humorous, contribute cumulatively to the novel's medieval flavor, as does Scott's account of Troubador poetry when the action moves to Provence and the court of King René.

Arthur Philipson's guide into the southern kingdom is a Provençal named Thiebault, who sings

> the history of a Troubadour, named William Cabestainy, who loved, *par amours*, a noble and beautiful lady, Margaret, the wife of a baron called Raymond de Roussillon. The jealous husband obtained proof of his dishonour, and, having put Cabestainy to death by assassination, he took his heart from his bosom, and causing it to be dressed like that of an animal, ordered it to be served up to his lady; and when she had eaten of the horrible mess, told her of what her banquet was composed. The lady replied, that since she had been made to partake of food so precious, no coarser morsel should ever after cross her lips. She persisted in her resolution, and thus starved herself to death. [Chap. 29]

This is a familiar story that Scott probably knew best in the Middle English version, *The Knight of Curtesy and the Fair Lady of Faguell* (in Ritson). A very early version involves the troubador Guilhem de Cabestanh. Thiebault concludes the story by telling "how every bold knight and true lover in the south of France assembled to besiege the baron's castle, stormed it by main force, left not one stone upon another, and put the tyrant himself to an ignominious death." Interestingly, Arthur is unable to appreciate a story of courtly love that glorifies an adulterous relationship: "Your Baron of Roussillon is a monster of cruelty," he tells Thiebault; "but your unfortunate lovers were not the less guilty. It is by giving fair names to foul actions that those who would start at real vice are led to practise its lessons, under the disguise of virtue." I suspect that Arthur is a spokesman here for Scott himself.

Rudolph Donnerhugel's account in chapter 11 of Anne's maternal grandparents reveals the story-pattern found in some Breton lais in which a mortal in difficulty encounters a friendly fairy-like creature who nevertheless imposes on him a taboo. The story of Sir Launfal is the most obvious example, as we have already seen, with Launfal in "obstructive circumstances" at King Arthur's court. The fairylike creature who becomes his mistress warns him that he must never speak of her to anyone. When Launfal does so by accident, she abandons him, and a crisis ensues—which is resolved when the lady appears at court and takes Launfal away with her.

"And so," Rudolph says to Arthur Philipson, "listen while I tell a tale, never sung or harped in hall or bower, and which, I begin to think, deserves as much credit, at least, as is due to the Tales of the Round Table, which ancient troubadours and minne-singers dole out to us as the authentic chronicles of your renowned namesake." Anne of Geierstein's grandfather, Baron Herman von Arnheim, is saddened when his mentor Dannischemend, a Persian sorcerer, must go away forever. Dannischemend promises that his daughter will take his place at the Castle of Arnheim and will help Herman in his occult studies. He warns Herman not to think of the girl in any other way, or there will be trouble. But the girl is so beautiful that Herman disregards the warning and marries her. Much negative gossip arises in connection with the new baroness because she seems superhuman. At the christening of their daughter the baron dips his hand in holy water, some of which spills on his wife's opal, which is believed to have magical properties, and she falls to the floor dreadfully ill. Shortly afterwards she dies, apparently, but instead of a body there is "about a handful of light grey ashes"; exactly three years later the baron dies also. In Rudolph's tale the taboo comes *before* the arrival of the fairy lady and is imposed not by her but by her father; otherwise, the basic pattern is the same as in the story of Launfal. The agent that brings about the crisis is holy water—an idea that Scott probably adapted from the romance about Richard the Lion-Hearted, in which Richard's mother, being detained in church during the Elevation of the Host (the presence of which she cannot bear), flies up through the roof and disappears. Rudolph's account of Anne's grandparents is a highly embellished version of her history; the real events are revealed later.

Other motifs from medieval literature include Archibald de Hagenbach's prophetic dream of "two men of middle stature, or somewhat under it" (chap. 13), signifying Arthur and the elder Philipson, who are about to fall into his power; and Charles of Burgundy "clothed with the jerkin and bonnet of a private soldier of the Walloon guard" (chap. 26) when he stealthily overhears and then interrupts the private conversation of Arthur and his father—a variation of the king-in-disguise motif (a trick the Duke plays very often, we are told). There are also good examples of rescue at the last moment: Arthur is saved by Anne from his precarious position on the dangerous precipice near Geierstein; the elder Philipson is saved from certain execution in De Hagenbach's prison when the Swiss take over La Ferette.

Also conspicuous is the motif of the perilous journey, especially that of Arthur and his father from La Ferette to Strasbourg. For a while they travel together along the west bank of the Rhine, barely escaping the snare laid for them by the deceitful pardoner, their guide. Ironically, the ploy the pardoner uses is to persuade them to stop to pray at the Chapel of Our Lady of the Ferry, which has a story behind it (told in some detail by the wily pardoner) resembling the medieval genre known as the miracle of the Virgin. Having been warned of danger by Anne of Geierstein, the Philipsons separate near the chapel, but the perils continue: the elder Philipson falls into the hands of the dreaded Vehme-gericht, and Arthur barely escapes capture when his horse is killed as he, Anne, and her party leave the Castle of Arnheim to escape from mutinous soldiers of the Rhingrave. Underlying much of the novel is the frequent medieval *topos* of youth versus age, the young Swiss clamoring for war with Burgundy while Arnold Biederman and other elderly Swiss diplomats strive fervently for peace— the young gradually succumbing to the influence of foreign culture and wealth, with Arnold lamenting the loss of the old virtues that made Switzerland a truly great nation.

In the introduction of 1831 Scott lists some of the historical sources to which he is indebted, including "the new Parisian edition of Froissart."[8] My concern is with his literary indebtedness: *Anne of Geierstein* is no exception to the long-time and profound influence of medieval literature on the Waverley Novels.

Count Robert of Paris (1831)

The setting for *Count Robert* is Constantinople, a scene of activity in the old romances for Valentine and Orson, Palmerin of England, Guy of Warwick, and Tirant lo Blanch. Tirant is eventually made Caesar of the Empire, a position held in this novel by Nicephorus Briennius, who is the husband of Anna Comnena, scholarly daughter of Emperor Alexius Comnenus. The time is the late eleventh century, when the armies of the First Crusade are passing through Constantinople on their way to the Holy Land.

The character for whom the novel is named is one of the more colorful leaders of the crusade—a man who has won great renown and "honor" in France, especially in his successful Malory-like encounters with challenging knights at the celebrated Chapel of Our Lady of the Broken Lances. "And ever and anon," he proudly explains to Alexius Comnenus,

> as a good knight arrives at this place, he passes in to the performance of his devotions in the chapel, having first sounded his horn three times, till ash and oak-tree quiver and ring. Having then kneeled down to his devotions, he seldom arises from the mass of Her of the Broken Lances, but there is attending on his leisure some adventurous knight ready to satisfy the new comer's desire of battle. This station have I held for a month and more against all comers, and all gave me fair thanks for the knightly manner of quitting myself towards them, except one, who had the evil hap to fall from his horse, and did break his neck; and another, who was struck through the body, so that the lance came out behind his back about a cloth-yard, all dripping with blood. [Chap. 9]

Robert almost becomes sidetracked from his mission in the Holy Land when he hears the cynical philosopher Agelastes—whom he likens to "one of those excellent men whom the knights of yore were wont to find sitting by springs, by crosses, and by altars, ready to direct the wandering knight where fame was to be found" (chap. 10)—tell of a princess who has long been the victim of an enchantment taking the form of a deep sleep (cf. *The Bridal of Triermain*). She "must be awakened," says Agelastes, "by the kiss of love"—to which the Count's wife quite naturally objects, so the adventure must go unattempted on his part. On another occasion he awakens to find himself, like many a knight in medieval romance, in a deep and dark dungeon, where he is threatened first by a tiger (which he kills) and then by a huge "Ourang-Outang" (which he wounds and tames). Encounters with vicious animals are frequent in romance; one thinks immediately of Guy of Warwick's slaying of the dun cow, and Tirant lo Blanch's similar adventure with a mastiff hound, and (more apropos to the present novel) the well-known episode in *Richard Coer de Lyon* in which Richard, while imprisoned in Germany, kills a vicious lion with his bare hands. Count Robert uses "a massive wooden stool" against the tiger and "a fragment of the bedstead" against the Ourang-Outang—the latter, once tamed, being somewhat reminiscent of the friendly ape in the prose romance *Milles et Amys*.[9]

Robert's wife, who accompanies him on most of his exploits, is a figure of heroic mold in her own right, as her Germanic name Brenhilda implies. She is frequently referred to as an amazon, and she is compared briefly but aptly with such larger-than-life women as Bradamante and Marphesa (from the great Orlando romances by Boiardo and Ariosto) and Thalestris, the Queen of the Amazons (who figures prominently in the romances about Alexander the Great). Robert won her hand in marriage after having overthrown her in a tournament in which numerous other suitors had failed.[10]

At least as important a character as Count Robert, and at least as heroic, is a young member of the Varangian Guard (the emperor's personal bodyguard) named Hereward, who, like most of his fellow soldiers, has found a new life in Constantinople in the wake of the Norman Conquest of England. Like the renowned Bevis he comes from the forests of Hampton; on one occasion he cautions Robert: "I am one man . . . you, sir, are another; but all our arithmetic will not make us more than two; and in this place, it is probable that a whistle from the Cæsar, or a scream from Agelastes, would bring a thousand to match us, if we were as bold as Bevis of Hampton" (chap. 18). Prior to the time of the novel, while he was still in England, he once saved his truelove Bertha from probable death when she was about to be attacked by a wild boar—the incident recalling similar incidents in romance. Hereward leaves for Constantinople only when it becomes absolutely clear to him that the cause of the Angles and Saxons is lost. As in *Guy of Warwick* and *Tirant lo Blanch*, the Empire of the East is in desperate straits, and Hereward acts as valiantly to save it from treason from within as do Guy and Tirant in their combat with hostile forces from without. He is depicted as a brave soldier who thinks in a straightforward manner, a man who assesses "men and things not according to the false estimate ascribed to them in this world, but to their real importance and actual value" (chap. 8). Hereward is not at all impressed with the hypocrisy and duplicity of the court, as is so visible in the character of his superior officer, Achilles Tatius, who turns out to be a traitor along with Agelastes and Nicephorus Briennius. In many ways, then, Hereward is very reminiscent of Quentin Durward, who in turn owes much (as we have seen) to the Squire of Low Degree. Hereward is less strongly reminiscent of the squire, for Scott does not allude even once to the medieval romance in the later novel, and Hereward does not aspire to the hand of a king's daughter; he cannot conceive of loving anyone other than his beloved Bertha, who disappeared after a bloody battle in England and who turns up in Constantinople as Agatha, favorite lady-in-waiting to Brenhilda, Countess of Paris.

These two equally attractive young men, Hereward and Robert, come into conflict but not over a lady; there is no Knight's Tale story-pattern here. The conflict is owing to the fact that Hereward is a Saxon and Robert a Frank, whom Hereward considers closely allied to and therefore little better than the hated Normans. They first get into a fight when Hereward discovers Robert in the dungeon of Blacquernal Palace; but then, like many warring knights in the *Morte Darthur*, they suddenly decide that they have no immediate or compelling cause for hostility, and moreover there is no one to watch them except the Ourang-Outang. At the end of the novel they are at it again, but now in the lists and in view of thousands of spectators, including the emperor. This solemn combat was originally to have been between Nicephorus Briennius and Brenhilda; owing to various complexities, however, Robert takes the place of his wife and Hereward the place of the Caesar, and the original reason for the combat is well-nigh lost sight of.[11] After a fierce struggle Count Robert gets the upper hand, but he desists from pursuing his advantage and the whole affair ends amicably, with Robert and Hereward gaining even greater respect for one another.

A few further touches contribute to the novel's medieval aura. The swords of many famous knights of romance have names, and Count Robert's trusty sword Tranchefer is no exception. Apparently Scott found this word in Lord Berners's translation of *Arthur of Little Britain*, where it is also the name of a sword.[12] A bard mentioned as having been in Brenhilda's service before the time of the novel has the name Lancelot. There are three allusions to Hereward's grandsire Kenelm, an ecclesiastic whose name recalls the ill-fated Saint Kenelm whom Chauntecleer tells Pertelote about in the Nun's Priest's Tale. Nicephorus Briennius comments to Agelastes that his philosophy "has never been tried with the exercise of a Xantippe" (chap. 18)—and we are reminded of the story of Socrates and Xantippe included in the notorious book of Jankyn, the Wife of Bath's fifth husband. For a short while we have the motif of the undesired marriage, with Alexius Comnenus planning to have Anna marry Ursel, his one-time political rival and long-time prisoner, once she is widowed by the execution of her husband-turned-traitor; but Alexius changes his mind, pardoning Nicephorus Briennius when his head is almost on the chopping block. Enmity ends in reconciliation, although the reconciliation is hardly heartfelt on the part of anyone.

For his historical information Scott relied on Anna Comnena's *Alexiad* (an inflated and flattering account of her father's reign), Edward Gibbon's *Decline and Fall of the Roman Empire*, and Charles Mills's *History of the Crusades*. History again provided Scott with one of his favorite situations, two opposing cultures—in this case the chivalric Christian crusaders from the West versus the wily, scheming Christians of the Eastern Empire. The romantic hero Hereward is caught in the middle, but he manages to come through unscathed, finally leaving the service of Alexius Comnenus to join Count Robert in the conquest of Jerusalem and at long last marrying his beloved Bertha. Like other Waverley Novels set in the Middle Ages, *Count Robert of Paris* is a conscious blending of history and elements from medieval literature, chiefly the romances.

Castle Dangerous (1831)

The time of Scott's last published novel is the first decade of the fourteenth century, the setting is Lanarkshire, and the historical events "on which the . . . novel mainly turns" are drawn from Barbour's *Bruce* and David Hume of Godscroft's *History of the Houses of Douglas and Angus*; but Scott has made many changes in his historical sources, amalgamating, for example, the well-known encounter between the English and the Scots in church on Palm Sunday (which ends in victory for the Scots and "Douglas' larder" and the castle being partly razed by Douglas himself) with another encounter, involving Sir John de Walton (in which the English are defeated by Scots disguised as carriers of victuals, De Walton is slain, his ladylove's letters are found on his person, and the castle is destroyed by Douglas to prevent its ever being used again by the English). The stark brutality of the historical record has been considerably toned down in the novel, or "softened," to use Scott's word. Indeed, his version of the conflict on Palm Sunday reads like medieval romance, with Douglas and De Walton fighting with almost incredible strength and endurance, like Malory's knights, and behaving toward each other in accordance with a code of chivalry seldom observed in real fights between the English and the Scots in the Border Country.

The conflict between youth and age is conspicuous here in the rivalry between De Walton's very young lieutenant, Sir Aymer de Valence, and the veteran archer Gilbert Greenleaf. Aymer also has difficulties with Father Jerome, the Abbot of Saint Bride's, and with his uncle, the Earl of Pembroke, who reminds him in a letter that it is "the duty of young men, whether in council or in arms, to be guided implicitly by their elders" (chap. 8). Aymer's impatience with authority and his overweening sense of his own importance endanger his relationship with De Walton, who is his friend as well as superior officer, but the enmity ends in reconciliation.

Also noteworthy is the frequent contrast between past and present. De Walton believes that minstrelsy was a noble pursuit in earlier centuries, "but in modern ministrelsy," he tells Greenleaf (meaning the minstrelsy of the early fourteenth century), "the duty of rendering the art an incentive to virtue is forgotten, and it is well if the poetry which fired our fathers to noble deeds does not now push on their children to such as are base and unworthy" (chap. 5). Sometimes Scott contrasts his own time with former times. In modern hunting, for example, "a fox, or even a hare, is . . . considered as a sufficient apology for a day's exercise to forty or fifty dogs, and nearly as many men and horse" (chap. 7), whereas in the Middle Ages the game was usually dangerous (a wild boar, perhaps) and thus demanded real bravery on the part of the hunters. In another connection Scott remarks that "exaggerated sentiments" once "inspired actions of extravagant generosity," but in his own time "everything is accounted absurd which does not turn upon a motive connected with the immediate selfish interests of the actor himself" (chap. 17). Invariably, the past times are nobler and worthier than the present, whether by "present" he means the time of his story or his own century.

The novel's heroine, the wealthy Lady Augusta of Berkely, has reason to think badly of her own day, because King Edward II has been trying to marry her off to a cousin of his favorite, Piers Gaveston. "Where are the champions of the renowned Edward the First?" asks her minstrel Bertram. "Where are the noble ladies, whose smiles used to give countenance to the Knights of Saint George's Cross? Alas! the spirit of love and of chivalry is alike dead amongst us—our knights are limited to petty enterprises—and our noblest heiresses are given as prizes to strangers, as if their own country had no one to deserve them" (chap. 11). Lady Augusta comes up with the idea of giving her hand in marriage, with the king's permission, to whatever knight can hold the Castle of Douglas (i.e., Castle Dangerous) in the king's name for a year and a day. Most knights hesitate, fearing the king's displeasure, but Sir John de Walton gallantly takes up the offer, initiating an affair of the heart that harks back to better, nobler times. One is reminded of a famous passage in the *Morte Darthur* in which Malory contrasts love in his own day (the fifteenth century) with genuine love in the time of King Arthur: "But nowadayes men can nat love sevennyght but they muste have all their desyres. That love may nat endure by reson, for where they bethe sone accorded and hasty, heete sone keelyth. And ryght so faryth the love nowadayes, sone hote sone colde. Thys ys no stabylyté. But the olde love was nat so. For men and women coude love togydirs seven yerys, and no lycoures lustis was betwyxte them, and than was love trouthe and faythefulnes. And so in lyke wyse was used such love in kynge Arthurs dayes."[13] The relationship between the lovers in *Castle Dangerous* is definitely of the old school. Since Lady Augusta is of higher rank than De Walton, he looks up to her and considers her the source of all his better thoughts and feelings, as a courtly lover should. But another aspect of courtly love is that the lady is not supposed to be easily won. Lady Augusta worries that she may have looked favorably on De Walton too quickly and thus lost his respect by not playing the game according to the rules. The problem arises partly because Scott has shortened the historical period of probation from seven years to the traditional year and a day in which knights of medieval romance must perform one feat or another.

Scott says of young Aymer de Valence that "he was mild, gentle, and 'meek as a maid,' and possessed exactly of the courteous manners ascribed by our father Chaucer to the pattern of chivalry whom he describes upon his pilgrimage to Canterbury" (chap. 2), but the comparison is not especially apt; Chaucer's Knight is an elderly man and, as Scott conceived of him, he lacks Aymer's personal deficiencies. When Bertram the Minstrel and Lady Augusta part company early in the story, he to go to Douglas Castle and she (in her disguise as the boy Augustine) to the Abbey of Saint Bride, Bertram "makes the motion" of throwing her a kiss, saying, "Believe me, all the old songs since Merlin's day shall not make me forget thee." During the hunting scene of chapter 7, De Walton addresses a stranger huntsman (who turns out to be Michael Turnbull, a Scot loyal to Douglas) as "one of the best pupils of Sir Tristrem." At the Abbey of Saint Bride, Lady Augusta meets and confides in Sister Ursula, who is really Margaret de Hautlieu—a name that brings to mind Artavan de Hautlieu, who fails to rescue a princess from enchantment in the story Agelastes relates to Count Robert of Paris and his wife. (It also recalls the name Hautdesert in *Sir Gawain and the Green Knight*, which Scott only knew *of*—see Chapter 1, above.)

Lady Augusta's disguise is again the motif of a young lady posing as a young man, and as a pilgrim to boot. The motif of the undesired marriage applies not only to King Edward's plans for Lady Augusta but also to Margaret de Hautlieu, who was almost forced into marrying an Englishman when she was already in love with Malcolm Fleming of Biggar, a Scottish loyalist. There are frequent references to Thomas of Erceldoune, since Bertram's reason for going to Douglas Castle is to find an old book that contains the "lay" of Sir Tristrem and Thomas's prophecies. Aymer de Valence's conversation by night with the aged sexton in the dilapidated kirk of Douglas recalls vaguely William of Deloraine's nocturnal experience at Melrose Abbey, in *The Lay of the Last Minstrel*, while the Black Douglas's attempt to make the freedom of his newly acquired prisoner, Lady Augusta, contingent on De Walton's surrendering Castle Dangerous to the Scots brings to mind the predicament of the Lady of Branksome Hall when her young son falls into the hands of the English. All these touches and others contribute to the novel's aura of romance.

More deserves to be said about Margaret de Hautlieu. In her unsuccessful attempt to elope with Malcolm Fleming, prior to the time of the novel, she was severely injured; her face was badly disfigured, and she lost the vision in one eye. She reminds Lady Augusta, who is well-versed in the minstrelsy of the times, of the Loathly Lady in *The Marriage of Sir Gawaine*. (None of the Middle English versions of the story are as old as the early fourteenth century, but the story itself is even older.) Margaret poses to Lady Augusta an intriguing question: since she herself would not think less of her lover if his face were scarred, is it not possible for him to love her despite her frightful appearance? The question might have been asked in one of Marie of Champagne's courts of love, and it is almost as difficult as "What do women most desire?" to which the knight in the old romance must find an answer in a year and a day. Lady Augusta manages to come up with a tactful, if flattering, reply. It appears that Margaret now holds no more interest for Malcolm Fleming than did the Loathly Lady for Sir Gawaine or Florent (in Gower's version) or the young unnamed knight of the Wife of Bath's Tale. But at the end of the novel Margaret has regained her beauty, not through magic or the removal of an enchantment but owing to the efforts of an excellent cosmetician or plastic surgeon—Scott refers only to "skilful hands." Chance then throws her into Malcolm's hands again—he rescues her from "certain ill-disposed caitiffs, who were carrying her by force through the forest"—and the novel ends with wedding bells ringing not only for Lady Augusta and Sir John de Walton but for the former loathly lady and her former lover. Despite all Lady Augusta's flowery talk about a woman's inner worth and talent and intellect and fine accomplishments (in answer to the difficult question), Malcolm Fleming clearly loves Margaret de Hautlieu more for her outward beauty than anything else.

The Siege of Malta

Scott wrote his last novel in the fall and winter of 1831-32, while he was in Malta and Naples in hopes of regaining his health after having suffered three strokes. The original manuscript, or most of it, is now in the Berg Collection of the New York Public Library. Also to be found there is a handwritten copy made in 1878, with radical revisions, and a 1932 typescript of the 1878 copy. Interest in this unpublished work was renewed in the 1970s, when Donald E. Sultana published a sixty-page "description of the contents," interspersed generously with quotations from the original manuscript,[14] and Jane Millgate prepared a fresh transcription of the entire manuscript.[15] The major event of the novel is the great siege of 1565, in which the Turks came very close to wresting Malta away from the brave Knights of St. John—the Christians managing finally to fend off the besiegers but only with great loss of life, especially in the small garrison defending Fort St. Elmo. Scott is indebted throughout to René d'Aubert de Vertot's *Histoire de Malthe* (which he took with him on his trip); toward the end his indebtedness amounts to virtual plagiarism.

Quite frequently the thought is expressed that olden times were better than the time of the novel, that the once highly prized chivalric code is eroding in 1565. Sultana argues that Scott's thoughts of this sort were stimulated by the events surrounding the controversial Reform Bill, to which he was adamantly opposed. How deeply Scott felt that his own era had gone bad is shown by a short passage in the *Journal*, quoted also by Sultana: "The time is gone of sages who traveled to collect wisdom as well as heroes to reap honour. Men think and fight for money" (October 18, 1831).[16] In the novel the contrast between olden times and 1565 is exemplified in the Maltese Knights themselves, who are widely believed by the Turks and many older Christians to have fallen off from the chivalry and extraordinary bravery associated with the European knights who fought in the Holy Land under the leadership of Richard the Lion-Hearted. The new Christian knights, the Turks believe, "no longer hold themselves bound to fight to the same extremity as they did in the ancient days of Melec-Ric [King Richard] and the other heroes of the days termed of chivalry."[17] Even Jean de la Valette, the Grand Master of the Order of St. John and Commander-in-Chief of the Maltese Knights, has serious misgivings at first about the reliability of the younger knights. And Don Manuel de Vilheyna, a distinguished Spanish Commander of the Order, "deplores not only that 'we should have relinquished or at least abandoned the dictates of honour and chivalry' but also that 'these infidel miscreants should have had the acuteness to perceive it.' "[18] In the words of Vilheyna's Brother Servant-at-Arms (or Squire), Juan Ramegas, "It seems they are presumptuous enough to think the young men of the Order of Malta are not brought up, as their fathers were, at the sword-belt of the man-at-arms, but at the apron-strings of the ladies, and so is shown by their chivalry."[19] The events of the siege prove, however, that the Turks and the doubting Christians are wrong. Inspired by their commander-in-chief's eloquent speech (chap. 7), the Knights of Malta fight and die as bravely as the crusaders of earlier times.

Whatever Scott may or may not owe to Vertot, the idea of Christian knights being thought by the Turks to lack the bravery and steadfastness of their predecessors has an interesting parallel in Nicolas de Herberay's *Dom Flores de Grece*, which Scott knew in the Paris edition of 1552. In its opening chapters we learn that the Turks and other infidels are planning to attack Christendom and especially to invade England and overthrow King Amadis, the English knights having acquired the reputation of being weak, as King Norandel is told by an important Turk whom he has captured in a sea battle: "We are well advertised that within this little time, Knighthood is rusted among them, that in a manner there is not any more talke ministred of wandring Knights; but all like carpet Knights, (in stead of following Arms, as in times past men were accustomed to do) study onely to sit by the fire and court fair Ladies, which maketh them so much the worse esteemed of." Having arrived safely at Constantinople, Norandel immediately reports to the Emperor Esplandran (i.e., Esplandian), son of King Amadis, what he has learned from his prisoner: "But yet am I in great fear as touching the Country of great Brittain; for (as Cosdroel hath very well noted unto mee) Arms are therein of late time so much left off and unfrequented, that at this present there is not a wandring Knight to bee found therein, as was accustomed to be, neither yet any other, doing that whereby in times past they were so much esteemed of, more then in any country of the World."[20] As in the opening chapters of *The Siege of Malta*, there is an uneasy feeling of suspense in the air owing to the imminence of the attack.

Vilheyna's nephew Francisco and his niece Angelica (also called Seraphina and Angelina) are in love with each other. Like Amadis of Gaul and Oriana, and like Julian Peveril and Alice Bridgenorth and other Scott lovers, they have been close since childhood, having been brought up together by Morayma, Angelica's Moorish governess. "Indeed during the happy years when the children *were* children, and engaged in the mimick sports of infancy and youth Francisco's make-believe plays were always made up by the help of his cousin Seraphina. If he was a Knight Errant his cousin was naturally the Enchanted Princess whom he was destined to relieve from a felon enchanter, and Morayma, who was no mean performer on the harp, supplied chorus and triumphal tunes on occasion."[21] Morayma provides instruction that is proper especially to ladies in medieval romance, and the medieval games continue:

She also instructed them both in the common elements of surgery, of which ladies were the depositories and in which they had great fame; further, many receipts were traditional among the Moors. Meanwhile she instructed the children in such arts as needlework, music, and even penmanship, and became one in their sports, in which, according to the tales which were told them on every hand, Angelica and Morayma, as a wandering Queen and Princess were discovered spellbound in some secluded glade of the forest by Don Francisco, a predestined Knight Errant, while the task of prolonging their confinement was entrusted to some strong fauteur. The simple amusement, one of that numerous set known as make-believe, amused the society in ten thousand different ways.[22]

When news comes to Spain that the Turks are approaching Malta, Vilheyna and Francisco must go where duty calls, and the idyllic life of the two young lovers must come to an end. "No, no, young lady," Ramegas explains to Angelica, "Francisco must learn to keep company with men and learn other amusements than fancy plays. And you, my fair Senhora, must play both Knight and Lady in the romance. You will not have me to act the false Enchanter."[23]

Scott quotes three stanzas from the old ballad "Hardyknute" as an opening motto, and he alludes once to "the Cid and other Spanish champions."[24] In chapter 6 there is a long discussion between Vilheyna and La

Valette about *Don Quixote*—Vilheyna explaining to the Grand Master that Cervantes' purpose was to ridicule not chivalry but rather "the *extravagances* of chivalry" and appealing to him not to do Cervantes "the wrong to regard him as an enemy to chivalry, although he had taste enough to point out the extravagant mode of composition, which was fashionable in setting it forth." Vilheyna argues that Don Quixote, "amid all his weaknesses," is "the real model of an accomplished gentleman." This, of course, was Scott's own view; he much admired Don Quixote's dedicated adherence in his own unchivalric times to the noble ideals of older times, and this sort of dedication is what *The Siege of Malta* is all about.[25] The extreme brutality at the end—with the Turks disemboweling dying Maltese Knights and attaching them to wooden planks to be floated down towards Fort St. Angelo in plain view of the Christians, and La Valette in reprisal ordering his Turkish captives to be beheaded and their "bloody heads" fired from cannons at the enemy—is all in Vertot; but such brutality has analogues in medieval romance as well: for example, the notorious cannibalism passage in *Richard Coer de Lyon*, well known to Scott, which I cited earlier. The absence of references to Chaucer and the sparsity of specific allusions to medieval romance can perhaps be explained by Scott's failing memory and the fact that he was away from his own library.

Sultana suggests several reasons for Scott's extreme reliance on Vertot in the closing chapters.[26] For one thing, "borrowing" was common in his day, especially from foreign authors. For another, Scott was anxious to finish the novel quickly so that he could get it into the hands of his publisher, Robert Cadell, in time to be included in the "magnum" edition of his works. As for the weakness of the ending—we lose sight of virtually all the original characters—Scott once admitted that he "never could lay down a plan—or, having laid it down . . . never could adhere to it."[27] I would suggest in addition that the gradual change from fiction to history might not have seemed so unusual to a man with Scott's profound knowledge of medieval literature, where the dividing line between romance and chronicle is sometimes faint. If we never learn whether Vilheyna gets to fight against the corsair Dragut, his old enemy, or whether he returns to Spain after the siege, or whether Francisco and Angelica are ever reunited, Scott may have been implying that their personal fortunes become insignificant as they are swept up in the relentless, mortal, almost suicidal conflict—that is, in the events of history. He had used this idea once before: in *The Lady of the Lake* the wedding of Tombea's Mary and young Norman, the heir of Armandave, is halted when Roderick Dhu's call to arms is proclaimed; their personal fortunes must fall by the wayside because of the impending clash between Roderick's forces and those of the king.

Unlike Chaucer, Scott has left us with no baffling retractions. While he was in Rome, not long before his ill-fated homeward journey, he told Edward Cheney, "I am drawing near the close of my career; I am fast shuffling off the stage. I have been perhaps the most voluminous author of the day; and it *is* a comfort to me to think that I have tried to unsettle no man's faith, to corrupt no man's principle, and that I have written nothing which on my deathbed I should wish blotted."[28]

7
STYLE AND STRUCTURE IN THE WAVERLEY NOVELS

SCOTT's debt to Chaucer and medieval romance extends beyond content to matters of style and structure in his novels, as well as in his poetry. An examination of his *style* reveals a number of words, phrases, and grammatical constructions that hark back to medieval literature[1]—as do such larger stylistic features as his way of describing characters; his use of *occupatio*, proverbs, and set speeches; and his propensity to philosophize, either as narrator or through one of his characters. By *structure* I mean organization, or the arrangement of parts, and such basic matters as how to begin or end a story. Scott's introductions and conclusions have striking parallels in medieval romance, and certain characteristics of the middle portions of his novels—such as effective repetition and the use of place as a unifying device—seem also to have been inspired, directly or indirectly, by the literature of the Middle Ages.

Style

Let us glance first at some of Scott's words. When Rudolph Donnerhugel, in *Anne of Geierstein,* heatedly calls Sigismund Biederman a "lazy losel" (chap. 9), the alert reader may recall that the noun *losel* occurs also in *The Faerie Queene;*[2] it means "a worthless or good-for-nothing man." William Stewart Rose uses the word in his *Partenopex de Blois,* near the end of Canto II, as well as in his *Amadis de Gaul,* where he glosses it as "scoundrel." Scott probably borrowed this rare term of disapprobation from Spenser and Rose, but it occurs also in Middle English literature: in Hoccleve's *Regement of Princes* (line 2097) and in the Prologue to the A-text of *Piers Plowman* (line 74). Scott's coupling of *losel* with the adjective *lazy* is felicitous; the resulting alliteration makes Donnerhugel's outburst more emphatic (and more memorable) than it would have been otherwise. One of Scott's favorite old words, Graham Tulloch reminds us, is *gramarye*, which appears in *The Lay of the Last Minstrel* and *The Talisman;* he even uses it in the *Journal.*[3] Scott could have found it in line 144 of Percy's ballad "King Estmere" in the *Reliques* ("My mother was a westerne woman, / And learned in gramarye") and also in Canto I of Rose's *Partenopex* ("They, batten'd with the spoil, by some strange sleight / Of grammary, evanish'd clean from sight"). Percy, Rose, and Scott all use the word in the sense of "occult learning, magic, or necromancy," but the Middle English meaning, according to the Oxford English Dictionary, was "grammar" or "learning in general." The modern reader may be baffled in the eighth chapter of *The Fortunes of Nigel* when Benjamin Suddlechop informs his wife Ursula, with reference to Margaret Ramsay's servant Jenny, that "the Scots laundry-maid from neighbour Ramsay's . . . must speak with you incontinent." But *incontinent* in the sense of "at once" is well documented in sixteenth- and seventeenth-century literature and in the old prose romances. In *Melusine* we are told that Geoffrey of the Great Tooth "dide blow vp hys trompettes, & armed hys peple, & went incontynent to sawte [i.e. assault] the toun,"[4] and in *Valentine and Orson* the word is used over and over again to mean "at once" or "immediately." Scott occasionally uses the old noun *faitour,* which is glossed variously as "cheat, deceiver, evil-doer, false man, imposter, vagabond, or villain." It appears in his work as early as *The Bridal of Triermain* (II.xi) and as late (as we have just seen) as *The Siege of Malta*. Its occurrence in *The Fair Maid of Perth* is typical. In the aftermath of Oliver Proudfute's encounter with the unruly Devil's Dick of Hellgarth, Henry Smith says to Oliver, "And yonder stands the faitour, rejoicing at the mischief he has done, and triumphing in your overthrow" (chap. 8). Scott probably remembered the word from *The Faerie Queene*,[5] but it occurs also in Middle English—for example, in *Piers Plowman:* "Faitoures for fere her-of flowen into bernes."[6]

None of the foregoing terms occurs in Chaucer, but other old words used by Scott are to be found in Chaucer as well as elsewhere in Middle English literature. One of these is *carl*, a word of Old Norse derivation meaning "fellow" or "guy" but often intended as a term of disrespect. When Christie of Clint-Hill, in *The Monastery*, asks Halbert Glendinning with regard to Henry Warden, "What old carle hast thou with thee?" (chap. xxiv), it is hard not to remember Chaucer's Miller, who was "a stout carl for the nones" (I, 545); or the "knave" Robyn in the Miller's Tale, who was "a strong carl for the nones" (I, 3469); or, especially, the insulting words of the proudest of the three revelers in the Pardoner's Tale to the strange old man: "What, carl, with sory grace! / Why artow al forwrapped save thy face? / Why lyvestow so longe in so greet age?" (VI, 717–19). Scott need not have borrowed this word from Chaucer, for it was in Scottish dialect, but his use of it does contribute to the archaic flavor of his language. Scott uses the Chaucerian word *gramercy,* meaning "thank you," in *Ivanhoe* (" 'Gramercy for thy courtesy,' replied the Disinherited Knight") and in *Kenilworth,* in addition to the example cited in Chapter 2 from *The Lay of the Last Minstrel,* where verbal irony is involved. The word *undo,* which Scott is supposed to have reintroduced in its literal sense into the language,[7] occurs also in Chaucer, but in chapter 20 of *Ivanhoe,* when the Black Knight tells the hermit, "But undo the door to him before he beat it from its hinges," I suspect that Scott had *The Squire of Low Degree* in mind: "Undo thy dore, my worthy wife! / I am besette with many a knife. / Undo your dore, my lady swete! / I am beset with enemies great"[8]—although the situations are quite different.

Tulloch is probably right in his contention that Scott borrowed such rare Middle English words as *heart-spone, thunder-dint, viretot, wastel-bread,* and *yeomanly* (as an adverb) from Chaucer. He points out, for example, that "the line in *Marmion:* 'Mid thunder dint and flashing levin' and the phrase in *Ivanhoe*: 'wild thunder-dint and levin-fire' are both almost word for word from the Wife of Bath's curse," directed toward one of her first three husbands: "With wilde thonder-dynt and firy levene / Moote thy welked nekke be tobroke!" (III, 276–77).[9] When George Heriot's sister Judith in *The Fortunes of Nigel* tells Margaret Ramsay, having arrived unexpectedly at Heriot's house to see Lady Hermione, "Here you come on the viretot, through the whole streets of London, to talk some nonsense to a lady . . ." (chap. 18), Scott can only have had Gervays' words to Absolon in mind, near the end of the Miller's Tale: "What eyleth yow? Som gay gerl, God it woot, / Hath broght yow thus upon the viritoot" (I, 3769-70). *Viritoot* apparently means "an unsettled state or condition," and *to bring upon the viritoot* means "to bring astir"—but this very strange word, so far as I know, has never been explained to everyone's satisfaction. Scott had used it many years before *Nigel* in a letter to Richard Heber: "Once more if you are upon what Chaucer calls the *Viretote* do extend your rambles hither."[10]

The history of *derring-do* is well known. Scott used this word in *Ivanhoe,*[11] and he is given credit for having reintroduced it into the language.[12] It had not been used since *The Faerie Queene,* Spenser having gotten it from Chaucer and having *misread* the passage in *Troilus and Criseyde* that he thought contained it:

> And certeynly in storye it is yfounde,
> That Troilus was nevere unto no wight,
> As in his tyme, in no degree secounde
> In durryng don that longeth to a knyght. [V.834–37]

The word *don* is actually an infinitive and should be translated "to do"; thus the whole line means "in daring to do that (which) belongeth to a knight." Spenser obviously thought that *durryng don* was a compound word; as such he borrowed it from Chaucer and used it in *The Shepheards Calender* and *The Faerie Queene;* as such it was revived by Scott; and as such it is used in the language today.[13]

The foregoing thirteen words and others that can be traced back directly or indirectly to Middle English all contribute to the archaic ring of Scott's language. So do certain phrases and grammatical constructions. In a small but telling way Scott gives a romantic aura to George Robertson (alias Staunton), villain-hero of *The Heart of Mid-Lothian*, by having him speak on at least two occasions a phrase that is frequent in the old romances. In an intense encounter with Reuben Butler early in the story, he says to Reuben, "Go thither, enquire for one Jeanie Deans, the daughter of the good man; let her know that he she wots of remained here from daybreak till this hour, expecting to see her, and that *he can abide no longer*" (chap. 11; emphasis added). Later, sensing danger, Robertson closes his melodramatic nocturnal meeting with Jeanie at Muschat's Cairn with the words "I dare stay no longer" (chap. 15). With a sense of urgency, Sir Tristrem speaks almost the same words to Ysonde when they are once discovered together by the king: "Y dar no leng abide."[14] Further examples, formulaic in nature, can be found in *Sir Launfal*—"He nolde no lengere abyde" (line 459); "Sche nolde no lengere abyde" (line 1011)—and the phrase occurs also in late prose romances: "We may here abide no longer (replyed Don Bellianus)."[15] George Robertson is not Scott's only character to use the phrase in a tense situation. When Father Philip, of *The Monastery*, sees that the Bible belonging to the Lady of Avenel is in English (the vulgar tongue), he departs from Glendearg quite unceremoniously: "Now, by mine order, it is as I suspected!—My mule, my mule!—I will abide no longer here—" (chap. 5).

In his long chapter "Period Grammar," Tulloch discusses in some detail a number of resemblances between Scott's English and Middle English. These include the use of a personal possessive pronoun immediately after a demonstrative pronoun ("this our host"); the occasional omission of relative pronouns in places where they would now be used; the occasional omission of articles where they would now be used; the use of *an* or *and* in the sense of "if"; the past and past participial form *builded;* hortatory subjunctives such as "wend we" and "leave we"; the subjunctive form *were* in places where *would be* would be (were) normal; the occasional use of an active infinitive in a passive sense—and so on.[16]

One of the most striking and widespread of such constructions in Scott is the use of two adjectives with a noun, one preceding the noun and the other following it after the conjunction *and*. In chapter 14 of *Rob Roy*, Andrew Fairservice says of the profession of a peddler, "It's a creditable calling and a gainfu'." Jenny Dennison calls Henry Morton "a brave lad, and a bonny" (chap. 10). "Reuben's a gude lad and a kind," says David Deans in chapter 47 of *The Heart of Mid-Lothian;* and in chapter 26 we find the same construction: " 'He's a gude creature,' said she, 'and a kind—it's a pity he has sae willyard a powny' "—Jeanie speaking with regard to Dumbiedikes. In *Kenilworth* Dickie Sludge describes Tressilian as "a true gentleman, and a bold" (chap. 10). The Abbot of *The Monastery* speaks of Walter de Avenel as "a good knight and a valiant" (chap. 5). And so on through the rest of the Waverley Novels. Even in one of the last of them, *Castle Dangerous*, we find Thomas Dickson saying of Bertram the Minstrel, "I have known him for twenty years, and never heard anything of him save that he was good man and true" (chap. 2)—in this instance the two indefinite articles being omitted. Examples of this construction in older literature are indeed numerous. They can be found in minstrelsy of the Scottish border: "He was a stalwart knight, and strong" (*Thomas the Rhymer*, II.iii). They are prevalent in the *Canterbury Tales*: "He was a gentil harlot and a kynde" (description of the Summoner in the General Prologue, I, 647); "Ther was a monk, a fair man and a boold" (Shipman's Tale, VII, 25); "An oold man and a povre with hem mette" (Pardoner's Tale, VI, 713). And they appear in the prose romances: " 'Sir,' seyde sir Trystrames, 'this is a foule custom and an horryble' " (Malory, *Works*, p. 259); " 'Hit is pité,' seyde sir Lameroke, 'that ony suche false kynge cowarde as kynge Marke is shulde be macched with suche a fayre lady and a good as La Beall Isode is' " (*ibid.*, p. 355); "[Tremoran] rode a bustard-coloured horse, which was a fair steed and a large" (Southey's edition of *Palmerin of England*, I, 238–39).

Another Middle English construction borrowed and adapted by Scott in *The Lady of the Lake* (see Chapter 2) is by no means limited to the poetry. Let's call it the "woe worth" construction. Sir Piercie Shafton uses it in chapter 29 of *The Monastery*, while speaking to Mysie: "Woe worth the hour that Piercie Shafton, in attention to his own safety, neglected the accommodation of any female, far less of his most beneficent liberatrice!" Quentin Durward says of his uncle, Ludovic Lesly: "But now I have seen him, and, woe worth him, there has been more help in a mere mechanical stranger, than I have found in my own mother's brother" (chap. 6). The best example I know from Middle English is the one already quoted in Chapter 2: "Wo worth the faire gemme vertulees! / Wo worth that herbe also that dooth no boote!" etc.—Pandarus speaking to Criseyde in *Troilus and Criseyde* (II.344ff.). So we have still another way in which the language of the Waverley Novels harks back to earlier times.

Vinaver and other students of Malory have been struck with Malory's predilection for the *-ing* form of the verb, especially in the description of knightly combat.17 Here, for example, is part of the account of Sir Gareth's fight with the Rede Knyght: "And eythir gaff other sad strokys now here now there, trasyng, traversyng, and foynyng, rasyng and hurlyng lyke two borys, the space of two owrys." When Gareth finally encounters the formidable Rede Knyght of the Rede Laundys, there is more of the same, as might be expected: "And than thus they fought tyll . . . they lacked wynde bothe, and than they stoode waggyng, stagerynge, pantynge, blowynge, and bledyng, that all that behelde them for the moste party wepte for pyté. So whan they had rested them a whyle they yode to batayle agayne, trasyng, traversynge, foynynge, and rasynge as two borys."18

Perhaps Scott, like Malory, realized the musical effect of the *-ing* ending as well as the sense of immediacy it conveys. In any case he made much use of it, especially to depict colorful and vigorous action, as in his memorable description of Holyrood in *The Abbot*: "Besides, there was the mustering and disposition of guards and soldiers—the dispatching of messengers, and the receiving them—the trampling and neighing of horses without the gate—the flashing of arms, and rustling of plumes, and jingling of spurs, within it" (chap. 18); or in the following passage from *The Betrothed*: "The cavaliers came up to join the retinue of Lady Eveline, with armour glittering in the morning rays, trumpets sounding, horses prancing, neighing" (chap. 15); or in the account of the hunt in *Castle Dangerous:* "Altogether, the ringing of bugles, the clattering of horses' hoofs, the lowing and bellowing of the enraged mountain cattle, the sobs of deer mangled by throttling dogs, the wild shouts of exultation of the men, made a chorus which extended far through the scene in which it arose" (chap. 7); or in the lively description in *Guy Mannering* of Clerihugh's Tavern, in Edinburgh: "At present, the interior of the kitchen was visible by its own huge fires,—a sort of Pandemonium, where men and women, half undressed, were busied in baking, broiling, roasting oysters, and preparing devils on the gridiron; the mistress of the place, with her shoes slip-shod, and her hair straggling like that of Megæra from under a round-eared cap, toiling, scolding, receiving orders, giving them, and obeying them all at once, seemed the presiding enchantress of that gloomy and fiery region" (chap. 36).

The effect is partly humorous in the last example. It is even more so when Waverley enters the village of Tully-Veolan for the first time and hears the "screaming" of children and the "growling remonstrances" of the old grandams, while "another part in this concert was sustained by the incessant yelping of a score of useless curs, which followed, snarling, barking, howling, and snapping at the horses' heels" (chap. 8). We have already observed, in connection with Bucklaw's breaking a stag, that Scott can use the *-ing* form with mock-heroic effect—a welcome relief in a novel as darkly pessimistic as *The Bride of Lammermoor* (see Chapter 4).

It is clear, then, that a number of Scott's words, phrases, and grammatical constructions are either borrowed from Middle English or at least have noticeable parallels in Chaucer and the old romances. "He who would imitate an ancient language with success," Scott once wrote, "must attend rather to its grammatical character, turn of expression, and mode of arrangement, than labour to collect extraordinary and antiquated terms."[19] An archaic aura was what he needed to make the language of the Waverley Novels different from the ordinary language of his day—more curious, more poetic, more "romantic," if you will—and his detailed knowledge of Chaucer and the old romances provided him with an important linguistic tool for achieving the desired effect. In passages of dialogue he wanted to avoid the quasi-modern, pseudophilosophical jargon—"this *twaddling* stuff"—which he found so objectionable in the speeches of the historical personages, especially John of Gaunt, who people the pages of Godwin's *Life of Chaucer.*[20]

Larger Elements of Style

Moving now to larger elements of style, we may look once more at Scott's use of the mock-heroic. The best example I know is Scott's account of the preparations for the defense of Tillietudlem against a possible assault by the Covenanters, in chapter 19 of *Old Mortality*. Tillietudlem is no Troy, and the castle's commander-in-chief—crusty old Major Bellenden—is no Hector, but Scott describes the events of the day in heroic fashion—and with just the right satirical touch:

With eleven men . . . himself included, Major Bellenden determined to hold out the place to the uttermost.
   The arrangements for defence were not made without the degree of fracas incidental to such occasions. Women shrieked, cattle bellowed, dogs howled, men ran to and fro, cursing and swearing without intermission, the lumbering of the old guns backwards and forwards shook the battlements, the court resounded with the hasty gallop of messengers who went and returned upon errands of importance, and the din of warlike preparation was mingled with the sound of female laments.
   Such a Babel of discord might have awakened the slumbers of the very dead, and therefore was not long ere it dispelled the abstracted reveries of Edith Bellenden. She sent out Jenny to bring her the cause of the tumult which shook the Castle to its very basis; but Jenny, once engaged in the bustling tide, found so much to ask and to hear that she forgot the state of anxious uncertainty in which she had left her young mistress. Having no pigeon to dismiss in pursuit of information when her raven messenger had failed to return with it, Edith was compelled to venture in quest of it out of the ark of her own chamber into the deluge of confusion which overflowed the rest of the Castle. . . .
   To the battlements, therefore, she made her way, impeded by a thousand

obstacles, and found the old gentleman [her uncle] in the midst of his natural military element, commanding, rebuking, encouraging, instructing, and exercising all the numerous duties of a good governor.

Here too the *-ing* form of the verb contributes significantly to the mock-heroic effect. One cannot say categorically that Scott borrowed his mock-heroic technique from medieval literature, for he certainly would have known Gray's "Ode on the Death of a Favorite Cat, Drowned in a Tub of Gold Fishes" and Pope's *Rape of the Lock*; but he also had an excellent model in the Nun's Priest's Tale, especially the brilliant account of the chase after the fox, in which men and women shout and shriek and whoop, hens cry and "maken wo," ducks quack, dogs bark, and the resulting noise is so "hydous," or frightful, "it semed as that hevene sholde falle" (see VII, 3375–3401).

Description in general in the old romances, however, came under Scott's censure:

In every composition of the later age, but more especially in the popular romances, a tedious circumlocutory style is perhaps the most general feature. Circumstantial to a degree of extreme minuteness, and diffuse beyond the limits of patience, the minstrels never touch upon an incident without introducing a prolix description. This was a natural consequence of the multiplication of romantic fictions. It was impossible for the imagination of the minstrels to introduce the variety demanded by their audience, by the invention of new facts, for every story turned on the same feats of chivalry.[21]

"Even Chaucer," Scott adds in a footnote, "was infected by the fault of his age, and, with all his unrivalled capacity of touching the real point of description, he does not always content himself with stopping when he has attained it. It has been long since remarked, that when he gets into a wood, he usually bewilders both himself and his reader." Some readers may feel that Scott himself is not free of the fault of which he accuses Chaucer; however, it cannot be said that his descriptions lack variety. In depicting his characters he carries on a tradition that can be traced back at least as far as Geoffrey of Vinsauf's *Poetria Nova* (c. 1210), which influenced countless medieval writers in England and elsewhere (who in turn influenced later writers), and which influenced Scott directly or indirectly (probably by way of eighteenth-century novelists). Although he once wrote that "the light afforded by . . . Geoffrey . . . is dimmed by such a conglomeration of uninteresting and unintelligible matter, that we gladly fly for relief to the delightful pages of the gallant Froissart,"[22] Scott regularly uses what Geoffrey called *effictio* (the description of a person's outward appearance) or *notatio* (the description of a person's character) or a combination of the two. In the examples I have examined, he appears to have a preference for *effictio*, but as in Chaucer's famous portrait of the Prioress, the description of a person's outward appearance is often an index to that person's character.

One of Scott's best applications of *effictio* is his description of the soldier of fortune, Dugald Dalgetty, near the beginning of chapter 2 of *A Legend of Montrose:*

He had a bright burnished head-piece, with a plume of feathers, together with a cuirass, thick enough to resist a musket-ball, and a back-piece of lighter materials. These defensive arms he wore over a buff jerkin, along with a pair of gauntlets, or steel gloves, the tops of which reached up to his elbow, and which, like the rest of his armour, were of bright steel. At the front of his military saddle hung a case of pistols, far beyond the ordinary size, nearly two feet in length, and carrying bullets of twenty to the pound. . . .
The appearance of the horseman himself corresponded well with his military equipage, to which he had the air of having been long inured. He was above the middle size, and of strength sufficient to bear with ease the weight of his weapons, offensive and defensive. His age might be forty and upwards, and his countenance was that of a resolute weather-beaten veteran, who had seen many fields, and brought away in token more than one scar.

One recalls also the detailed description (*effictio*) of Old Mortality: "A blue bonnet of unusual dimensions covered the grey hairs of the pious workman," and so on (chap. 1); the memorable descriptions of Gurth and Wamba in chapter 1 of *Ivanhoe*, and of Rowena (chap. 4), Isaac the Jew (chap. 5), Rebecca (chap. 7), and Lucas Beaumanoir, the Grand Master (chap. 35); of Halbert Glendinning in chapter 19 of *The Monastery*, the paragraph beginning "Halbert was now about nineteen years old, tall and active rather than strong," and the next paragraph detailing his dress. Any list of this sort should also mention Anthony Foster, in chapter 3 of *Kenilworth;* Jenkin Vincent (or Jin Vin), in the opening chapter of *Nigel*; Quentin Durward's uncle, Ludovic Lesly (chap. 5), and the Bohemian, Hayraddin Maugrabin (chap. 15); Damian de Lacy, of *The Betrothed* (chap. 9); Kenneth and the supposed emir, in the first two chapters of *The Talisman*; Anne of Geierstein, in the novel of the same name (chap. 3); and the minstrel Bertram, in the first chapter of *Castle Dangerous*. The portrait of King James I in *The Fortunes of Nigel* begins as *effictio*, but then comes the famous paragraph of *notatio*, beginning "But such inconsistencies in dress and appointments were mere outward types of those which existed in the royal character" and ending "he was the wisest fool in Christendom" (chap. 5). Scott combines the two methods also in *The Abbot*, where one word-portrait begins "Sir Halbert Glendinning was the same, yet a different person from what he had appeared in his early years" (chap. 3).

We have already seen in examining his poetry that Scott knew how to take advantage of the age-old device of *occupatio*, which is also noted by Geoffrey of Vinsauf and used by virtually all the Middle English writers. Chaucer, who was probably Scott's model, spends some forty-five lines in claiming *not* to describe Arcite's funeral. In the Waverley Novels this standard method of condensing is sometimes used by the narrator (Scott himself or a persona) and sometimes by a character in the story. A typical example comes near the end of *Waverley*, when Scott writes: "We shall not attempt to describe the meeting of the father and daughter,—loving each other so affectionately, and separated under such perilous circumstances. Still less shall we attempt too analyze the deep blush of Rose, at receiving the compliments of Waverley, or stop to inquire whether she had any curiosity respecting the particular cause of his journey to Scotland at that period. We shall not even trouble the reader with the humdrum details of a courtship Sixty Years since" (chap. 67). Another example, almost in the manner of the Knight's Tale, begins "We are, therefore, so far from attempting to trace the dull progress of Messrs. Clippurse and Hookem, or that of their worthy official brethren who had the charge of suing out the pardons of Edward Waverley and his intended father-in-law, that we can but touch upon matters more attractive" (chap. 70).

In *Rob Roy*, Francis Osbaldistone gives the reader a lot of information about Loch Lomond while pretending not to: "I will spare you the attempt to describe what you would hardly comprehend without going to see it, but certainly this noble lake, boasting innumerable beautiful islands, of every varying form and outline which fancy can frame,—its northern extremity narrowing until it is lost among dusky and retreating mountains, while, gradually widening as it extends to the southward, it spreads its base around the indentures and promontories of a fair and fertile land,—affords one of the most surprising, beautiful, and sublime spectacles in nature" (chap. 36). Dugald Dalgetty uses the device in straightforward fashion at the end of the speech that closes the second chapter of *A Legend of Montrose*: "So your lordship has an outline of my brief story, excepting my deportment in those passages of action in the field, in leaguers, storms, and onslaughts, whilk would be wearisome to narrate, and might, peradventure, better befit any other tongue than mine own"; and Scott as narrrator uses it with variation at the end of chapter 11, describing the beauties of the "noble" scenery surrounding Loch Fine which Captain Dalgetty might have "admired" or "marked" or "noticed" "if he had been so minded." There are further striking examples in chapter 20 of *St. Ronan's Well*, where Scott prefaces the details of preparations for a party by saying, "We must not pause to dilate upon the various labours of body and spirit which preceded the intervening space"; and in the last chapter of *The Talisman*: "But we cannot stop to describe the cloth of gold and silver, the superb embroidery in Arabesque, the shawls of Cashmere, and the muslins of India, which were here unfolded in all their splendour; far less to tell the different sweetmeats, ragouts edged with rice coloured in various manners, with all the other niceties of Eastern cookery."

Scott's very last novel, *The Siege of Malta*, is no exception: "I might describe the whole of the fortifications but it would fill my pages with hard names which would serve rather to embarras [sic] than to instruct. It is sufficient to say that they bore a strong resemblance to those used in the Middle Ages when the style of defence against gunpowder began to be adopted and improved upon."[23] And again: "Other General Officers there were who, inspired by a share of the ardent courage so boldly evinced by the most distinguished leaders, rose above the character which they had on less fortunate occasions formed to themselves, but we would not willingly be so prolix as to be tiresome."[24] Interestingly, even if Scott had known no Middle English, he would have found examples enough of *occupatio* in Rose's *Partenopex de Blois* and *Amadis de Gaul*. Not irrelevant to the present discussion is one example from his *Amadis:*

> To tell, as meet, the costly feast's array,
> My tedious tale would hold a summer's day.
> I let to sing, who mid the courtly throng
> Did most excel in dance, or sprightly song:
> Who first, who last, were seated on the dais,
> Who carp'd of love or arms in curtiest phrase,
> What merry minstrels harp, what brachets lie
> The feet beneath, what hawks are perch'd on high. [p. 157]

Rose adds in a note, "I need scarcely observe, that these lines are an imitation of a passage in the Knight's Tale of Chaucer" (p. 185).

A Scott character occasionally uses self-deprecation, one of the many conventional topics, or *topoi*, to be found in medieval literature.[25] It comes at the beginning of Lord Menteith's harangue in chapter 7 of *Montrose*: "With great modesty, and at the same time with spirit, that young lord said, 'he wished what he was about to propose had come from some person of better known and more established character.' " And Scott himself uses it in his introduction of 1831 to *Anne of Geierstein* with regard to his failing memory. In the case of Menteith the self-deprecation is not sincere; it is an assumed pose, as indeed it normally is.

More important to the present discussion is Scott's use of proverbs that go back to medieval times. We have already noticed a few. Ellieslaw's observation in *The Black Dwarf* that Westburnflat "had other tow on his distaff last night" (chap. 12) can be found in the Miller's Tale (I, 3774) and in Hoccleve's *Regement of Princes* (line 1226). And just before Caleb Balderston steals the wildfowl from the Girders' kitchen, Scott comments that "necessity was equally imperious and lawless," reminding us of John's words in the Reeve's Tale: "Nede has na peer" (I, 4026). The miller Symkyn in the same tale furnishes another proverb—"The gretteste clerkes been noght wisest men" (I, 4054)—that Scott uses, as we have already seen, in *The Monastery* and *Kenilworth*.

When the doughty patriarch Magnus Troil is captured by pirates, in *The Pirate*, Scott wisely observes that "the willow which bends to the tempest often escapes better than the oak which resists it; and so, in great calamities, it sometimes happens, that light and frivolous spirits recover their elasticity and presence of mind sooner than those of a loftier character" (chap. 36). One is reminded of words spoken by Pandarus, that master of proverbial expression, to Troilus with regard to the winning of Criseyde:

> And reed that boweth down for every blast,
> Ful lightly, cesse wynd, it wol aryse;
> But no nyl nought an ook, whan it is cast."
> [*Troilus and Criseyde*, II.1387-89]

When Quentin Durward first enters the great hall of Schonwaldt, he is seated next to the Bishop's chaplain, "who welcomed the stranger with the old college jest of *Sero venientibus ossa* [For latecomers, the bones], while he took care so to load his plate with dainties, as to take away all appearance of that tendency to reality, which in Quentin's country, is said to render a joke either no joke, or at best an unpalatable one" (chap. 19). A footnote geared to this sentence reads, " 'A sooth boord (true joke) is no boord,' says the Scot." Scott may have known this proverb from the Cook's Prologue, where it appears in Flemish garb as Roger the Cook answers the Host's allegations of malpractice in his kitchen: "Thou seist ful sooth ... by my fey! / But 'sooth pley, quaad pley,' as the Flemyng seith" (I, 4356-57), *quaad* meaning "bad." Scott repeats the proverb in *Redgauntlet*: Provost Crosbie says "The sooth bourd is nae bourd" to the Laird of Summertrees, who has made some remark that offends Mrs. Crosbie (chap. 11).

In *The Fortunes of Nigel* Richard Moniplies says to John Christie, "It's an ill bird that fouls its own nest" (chap. 26) when Christie thinks Nigel has seduced Mrs. Christie and speaks ill of his former Scottish guests, Nigel and Richard. This proverb occurs also in *Redgauntlet*—spoken by the elder Fairford shortly after Alan Fairford has bolted and left his client Peter Peebles in the lurch: "It's an ill bird that defiles its ain nest. I must cover up the scandal as well as I can" (chap. 2)—and I have already noted an instance in *Rob Roy* (see Chapter 4). Scott perhaps remembered Hoccleve's *Letter of Cupid*—"Men seyn þat brid or foul is deshonest, / what so it be and holden ful cherlissh, / þat wont is to deffoule his owne nest" (lines 184–86)—but it occurs elsewhere too in literature before 1500.[26] I have already cited the Earl of Douglas's unkind words about Henry Smith in *The Fair Maid of Perth*—"A churl will savour of churl's kind" (chap. 34)—which recall the Summoner's Tale: "I seye, a cherl hath doon a cherles dede" (III, 2206). In sum, Scott's frequent use of old proverbs is still another link in the chain that connects the Waverley Novels with the literature of the Middle Ages.

Throughout this study I have called attention to various medieval genres that Scott adapted to his needs. His long poems are imitations of medieval metrical romances, and one of them, *The Lady of the Lake*, contains a hymn to the Virgin. The "ditty" about Anna-Marie, which is sung by Wamba and King Richard in chapter 40 of *Ivanhoe*, is a variation of the medieval *aubade*, a song of lovers at daybreak. Father Eustace and the Protestant Henry Warden, of *The Monastery*, engage in a quasi-medieval debate (chaps. 31–32); so do Hugo de Lacy and Archibishop Baldwin in *The Betrothed* (chap. 18).

One also finds in the Waverley Novels a number of more or less formal biddings of farewell, sometimes very short and sometimes of greater length. Here are some examples:

Jeanie Deans to Mrs. Saddletree, when the idea dawns on her to try to procure a pardon for Effie:

Fare ye weel, Mrs. Saddletree; and may ye never want a friend in the hour o' distress! [*The Heart of Mid-Lothian*, chap. 25]

Cedric taking leave of Athelstane and Wamba at Torquilstone:

"Noble Athelstane, farewell; and farewell, my poor boy, whose heart might make amends for a weaker head—I will save you, or return and die with you. The royal blood of our Saxon kings shall not be spilt while mine beats in my veins; nor shall one hair fall from the head of the kind knave who risked himself for his master, if Cedric's peril can prevent it.—Farewell."

"Farewell, noble Cedric," said Athelstane; "remember it is the true part of a friar to accept refreshment, if you are offered any."

"Farewell, uncle," added Wamba; "and remember *Pax vobiscum*." [*Ivanhoe*, chap. 26]

The Earl of March, upon leaving King Robert III and the Scottish court:

Farewell, my liege. My counsels here avail not—nay, are so unfavourably received that perhaps further stay were unwholesome for my safety. May God keep your Highness from open enemies and treacherous friends! I am for my Castle of Dunbar, from whence I think you will soon hear news. Farewell to you, my Lords of Albany and Douglas; you are playing a high game, look you play it fairly. Farewell, poor thoughtless Prince, who art sporting like a fawn within spring of a tiger! Farewell, all. George of Dunbar sees the evil he cannot remedy. Adieu, all. [*The Fair Maid of Perth*, chap. 13]

The elder Philipson to the sleeping Arnold Biederman, and the thoughts of Arthur Philipson, just before father and son depart at dawn from Graffs-lust:

"Farewell, mirror of ancient faith and integrity—farewell, noble Arnold,—farewell, soul of truth and candour—to whom cowardice, selfishness, and falsehood are alike unknown!"

And farewell, thought his son, to the loveliest, and most candid, yet most mysterious of maidens!—But the adieu, as may well be believed, was not, like that of his father, expressed in words. [*Anne of Geierstein*, chap. 13]

Anne to Arthur Philipson, when she is forced to abandon her castle:

Farewell!—Farewell! Accept this token of friendship, and wear it for my sake. May you be happy! [*Anne of Geierstein*, chap. 23]

Everyone will recall Othello's well-known and moving farewell speech in the "temptation scene" (Act III, scene iii):

> I had been happy if the general camp,
> Pioners and all, had tasted her sweet body,
> So I had nothing known. Oh, now forever
> Farewell the tranquil mind! Farewell content!
> Farewell the plumed troop and the big wars
> That make ambition virtue! Oh, farewell,
> Farewell the neighing steed and the shrill trump,
> The spirit-stirring drum, the ear-piercing fife,
> The royal banner and all quality,
> Pride, pomp, and circumstance of glorious war!
> And, O you mortal engines, whose rude throats
> The immortal Jove's dread clamors counterfeit,
> Farewell! Othello's occupation's gone!

I think it just as likely, though, that Scott's inspiration came from medieval literature. A brief example occurs in *Troilus and Criseyde* when Troilus, thinking that Criseyde is dead, is about to take his own life:

> And thow, cite, which that I leve in wo,
> And thow, Priam, and bretheren al yfeere,
> And thow, my moder, farewel! for I go;
> And Atropos, make redy thow my beere. [IV.1205–08]

Valentine, having been taken prisoner by the Saracens, bewails his lot at some length: "I am of all pleasure vnwrapped and separed from my friendes, and am in the handes of myne enemies. Farewel my fader noble emperour of Grece, for in me you shal haue no more a chylde. Farewell the noble Bellyssant my mother, for you had neuer for me but a lytle pleasure nor comforte, and you shal neuer haue more but sorow and distresse. Fare well my valyaunt broder Orson that hath loued me with so good heart."[27]

And Raymondin, having broken the all-important taboo and beholding his wife a serpent "fro the nauel dounward," immediately repents: "Halas, Melusyne . . . of whom all the world spake wele, now haue I lost you for euer. Now haue I fonde the ende of my Joye / and the begynnyng is to me now present of myn euerlastyng heuynes / Farewel beaute, bounte, swetenes, amyablete / Farwel wyt, curtoysye, & humilite / Farwel al my joye, al my comfort & myn hoop / Farwel myn herte, my prowes, my valyaunce."[28]

By far the most striking example I have found is in *The Squyr of Lowe Degre*, where the King's daughter of Hungary is lamenting the loss of her lover, many years after his supposed death:

> And, squier, for the love of thee,
> Fy on this worldes vanité!
> Farewell golde, pure and fine;
> Farewell velvet and satine;
> Farewell castelles and maners also;
> Farewell huntinge and hawkinge too;
> Farewell revell, mirthe, and play;
> Farewell pleasure and garmentes gay;
> Farewell perle and precious stone;
> Farewell my juielles everychone;
> Farwell mantell and scarlet reed;
> Farewell crowne unto my heed;
> Farewell hawkes and farewell hounde;
> Farewell markes and many a pounde;
> Farewell huntinge at the hare;
> Farewell harte and hinde for evermare.[29]

In view of Scott's profound knowledge of all the works quoted, it is hard to believe that he would not have been aware of the tradition of farewell speech s. I would argue that the farewell speeches of the Waverley Novels were directly inspired by medieval romance.

The foregoing discussion leads us naturally into a larger topic: Scott's novels abound in what one might call set speeches, sometimes addressed to one or more other persons and sometimes spoken in a soliloquy. These speeches can be highly rhetorical and impassioned, or moderately rhetorical, or quietly meditative. The famous malediction that Meg Merrilies pronounces upon Godfrey Bertram, the old Laird of Ellangowan in *Guy Mannering* (chap. 8), is impassioned to the point of being virtually operatic:

Ride your ways . . . ride your ways, Laird of Ellangowan, ride your ways, Godfrey Bertram! This day have ye quenched seven smoking hearths,—see if the fire in your ain parlour burn the blyther for that. Ye have riven the thack off seven cottar-houses,—look if your ain roof-tree stand the faster. Ye may stable your stirks in the shealings at Derncleugh,—see that the hare does not couch on the hearthstane at Ellangowan. Ride your ways, Godfrey Bertram,—what do ye glower after our folk for? There's thirty hearts there that wad hae wanted bread ere ye had wanted sunkets, and spent their life-blood ere ye had scratched your finger. Yes, there's thirty yonder, from the auld wife of an hundred to the babe that was born last week, that ye have turned out o' their bits o' bields, to sleep with the tod and the black-cock in the muirs! Ride your ways, Ellangowan. Our bairns are hinging at our weary backs: look that your braw cradle at hame be the fairer spread up,—not that I am wishing ill to little Harry, or to the babe that's yet to be born,—God forbid,—and make them kind to the poor, and better folk than their fathers! And now, ride e'en your ways; for these are the last words ye'll ever hear Meg Merrilies speak, and this is the last reise that I'll ever cut in the bonny woods of Ellangowan.

Part of the effect here obviously comes from the almost liturgical repetition of "Ride your ways." Another speech of passionate intensity is Magdalen Græme's memorable address in *The Abbot* (chap. 32) to Mary, Queen of Scots, at Lochleven:

Arise . . . Queen of France and of England! Arise, lioness of Scotland, and be not dismayed, though the nets of the hunters have encircled thee! . . . Let the Lady of Lochleven double her bolts and deepen her dungeons, they shall not retain thee—each element shall give thee its assistance ere thou shalt continue captive—the land shall lend its earthquakes, the water its waves, the air its tempests, the fire its devouring flames, to desolate this house, rather than it shall continue the place of thy captivity.—Hear this and tremble, all ye who fight against the light, for she says it, to whom it hath been assured!

The "astonished" physician in attendance observes, "If there was ever an *Energumene*, or possessed Demoniac, in our days, there is a devil speaking with that woman's tongue."

One recalls also the operatic speeches and soliloquies of Richard Varney, in *Kenilworth*, as well as the brief, impassioned meditation of Tressilian at Cumnor-Place: "These are the associates, Amy . . . to which thy cruel levity—thine unthinking and most unmerited falsehood, has condemned him, of whom his friends once hoped far other things, and who now scorns himself as he will be scorned by others, for the baseness he stoops to for the love of thee!" (chap. 4); it is broken off by Amy Robsart's sudden entrance. And there is Catharine Glover's righteous indignation in *The Fair Maid of Perth*—"And is it even so? . . . and can so much of the wishes, hopes, and prejudices of this vile world affect him who may be called to-morrow to lay down his life for opposing the corruptions of a wicked age and backsliding priesthood?"—when Father Clement suggests the possibility of her marrying the lascivious Duke of Rothsay (chap. 14). Somewhat less rhetorical is Nigel Olifaunt's soliloquy at Alsatia, the haven for criminals in London, when he is at the low ebb of his fortunes; this comes right after Scott's explanation of why he uses soliloquies: "In narrative, no doubt, the writer has the alternative of telling that his personages thought so and so, inferred thus and thus, and arrived at such and such a conclusion; but the soliloquy is a more concise and spirited mode of communicating the same information." (chap. 22). Other soliloquies include the agitated reflection of Edward Christian, in *Peveril of the Peak* (chap. 29), just after Major Bridgenorth has criticized him for being overly zealous in his wish for revenge (beginning "I ought to have persuaded him to return" and ending "And after all, what I am labouring to bring about is best for himself, the wench, and above all, for me, Edward Christian"); and the spirited monologue of the villainous Henbane Dwining, in chapter 22 of *The Fair Maid of Perth*, on the power he will obtain from the wealth he is accumulating; and so on and so on and so on.

We are dealing here in part with the influence of Elizabethan and Jacobean drama, most notably Shakespearean soliloquy, but medieval romance is full of set speeches as well. One thinks immediately of the complaints of Palamon and Arcite in prison in Athens, and of the speech of Arcite when he is dying, and of the touching laments of Troilus when he learns that Criseyde will have to depart from Troy. Set speeches are perhaps even more striking in the prose romances. There are the heart-rending laments of Bellyssant, in *Valentine and Orson*, in response to her husband the emperor's cruel mistreatment and to the loss of her newly born children; here is one example:

Alas said she, there is not in the world a more discomforted lady than I am, for from syde to side I am deuoyde of Ioye, of pleasure, of myrthe, and am replete wyth doloure and misery, and of intollerable dystresse, greued wyth all trybulacyons, and amonge all desolates, the moost desolate. Alas Emperour you are the cause to auaunce my death wrongfully, and without cause, & by euyl counsell haue depryued me from your company, for on my soule neuer the dayes of my life dydde I faute wyth my body. I haue nowe loste by you your propre chyldren legityme, yssued out of bloud ryall, by whom I trusted ones to be venged. Come death vnto me for to finisshe my dolour for the death shall be more agreeable vnto me, than to liue in this martyre.[30]

In *Melusine* the complaint of Raymondin, which begins with the farewell speech quoted above, continues for another twenty lines of heartfelt agony expressed in highly rhetorical language. And in the same romance, after her father King Frederick has been killed by the King of Cracow, there is the pitiful lament of Eglantyne, ending with an impassioned prayer to the

Virgin: "O ryght noble, ryght puyssaunt, & ryght excellent pryncesse! virgyne & moder of god! Marye, my lady & maistresse / haue compassion on me! poure orphenyn & faderles."[31]

The most impassioned, most highly rhetorical set speeches I have found are in the late prose romance *The Renowned History of the Seven Champions of Christendom*.[32] Here, for example, is the lament of St. George of England's father, when he learns that his child has been stolen:

O heavens! why cover ye not the earth with everlasting night? Why do these eyes accursed behold the sun? O that the waves of Œnipus would end my days; or yon high mountains crush me with their fall! Or, heavens! let me rove a wretched exile and forlorn, in solitary woods to make my moan; the senseless trees, the savage and untamed beasts, would grieve at miseries like mine. What monster has bereaved me of my child? What tyrant's glutted with his blood? O that the winds would bring me tidings of him, though from the most distant quarters of the world, thither would I fly to see him; or were he hid beneath the ocean's deepest floods, thither would I dive to bring him forth; or if, like feathered fowls, he winged the liquid air, thither would I mount to catch him in my arms, and embrace him that never yet mine eyes beheld. But why do I rave, and vainly thus exclaim, when neither earth, nor air, or seas, or anything in earth, air, or seas, can bring me comfort? [Chap. 1]

The effect is achieved by rhetorical questions, emotional exclamations, alliteration, anaphora, and other forms of repetition, to name the most prominent devices. Not less melodramatic is the lamentation (in chap. 2) of Kalyb, the Lady of the Woods, who stole the child and who is finally imprisoned in a cave:

O miserable Kalyb . . . cursed be thy destiny, for now thou art enclosed within a desolate and darksome den! where neither sun can lend thee comfort with his enlivening beams, nor the cool breath of air refresh thy parched and burning body; thou art thyself, by magic art, empaled and rooted in the centre of earth, who wert thyself the wonder of the times for magic. I, that by art have made my journey to the lowest depths of hell, where multitudes of black and ugly spirits have trembled at my charms; I that have bound the Furies in my iron chains, and caused them to attend my pleasure through the wilds of Egypt, or where the tawny Moor inhabits, am now myself constrained to languish in eternal darkness. Woe to my soul! woe to my charms! and woe to all my magic spells! for they have bound me in this hollow rock. Let the sun grow pale, and the earth be covered with eternal darkness. Let the firmament be turned to pitch; roar hell! quake earth! swell seas! and all ye stars and planets burst from your spheres! Let all nature be convulsed and tortured with the misery of wretched Kalyb!

And still later in the story (chap. 3) there is the complaint of St. George when he is in prison in Persia:

O cruel destiny! Why am I punished in this sort? Have I conspired against the majesty of heaven, that it has hurled such vengeance on my head? O! shall I never regain my former liberty, that I may be revenged on those who have imprisoned me? Frown, angry heavens, on these bloody-minded infidels, these daring rebels against the truth of thy divinity; these professed enemies of Christ. And may the plagues of Pharoah light upon their country, and the miseries of Œdipus upon their princes. Let them be witnesses of their daughters' ravishments, and behold their cities flaming like the burning battlements of Troy.

These speeches not only have models in medieval romance, but they have undoubtedly been influenced by sixteenth-century drama as well.

Twentieth-century readers who have grown up on psychologically oriented literature and stream of consciousness are sometimes put off by the highly rhetorical set speeches in Scott, which they find unnatural. The quotations above are instructive in that they remind us that Scott was working in a quite different tradition. I am not able to come up with *specific* set speeches in the old romances that Scott had in mind in writing his own set speeches, and the situations in which his occur are more varied than those of romance, which so often hinge on the speaker's having lost a loved one, or his children, or his freedom; but there is a similarity in manner that can hardly be fortuitous. I am convinced that there is a definite connection between Scott's set speeches and those of earlier literature—that we are dealing here with a tradition that can be traced from Scott back through Shakespeare and drama-influenced sixteenth-century romance to the verse and prose romances of the Middle Ages. And this tradition is very much a part of Scott's style.

Some of the quietly meditative set speeches have a philosophical bent. Such is the meditation of Harry Bertram in *Guy Mannering* as he looks out upon the ocean's waves, "crossing, bursting, and mingling with each other," from his room of confinement at Portanferry: " 'A wild and dim spectacle,' said Bertram to himself, 'like those crossing tides of fate which have tossed me about the world from my infancy upwards!' " (chap. 48). Near the end of *Old Mortality* (chap. 41), a turbulent mountain stream causes Henry Morton to ponder the brevity of life:

"Murmurer that thou art," said Morton, in the enthusiasm of his reverie, "why chafe with the rocks that stop thy course for a moment? There is a sea to receive thee in its bosom; and there is an eternity for man when his fretful and hasty course through the vale of time shall be ceased and over. What thy petty fuming is to the deep and vast billows of a shoreless ocean, are our cares, hopes, fears, joys, and sorrows to the objects which must occupy us through the awful and boundless succession of ages!"

Other "moral observations,"[33] come from Scott as narrator. After telling how easily Mary Avenel and Mysie Happer became friends, in *The Monastery* (chap. 14), Scott observes: "In youth, however, there is a sort of free-masonry, which, without much conversation, teaches young persons to estimate each other's character, and places them at ease on the shortest acquaintance. It is only when taught deceit by the commerce of the world, that we learn to shroud our character from observation, and to disguise our real sentiments from those with whom we are placed in communion." Later in the same chapter he muses on Edward Glendinning's difficulty in the presence of Sir Piercie Shafton: "But, alas! where is the man of modest merit, and real talent, who has not suffered from being outshone in conversation, and outstripped in the race of life, by men of less reserve, and of qualities more showy, though less substantial? and well constituted must the mind be, that can yield up the prize without envy to competitors more worthy than himself." In the next chapter he says about Edward, in a different situation, "He was yet to learn how long it is ere our reason is enabled to triumph over the force of external circumstances, and how much our feelings are affected by novelty, and blunted by use and habit." And later, he offers a somewhat similar observation with regard to Mary Avenel: "She felt as those who, loving for the first time, have lost what they loved, before time and repeated calamity have taught them that every loss is to a certain extent reparable or endurable" (chap. 30). The wistful tone of Scott's observations continues in the sequel, *The Abbot:* "Sir Halbert Glendinning looked at the demeanour of his new attendant [Roland Græme] with that sort of melancholy pleasure with which those who have long followed the pursuits of life, and are sensible of their vanity, regard the gay, young, and buoyant spirits to whom existence, as yet, is only hope and promise" (chap. 16).

In the next brilliant novel Scott says of Amy Robsart, who, "poorly led" and having just escaped from Cumnor-Place, is approaching the castle of her husband, Kenilworth, where preparations are under way for the queen's official visit: "No infliction can be so distressing to a mind absorbed in melancholy, as being plunged into a scene of mirth and revelry, forming an accompaniment so dissonant from its own feelings" (chap. 25). Such were Troilus's feelings at the house of Sarpedoun, where Pandarus hoped to cheer him up after Criseyde's departure from Troy. "Yet," Scott continues, "in the case of the Countess of Leicester, the noise and tumult of this giddy scene distracted her thoughts, and rendered her this sad service, that it became impossible for her to brood on her own misery, or to form terrible anticipations of her approaching fate." Scott saves his most poignant observation for Edmund Tressilian, Amy's rejected suitor:

Nothing is perhaps more dangerous to the future happiness of men of deep thought and retired habits, than the entertaining an early, long, and unfortunate attachment. It frequently sinks so deep into the mind, that it becomes their dream by night and their vision by day—mixes itself with every source of interest and enjoyment; and, when blighted and withered by final disappointment, it seems as if the springs of the spirit were dried up along with it. This aching of the heart, this languishing after a shadow which has lost all the gaiety of its colouring, this dwelling on the remembrance of a dream from which we have been long roughly awakened, is the weakness of a gentle and generous heart, and it was that of Tressilian. [Chap. 27]

The passage rings true, and Tressilian seems a projection of what Scott himself might have become if he had let himself be overwhelmed by disappointment at being rejected by Miss Williamina Belsches.

There are many more "moral observations" in the Waverley Novels, and they are "of all sorts."[34] "All men, I believe, enjoy an ill-natured joke," Scott says in *The Fair Maid of Perth* (chap. 8), with regard to the joke played on Oliver Proudfute by Henry Smith and the others in allowing him to be knocked off his horse by Devil's Dick of Hellgarth. Scott could not have been unaware of the frequent passages of philosophical observation in medieval romance, especially the prose romances. There is Malory's unflattering comparison of "love" in his own day with the genuine love prevalent in the time of King Arthur (see the discussion of *Castle Dangerous* in Chapter 6), and *Palmerin of England* is full of brief passages of moral reflection, such as the following:

For that the report of noble deeds doth urge the minds of the courageous to be equal with those who bear most commendation of their approved valiancy. And this is the good fruit of imagination and of ancient histories. [I, 289]

But such are the changes and mutabilities of Fortune, who, when the heart is drowned in grief past any good hope, she sendeth a happy success to requite the former mischance; and likewise, where most pleasure hath residence, there she provideth the greatest mishap. [I, 401]

For when things are of importance, much time should be expended in considering them, and little in executing. [I, 445]

Scott's passages of moral and philosophical reflection are more profound than those found in medieval romance, but the prototypes were certainly there, whatever additional influence the novels of Fielding, Smollett, Sterne, and others must have had on him in this important aspect of his style.

In view of the immense influence of medieval literature on Scott and in the wake of the Robertsonian approach to medieval literature, one might wonder whether any of the Waverley Novels were meant to be read allegorically. The answer is No. Scott himself had a low opinion of attempts to allegorize medieval literature. Or so at least his criticism of Jean Maugin's modernized version of the prose *Tristan*, published in 1554, would imply: "It is far inferior to the original work. Allegory was then the prevailing taste, and, though, it seems hard to wring a moral meaning out of the illicit amours of Tristrem and Yseult, Jean Maugin has done his best. Sir Tristrem is the emblem of the Christian perfection of chivalry, his fair paramour of—heaven knows what!"[35]

Structure

As an introduction to matters of structure, let us recall the way in which Scott begins *Old Mortality*. It is purported to be edited by one Jedediah Cleishbotham from the manuscript of a recently deceased teacher, Peter Pattieson, who based his story on the anecdotes of Robert Paterson, better known as Old Mortality. "Modern authors were not the first," Scott wrote in the Essay on Romance, "who invented the popular mode of introducing their works to the world as the contents of a newly-discovered manuscript." He then gives the account of how the medieval French romance *Perceforest* came into being (which is quoted at the end of Chapter 3). The versions of the Trojan War by Dictys Cretensis and Dares Phrygius, highly respected in the Middle Ages, were also presented to the world as the contents of newly discovered manuscripts—written by men who were supposed to have been participants or eyewitnesses and thus more reliable authorities than Homer, who lived three hundred years afterwards. Indeed, the *raison d'être* for this sort of ruse is to create an aura of authenticity; for Scott it had the additional attraction of helping him remain the Great Unknown.

One noticeable structural characteristic of Scott's novels is that they are rather slow in getting started; the reader does not know for a long time where the various strands of the story are leading. One has to read patiently through one-third of *Waverley* before anything happens—apparently happens, I should say, because a lot *is* going on that Waverley does not know about until later, and the reader is lulled into the quagmire along with the hero. Protracted beginnings can be observed also in romance; they are even necessary, according to the author of *Don Flores of Greece:*

If all waies were straight, and that wee needed not often times either to passe over mountains, or compasse about rivers, marshes, and ditches, to arrive where we desire to bee, we should rest us sometimes, and the pains wee took would be lesse tedious, and not seem so long, as oftentimes it is found to be. This I say, to the end that before we enter into the very depth of our History, and the true discourse of this Book, wee have been forced to choose out crooked waies and follow obscure paths, thereby drawing somewhat out of the way to make the matter more easie and intelligible: but seeing we are re-entred into the high way, beleive [*sic*] me the rest of the way you have to walk, is much more easie and pleasant than that which already wee have travelled: which to prove true, let us now return unto our matter.[36]

Scott has his own explanation near the end of *Waverley* (chap. 70), where he is excusing himself for not relating in detail the final events of the story:

I must remind my reader of the progress of a stone rolled down hill by an idle truant boy (a pastime at which I was myself expert in my more juvenile years); it moves at first slowly, avoiding by inflection every obstacle of the least importance; but when it has attained its full impulse, and draws near the conclusion of its career, it smokes and thunders down, taking a rood at every spring, clearing hedge and ditch like a Yorkshire huntsman, and becoming most furiously rapid in its course when it is nearest to being consigned to rest for ever. Even such is the course of a narrative, like that which you are perusing. The earlier events are studiously dwelt upon, that you, kind reader, may be introduced to the character rather by narrative than by the duller medium of direct description; but when the story draws near its close, we hurry over the circumstances, however important, which your imagination must have forestalled, and leave you to suppose those things which it would be abusing your patience to relate at length.

More about Scott's endings anon. His *middle* chapters follow a method typical of Malory and more especially of the long French prose romances. In *Redgauntlet*, for example, he tells us at some length (chaps. 3–9) about the adventures of Darsie Latimer. Then he leaves Darsie to relate at length (chaps. 10–16) what his friend Alan Fairford is doing. At the beginning of chapter 17 he returns to Darsie: "Our history must now, as the old romancers were wont to say, 'leave to tell' of the quest of Alan Fairford, and instruct our readers of the adventures which befell Darsie Latimer, left as he was in the precarious custody of his self-named tutor." The two friends come together in the same place in chapter 19, at Crackenthorp's pub. Scott uses this same method of following different strands of a story in *Ivanhoe*. After the tournament at Ashby there is a chapter devoted to the feast at which Cedric and the Saxons are insulted by their Norman hosts. There follows a chapter in which Maurice de Bracy plans to waylay Rowena, with the help of Brian de Bois-Guilbert. Then Scott returns to the Black Knight (Richard I), who had disappeared from the scene of the tournament: two colorful chapters relate his stay with the hermit. In the next two chapters Scott returns to Cedric and his party, who leave Ashby for home and are joined by Isaac and Rebecca and the wounded Ivanhoe.

They do not get very far before they are attacked and captured by De Bracy and Bois-Guilbert and are taken to Torquilstone, where the story divides into still more strands. A chapter is devoted to Cedric and Athelstane, who are kept separate from Rowena and the others; then, in the dungeon of the castle, Reginald Front-de-Bœuf tries through torture to extort money from Isaac. Next comes a chapter in which Rowena, in another part of the castle, is wooed by De Bracy; it is followed by the famous scene in which Rebecca, confined high up in one of the towers, is approached by Bois-Guilbert, whom she roundly refuses, threatening to jump from the window. The assault on Torquilstone by Robin Hood, the Black Knight, Cedric (who has escaped), and their allies brings all the various strands of the story together again.

Twentieth-century readers of the Waverley Novels are likely to be struck by the numerous poems and bits of poetry interspersed among the much longer passages of the prose narrative. Here again there are parallels in romance. *Antar, A Bedoueen Romance* incorporates Antar's own poems (see Chapter 1) and in *The Seven Champions of Christendom* there is occasional poetry: the voice from the mulberry tree, for example, sounds forth in verse. Enchantment and transformation are involved in the later romance, inasmuch as the mulberry tree is actually Princess Eglantine, the proud daughter of the King of Thessaly. Scott also has a tendency to use verse when something supernatural is in the wind. The old prophecies of *Guy Mannering* and *The Bride of Lammermoor* (cited below) are examples; in *The Monastery* Halbert Glendinning summons the White Lady in verse, and she answers him in like manner—the poetry helping to make the supernatural palatable, if not credible.

Another way Scott used to help make the supernatural convincing was to prepare for the really unusual by relating generally believed supernatural stories. Thus the account of the legend of the fountain, in *The Bride of Lammermoor,* prepares us for Old Alice's mysterious appearance to Edgar shortly after her death. And in *The Monastery* a brief account of "the savage and capricious Brown Man of the Moors" (chap. 2), together with the other otherworldy creatures that were believed to inhabit Glendearg, helps prepare us for the appearances of the White Lady. Scott may have been following here the lead of Jean d'Arras, who, in the first chapter of *Melusine,* discusses this very method of making the marvelous appear believable and relates briefly a story of faerie by the highly respected Gervaise of Tilbury which is similar to the one he is about to tell.[37]

As in the poems, Scott uses repetition to good effect. In *Waverley* there is occasional reference to the novel's subtitle, *'Tis Sixty Years Since:* "We shall not even trouble the reader with the humdrum details of a courtship Sixty Years since"; "Let us devoutly hope that . . . we shall never see the scenes or hold the sentiments that were general in Britain Sixty Years since" (chap. 67). Andrew Fairservice uses the phrase "since the sad and sorrowfu' Union" more than once in *Rob Roy;* it plays its part in Scott's depiction of Andrew's personality. Before she is introduced, there are at least three references to Mrs. Glass, the Scottish tobacconist "at the sign o' the Thistle"; it is she whom Jeanie Deans is supposed to stay with in London, in *The Heart of Mid-Lothian,* and the repetition of the phrase contributes in a small way to the drama that is unfolding.

Sometimes a larger unit is involved. When Harry Bertram of *Guy Mannering* first arrives at Ellangowan, not knowing yet who he is, the strange familiarity of the locality reminds him of "an old prophecy, or song, or rhyme":

> The dark shall be light,
> And the wrong made right,
> When Bertram's right and Bertram's might
> Shall meet on—[Chap. 41]

At this point his memory fails him, but the completion of the prophecy is recited twice by Meg Merrilies—"And Bertram's right and Bertram's might / Shall meet on Ellangowan's height" (chap. 46)—and the whole stanza appears in Meg's letter to Guy Mannering, which is read aloud by the lawyer Pleydell in the chapter immediately preceding the wonderful recognition and reunion scene. Just before Meg appears to the Dominie at Derncleugh, Scott uses another form of repetition to create suspense:

What, then, was his astonishment, when, on passing *the door—that door* which was supposed to have been placed there by one of the latter Lairds of Ellangowan to prevent presumptuous strangers from incurring the dangers of the haunted vault; *that door,* supposed to be always locked, and the key of which was popularly said to be deposited with the presbytery,—*that door, that very door,* opened suddenly, and the figure of Meg Merrilies, well known, though not seen for many a revolving year, was placed at once before the eyes of the startled Dominie! [Chap. 46; emphasis added]

Her first words—"I kenn'd ye wad be here. . . . I ken who ye seek"— help to set the stage for her heartrending "I kenn'd it would be this way" a few chapters later, in the smugglers' cave, after she has been shot by Dirk Hatteraick.

And there is much more repetition in the Waverley Novels, including the haunting prophecy about the last Laird of Ravenswood, in *The Bride of Lammermoor,* and the already quoted eight-line spell that Halbert Glendinning recites whenever he summons the White Lady, in *The Monastery*. Of course, repetition is a staple of ballads; it is also much used in the old romances, both in verse and in prose. I think at once of the frequent references to "the knight with the lion" in *Ywain and Gawain*, and the suspense that builds up in Malory's *Tale of Sir Gareth* about the Red Knight of the Red Launds, who (we are told several times) has "seven mennys strength," and Sir Bors's often repeated promise to defend Guinevere against the accusal of Sir Mador "onles there by aventure com a bettir knyght than I am to do batayle for you"; but examples are legion.

Another kind of repetition can be seen in Scott's use of a particular place as a focal point for important events in a story, and this is a structural technique that he may have learned from medieval romance. J.W. Thomas points out that in Eilhart von Oberge's *Tristrant*, "four of the more noteworthy occurrences—the aborted murder of Brangene, the deception of Mark at the linden, the delivery of the priest's letter, and the penultimate meeting of hero and heroine—take place in an orchard with a brook which was right beside the palace at Tintanjol."[38] I have found no indication that Scott was familiar with Eilhart, but he certainly knew the Knight's Tale, in which a beautiful natural setting near Athens is the site of three important events: the duel between Palamon and Arcite that is broken up by Theseus, the tournament in which Palamon and Arcite contend for the hand of Emily, and the cremation of Arcite's body on a huge funeral pyre. Similarly, in *The Talisman* an oasis known as the Diamond of the Desert is the site of Sir Kenneth's early encounter with the supposed Saracen emir, who in the disguise of the physician El Hakim later comforts a disgraced Kenneth at that very spot, and who there presides in his proper person—Saladin, the Soldan of the East—during the judicial combat in which Sir Kenneth vanquishes Conrade of Montserrat. Scott knew that a specific place used in this way gives a story a certain unity and concentration.

Much of the important action in *The Antiquary* occurs at the ruins of St. Ruth's Priory, where there is a duel between Lovel and Captain M'Intyre, where the scoundrelly Dousterswivel has hoodwinked Sir Arthur Wardour into believing there is buried treasure, where Dousterswivel is knocked unconscious by Steenie Muckelbackit, and where he awakens during the secretly conducted Roman Catholic funeral service for the recently deceased Countess of Glenallan. In *The Bride of Lammermoor* the fountain in the forest near Ravenswood is a place believed to be fatal to the Ravenswood family: it is where an ancestor of Edgar had an unfortunate liaison with a fairy mistress, where Lucy is revived after the incident with the wild bull, where Lucy and Edgar plight their troth, and where Edgar sees the apparition of Old Alice just after her death. In *The Monastery* the glen of Corri-nan-shian is a place of special significance. Early in the novel Father

Eustace has an encounter there with the White Lady. It is where Halbert Glendinning on two occasions summons the White Lady, where Halbert fights a duel with Sir Piercie Shafton, and where Edward Glendinning twice encounters the White Lady and hears her prediction of trouble for Halbert and Mary Avenel.

Things are more complicated in *Guy Mannering* because there are at least four places of special importance. When Harry Bertram, the missing heir, returns to Ellangowan after long absence, still not knowing who he is, "it happened that the spot upon which [he] chanced to station himself for the better viewing the castle was nearly the same on which his father had died" (chap. 41). The "top of a small hillock which overhung the road" near Ellangowan is where Meg Merrilies pronounces her impassioned malediction upon the old Laird; later she speaks with Dominie Sampson at that place, and it is very near this hillock that she suddenly appears to Harry Bertram and his friends: "It is *here* we should meet, on this very spot where my eyes last saw your father. Remember your promise, and follow me" (chap. 52). There is also the cave not far from Ellangowan in which Harry Bertram as a small boy was kept for a while after he had been kidnapped; it is also where the smuggler and kidnapper Dirk Hatteraick is finally captured, and where Meg Merrilies is mortally wounded. Finally, there is the Kaim of Derncleugh, where Meg protects Bertram for a few days after his return. It is where Sampson encounters her much later in the story; it is where she receives Bertram and Dandy Dinmont after the sudden appearance just noted; and it is where she dies.

"The Tale of 'Waverley,' " Scott wrote in the general preface, "was put together with so little care that I cannot boast of having sketched any distinct plan of the work." And yet, as I have shown in my earlier discussion of *Waverley*, he carefully brings all the characters together for the finale, very much in the manner of medieval romance. He describes his way of writing in more detail in his *Journal*, with particular reference to *Woodstock*, but he no doubt had his other novels in mind too: "I never could lay down a plan—or having laid it down I never could adhere to it; the action of composition always dilated some passages and abridged or omitted others and personages were rendered important or insignificant not according to their agency in the original conception of the plan but according to the success or otherwise with which I was able to bring them out. I only tried to make that which I was actually writing diverting and interesting, leaving the rest to fate" (*Journal*, p. 86). There is some truth in all this, and yet the novels are not so haphazard in organization as he would have us believe. Some of the others have conclusions as carefully wrought as the ending of *Waverley*. In the final chapters of *Redgauntlet*, Joe Crackenthorp's pub is the setting for the gathering of virtually all the novel's characters—the pauper litigant Peter Peebles, the Quaker Joshua Geddes, Nanty Ewart (captain of the smuggling vessel "Jumping Jenny"), Redgauntlet, Darsie Latimer, Alan Fairford, Cristal Nixon, Prince Charles Edward, and other conspirators whom we encounter for the first time. All the strands of the story are brought together; all complications are resolved. The same procedure is conspicuous in *Castle Dangerous*, where virtually all the main characters congregate for the Palm Sunday service at the Church of Douglas; they include John de Walton, Aymer de Valence, the old archer Gilbert Greenleaf, the minstrel Bertram, Thomas Dickson, Michael Fleming, Lady Augusta Berkely, and Margaret de Hautlieu. The conflict over the castle between the Scots and the English usurpers is resolved when the English receive orders to surrender the castle, and there is a "distribution of happiness at the conclusion of the piece."[39] In *The Pirate* all the characters come together at Kirkwall, in the Orkney Islands, for the final resolution of a rather complicated plot.

R.D.S. Jack has observed that this bringing together of all the strands of a story at the end is something that Scott admired in Italian romance.[40] It is also a characteristic of medieval romance, very noticeable in *Le Bone Florence of Rome*, Malory's *Tale of Sir Gareth*, and *Palmerin of England*. In *Le Bone Florence* the heroine, living incognita in a nunnery, has acquired fame as a healer. Her husband Esmere and all the men who have done her wrong—her brother-in-law Mylys, the knight Machary, her page Clarebalde, and the evil mariner—are broken down with illness and infirmity, and they come to her by chance at the same time to be cured. Machary is accompanied by Sir Tyrry and his wife Eglantine, who had been friendly to Florence. This gathering of characters brings the strands of the story together, and the resolution is at hand. Florence says that she cannot cure the men unless they confess their sins fully. They do so, much to the astonishment of Esmere, Tyrry, and Eglantine. In conclusion, Esmere orders a fire to be lighted, and the wrongdoers are burned up. One has to turn to Hoccleve's version of this part of the story, his *Tale of Jereslaus' Wife*, to find a final distribution of happiness for all concerned: *his* wrongdoers get off scot-free. In the *Tale of Sir Gareth* there is also a final distribution of happiness, as all the knights whom Gareth has defeated—the Grene Knyght, the Rede Knyght, Sir Persaunte of Inde, and the Rede Knyght of the Rede Laundis—come to King Arthur's court, along with scores of their vassal knights, to pay homage to Gareth and to serve at his wedding (actually a triple wedding). In *Palmerin of England* all the strands of the story are brought together near the end of Part I, with the events leading up to and including the defeat of the giant Dramuziando. This occasion is happy, but the romance does not end happily: in the closing chapters of Part IV all the leading characters are at Constantinople for the final tragic battle against the Turks, which the Christians win only at very great cost, those who are still alive wanting to die. Not all old romances end with a distribution of happiness, but neither do all of the Waverley Novels.

In addition, then, to story-patterns, motifs, character types, and detail of one sort or another, there are elements of style and structure (as in the poems) that derive directly or indirectly from Chaucer and medieval romance and are an important part of each novel's texture. It remains to be explained what all this means and why it is important.

8

CONCLUSION

IN HIS pioneering study of Shakespeare's influence on Scott, Wilmon Brewer first goes through Scott's poems and novels one by one and tells what they owe to Shakespeare's plays. Later he reverses his method and puts the plays in the forefront.[1] Taking a hint from Brewer, I shall now turn things around and glance very briefly at the medieval romances in roughly a descending order of the amount and importance of their influence on Scott.

At the top of the list are the Tristan-story and Chaucer's Knight's Tale. The influence of the Tristan-story is very pervasive in Scott, as might be expected, since as a young man he edited the Middle English poetical version. As we have seen, he draws most heavily on Tristan in *The Betrothed*. The novel's young hero, out of a sense of duty, helps his uncle woo the heroine, even though he is in love with her himself and she with him; later in the novel she is betrothed to the uncle. We are constantly reminded of Tristan, Iseult, and King Mark, and the similarity in situation enhances and deepens the novel.[2] The Knight's Tale provided Scott with a story-pattern that he used in at least a dozen of his works. In the form closest to Chaucer it involves two equally or almost equally attractive young men who are in love with the same girl and are trying to win her hand in marriage, but Scott varied the basic pattern in almost every conceivable way.[3]

Next on anyone's list should come *Bevis of Hampton*, *Amadis of Gaul*, *Richard Coer de Lyon*, and the prose romances *Valentine and Orson* and Malory's *Morte Darthur*, although not necessarily in this order. In the preface to a 1637 edition of Valentine and Orson, the printer tells his readers:

If you desire to see the cares and troubles of kings, here they are: If you desire to know the battels of Martiall Champions here they are: If of Courtly Tournaments and Combats of Princes heere thy [*sic*] are: If of the sorrows of distressed Ladyes, here they are: If of strange births & savage educations, heere they are: If of friends long lost, & of their joyfull meetings againe, here they are: If the reward of Traitors & treasons, here they are: If of long captivities and imprisonments, here they are.[4]

Much the same could be said about the Waverley Novels—and about the *Morte Darthur*, which also had a profound influence on Scott. In some ways Scott's temperament was closer to the prose romances of the fifteenth and sixteenth centuries than to the earlier verse romances. In the later romances there was more emphasis on "action" and "historical fact" than on the "remote" and the "unobtainable." Larry Benson has reminded us that the prose romances "emphasize realistic geographical settings, deal with the possible more often than the marvelous, and frequently employ realistic details of action, manners, and speech."[5]

Next in importance to Scott is a group of verse romances including *Sir Gowther, The Marriage of Sir Gawaine, Guy of Warwick, Le Bone Florence of Rome, The Squire of Low Degree,* and *Sir Eglamour of Artois,* again not necessarily in this order. As for other romances, *Rauf Coilyear* contains the motif of the king in disguise, found also in ballads, which Scott used to good advantage in *Quentin Durward* and (before the rediscovery of *Rauf*) in *The Lady of the Lake* and *Ivanhoe. Tirant lo Blanch,* which he was reading when he wrote *Marmion,* is still another source, along with *Bevis* and *Guy of Warwick,* for the scene at Rotherwood in which Ivanhoe, disguised as a palmer, is questioned about the goings-on in Palestine. Also important to Scott were *Aucassin and Nicolette, Floris and Blancheflur, Huon of Bordeaux, King Horn, Melusine, Palmerin of England, Partenopex de Blois,* and *Sir Launfal.* I suspect that he learned most of what he knew about courtly love from *Le Petit Jehan de Saintré. Golagrus and Gawain* provided him with an incident of comic relief that he used in *The Bride of Lammermoor;* Marie's *Lai of Yonec* lies behind a strange incident in *The Pirate;* and in *Sir Triamour* the ability of a dog to single out and attack the villain who has done it wrong undoubtedly inspired the similar incident in *The Talisman.* Parallels for one thing or another in the Waverley Novels can be found in a host of other romances; they include *Agesilan of Colchos, Amadis of Greece, Antar, Don Flores of Greece, Esplandian, Florisel de Niquea, Gamelyn, Das Heldenbuch, The Knight of the Swan, Roswall and Lillian, Sir Orfeo,* and *Ysaie le Triste.*

Why should all this be important? Let me begin by talking around the question. Just before entering into his well-known and delightful "analysis" of *The Antiquary,* E.M. Forster states that there are two reasons why Scott is famous: (1) he reawakens in many people pleasant memories from their childhood, when the Waverley Novels were read aloud to them; and (2) he indeed can tell a good story—he has "the primitive power of keeping the reader in suspense and playing on his curiosity."[6] Forster was writing "sixty years since"; it might be hard today to find anyone who heard Scott's novels read to him as a child. I understand, though, what Forster is saying, because I had a somewhat similar experience when I reread *Great Expectations* at age forty in preparation for teaching it to sophomores. I had first become acquainted with this novel when I was fifteen, and in reading it again I found that many thoughts and feelings that I had shoved into an out-of-the-way corner of my mind, and had apparently forgotten, somehow began to reemerge. It was a strange experience and in some ways pleasant, but not altogether so, since some of the memories were not happy. When people of my generation read Scott, however, there is no sunken reservoir of this sort to be stirred up, because the only work of Scott we were exposed to as young people was *Ivanhoe*, when we were in the ninth grade, and only in a very much abridged version. And yet, when I began to read Scott in my twenties, something did happen. There was something about his stories—whether they were of escape in the nick of time, or of the expulsion of a young man who later returns to try to regain what is rightfully his, or of a girl about to be forced into a marriage she does not want, or of betrayal, faithfulness, love, hate, or murder—that reminded me of other stories I had been exposed to as a child—fairy tales, children's stories, maybe a Saturday afternoon movie. Reading Scott did bring back memories from my remote past, and his novels indeed held for me some sort of basic or "primitive" appeal.

The key to understanding may lie in the word *primitive*. Northrop Frye, who belongs to the generation of my parents, has very sensitively described his connection with Scott. He read all the Waverley Novels as a boy "with utter fascination," then went through a phase of critical snobbery when he was in college, but returned to Scott in later life, almost by chance (if there really is such a thing), and was fascinated once again: "The same building blocks appeared every time: light and dark heroines, outlawed or secret societies, wild women chanting prophecies, heroes of mysterious and ultimately fortunate birth; but the variety with which they were disposed was what now impressed me."[7] Frye appears to be thinking mainly of *Guy Mannering*, and indeed there *is* a deep-seated appeal to this novel. A correct order has been disrupted, and we enjoy seeing it straightened out. Moreover, the good fortune of Harry Bertram—the discovery that he is the long-lost heir—fulfills the childhood dreams of many of us that we too might some day turn out to be long-lost heirs or persons of noble birth or of importance. The "building blocks" or "traditional fictional formulas" that Scott has used in *Guy Mannering* are all to be found in medieval romance and even earlier, as Frye says, in the Greek romances, where "we find stories of mysterious birth, oracular prophecies about the future contortions of the plot, foster parents, adventures which involve capture by pirates, narrow escapes from death, recognition of the true identity of the hero and his eventual marriage with the heroine."[8] There are, as we have seen, many more such building blocks: the perilous journey, the hero's secret love for an enemy's daughter, his winning her for his wife despite seemingly insurmountable obstacles, combat between father and son or brother and brother, disguises sometimes involving an apparent change in sex, faithful squires, faithful ladies-in-waiting, wicked tale-bearers—and the list goes on and on. Most of these building blocks too can be found in *Guy Mannering*.

In reading Scott we are linked up, as if by some sort of magic spell, with the realm of medieval romance and beyond it to the realm of folktale and myth—a realm that is remote and yet sometimes terrifyingly near. Harry Bertram's story is one of mythical descent from the world of ordinary human experience into the world of darkness.[9] The break from ordinary life comes when young Bertram is kidnapped. The first level in his descent is the smuggler's cave not far from Ellangowan, and before his reemergence into ordinary life can be completely effected, he must have another experience in this cave: this occurs in the scene near the end when Dirk Hatteraick is captured and Meg Merrilies is mortally wounded. Waverley's trip into the Highlands is another mythical descent; and while there is no dramatic break (such as kidnapping) from the world of ordinary experience, I think it significant that Waverley's seal is stolen while he is in the dark cave of Donald Bean Lean, and loss of the seal makes his reemergence into ordinary life extremely difficult. Frye suggests that Rebecca, on the other hand, is a creature from a higher plain of existence who has descended to the world of ordinary experience, bringing with her an almost supernatural power to heal the sick and the wounded, to relieve mankind from misery, to redeem the world to which she has descended—but she is misunderstood and is almost burned at the stake.[10] The Norman baron Front-de-Bœuf, whose immense size is emphasized by Scott, has a family resemblance to the evil giants of romance, folktale, and myth who hold women captive in their castles or caves and force them to satisfy their ravenous sexual appetites.[11] Norna of the Fitful-head is a descendant of the sorceresses and magicians that figure so prominently in romance.[12]

"The journeys of Alan and Darsie belong to the world of Romance," Mark A. Weinstein has recently averred in a provocative essay on *Redgauntlet*; they illustrate

practically all of the "formidable techniques" that Northrop Frye has described in his section on the descent to a subterranean world: the mysterious birth of the hero, the change in fortune or social context, the fall from privilege to a struggle for survival, the separation from his true family during which the hero "may find himself falling in love with his sister," the break in the continuity of identity, the metamorphoses into other characters, the sexual disguise, the progressive loss of freedom, the "twin theme" in which "one brother goes out on a quest or in search of adventure, the other remaining home, though able to tell from some sign how his brother is faring, and going into action when help is needed" [as in *Amis and Amiloun*], the "night world, often a dark and labyrinthine world of caves and shadows" where cruelty and horror predominate, the world of increasing alienation and loneliness in which "the hero is not only separated from the heroine or his friends, but is often further isolated by being falsely accused of major crimes," and, at the lower levels of the subterranean world, "the Narcissus or twin image darkens into a sinister doppelganger figure [one thinks of the resemblance between Darsie and Redgauntlet], the hero's shadow and the portent of his own death or isolation."[13]

So we are dealing not just with memories from childhood when we read Scott but with archetypal story-patterns and motifs and situations and age-old character types that have been part of the human condition, of our culture, of our civilization from earliest times. In the final analysis it does not matter if Scott digresses, or if he is long-winded, or if he is too moralistic, or if he does not get into the minds of his characters, or if he commits other alleged faults. Something else is involved here. Scott speaks to us on a different wavelength. What he says may not always conform to modern critical notions of what is proper in literature, but his appeal is direct, immediate, strong, deep-seated, primitive, elemental—and that's what really matters.

We might say, then, that *it is mostly at an intuitive level that* Scott *works his magic*. (This is an experiment, and I shall explain in a moment why I am using italics.) *To those who respond to* him *at all there is an emotional and instinctive contact which quite simply cannot be described: it can only be experienced. We are dealing with characters* in the Waverley Novels *who reveal and reflect our own emotional states*. Scott *reaches deep into the subconscious*. We must also remember that there is another important dimension to Scott's work: his poetry—and I do not mean the ballads and long narrative poems, nor the short poems that are interspersed throughout his novels, but the novels themselves. Scott's best poetry is the prose that he wrote in the best of his novels. *He was able* through his poetical prose *to reach emotional depths entirely beyond description in* ordinary prose. *What* Scott *did in* the best of the Waverley Novels *was to connect two basic human instincts or responses—the response to* poetry, *which is indefinable, and the response to the retelling of a myth, which is something all of us share in common, because myths only exist out of necessity, out of the need to express anxieties and ambitions by means of symbols. In* the Waverley Novels Scott *was dealing with irrationalities, primitive fears and instincts, which we all share and recognize because they are inherited*. The best of his novels are a retelling of *myth, and the emotions* they seek *to arouse are buried deep in human consciousness. What we sense about them matters very much more than anything we can say about them. Something more elemental than logic is involved.* The Waverley Novels deal in *physical fear, mental fear, greed, envy, corruption, treachery, betrayal, physical love, compassion, murder, hatred,* and *forgiveness.* They are *about humanity, and that is why* they are *important.*

What I have done here is to borrow freely the language of John Culshaw in discussing Wagner's *Ring of the Nibelung* and freely apply it to Scott. All the italicized words come from Culshaw's *Reflections on Wagner's "Ring,"* a book comprising the four intermission lectures he prepared for Saturday matinee broadcasts from the Metropolitan Opera in 1974–75. I heard these splendid lectures and thought at the time that Culshaw, more than anyone I had ever before heard or read, really understood and was able to articulate what was important in Wagner. When I read Culshaw's book several years later, the thought occurred to me that much of what he had said about Wagner was also true of Scott in his best novels; hence my experimental paragraph, which says in Culshaw's words what *I* have tried to say earlier in this chapter.[14]

The word *humanity* is another key to an understanding of Scott, and at this point we must return to Chaucer. Scott's indebtedness to Chaucer is considerably greater than the sum of his specific allusions and borrowings. We find Chaucer an impressive writer because of his absolute mastery of the language, of style and rhetoric, and because of his immense learning. We are still reading him today, after six hundred years, because of his wisdom, his sense of humor, his wholesomeness, his broadness of vision, his largeness of spirit, and his sense of the dignity of the individual. We love him because of his deep and compassionate understanding of his fellow human beings, with all their quirks and foibles. The same can be said about Shakespeare—and, I think, about Sir Walter Scott. Dryden's famous remark "Here is God's plenty" applies as happily to Shakespeare and Scott as it does to Chaucer. It's no wonder that Scott was irked with Godwin's *Life of Chaucer.* Godwin had somehow missed what was essential in the work of the great fourteenth-century poet "who loved his fellow-men, both good and bad," a famous scholar has said, "and found no answer to the puzzle of life but in truth and courage and beauty and belief in God."[15]

I would not want to try to explain Scott's belief in God any more than I would Chaucer's, but a love for his fellow men and a love for truth, courage, and beauty are certainly feelings that Scott shared with Chaucer. In his efforts to express them, Scott's debt to medieval literature was immense and profound. I have tried to show that it is the single most important, most essential literary source for the Waverley Novels—that it is their very warp and woof. Although Shakespeare's influence on Scott was also immense, the influence of medieval literature is more pervasive, more deep-seated, more elemental. I think it is the key to Scott's immense appeal—the very dimension to Scott which enabled him to cast an everlasting spell on his contemporaries, even on such great men as Byron and Goethe, and which has charmed generations of readers to the present day.

Northrop Frye returned to Scott after an esteemed friend had confessed to him, "I love Scott." A distinguished professor of law recently told me that he read all the Waverley Novels, some of them more than once, when he was recovering from a long illness. He said that he loved Scott. I am sure it must be clear by now that I love Scott too. In a sense this book has been my attempt, imperfect as it is, to explain why.

"I have now finished what I proposed to write"—with these words John Dunlop approaches the end of his monumental *History of Fiction*. He concludes:

To some of my readers I may appear, perhaps, to have dwelt too shortly on some topics, and to have bestowed a disproportionate attention on others; nor is it improbable that in a work of such extent and variety, omissions may have occurred of what ought not to have been neglected. Such defects were inseparable from an enquiry of this description, and must have, in some degree, existed even if I could have bestowed on it undivided attention, and if . . . it had been my sole employment. I shall consider myself, however, as having effected much if I turn to this subject the attention of other writers. . . . A work, indeed, of the kind I have undertaken, is not of a nature to be perfected by a single individual, and at a first attempt, but must be the result of successive investigations. By the assistance of preceding researches on the same subject, the labour of the future enquirer will be abridged, and he will thus be enabled to correct the mistakes, and supply the deficiencies, of those who have gone before him.

With this apology and this hope, I too take my leave.

NOTES

QUOTATIONS from Scott's poetry follow the standard Oxford edition, *The Poetical Works of Sir Walter Scott*, by J. Logie Robertson (London, 1904). Quotations from the Waverley Novels are taken from the 48-volume Border Edition, by Andrew Lang (London, 1892-94), but chapters are cited by the continuous numbering that is used in most editions. (I give chapter rather than page numbers so that passages can easily be looked up in almost any edition and with only a minimum of bother in editions where chapter numbering begins anew with each volume of a novel.) For Scott's essays on Romance and on Chivalry, and for his periodical criticism, I use the texts as collected in *The Miscellaneous Prose Works*. For Chaucer, I rely on F.N. Robinson's standard text unless there is some reason to cite an earlier edition; and for the romances, I quote from recent editions, again unless there is good reason to use an earlier one. For the sake of uniformity, I have generally adopted the titles of Middle English verse romances as they appear in J. Burke Severs's *Manual of Writings in Middle English*.

1. Scott's Knowledge of Medieval Literature

1. Friedrich Sommerkamp's industrious study "Sir Walter Scott's Englische und Deutsche Belesenheit" (Ph.D. diss., Berlin, 1924), is woefully lacking with regard to Scott's knowledge of specific medieval romances; see, e.g., pp. 101-2. Graham Tulloch's chapter entitled "Scott's Reading of Medieval and Renaissance Authors," in *The Language of Walter Scott: A Study of His Scottish and Period Language* (London: André Deutsch, 1980), is useful but sketchy. Arthur Johnston, in *Enchanted Ground: The Study of Medieval Romance in the Eighteenth Century* (London: Athlone, 1964), presents some of the material with which I am here concerned, but his approach, organization, emphasis, and purpose are very different from mine.

2. Sir Walter Scott, ed., *Minstrelsy of the Scottish Border*, 4 vols., ed. T.F. Henderson (Edinburgh, 1902; Singing Tree rpt., 1968); hereafter, *Minstrelsy*.

3. *The Miscellaneous Prose Works of Sir Walter Scott, Bart.*, 28 vols. (Edinburgh: Adam & Charles Black, 1851-55); hereafter, *Miscellaneous Prose Works*.

4. *The Letters of Sir Walter Scott*, 12 vols., ed. H.J.C. Grierson (London: Constable, 1932-37; AMS rpt., 1971); hereafter, *Letters*. James C. Corson, *Notes and Index to Sir Herbert Grierson's Edition of the Letters of Sir Walter Scott* (Oxford: Clarendon, 1979); hereafter, *Notes and Index*. In the unpublished parts of letters to Ellis dated March 2 and

October 17, 1802, Scott discusses, respectively, the romance of *Guy of Warwick* as it appears in the Auchinleck MS and the Auchinleck fragment of *Richard Coer de Lyon*. Both letters are in the Pierpont Morgan Library (New York); photostats can be found in the National Library of Scotland (Edinburgh), which houses the most complete collection of Scott's letters.

5. John Gibson Lockhart, *Memoirs of the Life of Sir Walter Scott, Bart.*, 2d ed., 10 vols. (Edinburgh, 1839); hereafter, *Life of Scott*.

6. J.G. Cochrane, *Catalogue of the Library at Abbotsford* (Edinburgh, 1838); hereafter, Abbotsford Library *Catalogue*.

7. See James C. Corson, "Scott's Boyhood Collection of Chapbooks," *Bibliotheck* 3 (1962): 202-18. The most thorough study to date of chapbook literature is Rainer Schöwerling, *Chapbooks: Zur Literaturgeschichte des einfachen Lesers*, Regensburger Arbeiten zur Anglistik und Amerikanistik, 18 (Frankfurt am Main: Peter D. Lang, 1980).

8. Louis Elisabeth de la Vergne (Comte de Tressan), ed., *Corps d'Extraits de Romans de Chevalerie*, 4 vols. (Paris, 1782); hereafter, Tressan.

9. Pierre Jean Baptiste Le Grand d'Aussy, ed., *Fabliaux ou Contes du XIIe et du XIIIe Siècle, Fables et Romans du XIIIe*, 5 vols. (Paris, 1781); hereafter, Le Grand.

10. Gregory Lewis Way, trans., *Fabliaux or Tales, Abridged from French Manuscripts of the XIIth and XIIIth Centuries, by M. Le Grand*, 2 vols. (London, 1796, 1800); hereafter, Way.

11. *Letters*, 12:165-66. In 1800 Scott had not yet had the pleasure of meeting George Ellis but knew of his important work in progress and eagerly looked forward to its completion.

12. I cite a later edition: Thomas Percy, ed., *Reliques of Ancient English Poetry*, 3 vols., ed. Henry B. Wheatley (London, 1886); hereafter, *Reliques*.

13. John Pinkerton, ed., *Scotish Poems, Reprinted from Scarce Editions*, 3 vols. (London, 1792); hereafter, *Scotish Poems*.

14. Joseph Ritson, ed., *Ancient Engleish Metrical Romanceës*, 3 vols. (London, 1802); hereafter, Ritson.

15. George Ellis, ed., *Specimens of Early English Metrical Romances, Chiefly Written during the Early Part of the Fourteenth Century*, 3 vols. (London, 1805); hereafter, Ellis.

16. Henry Weber, ed., *Metrical Romances of the Thirteenth, Fourteenth, and Fifteenth Centuries*, 3 vols. (Edinburgh, 1810); hereafter, Weber.

17. There is no greater testimony to the genuine usefulness of the collections by Weber, Ritson, and Ellis than the fact that they were all "on reserve" as late as 1961-62 for an unforgettable seminar on the Middle English Breton lais, conducted by Professor Walter F. Schirmer at the University of Bonn. Kurt Gamerschlag is currently preparing a monograph on Weber. He believes that Weber himself did the verse translations of the *Nibelungen Lied* but that they may have been touched up by Scott.

18. E.V. Utterson, ed., *Select Pieces of Early Popular Poetry: Re-published Principally from Early Printed Copies in the Black Letter*, 2 vols. (London, 1817); hereafter, *Select Pieces*.

19. John Dunlop, *The History of Fiction: Being a Critical Account of the Most Celebrated Prose Works of Fiction, from the Earliest Greek Romances to the Novels of the Present Age*, 2d ed., 3 vols. (Edinburgh, 1816); hereafter, *History of Fiction*.

20. Etienne Barbazan, ed., *Fabliaux et Contes des Poètes François des XI, XII, XIII, XIV, et XVe Siècle*, 4 vols. (Paris, 1808); hereafter, Barbazan.

21. Donald E. Sultana, *"The Siege of Malta" Rediscovered* (Edinburgh: Scottish Academic Press, 1977), p. 68.

22. J. Burke Severs, ed., *A Manual of the Writings in Middle English, 1050-1500*, Fascicule 1: *Romances* (New Haven: Connecticut Academy of Arts and Sciences, 1967); hereafter, Severs's *Manual*.

23. Thomas Warton, *History of English Poetry from the Twelfth to the Close of the Sixteenth Century*, 4 vols., ed. C. Carew Hazlitt (London, 1871; Georg Olms rpt., 1968); hereafter, Warton.

24. Quoted from the edition included as vol. 5 in *The Poetical Works of Sir Walter Scott, Bart.* (Edinburgh: Adam & Charles Black, 1880). Scott wrote to Ellis, March 27, 1801: "Permit me to state a query to you about Sir Gawaine. *Our* Traditions & father Chaucer himself represent him as the flower of Courtesy. On the contrary the Morte Arthur & other French Romances & translations stigmatize him as a foul Murtherer of Women & of disarmed knights—a worthy Brother in short of the Traitor Modred. How comes this?" This same question comes up every time I teach Malory, because the Gawain of poesy is quite different in character from the Gawain of the prose romances.

25. See Eugène Vinaver, "A Romance of *Gaheret*," *Medium Ævum* 1 (1932): 157-67.

26. Joseph A. Vaeth, *"Tirant lo Blanch": A Study of Its Authorship, Principal Sources, and Historical Setting* (New York: Columbia Univ. Press, 1918; AMS rpt., 1966). The first English translation of *Tirant*, by David H. Rosenthal (New York: Schocken, 1984), appeared after I had completed my research for this book.

27. *The Journal of Sir Walter Scott*, ed. W.E.K. Anderson (Oxford: Clarendon, 1972), p. 667 n.2; hereafter, *Journal*.

28. W.A. Clouston, *Popular Tales and Fictions: Their Migrations and Transformations*, 2 vols. (Edinburgh, 1887), 1:50.

29. In *The Works of John Dryden*, 18 vols., ed. Sir Walter Scott, rev. George Saintsbury (Edinburgh, 1882-93), 11:221. (Scott's edition of Dryden was originally published in 1808.)

30. Terry Jones, *Chaucer's Knight: The Portrait of a Medieval Mercenary* (Baton Rouge: Louisiana State Univ. Press, 1980), p. 187.

31. See Scott's letter to Anna Seward, February 20, 1807 (*Letters*, 1:354).

32. From Scott's review (1804) of Ellis's *Specimens of the Early English Poets* (*Miscellaneous Prose Works*, 17:11).

33. See Scott's letter to Ellis, October 17, 1802 (*Letters*, 12:220), and Corson's note (*Notes and Index*, p. 323).

2. The Narrative Poetry

1. My approach is almost totally different from J.H. Alexander's in "A Study of Scott's Poetic Treatment of the Middle Ages and Its Relation to the Poetry of the 'Medieval Revival' " (B.Litt. thesis, Oxford University, 1964). Alexander is interested more in how Scott's medievalism relates to that of his immediate predecessors and in how his poetry was received by contemporary critics.

2. Sir Thomas Malory, *Works*, ed. Eugène Vinaver, 2d (one-volume) ed. (London: Oxford Univ. Press, 1971), p. 4; hereafter, *Works*.

3. The following four paragraphs are adapted from my paper "Wordsworth's Tail-Rhyme 'Lucy' Poem," *Studies in Medieval Culture* 4 (1974): 561-68. I wish to thank the Medieval Institute Publications, Western Michigan University, for allowing me to reproduce this material.

4. The group includes *Amis and Amiloun, Athelston, Le Bone Florence of Rome, Emare, The Erl of Tolous, Guy of Warwick* (Parts II and III), *Horn Child, Ipomadon, The King of Tars, Libeaus Desconus, Octavian, Otuel and Roland, Roland and Vernagu, The Sege of Melayne, Sir Amadace, Sir Cleges, Sir Eglamour, Sir Gowther, Sir Isumbras, Sir Launfal, Sir Torrent of Portyngale,* and *Sir Triamour*.

5. *Amis and Amiloun,* ed. Eugen Kölbing (Heilbronn, 1884), lines 1-12.

6. For the following discussion I am in some measure indebted to A. McI. Trounce, "The English Tail-Rhyme Romances," *Medium Ævum* 1 (1932): 169ff. (the article is continued in vols. 2 and 3), and to A.J. Bliss, ed., Thomas Chestre's *Sir Launfal* (London, 1960), pp. 35-36. See also Kölbing, *Amis and Amiloun,* pp. xxxvii-lxxii. For references to *Emare,* see the edition by A.B. Gough (London, 1901); for the *Erl of Tolous* see the text printed in Walter Hoyt French and Charles Brockway Hale, eds., *Middle English Metrical Romances* (New York, 1930); for *Sir Launfal* see the Bliss edition.

7. II.cv, from the *Poetical Works,* 5:247. (This edition of *Sir Tristrem* is perhaps more accessible than the earliest editions.) The word *on* in the third line means "one." *Ferli* in line 6 has the sense of "wondrously" or "amazingly."

8. Georg Martin Hofmann, *Entstehungsgeschichte von Sir Walter Scotts "Marmion"* (Ph.D. diss., Königsberg, 1913).

9. Another slight touch to the portrait of Friar John of Tillmouth is owing to Rabelais, as Scott shows us in his Note xvii.

10. In Southey's edition (1807), I, viii.

11. Quoted from the Scolar facsimile of the original edition (1700) of John Dryden, *Fables Ancient and Modern,* p. 235; hereafter, *Fables.*

12. Alexander, "Scott's Poetic Treatment," p. 103.

13. See Margaret J.C. Reid, *The Arthurian Legend: Comparison of Treatment in Modern and Mediæval Literature: A Study in the Literary Value of Myth and Legend* (Edinburgh: Oliver & Boyd, 1938), pp. 42-44.

14. As printed in *The Bridal of Triermain, or The Vale of St. John* (Edinburgh: Ballantyne, 1813). This point is made by Kurt Gamerschlag, "Versions of Ideal Man: *The Bridal of Triermain* and Its Adaptations," in *Scott and His Influence,* ed. J.H. Alexander and David Hewitt (Aberdeen: Association for Scottish Literary Studies, 1983), p. 506 n.16. The title-page to the third edition of *Sir Tristrem* (Edinburgh: Constable, 1811) also has a stanza from *Sir Thopas*:

> Now, hold your mouth, pour charitie,
> Both Knight and Lady fre,
> And herkneth to my spell;
> Of battaille and of chivalry,
> Of Ladies' love and druerie,
> Anon I wol you tel.

15. From the 1830 introduction to *The Lord of the Isles.*

16. Scott's Gothic tragedy *The House of Aspen* (which is in prose) is derived from the German of Veit Weber. The time is the Middle Ages, and a number of motifs vividly

recall medieval romance. The evil Roderic makes war on Rudiger in an attempt to win the hand of Gertrude, the niece of Rudiger's wife Isabella, but Gertrude is betrothed to Henry, who is a son of Rudiger and Isabella: the motif is familiar. Isabella's first husband was Arnolf of Ebersdorf, whom she did not want to marry: again the undesired marriage. Gertrude dreams that Isabella is being buried alive and that her son George and faithful retainer Martin are shoveling the earth in on her: the dream foreshadows what occurs later. As in some medieval romances (and some of Scott's novels), place is a device of unity: it seems that Martin gathered the hemlock leaves used for the poison brewed for Arnolf at the very place (a marsh) where he is later surprised and taken prisoner by Roderic.—I hesitate to comment further on Scott's plays until the publication of Neil Key's long-in-the-making study of Scott as a dramatist.

3. The Early Novels

1. Alice Chandler, *A Dream of Order: The Medieval Ideal in Nineteenth-Century English Literature* (Lincoln: Univ. of Nebraska Press, 1970), pp. 25-47.

2. The phrase, or something very like it, is of course Charles Muscatine's, in "Form, Texture, and Meaning in Chaucer's *Knight's Tale*," *PMLA* 65 (1950): 911-29.

3. Robin Mayhead, *Walter Scott* (Cambridge: Cambridge Univ. Press, 1973), pp. 18, 31.

4. Walter W. Skeat, ed., *The Romans of Partenay*, Early English Text Society, Original Series, no. 22 (London, 1866; rev. ed., 1899), pp. xv, xvii. The society's editions are hereafter cited as E.E.T.S., O.S. or E.S. (Extra Series).

5. For a thorough discussion of the Bodach Glas, see Coleman O. Parsons, *Witchcraft and Demonology in Scott's Fiction* (Edinburgh: Oliver & Boyd, 1964), pp. 75-79.

6. Donald Sands, ed., *Middle English Verse Romances* (New York: Holt, Rinehart & Winston, 1966), p. 55.

7. Larry D. Benson, *Malory's "Morte Darthur"* (Cambridge, Mass.: Harvard Univ. Press, 1976), p. 102.

8. Another possible echo from medieval literature occurs in chapter 15, when Mr. Mac-Morlan begins to suspect a budding relationship between Lucy Bertram and Charles Hazlewood: " 'O ho!' thought Mac-Morlan; 'sits the wind in that quarter?' " Cf. King Arthur's words to Gareth in Malory's *Tale of Sir Gareth*: "What, nevew? . . . Is the wynde in that dore?" (*Works*, p. 223). But the expression occurs in later literature too; it is proverbial.

9. See, e.g., Clouston, *Popular Tales and Fictions*, 2:379-412, esp. the interesting chapter on Chaucer's Pardoner's Tale, including a note on "Resuscitation in Folk-Lore."

10. Benson, *Malory's "Morte Darthur,"* pp. 117-28.

11. *Valentine and Orson*, trans. Henry Watson, ed. Arthur Dickson, E.E.T.S., O.S., no. 204 (London: Oxford Univ. Press, 1937 [for 1936]; Kraus rpt., 1971), p. 201.

12. Francis E. Utley, *The Crooked Rib: An Analytical Index to the Argument about Women in English and Scots Literature to the End of the Year 1568* (Columbus: Ohio State Univ. Press, 1944).

13. From Charles W. Dunn's summary in Severs's *Manual*, pp. 22-23.

14. Harry Ahlers, "Untersuchungen zu Scott's Roman *The Antiquary*" (Ph.D.

diss., Kiel, 1920), p. 100: "Since from the beginning we expect from him, as an antiquary and scholar, a rich store of facts, they seem to us hardly importunate despite their large number."

15. Dryden, *Fables*, p. 79.

16. See Christabel F. Fiske, *Epic Suggestion in the Imagery of the Waverley Novels* (New Haven: Yale Univ. Press, 1940; Kraus rpt., 1973), pp. 2-3.

4. Novels of the Broken Years

1. Ballantyne, quoted in Lockhart, *Life of Scott*, 6:89.

2. From Edward Cheney's reminiscences, quoted in Lockhart, *Life of Scott*, 10:187.

3. Henry Weber, *Illustrations of Northern Antiquities* (Edinburgh, 1814), appendix 2.

4. Dryden, *Fables*, p. 32.

5. The word *combre-world* occurs also in Hoccleve's lament for Chaucer, in the *Regement of Princes*, line 2091. (It is interesting too that the word *bereaved* is used by all three writers in close proximity to the expression in question.)

6. Alan S. Fedrick's translation (Harmondsworth, Eng.: Penguin, 1970), p. 71.

7. See Scott's edition of *Sir Tristrem*, III.xxii-xxiii.

8. Robert Copland, *The History of Helyas, Knight of the Swan*, ed. William John Thoms from the old edition by William Copland (London: William Pickering, 1827), p. 46. This episode is not in *Chevalere Assigne*, the poetical version of the story.

9. See G.V. Smithers, "Story-Patterns in Some Breton Lays," *Medium Ævum* 22 (1953): 61-92.

10. The oldest copy of this romance is dated 1597, but it may be a second edition. I used an edition published in London in 1824. Scott owned the London edition of 1670, which is bound up in the second volume of the Stansby *Morte Darthur* at Abbotsford. He also had a chapbook version printed at Newcastle, according to Corson's unpublished catalogue.

11. See H.S. Bennett's sketch of Margaret Paston in *Six Medieval Men and Women* (Cambridge, 1955; Atheneum rpt., 1962), pp. 100-23.

12. F.J. Amours's text, in *Scottish Alliterative Poems in Riming Stanzas* (Edinburgh, 1897; Johnson rpt., 1966), lines 79-83; Louis B. Hall's translation, in *The Knightly Tales of Sir Gawain* (Chicago: Nelson-Hall, 1976), p. 83.

13. Jones, *Chaucer's Knight*.

14. Roland Abramczyk, *Über die Quellen zu Walter Scotts Roman "Ivanhoe"* (Ph.D. diss., Leipzig, 1903).

15. *Bevis of Hampton*, ed. Eugen Kölbing from the Auchinleck text, E.E.T.S., E.S., nos. 46 (1885), 48 (1886), and 65 (1894); Kraus rpt. in one volume, 1975.

16. Samuel Rowland[s], *The Famous History of Guy of Warwick* (London: G. Conyers, n.d.), p. 25; the British Library Catalogue suggests the date 1680; the National Union Catalogue suggests 1690. For the quotation that follows, from the version in couplets, see Samuel Rowland[s], *The Famous History of Guy Earl of Warwick* (London: G. Conyers, n.d.), pp. 74-75; both the British Library Catalogue and the National Union Catalogue suggest the date 1680. Rowlands's *stanzaic* version, reprinted from the Edward Brewster edition of 1682 by the Hunterian Club, in *The Complete Works of*

Samuel Rowlands (Glasgow, 1880), vol. 3, is more expansive, but the thirty-one lines corresponding to the nineteen that I have quoted give no additional information worthy of note.

17. From the summary in Vaeth, *"Tirant lo Blanch": A Study*, pp. 16-18.

18. *Roberte the Deuyll: A Metrical Romance* (London, 1798), p. 37, printed from a manuscript that "appears to have been transcribed, word for word, from an edition in quarto printed either by *Wynken de Worde* or *Pynson*" (according to the Advertisement).

19. Vaeth, *"Tirant lo Blanch": A Study*, p. 24.

20. See Malory, *Morte Darthur*, Book X, chap. 44, in Caxton editions. Sir Galahaut the Haut Prince stops a fight between Sir Palomides and a strange knight, who gets the upper hand and turns out to be Sir Lamorak.

21. See I, xii, in Southey's edition. The Emperor of Greece requests that the fighting stop between Palmerin and the Knight of the Savage Man (who turns out to be his brother), "perceiving it drew towards night, and fearing the endamagement that might come to either of them."

22. Irvine Gray's translation (London: Routledge, 1931), p. 158 (chap. 42). Other instances of a king's stopping a tournament occur in chaps. 50-51, when Saintré is jousting with the Lord of Loysseleuch.

23. See Elizabeth Walsh, "The King in Disguise," *Folklore* 86 (1975): 3-24.

24. See lines 739-96, which can be conveniently read in *"Richard the Lion-Hearted" and Other Medieval English Romances*, trans. Bradford B. Broughton (New York: Dutton, 1966), pp. 168-69.

25. This was brought to my attention by Paul Schleifer when he was a Ph.D. candidate in English at the University of Georgia. I have since learned that Scott knew the story (see Chapter 1).

26. Mentioned by Parsons, *Witchcraft and Demonology*, p. 149. Parsons also calls attention (p. 175) to the anachronistic remark of Wamba in chap. 1 when he and Gurth first hear (but do not yet see) horsemen approaching: "Perhaps they are come from Fairy-land with a message from King Oberon." It is anachronistic in that "twelfth-century Wamba refers to the king of the fairies in thirteenth-century *Huon de Bordeaux*."

27. Malory, *Morte Darthur*, Book XVI, chap. 12, in Caxton editions; page 571 in *Works*.

28. It is also in *Paradise Lost*, I, 584; see Merritt Y. Hughes's note, in his standard edition, for other possibilities.

5. Novels of the High-Noon Period

1. The historian Mézeray, as quoted in translation by Skeat, *The Romans of Partenay* (rev. ed.), p. xv. Cf. my brief discussion (Chapter 3) of the Bodach Glas, in *Waverley*.

2. Smithers, "Story-Patterns in Some Breton Lays," pp. 62, 65, 67.

3. This is a later romance: *The Honour of Chivalry; or, The Famous and Delectable History of Don Bellianis of Greece*. I read several chapters in an edition of 1683, now in the National Library of Scotland, which once belonged to G.L. Way. (Captain Coxe apparently read this and the other romances in chapbook versions.)

4. Malory, *Works*, p. 231.

5. Karl Albert Paul Müller, *Die Quellen zu Walter Scotts Roman "The Fortunes of Nigel"* (Ph.D. diss., Leipzig, 1913).
6. William Stewart Rose's translation of *Amadis de Gaul* (London, 1803), pp. 34-35.
7. See Scott's introduction of 1831; and Hans Lorenz Lorenzen, *"Peveril of the Peak": Ein Beitrag zur literarischen Würdigung Sir Walter Scotts* (Ph.D. diss., Kiel, 1912), pp. 95-104.
8. The original Middle English poem is thought to have been composed between 1450 and 1500. No MS of it is extant, but there is a condensed version in the Percy Folio MS (which was not printed until after Scott's death). Interestingly, an early chapbook version of the *Octavian* romance *was* published in Strasbourg, in 1535, according to E.M. Goldsmid in a note to his edition (Edinburgh: Aungervyle Society, 1882) of J.J. Conybeare's version of the story, which was first printed in 1809 (see Chapter 1); Conybeare was informed by Henry Weber that the story was still known in Germany in a chapbook version. For a discussion of the freedom with which Scott quotes from *The Squyr of Lowe Degre*, see Tulloch, *The Language of Walter Scott*, p. 106. The four lines that Tulloch thinks Scott "has made up or remembers from elsewhere" are in fact in Ritson (3:169), though the phraseology is somewhat different.
9. In *Valentine and Orson* there is a "grene knyght" who, having conquered his adversaries, "maketh them to be hanged on a tree that is in the place on the whiche tree is hanged dyuers knyghtes to the nombre of two & thyrty" (Arthur Dickson's edition, chap. 20).
10. See Lockhart, *Life of Scott*, 7:208-9; and Edgar Johnson, *Sir Walter Scott: The Great Unknown*, 2 vols. (New York: Macmillan, 1970), 2:918.
11. See the section "Launcelot and Elaine" in Malory, *Works*, or Books XI and XII in Caxton editions.
12. See Felix Knothe, *Untersuchungen zu "Redgauntlet" von Walter Scott* (Ph.D. diss., Kiel, 1913), pp. 60-61.
13. Malory, *Works*, pp. 382, 387-88.
14. Benson, *Malory's "Morte Darthur,"* pp. 191-92.
15. The haunted chamber episode has at least one analogue in medieval romance: in *Ysaie le Triste*, Ysaie's son Marc undergoes a somewhat similar ordeal; see Dunlop, *History of Fiction*, 1:286, 492-95.
16. Gillian is a Wife of Bath type; Scott never explicitly compares the two, but it is hard not to think of the "long preamble" to the wife's tale when Eveline says to Rose, "Do not liken your mistress to those provident dames who, while one husband yet lives, though in old age or weak health, are prudently engaged in plotting for another" (chap. 28). The similarity is noted by Parsons in his *Witchcraft and Demonology*, p. 278 n.18.
17. See Ludwig Aigner, "Studien zu Walter Scott's 'The Talisman' " (unpubl. Ph.D. diss., Munich, 1920), esp. B.IV: "Die Haupttatsachen und -Ereignisse in 'The Talisman' und ihre Grundlagen in Geschichte und Fabel." This is a diligent and useful study, although not attractive to the eye because it is so carelessly typed.
18. See Broughton's translation, *Richard the Lion-Hearted*, lines 5951ff.
19. Vaeth, *"Tirant lo Blanch": A Study*, p. 50.
20. See Aigner, "Studien zu 'The Talisman,' " pp. 51-53, plus the additional sheet (*Einlage*) to p. 53.
21. This scene may owe something, as Aigner observes (*ibid.*, p. 55), to the romance hero's severing of the thick iron chain that barred the harbor at Acre.

22. See *ibid.*, p. 85.—One also thinks of some of the Arabian, Persian, and Oriental tales that were readily available to Scott in Henry Weber's mammoth three-volume *Tales of the East* (Edinburgh: Ballantyne, 1812). (The first volume includes the tale from the *Arabian Nights* that is alluded to by Clara Mowbray; see the discussion of *St. Ronan's Well* above.)

6. Novels of the Dark Days and Servitude

1. Johnson, *Sir Walter Scott*, 2:1055-56.
2. See W.A. Clouston, *On the Magical Elements in Chaucer's "Squire's Tale," with Analogues*, in the second part of F.J. Furnivall's edition of John Lane's continuation of the Squire's Tale, Chaucer Society, Series 2, nos. 23 & 26 (London, 1888, 1890), esp. pp. 299-333. In "The Story of Prince Ahmed and the Fairy Pari Banou" (see the discussion of *St. Ronan's Well*), there is an "ivory perspective glass" purchased by Prince Ali through which one can see whatever he wishes to see. Wishing to see his father the sultan, Ali looks through the glass and beholds him sitting in council. Then, wishing to see the princess Nouronnihar, he beholds her in the presence of her ladies-in-waiting. Apparently the animated pictures do not last long, although no time limit is specified.
3. See Dunlop, *History of Fiction*, 1:492-95.
4. For detailed information on the historical background, see Walter Ehrich, "Untersuchungen zu Scotts Roman 'St. Valentine's Day, or The Fair Maid of Perth' " (unpubl. Ph.D. diss., Kiel, 1914).
5. "Earl Richard" is included in *Minstrelsy*, 3:238-39.
6. Weber, *Illustrations of Northern Antiquities*, p. 189.
7. Ehrich, "Untersuchungen zu 'The Fair Maid of Perth,' " p. 103, citing G. Le Grys Norgate's *The Life of Sir Walter Scott* (London, 1906), p. 288.
8. For further information about Scott's historical sources, see Carl Bröker, *Scotts "Anne of Geierstein"* (Ph.D. diss., Kiel, 1927), esp. the section entitled "Technik des Romans."
9. See Dunlop, *History of Fiction*, 1:430-41.
10. The women in Malory's *Morte Darthur* do not fight, but many female warriors besides those mentioned can be found in medieval romance. Amazon types appear in *Ysaie le Triste*, for example. And in the first chapter of *Antar* there is an armed encounter between Queen Robab and King Jazeemah, who hope thus to prevent bloodshed between their respective peoples; the lady wins, but fighting does after all commence between the two sides. Scott no doubt remembered Spenser as well, especially the combat between Artegall and the Amazon Radigund in Book V of *The Faerie Queene*.
11. In the original version of the novel, which was drastically expurgated by Lockhart, Scott intended the combat between Robert and Hereward to be preceded by one between Brenhilda (who is pregnant) and Anna Comnena. See Kurt Gamerschlag, "The Making and Un-Making of Sir Walter Scott's *Count Robert of Paris*," in *Studies in Scottish Literature* 15 (1980): 95-123, esp. 108.
12. See Tulloch, *The Language of Walter Scott*, p. 36.
13. Malory, *Works*, "The Knight of the Cart," p. 649 (Book XVIII, chap. 25, in Caxton editions).
14. See Sultana, *"The Siege of Malta" Rediscovered*, pp. 130-91. (I am much indebted to Dr. Sultana's stimulating book.)

15. Jane Millgate, "*The Siege of Malta*: A Transcription with Introductory Commentary" (1979), an unpublished typescript in the New York Public Library. See also Millgate's "The Limits of Editing: The Problem of Scott's *The Siege of Malta*," in the *Bulletin of Research in the Humanities* 82 (1979): 190-212. The reasons why the novel has never been published and the arguments for and against its publication do not concern us here; these matters have already received detailed consideration by Dr. Sultana and Dr. Millgate.

16. Scott, *Journal*, p. 668; Sultana, *"The Siege of Malta" Rediscovered*, facing p. 1. See Sultana's index for references to the Reform Bill.

17. Sultana, *"The Siege of Malta" Rediscovered*, p. 149.

18. *Ibid.*, p. 152.

19. *Ibid.*, p. 139.

20. These quotations are from a seventeenth-century translation: Nicholas de Hereby [sic], *The Most Excellent History of the Valiant and Renowned Knight, Don Flores of Greece, Knight of the Swans, Second Sonne to Esplandran, Emperour of Constantinople*, trans. W.P., 3rd ed. (London, 1664), pp. 10, 13.

21. From the 1932 typescript, pp. 4-5; cf. Millgate's transcription, p. 6. I realize that the 1932 typescript has no textual status, but it reads smoothly in comparison with Scott's original as transcribed meticulously, with all its mistakes, by Dr. Millgate. I wish to thank the New York Public Library (Astor, Lenox, and Tilden Foundations) for letting me see Scott's autograph MS, the 1932 typescript, and Dr. Millgate's recent transcription (which are all in the Henry W. and Albert A. Berg Collection) and for allowing me to quote from the 1932 typescript. In a separate communication Dr. Millgate has kindly given me permission to quote from her transcription.

22. From the 1932 typescript, p. 41 (cf. Millgate, p. 96). Scott's holograph has *Ageolina* here rather than *Angelica* or *Angelina*; *fauteur* should be *faitour* (i.e., "false man").

23. From the 1932 typescript, p. 43 (cf. Millgate, p. 98).

24. Sultana, *"The Siege of Malta" Rediscovered*, pp. 137, 138.

25. *Ibid.*, pp. 79-80, 151-53.

26. *Ibid.*, p. 191.

27. As quoted in *ibid.*, p. 177.

28. Lockhart's *Life of Scott*, 10:196; quoted also in Sultana, *"The Siege of Malta" Rediscovered*, p. 107.

7. Style and Structure in the Waverley Novels

1. Much of this material has received attention in Graham Tulloch's excellent study, *The Language of Walter Scott*, esp. chapters entitled "Period Vocabulary" and "Period Grammar." Since I have collected my data independently, however, and since the subject is as important as it is interesting, I present here what I have found, giving my more thorough attention to matters that Tulloch either does not emphasize or has not noticed.

2. E.g., in Book II, III.iv, and in Book VI, V.x.

3. Tulloch, *The Language of Walter Scott*, pp. 27-28.

4. Jean d'Arras, *Mélusine*, ed. A.K. Donald, E.E.T.S., E.S., no. 68 (London, 1895), p. 276.

5. Book I, IV.xlvii; Book IV, I.xliv; Book VI, I.xviii.

6. Passus 6 of the B-text, as quoted by John Burrow, "The Action of Langland's Second Vision," in *Style and Symbolism in "Piers Plowman": A Modern Critical Anthology*, ed. Robert J. Blanch (Knoxville: Univ. of Tennessee Press, 1969), p. 217; the word in question is translated as "the false men."

7. See Paul Roberts, "Sir Walter Scott's Contributions to the English Vocabulary," *PMLA* 68 (1953): 195.

8. Lines 539-42, as they appear in Sands, *Middle English Verse Romances*, p. 264.

9. Tulloch, *The Language of Walter Scott*, 34-35, 124.

10. In a letter of August 18, 1806; see Scott, *Letters*, 12:289-90.

11. It is spoken by Ivanhoe in the famous conversation with Rebecca at Torquilstone, chap. 29. Scott glosses the word as "desperate courage."

12. Roberts, "Scott's Contributions," p. 195.

13. It is not in everyone's active vocabulary, as I have found in talking with American undergraduate students.

14. III.xxviii, line 2, in Scott's edition of 1880.

15. *The Honour of Chivalry; or, The Famous and Delectable History of Don Bellianus of Greece* (London: Tho. Passinger, 1683), p. 37. The quotations from *Sir Launfal* follow the edition by A.J. Bliss.

16. Tulloch, *The Language of Scott*, pp. 144-65.

17. See Eugène Vinaver's critical study: *Malory* (Oxford: Clarendon, 1929; rpt., 1970), p. 108 n.1.

18. Malory, *Works*, pp. 188, 198.

19. In "Laurence Templeton's Dedicatory Epistle to the Rev. Dr. Dryasdust," prefixed to *Ivanhoe*.

20. For Scott's review of Godwin for the *Edinburgh Review*, 1804, see *Miscellaneous Prose Works*, 17:55-80, esp. 72-73.

21. Scott, Introduction to *Sir Tristrem* (1880), p. 85 (pp. lxxxiii-lxxxiv in the 3rd ed., 1811).

22. In the "Dedicatory Epistle" to *Ivanhoe*.

23. From the 1932 typescript, p. 109. The passage in Millgate's transcription (p. 55) reads as follows: "I might describe the sale of the fortifications but it would only serve to embarass my pages with hard names which woud serve rather to embarass than instruct him. It is sufficient to say that they bore a strong resemblances to those used in the in the middl ages when the stile of defence against gunpowd began to be adopted and improved upon." Professor Millgate thinks now that Scott wrote "stile" rather than "sale" (the fifth word), as in the phrase "stile of defence" a few lines later.

24. From the 1932 typescript, p. 154.

25. See Ernst Robert Curtius, *European Literature and the Latin Middle Middle Ages*, trans. Willard R. Trask (New York: Pantheon, 1953), esp. pp. 83-85; see also pp. 159-60.

26. See Bartlett Jere Whiting, *Proverbs, Sentences, and Proverbial Phrases* (Cambridge, Mass.: Harvard Univ. Press, 1968). My quotation from Hoccleve follows Sir Israel Gollancz's text, which is based on Huntington Library MS. HM 744, an autograph MS. See the E.E.T.S. revised reprint of Hoccleve's *Minor Poems* (1970), p. 299.

27. *Valentine and Orson*, p. 196.

28. *Melusine*, p. 298.

29. Lines 939-54, in Sands, *Middle English Verse Romances*.

30. *Valentine and Orson*, p. 36.
31. *Melusine*, pp. 227-28.
32. The oldest extant copy is dated 1597, but it may not be a first edition. I have used an edition published in London in 1824.
33. From the introduction to *The Betrothed*.
34. *Ibid*.
35. From Scott's introduction to *Sir Tristrem* (1880), p. 80 (p. lxxix in the 3rd ed., 1811).
36. Nicolas de Herberay, *Don Flores of Greece*, trans. W.P., 3rd ed. (London, 1664), p. 40. (Scott knew the French original.)
37. See *Melusine*, pp. 2-6.
38. Eilhart von Oberge, *Tristrant*, trans. J.W. Thomas (Lincoln: Univ. of Nebraska Press, 1978), p. 14.
39. The phrase is Scott's; see the introduction to *The Betrothed*.
40. R.D.S. Jack, *The Italian Influence on Scottish Literature* (Edinburgh: Edinburgh Univ. Press, 1972), p. 215.

8. Conclusion

1. Wilmon Brewer, *Shakespeare's Influence on Sir Walter Scott* (Boston: Cornhill, 1925; AMS rpt., 1974).
2. I have already written on this topic in "Scott's Use of the Tristan-Story in the Waverley Novels," *Tristania* 6, no. 1 (1980): 19-29, and I wish to thank that journal's editor, Lewis A.M. Sumberg, for allowing me to draw on my earlier article throughout this book.
3. Sometimes there are two attractive young ladies and one eligible young man, as in *The Lord of the Isles* and *The Pirate*.
4. *Valentine and Orson: The Two Sonnes of the Emperour of Greece* (London: T. Purfoot, 1637). This passage in the edition at Abbotsford (see Chapter 1) reads almost the same but has a few additional phrases.
5. Benson, *Malory's "Morte Darthur,"* p. 138.
6. E.M. Forster, *Aspects of the Novel* (New York: Harcourt, Brace, 1927), p. 53.
7. Northrop Frye, *The Secular Scripture: A Study of the Structure of Romance* (Cambridge, Mass.: Harvard Univ. Press, 1976), p. 5.
8. *Ibid.*, p. 4.
9. I am borrowing some of Frye's terminology; see esp. *ibid.*, pp. 97ff.
10. *Ibid.*, p. 87.
11. *Ibid.*, pp. 133, 135.
12. *Ibid.*, p. 144.
13. Mark A. Weinstein, "Law, History, and the Nightmare of Romance in *Redgauntlet*," in Alexander and Hewitt, *Scott and His Influence*, pp. 146-47. Weinstein has a footnote referring to Frye's *Secular Scripture*, pp. 97-126. The first set of brackets encloses an insertion on my part suggested by Frye, p. 111; the second set encloses Weinstein's interpolation. Weinstein goes on to argue that "*Redgauntlet* lacks the reversal of movement, the theme of ascent, from which Romance derives so much of its effect."

14. John Culshaw, *Reflections on Wagner's "Ring"* (New York: Viking, 1976). Most of the italicized words come from the chapter on *Götterdämmerung*. I have substituted Scott's poetical prose for Wagner's music; otherwise the changes are few.

15. George Lyman Kittredge, *Chaucer and His Poetry* (Cambridge, Mass.: Harvard Univ. Press, 1915; 8th printing, 1939), p. 218.

INDEX

Abbot, The (Scott), 141-46, 147, 148-49, 150, 170, 218, 221; "moral observations" in, 232
Abramczyk, Roland, 126-27, 132, 134
Agesilan of Colchos, 115, 243
Alchemist, The (Jonson), 101
Alexander romance, 3, 8, 17, 202-03
Alxinger, Johann Baptist von, 14
Amadis de Gaul, 12, 66, 92, 142, 146, 148, 155, 161, 166, 168, 185, 189, 242; Southey's version, 1, 10, 12; Rose's version, 1, 10, 12, 51, 132-33, 157, 213, 223; and *Guy Mannering*, 92, 93; and *Mid-Lothian*, 116-17. *See also* Herberay, Nicolas de
Amadis of Greece, 115, 117, 243
Amis and Amiloun, 3, 9, 12-13, 171, 246; quoted, 45; and *Marmion*, 52
animal companions: in *Guy Mannering*, 94; in *The Talisman*, 179; in *Woodstock*, 184-85; in *Count Robert*, 202, 204
Anne of Geierstein (Scott), 77, 183, 197-201, 213, 221, 223, 226
Antar, 32, 236, 243, 256 n 10
Antiquary, The (Scott), 97-101, 105, 106, 243; place as focal point in, 238
Arabian Nights, 166
Ariosto, Ludovico, 110, 191, 202
Arthur and Merlin, 3, 7, 9, 13
Arthur of Little Britain (Artus de Bretagne): Tressan's version, 4, 24; Lord Berner's translation, 11, 24, 204
Arthur; or, The Northern Enchantment (Hole), 71
Ascham, Roger, 184
Athelston, 30, 136
Aucassin and Nicolette, 4, 13, 66, 243; Way's version, 4, 133; Barbazan's version, 13
Auchindrane, or The Ayrshire Tragedy (Scott), 84
"Ave Maria" (Scott). *See Lady of the Lake, The*
Awntyrs off Arthur, The, 5, 22

Ballantyne, James, 38, 108, 167
Barbazan, Etienne: his *Fabliaux et Contes*, 13, 14, 24
Bellenden, John, 191
Belsches, Williamina, 91, 233
Benson, Larry D., 92, 94, 175, 243
Beowulf, 136
Berners, Lady Juliana, 36
Berners, Lord. *See* Bourchier, John
Betrothed, The (Scott), 4, 84, 138, 172-77, 181, 182, 191, 218, 221, 225, 242
Bevis of Hampton, 3, 7, 9, 13-14, 59, 84, 91, 92, 99, 148, 158, 184, 203, 242; and *Marmion*, 51; and *The Bride of Lammermoor*, 119, 120-21; and *Ivanhoe*, 127-28, 135
Bibliothèque Bleue, 4, 24, 28
Bibliothèque Universelle des Romans, 4, 13-30 passim
Black Dwarf, The (Scott), 101-02, 112, 120, 223
Blondel, 51, 171, 180
Boece, Hector, 191
Boiardo, Matteo Maria, 191, 202
Bone Florence of Rome, Le, 5, 24, 164, 240, 243; and *Ivanhoe*, 134; and *The Betrothed*, 174
Book of St. Albans (Lady Juliana Berners), 36
Bourchier, John (Lord Berners), 16, 27. *See also Arthur of Little Britain*
Brewer, Wilmon, 242
Bridal of Triermain, The (Scott), 70-74, 78, 202, 214
Bride of Lammermoor, The (Scott), 108, 118-24, 218, 236, 237, 243; place as focal point in, 238
Brother Robert: his Tristan-story, 3, 23
Bruce, The (Barbour), 14, 90, 205; and *The Lord of the Isles*, 75-76, 79
Buchan, John, ix

Buchanan, George, 191
Byron, Lord, 70, 248

Cadell, Robert, 211
Canterbury Tales, The (Chaucer), 33, 35, 36, 180, 217
—Canon's Yeoman's Prologue, 147;
—Canon's Yeoman's Tale, 101
—Clerk's Tale (and Griselda), 4, 61, 73, 188, 193; and *The Antiquary*, 97, 99-100
—Cook's Prologue, 224
—Franklin's Tale, 34, 72
—Friar's Tale, 102, 112, 171
—General Prologue (and its pilgrims), 35, 78, 111; and *The Lay of the Last Minstrel*, 43-44; Squire, 53, 198-99; Friar, 53-54; Host (Harry Bailey), 54, 111, 146, 198; Knight, 54, 125, 126, 136, 183, 199, 206-07; Prioress, 54, 196, 221; Miller, 102, 141, 214; Summoner, 112, 217; Monk, 136; Wife of Bath, 143; Pardoner, 143, 181, 198; Physician, 53, 184, 196
—Knight's Tale, 34, 35, 62, 112, 160, 167, 190, 238, 242; and *The Lay of the Last Minstrel*, 43, 45, 48; and *Rokeby*, 68; and *Waverley*, 88-90, 94; and *Old Mortality*, 103-04; and *Ivanhoe*, 130; and *Redgauntlet*, 169-70. *See also* Knight's Tale story-pattern
—Man of Law's Tale, 62, 132, 178, 181; and *Marmion*, 55
—Merchant's Tale, 33, 136, 164; and *The Betrothed*, 176
—Miller's Tale, 102, 160, 214, 215, 222
—Nun's Priest's Tale, 35, 59, 62, 63, 68, 83, 113, 158, 184, 194, 195, 204, 220
—Pardoner's Tale, 82, 214, 217
—Physician's Tale, 147, 164
—Prioress's Prologue, 63
—Reeve's Tale, 124, 141, 148, 224
—Second Nun's Prologue, 63
—Second Nun's Tale, 195
—Shipman's Tale, 217
—*Sir Thopas*, 29, 33, 47, 55, 73, 111
—Squire's Tale, 190-91
—Summoner's Tale, 123, 195, 196, 224
—Wife of Bath's Prologue, 34, 68, 100, 111, 136, 195, 204, 215, 256 n 16; and *Kenilworth*, 147-48
—Wife of Bath's Tale, 17, 34, 35, 36, 72, 153, 208
Capellanus, Andreas, 104, 135
Cary, Henry Francis, 36
Castle Dangerous (Scott), 183, 205-08, 217, 218, 221; conclusion of, 240
Caxton, William, 18, 24, 51

Cervantes, Miguel de, 29, 188. *See also Don Quixote*
Chalmers, Alexander, 31, 33
Chandler, Alice, 86
Chaucer, Geoffrey, 100, 247; editions of, at Abbotsford, 24, 33; his *Book of the Duchess*, 100, 171; his *House of Fame*, 181; words of, borrowed by Scott, 214-15. *See also Canterbury Tales; Troilus and Criseyde*
Cheney, Edward, 36, 212
Cheuelere Assigne, 11, 24, 133
Chrétien de Troyes, 25-26
Chronicle of England, 36
Chronicles of the Canongate, First Series (Scott), 183, 187-91
Clariodus, 3, 14
Clarissa (Richardson), 134
Cleanness (or *Purity*), 181
Clouston, W. A., 32, 257 n 1
Coleridge, Samuel Taylor, 155, 166
Comnena, Anna: her *Alexiad*, 204
Constable, Archibald, 22
Conybeare, J.J., 25, 256 n 8
Copland, Robert, 26
Copland, William, 5, 7, 26, 161
Corson, James C., 2, 14, 15, 20, 23, 29, 37
Countess of Vergy, The, 4
Count Robert of Paris (Scott), 201-04, 207
courtly love, 84, 104; illustrated in *Le Petit Jehan de Saintré*, 19-243; in *Ivanhoe*, 135; in *The Talisman*, 179; in *The Fair Maid of Perth*, 195; in *Castle Dangerous*, 206
Cowley, Abraham, 158
Culshaw, John, 246-47
Cursor Mundi, 36

Dante, 36, 155; and *Rob Roy*, 110
"Death of the Laird's Jock" (Scott), 190, 191
De la Sale, Antoine, 131. *See also Petit Jehan de Saintré, Le*
disguises: heroine as male, 76, 207; hero in female, 114-15, 171; hero as black person, 179. *See also* king in disguise
Dom Flores de Grece, 12, 26, 234-35, 243; and *The Siege of Malta*, 209-10
Don Bellianis of Greece, 148, 216
Don Quixote (Cervantes), 19, 38, 153, 155, 159, 166; as frame of reference in *Redgauntlet*, 169; and *The Siege of Malta*, 211
Doolin von Maynz (Alxinger), 14
Doom of Devorgoil, The (Scott), 85
Douce, Francis, 7
dreams, prophetic or foreboding: in *The Lady of the Lake*, 60; in *Old Mortality*, 106; in *The Pirate*, 153; in *Anne of Geierstein*, 200

Dryden, John, 36, 247. See also *Fables*
Dunbar, William, 37, 54
Dunlop, John: his *History of Fiction*, 11, 14, 26, 28, 115, 117, 120, 145, 167, 248

Earl of Toulous, The 5, 24, 46
Eger and Grime. See *Sir Eger, Sir Grahame, and Sir Gray-Steel*
Ellis, George, 4, 50; his *Specimens*, 1, 6-8, 13-25 *passim*, 178, 192; correspondence with Scott, 2, 8, 13-27 *passim*
Emare, 5, 24, 46, 55
enmity and reconciliation: in *The Lay of the Last Minstrel*, 42; in *The Lady of the Lake*, 60; in *The Doom of Devorgoil*, 85; in *Guy Mannering*, 94-95; in *The Black Dwarf*, 101; in *Rob Roy*, 108-09; in *The Talisman*, 178-179; in *Count Robert*, 204
Epicœne, or the Silent Woman (Jonson), 76
Esplandian, 12, 26, 243
Evans, Thomas: his *Old Ballads*, 1, 15-16, 23
expulsion (or exile) and return: in *Rokeby*, 66; in *Guy Mannering*, 91-92; in *The Antiquary*, 98-99; in *Old Mortality*, 105; in *The Betrothed*, 176-77
Eyrbiggia-Saga: Scott's abstract of, 136

Fables (Dryden): *The Wife of Bath's Tale*, 17, 35; Preface to, 33, 35, 247; *Palamon and Arcite*, 34, 45, 103, 111, 130; *The Character of a Good Parson*, 35; *The Flower and the Leaf*, 35; *The Cock and the Fox*, 35, 45, 62-63
Fair Maid of Perth, The (Scott), 183, 191-97, 198, 214, 225, 225-26, 228, 229, 233
farewell speeches: in Scott, 225-26; in *Othello*, 226; in medieval romance, 226-27
Fielding, Henry, 233
Field of Waterloo, The (Scott), 63
Fleur des Batailles, La, 14; Tressan's version, 4; Alxinger's version (*Doolin von Maynz*), 14
Floris and Blancheflur, 3, 9, 66, 133, 243; Tressan's version, 4; Ellis's version, 7
Florisel de Niquea, 122, 167-68, 243
Fordun, John of, 83
Forster, E.M., 243-44
Fortunes of Nigel, The (Scott), 138, 154-56, 157, 182, 214, 215, 221, 224, 229
Fouqué, Friedrich, 139
Foure Sonnes of Aymon, The. See *Quatre Fils d'Amyon, Les*
Freine, 3, 8, 16; Ellis's version, 7
Friars of Berwick, The (Dunbar?), 54
Froissart, Jean, 68, 83, 105, 177, 201, 220
Frye, Northrop, 244-48 *passim*

Gamelyn, 24, 33, 62, 67, 98, 243

Gamerschlag, Kurt, 250 n 17, 252 n 14, 257 n 11
Gentle Shepherd, The (Ramsay), 92
Geoffrey of Monmouth, 6, 136
Geoffrey of Vinsauf, 56, 68, 69, 77, 220, 222
Gervaise of Tilbury, 38, 236
Gesta Romanorum, 164, 179
Gibbon, Edward, 204
Gil Blas (Le Sage), 112
Godwin, William: his *Life of Chaucer*, 1, 33, 219, 247
Goethe, Johann Wolfgang von, 157, 248
Götz von Berlichingen (Goethe), 134
Golagrus and Gawain, 5; and *The Bride of Lammermoor*, 124, 243
Gottfried von Strassburg, 3, 23
Gower, John, 37, 45, 55, 63, 186; his Tale of Florent, 17, 35-36, 37, 208
Graelent. See *Gruelan*
Gray, Thomas, 220
Grene Knight, The, 32
Grierson, Sir Herbert, 1-2; correspondence with, Scott, 31
Grimm, Jakob, 14, 27
Griselidis, 4
Gruelan, 119; Way's version, 4, 22
Guerin de Montglave, 15; Tressan's version, 4
Guy Mannering, 91-97, 105, 156, 218, 231, 236, 244-45; Meg's malediction, 227-28; repetition in, 237; place as focal point in, 239
Guy of Warwick, 3, 7, 15, 19, 29, 91, 119, 144, 148, 155, 158, 184, 243; and *Ivanhoe*, 128-29, 132, 135, 136; and *Count Robert*, 201, 203
Gyron le Courtois, 26

Halidon Hill (Scott), 83-84
Halliwell, J.O., 32, 33
Harold the Dauntless (Scott), 80-83
Hartshorne, C.H.: his *Ancient Metrical Tales*, 14, 30
Havelok, 30-31, 99, 126
Hawthorne, Nathaniel, 171
Heart of Mid-Lothian, The (Scott), 108, 113-18, 137, 151, 215, 217, 225, 237
Heber, Richard, 50; correspondence with Scott, 2, 4, 11-28 *passim*, 34, 215
Heldenbuch, Das, 115, 126, 127, 133, 140, 243
Helyas, The Knight of the Swan, 26-27, 119, 132, 133, 176, 243; and *The Heart of Mid-Lothian*, 115-16
Henderson, T.F., 28
Henryson, Robert, 37; his *Testament of Cresseid*, 37

Henry the Minstrel (Blind Harry), 90, 194
Herberay, Nicolas de, 10, 26, 209; his *Amadis de Gaul*, 12, 26
"Highland Widow, The" (Scott), 183, 187-88
"Hildebrand, The Song of Old," 110, 117, 146
Hoccleve, Thomas, 37, 63, 164, 240; his *Regement of Princes*, 3, 37, 102, 141, 186, 213, 222; his *Letter of Cupid*, 37, 224-25
Hole, Richard, 71
Horn Child, 3, 5, 15, 60
House of Aspen, The (Scott), 252-53
Hume, David, of Godscroft, 205
Hundreth Good Pointes of Husbandrie (Tusser), 153
Hunting of the Felon Sow of Rokeby, The, 15-16, 67, 68-69
Huntyng of the Hare, The, 3, 9, 16
Huon of Bordeaux, 16, 88, 109, 197, 243; Tressan's version, 4

Ipomadon. See *Lyfe of Ipomydon, The*
Ivanhoe (Scott), 19, 83, 108, 126-37, 182, 215, 221, 225, 235, 243, 244, 245

Jack, R.D.S., x, 240
Jamieson, John: edits *Bruce*, 14
Jamieson, Robert, 9
Jean d'Arras. See *Melusine*
Jean de Calais: in *Bibliothèque Bleue*, 4
Johnson, Richard, 120. See also *Seven Champions of Christendom, The*
Jones, Terry, 34, 124-25
Jonson, Ben, 76, 101, 154, 156
Jourdain de Blaves, 26

Kenilworth (Scott), 138, 146-50, 164, 193, 215, 217, 221, 228; "moral observations" in, 232-33
King Horn, 5, 15, 25, 60, 91, 92, 120, 243
king in disguise: in *The Lady of the Lake*, 60; in *Ivanhoe*, 131; in *Quentin Durward*, 162-63; in *Woodstock*, 185-86
King of Tars, The, 3, 5, 25
King Orfeo. See *Sir Orfeo*
Kirkman, Francis, 12
Knight of Curtesy, The, 5, 25, 125, 199
Knight of the Swan, The. See *Helyas*
Knight's Tale story-pattern (or variations): in *The Lady of the Lake*, 60; in *Rokeby*, 66; in *The Lord of the Isles*, 76; in *Waverley*, 88; in *The Antiquary*, 99; in *Old Mortality*, 102-03; in *Rob Roy*, 111; in *Montrose*, 125; in *The Monastery*, 138-39; in *The Pirate*, 152-53; in *St. Ronan's Well*, 167; in *Redgauntlet*, 169; in

The Surgeon's Daughter, 189; in *The Fair Maid of Perth*, 193-95; in *Anne of Geierstein*, 197

Lady of the Lake, The (Scott), 1, 24, 28, 57-63, 64, 70, 74, 77, 131, 211, 217, 225, 243; "Ave Maria," 58, 63, 225
Laing, David, 19, 20, 22, 30, 38; correspondence with Scott, 24, 30, 31
Lancelot du Lac, 27, 28, 29
Lancelot of the Laik, 32
Lay of the Last Minstrel, The (Scott), 1, 40-49, 56, 57, 62, 63, 64, 70, 74, 207, 214, 215
Legend of Montrose, A (Scott), 108, 124-26, 222, 223; description of Dalgetty, 221
Le Grand d'Aussy: his *Fabliaux ou Contes*, 4, 10, 13-25 passim, 177
Le Sage, Alain René, 188. See also *Gil Blas*
Leslie, John, 191
Lewis, Matthew Gregory, 132
Leyden, John, 18, 20
Leyden, Robert, 18
Libeaus Desconus, 5, 16-17, 71, 92, 170
Lindsay, Sir David, 110
"Lochinvar" (Scott). See *Marmion*
Lockhart, John Gibson, ix, 2, 5, 36; on Ritson, 5; on Weber, 8, 9-10
Lohengrin (medieval romance), 27, 119
Lord of the Isles, The (Scott), 74-79
Lydgate, John, 37, 63; his *Siege of Thebes*, 33, 68, 186, 187; his *Temple of Glas*, 37, 181
Lyfe of Ipomydon, The, 7, 9, 17, 130

Mabinogion, The, 27, 132
MacDuff's Cross (Scott), 84
Madden, Frederic, 30, 31
Malory, Sir Thomas. See his *Morte Darthur, Le*
Mandeville, Sir John: his *Travels*, 3, 37, 181
Marie de France, 51; lais of, 4, 6-7, 16, 22; *Lanval*, 4, 7, 16, 119, 200; *Yonec*, 7, 152, 243
Marie of Champagne, 208
Marmion (Scott), 1, 13, 29, 49-57, 62, 63, 64, 70, 74, 110, 215, 243; "Lochinvar," 50, 57, 120
Marriage of Sir Gawaine, The, 17, 35-36, 72, 74, 93, 97, 243; in *Castle Dangerous*, 207-08
Meliador (Froissart), 177
Meliadus de Leonnoys, 23, 27
Melusine, 27, 88, 90, 109, 119, 139, 163, 175, 214, 243; farewell speech in, 227; lament of Eglantyne, 229-30
Milles et Amys, 202
Millgate, Jane, 208, 258 nn 15, 21, 259 n 23
Mills, Charles, 204

Milton, John, 69; echoes of, in *The Lord of the Isles*, 78
missing heir, 85, 126. *See also* expulsion and return
misspent youth: in *Kenilworth*, 146; in *Woodstock*, 184; in Chronicles of the Canongate, First Series, 187; in *The Fair Maid of Perth*, 193
Monastery, The (Scott), 138-41, 142, 148, 214, 215, 217, 221, 225, 228, 236, 237; "moral observations" in, 232; place as focal point in, 238-39
Monk, The (Lewis), 132
Montvalo, Garciordonez de, 10
Moraes, Francisco de, 18
"moral observations": in Malory, 206; in Scott, 231-33; in *Palmerin of England*, 233
Morte Arthur (Stanzaic), 7, 18
Morte Arthure (Alliterative), 32
Morte Darthur, Le (Malory), 11, 17-18, 29, 83, 106, 123, 148, 156, 158, 159, 163, 171, 175, 176, 180, 196-97, 202, 203, 233, 242-43; and *The Lay of the Last Minstrel*, 42-43; and *Marmion*, 50-51, 57; and *The Lady of the Lake*, 59, 62; and *The Bridal of Triermain*, 71-72, 74; *Tale of Sir Gareth*, 91, 96-97, 109, 135, 162, 238, 240; *Book of Sir Tristram*, 94-95, 143, 148, 154, 173, 217; *Tale of King Arthur*, 102; and *Ivanhoe*, 130, 133, 134, 135; and *St. Ronan's Well*, 167, 168; and *Anne of Geierstein*, 197-98; and *Castle Dangerous*, 205, 206, 207; *-ing* verbs in, 217-18
Munday, Anthony, 18
"My Aunt Margaret's Mirror" (Scott), 190

Nibelungenlied, Das, 143, 192-93

occupatio: in *The Lay of the Last Minstrel*, 48; in *Rob Roy*, 111-12, 222; in *St. Ronan's Well*, 167, 222; in *Waverley*, 222; in *Montrose*, 222; in *The Talisman*, 222; in *The Siege of Malta*, 223; in Rose's *Amadis*, 223
Octavian, 9, 25, 94, 195
Odyssey, The, 104, 129
Ogier le Danois, 27-28; allusion to Ugero the Dane, 197
Old Mortality (Scott), 102-07, 138, 183, 221, 231, 234; mock-heroic element in, 219-20
Orlando Furioso (Ariosto), 110, 191, 202
Orlando Innamorato (Boiardo), 191, 202
Othello (Shakespeare), 66, 149, 226
Otuel a Knight, 3, 7, 9, 18
Owain Miles, 3, 9, 38, 64
Owen, William, 27

Palmerin of England: Southey's version of, 10, 18-19, 62, 120, 201, 217, 240-41, 243
Partenopex de Blois, 19, 243; Le Grand's version, 4, 19; Rose's version, 10, 16, 19, 51, 164, 213, 214, 223; and *The Lady of the Lake*, 59
Paston Letters, 121
Pearl, 56
Perceforest, 28, 62; and *Old Mortality*, 106-07, 234
Percy, Thomas, 21, 32, 92; his *Reliques*, 5, 16, 18, 23, 24, 30, 38, 144, 214. See also *Marriage of Sir Gawaine, The*
perilous journey: in *Waverley*, 87; in *Rob Roy*, 109; in *Mid-Lothian*, 114; in *Redgauntlet*, 172
Petit Jehan de Saintré, Le, 19, 130-31, 159, 164, 243; Tressan's version, 4
Peveril of the Peak (Scott), 138, 156-60, 183, 229
Piers Plowman (Langland), 38, 153, 213, 214
Pinkerton, John: his *Scottish Poems*, 5, 14, 22; his *Bruce*, 14, 75; his *History of Scotland*, 83
Pirate, The (Scott), 76, 150-54, 224, 240, 243
Pistill of Susan, The, 38; allusion to "the chaste Susannah," 176
Polwhele, Richard: correspondence with, Scott, 17, 22, 25
Pope, Alexander, 220
proverbs in Scott, 223-25
Pynson, Richard, 7

Quatre Fils d'Aymon, Les, 24; version in *Bibliothèque Bleue*, 4
Queenhoo-Hall (Strutt), 86
Quentin Durward (Scott), 1, 23, 138, 160-65, 166, 182, 197, 203, 221, 224, 243

Ramsay, Allan, 92
rash promise: in *Montrose*, 125; in *The Betrothed*, 175
Rauf Coilyear, 19, 60, 131, 163, 243
Redgauntlet (Scott), 138, 168-72, 224, 235, 245-46; conclusion of, 239-40
Reinbrun, 3, 19, 91-92
rescue (or escape) in nick of time: in *Rokeby*, 66-67, 69; in *The Lord of the Isles*, 76; in *Guy Mannering*, 94; in *Old Mortality*, 105; in *Woodstock*, 186; in *Anne of Geierstein*, 200
resuscitation of the dead: in *Guy Mannering*, 94; in *Old Mortality*, 105; in *Ivanhoe*, 132
reunion and reconciliation: in *Guy Mannering*, 95; in medieval romance, 95-97
Richard Coer de Lyon, 3, 7, 8-9, 19-20, 125, 140, 200, 202, 211; and *Ivanhoe*, 130, 131; and *The Talisman*, 177-78

Richard sans Peur, 28; version in *Bibliothèque Bleue*, 4, 28
Richardson, Samuel, 134
Ritson, Joseph, 2, 5-6, 38; his *Metrical Romanceës*, 1, 5-6, 13-25 *passim*, 36
Roberd of Cisyle, 7, 9, 20
Robertson, D.W., 223
Robert the Devil, 22, 61, 76, 81-82, 142-43, 158, 196; version in *Bibliothèque Bleue*, 4; and *Ivanhoe*, 129
Rob Roy (Scott), 108-13, 137, 216-17, 222, 224, 237
Rokeby (Scott), 16, 23, 64-70, 74, 82
Roland, The Song of, 53, 132, 196
Roland and Ferragus (or *Vernagu*), 3, 7, 9, 20; quoted in notes to *The Lady of the Lake*, 59
Rose, William Stewart, 50; his *Amadis de Gaul*, 1, 10, 12, 51, 213, 223; his *Partenopex*, 10, 51, 59, 213, 214, 223; cites *Le Petit Jehan*, 19; quotes *Emare*, 24
Roswall and Lillian, 2, 7, 9, 20, 130, 143, 179, 243
Rowlands, Samuel: his version of *Guy of Warwick*, 128-29, 254 n 16

St. Ronan's Well (Scott), 165-68, 222
Sands, Donald B., 92
Scoti-Chronicon, The, 191
Scott, Sir Walter
—chapbooks, 2, 14, 15, 20, 23, 29
—correspondence: with Ritson, 2; with Heber, 2, 4, 11-28 *passim*, 34, 215; with Ellis, 2, 8, 13-27 *passim*; with Southey, 2, 27; with Grimm, 14, 27; with Polwhele, 17, 22, 25; with Percy, 21; with Laing, 24, 30, 31; with others, 19, 29-30, 31, 37
—essays: on Romance, 1, 11, 12-32 *passim*; on Chivalry, 1, 12-29 *passim*, 34; "On the Fairies of Popular Superstition," 13-28 *passim*, 33, 38
—*Journal*, 38-39, 209, 214, 239
—*Minstrelsy of the Scottish Border*, 1, 12-28 *passim*, 34, 35, 37, 38, 92, 171
—reviews: of Ellis's and Ritson's *Metrical Romances*, 1, 7, 13, 21, 24; of Rose's and Southey's *Amadis de Gaul*, 1, 10, 12, 36; of Evans's *Old Ballads*, 1, 16, 23; of Godwin's *Life of Chaucer*, 1, 34-35
See also poems, plays, and novels by title; *Sir Tristrem*: Scott's edition of
Scudéry, Madeleine de, 158
self-deprecation: in *Marmion*, 51; in *Waverley*, 91; in *Montrose*, 223; in *Anne of Geierstein*, 223

set speeches: in Scott, 227-28; in medieval romance, 229-31
Seven Champions of Christendom, The (Johnson), 120, 121, 127, 133, 140, 179, 236; set speeches in, 230-31
Seven Wise Masters, The, 2, 3, 7, 9, 20-21, 123
Seward, Anna, 36
Shadwell, Thomas, 154
Shakespeare, William, x, 101, 147, 184, 231, 242, 247, 248; *Othello*, 66, 149, 226; *The Winter's Tale*, 92
Siege of Malta, The (Scott), 84, 183, 208-11, 214, 223
Siege of Thebes, The. See Lydgate, John
Sir Amadace, 3, 9
Sir Cleges, 3, 8, 25
Sir Degare, 3, 10, 25
Sir Degrevant, 32-33, 130
Sir Eger, Sir Grahame, and Sir Gray-Steel (Eger and Grime), 7, 9, 21, 84, 144, 146; and *Redgauntlet*, 170
Sir Eglamour of Artois, 7, 9, 21, 29, 117, 148, 173, 243; and *Guy Mannering*, 92-93, 95-96, 97
Sir Ferumbras (The Sowdon of Babylon), 7, 9, 21
Sir Gaheret, 28-29
Sir Gawain and Sir Galeron of Galloway. See *Awntyrs off Arthur, The*
Sir Gawain and the Green Knight, 4, 31, 207; analogues to, 4
Sir Gowther, 3, 9, 10, 22, 61, 76, 81-82, 142-43, 157-58, 243
Sir Isumbras, 3, 7, 9, 10, 22
Sir Launfal (Chestre), 4, 5, 22, 46-47, 200, 215, 243
Sir Orfeo, 3, 5, 22, 61, 72, 104, 140, 172, 177, 243
Sir Pleindamour, 29
Sir Torrent of Portyngale, 33, 117
Sir Triamour, 7, 9, 10, 25, 117, 130; and *The Talisman*, 179, 243
Sir Tristrem (Middle English romance), 3, 56, 95, 171, 173, 207; Scott's edition of, 1, 2, 12-31 *passim*, 34, 36, 37, 48-49; and *The Lady of the Lake*, 60, 61; and *Mid-Lothian*, 114; and *The Bride of Lammermoor*, 122; and *Ivanhoe*, 135-36. See also Tristan-story
Sir Tundale, 9, 38, 64
Skeat, Walter W., 90
Smollett, Tobias George, 233
Southey, Robert, 3, 11; correspondence with Scott, 2, 27. See also *Amadis de Gaul*; *Palmerin of England*
Spenser, Edmund, 64, 69, 110, 213;

Spenserian stanzas, 64, 77, 78; his *Faerie Queene*, 213, 214, 215-16, 256 n 10; his *Shepheards Calender*, 216
Squire of Alsatia, The (Shadwell), 154
Squyr of Lowe Degre, The, 1, 5, 23, 169, 195, 215, 243; and *Quentin Durward*, 1, 23, 160, 161-62, 203; farewell speech in, 227
Sterne, Laurence, 233
Stothard, Thomas: his *Canterbury Pilgrims*, 33, 196
Strutt, Joseph, 86
Sultana, Donald E., 208-11 *passim*
Surgeon's Daughter, The (Scott), 183, 187, 189-90

taboos: in *The Lay of the Last Minstrel*, 42; in *The Bride of Lammermoor*, 119; in *Anne of Geierstein*, 200
Talisman, The (Scott), 138, 166, 177-82, 185, 195, 214, 221, 222, 243; place as focal point in, 238
"Tapestried Chamber, The" (Scott), 190, 191
Temple of Glas, The (Lydgate), 37, 181
Thomas, J.W., 238
Thomas of Britain, 2, 23
Thomas of Erceldoune, 3, 23, 98, 207
Thomas the Rhymer (ballad), 217
Thomas the Rhymer (Scott), 86
Thorkelin, G.J., 136
Tirant lo Blanch, 29, 178, 243; and *The Lay of the Last Minstrel*, 43; and *Marmion*, 51; and *Ivanhoe*, 129; and *Count Robert*, 201, 202, 203
Todd, Henry J., 33
Tournament of Tottenham, The, 23
Tressan, Comte de: his *Corps d'Extraits de Romans de Chevalerie*, 4, 12, 14-24 *passim*; compared with Ellis, 7-8
Trevisa, John, 38
Tristan-story, 5, 23, 94-95, 104-05, 106, 145, 148; Tressan's version, 4; Béroul's version, 23, 113; Eilhart von Oberge's *Tristrant*, 23, 238; and *The Lay of the Last Minstrel*, 42; and *Marmion*, 52; and *The Bridal of Triermain*, 74; and *The Bride of Lammermoor*, 121-22; and *Peveril of the Peak*, 159; and *Quentin Durward*, 164, 165; and *The Betrothed*, 172-73, 175, 242; Jean Maugin's version, 234. See also *Sir Tristrem*
Trivet, Nicolas, 63
Troilus and Criseyde (Chaucer), 33, 68, 79, 87, 113, 141, 147, 155, 195, 215, 224, 226, 232; Scott's opinion of, 36; "woe worth" construction in, 62, 140, 217
Troy-Book, 29
Tulloch, Graham, 214, 216

Tusser, Thomas, 153
"Two Drovers, The" (Scott), 183, 187, 188

undesired marriage: in *Marmion*, 57; in *The Lady of the Lake*, 59-60; in *Rokeby*, 66; in *The Doom of Devorgoil*, 85; in *The Black Dwarf*, 101; in *Old Mortality*, 105; in *The Bride of Lammermoor*, 120-21; in *Ivanhoe*, 131; in *Kenilworth*, 150; in *St. Ronan's Well*, 168; in *The Talisman*, 178
Undine (Fouqué), 139
Utterson, E.V.: his *Select Pieces*, 10, 22, 25; edits *Arthur of Little Britain*, 10-11, 24; edits *Cheuelere Assigne*, 11, 24

Valentine and Orson, 2, 23, 87, 96, 104, 109-10, 126, 144, 149-50, 153, 157, 164, 166, 181-82, 201, 214, 242-43; and *Rokeby*, 66; and *Mid-Lothian*, 117-18; and *The Bride of Lammermoor*, 120, 121; and *The Betrothed*, 173-74; farewell speech in, 226-27; lament of Bellyssant, 229
Vertot, René d'Aubert de, 208, 211
Vision of Don Roderick, The (Scott), 63-64, 69, 77

Wagner, Richard, 72, 83, 247
Wallace (Blind Harry), 90, 194
"Wandering Willie's Tale" (Scott), 171-72
Warner, William, 31
Warton, Thomas: his *History of English Poetry*, 15, 18, 23, 24, 25, 36
Waverley (Scott), 2, 86-91, 120, 169, 222, 235, 236-37, 239, 243
Way, Gregory Lewis: his *Fabliaux or Tales*, 4, 13-25 *passim*, 133, 161, 177
Weber, Henry, 8, 13-30 *passim*, 38, 110; his *Metrical Romances*, 8-9, 13-25 *passim*; *Illustrations of Northern Antiquities*, 9-10, 136, 192-93, 250 n 17
Weddynge of Sir Gawen and Dame Ragnell, The, 17, 33
Weinstein, Mark A., 245-46
Wilhelm Meisters Lehrjahre (Goethe), 157
William of Palerne, 29-30
Winter's Tale, The (Shakespeare), 92
Woodstock (Scott), 183-87, 239
Worde, Wynkyn de, 51, 161
Wyntoun, Andrew of, 191

Yonec, Lai of (Marie), 7; and *The Pirate*, 152, 243
Ysaie le Triste, 23, 30, 191, 243, 256 n 15, 257 n 10
Ywain and Gawain, 5, 24, 26, 94, 195, 238

www.ingramcontent.com/pod-product-compliance
Lightning Source LLC
Chambersburg PA
CBHW021836220426
43663CB00005B/268